DIEGO JOURDAN PEREIRA

THE BIG BOOK OF BRAIN-BOOSTING PUZZLES

WORD GAMES DESIGNED TO KEEP THE MIND YOUNG!

RACEHORSE PUBLISHING

Racehorse Publishing books may be purchased in bulk at special discounts for sales promotion, corporate gifts, fund-raising, or educational purposes. Special editions can also be created to specifications. For details, contact the Special Sales Department, Skyhorse Publishing, 307 West 36th Street, 11th Floor, New York, NY 10018 or info@skyhorsepublishing.com.

Racehorse Publishing™ is a pending trademark of Skyhorse Publishing, Inc.®, a Delaware corporation.

Visit our website at www.skyhorsepublishing.com.

10 9 8 7 6 5 4 3 2

Library of Congress Control Number: 2019951125

Cover and interior design by Diego Jourdan Pereira

Mechanical design by Kai Texel

Graveside font designed by Nate Piekos. Used under license.

Cover pencil photo ©hayatikayhan - Can Stock Photo Inc. Used under license.

Print ISBN: 978-1-63158-511-1

Printed in the United States of America

CONTENTS

III

O	E	Z	M	K	O	U	H	I
M	I	L	O	V	E	Z	I	T
Q	J	O	U	R	D	A	N	O
D	B	C	N	S	G	U	H	L
D	E	D	I	C	A	T	E	D
A	N	H	S	L	I	S	S	Y
P	T	X	M	W	J	N	M	Y

- Denotes a thing.
- Printed and bound.
- Quality of being.
- Inscribed by compliment.
- Intended for.
- Of me.
- Sister of father.
- Pronounced LIHS-iy.
- <u>Swamp Thing</u> villain in '82.
- Accompanying.
- Affection.

See page VI.

► INTRODUCTION

"A mind needs books like a sword needs a whetstone,
if it is to keep its edge."
–George R.R. Martin.

For years on end, every morning after breakfast, my grandfather Darío would walk to the living room, his newspaper and lead pencil in hand, and sit at the round table by the veranda to try and crack the crossword on the last page.

He understood nobody is supposed to know it all, that looking for answers is where the fun is. So, he kept on doing his daily puzzle, stalling dementia as best he could, till it got so bad he had to move to an assisted living residence, where he would spend the remainder of his life in comfort, passing in my Oma Hedy's arms a few years later.

This family tragedy made me realize my career in comic books had been nothing but a vain pursuit up to that point. However, the year 2012 would bring the gift of assisting cartoonist Bob Weber Jr. on his <u>Slylock Fox</u> syndicated feature, and with it a taste of puzzles and the infinite potential for true engagement with readers of every age group, which would send me on an alternative path.

From then on, I would learn more about the craft, studying from every out-of-print how-to book I could get my hands on, while training myself in the use of modern design software. My new chops were soon put to the test when offered the opportunity to write, design, and illustrate one of the biggest activity books for children around (my very own <u>Giant Book of Games & Puzzles for Smart Kids</u>), and again, when the opportunity to package this massive puzzle book aimed at adult and elderly readers presented itself a year later. But rather than setting out to reinvent the wheel, I decided to put my own spin on "tried and true" games which target cognitive skills vulnerable to aging such as attention (Matchmaker), language (Crossword), memory (Trivia), logic (Wordoku), and visual processing (Maze).

Some of these give way to new puzzles every hundred pages, to bring in fresh challenges while keeping a steady ship for the more conservative out there, yet all getting progressively harder over five levels (indicated by black chevrons at the bottom of each page) in order to build up the reader's problem-solving resolution, while also including fun "breathers" here and there, hoping <u>The Big Book of Brain-Boosting Puzzles</u> keeps everyone turning pages for more!

–Diego Jourdan Pereira

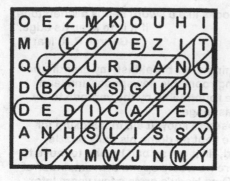

THIS BOOK IS DEDICATED TO MY AUNT, LISSY JOURDAN, WITH LOVE.

▶ CROSSWORD

1	2	3		4	5	6
7			8			
		9				
10						
		11				
12	13				14	
15				16		

ACROSS:
1. To increase.
4. Medical rescue.
7. Guideline.
9. Bro or sis (abbr.).
10. High-energy electron.
11. American Nurses Association (abbr.).
12. Venezuela capital.
15. Together with.
16. Founded (abbr.).

DOWN:
1. Coffee plant.
2. Undertake.
3. Despicable.
4. Hold closely.
5. Massachusetts (abbr.).
6. The most active
8. Moon goddess.
13. Indefinite article.
14. Compare and contrast.

WORDSEARCH

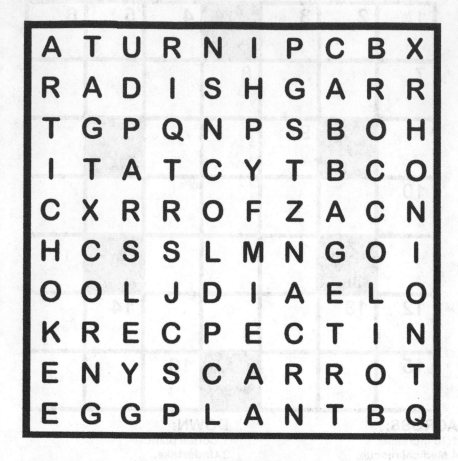

A	T	U	R	N	I	P	C	B	X
R	A	D	I	S	H	G	A	R	R
T	G	P	Q	N	P	S	B	O	H
I	T	A	T	C	Y	T	B	C	O
C	X	R	R	O	F	Z	A	C	N
H	C	S	S	L	M	N	G	O	I
O	O	L	J	D	I	A	E	L	O
K	R	E	C	P	E	C	T	I	N
E	N	Y	S	C	A	R	R	O	T
E	G	G	P	L	A	N	T	B	Q

FIND THE FOLLOWING VEGETABLES:

ARTICHOKE
BROCCOLI
CABBAGE
CARROT
CORN
EGGPLANT
GARLIC

ONION
PARSLEY
RADISH
SOY
SPINACH
TOMATO
TURNIP

► WORDOKU

FILL EVERY ROW, COLUMN, AND 3X3 SECTOR,
USING EACH GIVEN LETTER ONLY ONCE!

▶ QUOTES

HOW MANY OF THESE MOVIE QUOTES CAN YOU IDENTIFY?

"Toto, I've got a feeling we're not in Kansas anymore."

FILM:
. . . .

YEAR:
. . . .

ACTOR:
. . . .

FILM:
. . . .

YEAR:
. . . .

ACTOR:
. . . .

"We'll always have Paris."

"Mrs. Robinson, you're trying to seduce me. Aren't you?"

FILM:
. . . .

YEAR:
. . . .

ACTOR:
. . . .

▶ SILHOUETTES

GIVE EACH COUNTRY ITS CORRESPONDING NAME.

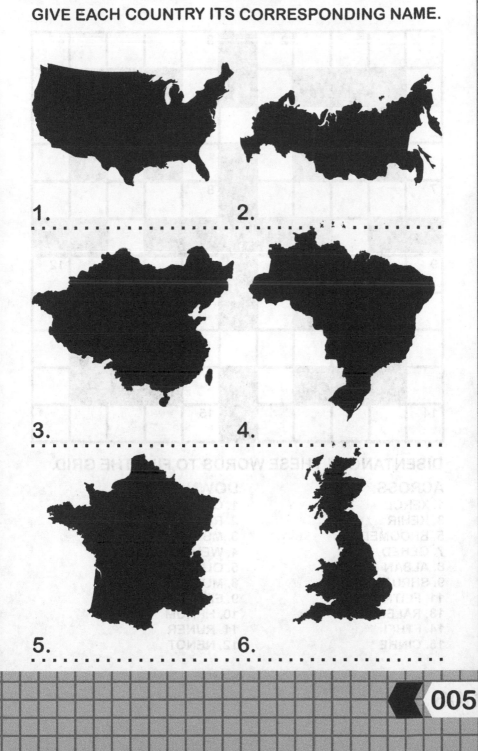

1.

2.

3.

4.

5.

6.

►UNSCRAMBLE

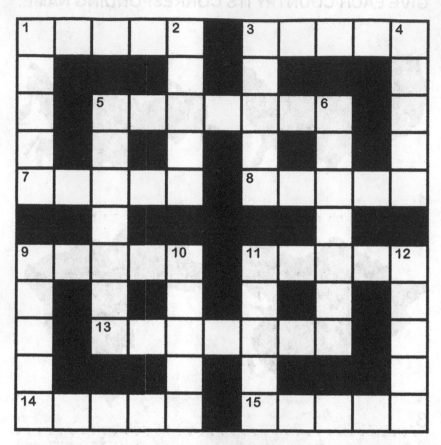

DISENTANGLE THESE WORDS TO FILL THE GRID.

ACROSS:
1. XEROB
3. KEHIR
5. BROOMED
7. GEHED
8. ALBAN
9. SHRUB
11. FEITR
13. RALEMNU
14. FTHFI
15. CINHE

DOWN:
1. CHUNB
2. RGEID
3. MBHBO
4. WELOR
5. OUBEDIN
6. MUDFLIN
9. EFRIB
10. HPHUM
11. RUNER
12. NENOT

▶ TRIVIA

FAMOUS PEOPLE FROM THE PAST.

1.

1492 ▶ Sailed west from Spain, reaching the island of Guanahani on October 12th, renaming it El Salvador.

2.

1776 ▶ Helped draft the Declaration of Independence, the U.S. Constitution, and invented bifocal glasses.

3.

1781 ▶ Defeated the British army commanded by Lord Cornwallis at the Battle of Yorktown.

4.

1876 ▶ Best known for writing <u>The Adventures of Tom Sawyer</u> and its sequel, <u>The Adventures of Huckleberry Finn.</u>

5.

1877 ▶ Invented the phonograph along with 1,093 other patents.

6.

1901 ▶ Created the United States Forest Service and established five national parks.

7.

1927 ▶ Demonstrated the first television signal transmission with his own scanning tube.

8.

1941 ▶ A successful movie star, she also became a pioneer in the field of wireless communications.

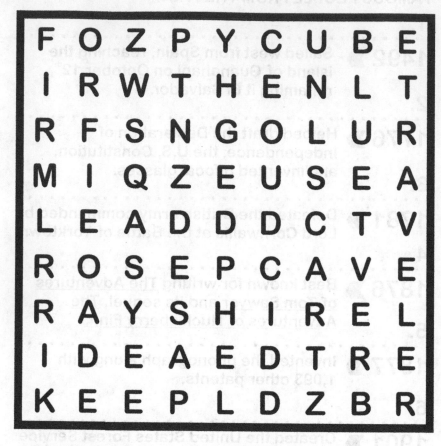

```
F O Z P Y C U B E
I R W T H E N L T
R F S N G O L U R
M I Q Z E U S E A
L E A D D D C T V
R O S E P C A V E
R A Y S H I R E L
I D E A E D T R E
K E E P L D Z B R
```

- Primary color.
- Pulled by a horse.
- Underground chamber.
- A block.
- Uninteresting.
- Colored.
- Steady.
- Recruit.
- Receives a guest.
- Original thought.
- Hold.
- By example.
- Schindler's—
- Faithful.
- Made dirty.
- Possessed.
- Energy beams.
- —and now.
- Makes a journey.
- Describes an action.

▶ RIDDLES

DO YOU REMEMBER THE ANSWERS TO THESE?

"The more there is
the less you see."

WHAT IS IT?

. . . .

"Runs over fields and woods
all day. At night it sits not
alone under the bed, with its
tongue hanging out, waiting
for a bone."

WHAT IS IT?

. . . .

"A box without hinges,
key or lid, yet a golden
treasure inside it hides."

WHAT IS IT?

. . . .

◤ MATCHMAKER

DRAW A LINE TO CONNECT EACH OF THE FIRST 10 PRESIDENTS OF THE UNITED STATES TO THE YEARS THEY SPENT IN OFFICE.

1. 1789-1799   William Henry Harrison

2. 1797-1801   John Quincy Adams

3. 1801-1809   Thomas Jefferson

4. 1809-1817   Martin Van Buren

5. 1817-1825   George Washington

6. 1825-1829   John Tyler

7. 1829-1837   James Monroe

8. 1837-1841   Andrew Jackson

9. 1841-1841   James Madison

10. 1841-1845   John Adams

► CROSSWORD

ACROSS:
1. Whole quantity.
3. What reason.
5. Old spider net.
9. Put in words.
10. Animal hide.
12. Method.
13. Raced.

DOWN:
1. Curved shape.
2. Contains books.
3. —you like it or not.
4. Affirmative.
6. Bound to repay.
7. Mental sharpness.
8. Honey insect.
10. The rule of—.
11. Bolt.

WORDSEARCH

```
G F B A T T E R T T
L E M Z E K H E F S
O N A M R C M L E L
V C L T T O O R W I
E E N A H E I A V D
H U C R K P S P C E
B N U I M F O U L H
B H R U P I T C H N
W T V I N N I N G D
S F E D U G O U T J
```

FIND 16 BASEBALL TERMS AND WRITE THEM BELOW:

....
....
....
....
....
....

WORDOKU

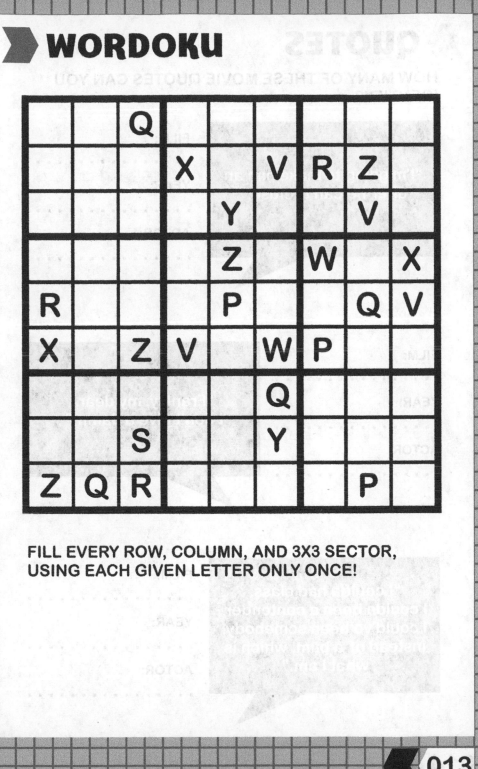

FILL EVERY ROW, COLUMN, AND 3X3 SECTOR,
USING EACH GIVEN LETTER ONLY ONCE!

QUOTES

HOW MANY OF THESE MOVIE QUOTES CAN YOU IDENTIFY?

"I'm going to make him an offer he can't refuse."

FILM:
. . . .

YEAR:
. . . .

ACTOR:
. . . .

FILM:
. . . .

YEAR:
. . . .

ACTOR:
. . . .

"Frankly, my dear, I don't give a damn."

"I coulda had class. I coulda been a contender. I could've been somebody, instead of a bum, which is what I am."

FILM:
. . . .

YEAR:
. . . .

ACTOR:
. . . .

▶ SILHOUETTES

GIVE EACH COUNTRY ITS CORRESPONDING NAME.

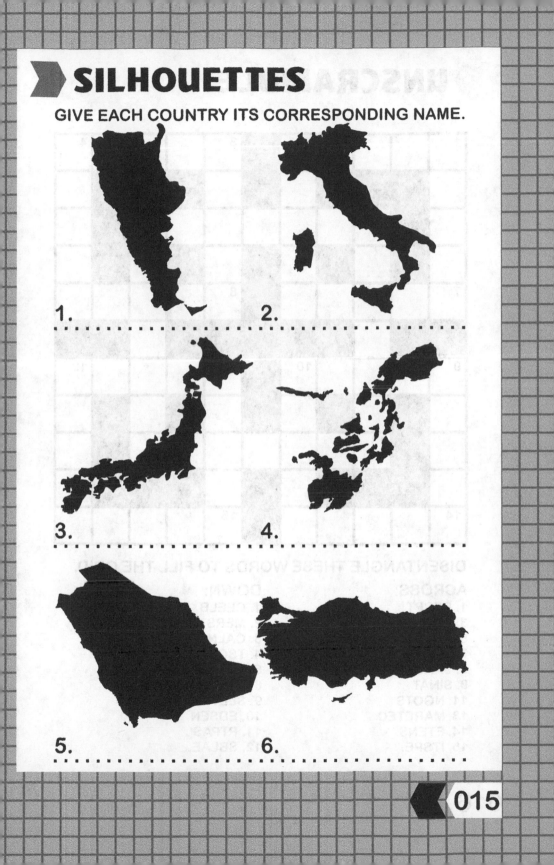

1.

2.

3.

4.

5.

6.

►UNSCRAMBLE

SILHOUE

GIVE EACH COUNTRY ITS CORRESPONDING NAME

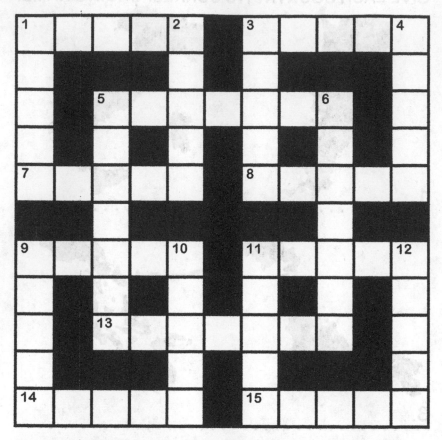

DISENTANGLE THESE WORDS TO FILL THE GRID.

ACROSS:
1. RECPT
3. LICCO
5. VANERTS
7. SEANB
8. SARGS
9. SINAT
11. NGOTS
13. MARETEC
14. ETENS
15. ITSPE.

DOWN:
1. CEELB
2. MERST
3. CALNG
4. TSOCS
5. TIPASSC
6. TERAINE
9. SLETE
10. EDSEN
11. RTPAS
12. SBLAE.

► TRIVIA

FAMOUS PEOPLE FROM THE PAST.

1. ....

49BC ► Expanded the Roman Republic through a series of battles across Europe before declaring himself dictator for life.

2. ....

1271 ► Traveled from Europe to Asia in 1271–95, remaining in China for seventeen of those years.

3. ....

1279 ► Ruled the largest contiguous land empire in history.

4. ....

1520 ► Became a prominent monarch of 16th-century Europe, presiding over the apex of the Ottoman Empire's power.

5. ....

1560 ► Founded the Presbyterian Church of Scotland.

6. ....

1855 ► A social reformer and statistician, she founded modern nursing.

7. ....

1855 ► Developed a style of poetry that was distinctly American and democratic.

8. ....

1863 ► Preserved the Union during the American Civil War and brought about the emancipation of slaves.

DEFINITION SEARCH

```
G Z X P S S O I L
F R E G N F P B K
L E G E G L U E B
D E L C C U R L Y
A D V L U Y U L B
H R P E L B H A U
O O C O R H E L L
L R H H H V R L L
D N H O O K D Y J
```

- Friend.
- Passageway.
- Alexander Graham—
- Light—
- Uncastrated bovine.
- Made of 6 equal squares.
- Stooge #3.
- Profound.
- Laid by birds and reptiles.
- Knocked down.
- Fixative.
- Opposite of Heaven.
- Group of mammals.
- Embrace.
- Sacred.
- Captain—
- Curved glass.
- Bar on pivot.
- Tall and slender grass.
- Ground.

▶ RIDDLES

DO YOU REMEMBER THE ANSWERS TO THESE?

"The sun bakes them,
The hand breaks them,
The foot treads on them,
and the mouth tastes them."

WHAT IS IT?

. . . .

"Soars without wings,
sees without eyes,
travels without leaving
home."

WHAT IS IT?

. . . .

"The rich men want it,
the wise men know it,
the poor all need it,
the kind men show it."

WHAT IS IT?

. . . .

▶ MATCHMAKER

DRAW A LINE TO CONNECT EACH OF THE NEXT 10 PRESIDENTS OF THE UNITED STATES TO THE YEARS THEY SPENT IN OFFICE.

11. 1845-1849	James Abram Garfield
12. 1849-1850	Zachary Taylor
13. 1850-1853	Ulyses Simpson Grant
14. 1853-1857	James Buchanan
15. 1857-1861	Rutherford B. Hayes
16. 1861-1865	Millard Fillmore
17. 1865-1869	Abraham Lincoln
18. 1869-1877	Andrew Johnson
19. 1877-1881	James Knox Polk
20. 1881-1881	Franklin Pierce

CROSSWORD

ACROSS:
1. Further negative.
5. Head.
8. Functioning correctly.
11. Russian queen.
13. Assemble together.
15. Drill bit.
16. Nipple.
17. Legend.
20. Traveling by boat.
22. Holy bovine (2 words).
24. Lyric poem.
25. Organ of sight.

DOWN:
1. Opposite of yes.
2. Choose.
3. To come up above.
4. Liable to change.
5. Coin worth.
6. Reproductive cells.
7. Exist.
9. Bolted.
10. Slang for breast.
12. NCIS network.
14. Mineral spring.
18. Breeze.
19. Cover
20. Dejected.
21. Gentile.
22. South (abbr.).
23. Us.

021

WORDSEARCH

```
C A R A V A G G I O V
P E D A V I N C I Z M
O D Z U S V D S E C I
L A B A R I V E R A I
L U C R N E M V G L Q
O M H N A N R O A A J
C I A V S N E D N O S
K E G L B A C O N E S
B R A Q U E E U E G T
R B L Y P I C A S S O
B A L T H U S P B I M
```

FIND 16 FAMOUS ARTISTS AND WRITE THEM BELOW:

....
....
....
....
....
....
....
....

WORDOKU

FILL EVERY ROW, COLUMN, AND 3X3 SECTOR,
USING EACH GIVEN LETTER ONLY ONCE!

▶ QUOTES

HOW MANY OF THESE MOVIE QUOTES CAN YOU IDENTIFY?

"May the Force be with you."

FILM:
. . . .

YEAR:
. . . .

ACTOR:
. . . .

FILM:
. . . .

YEAR:
. . . .

ACTOR:
. . . .

"Mama always said life was like a box of chocolates. You never know what you're gonna get."

"Get your stinking paws off me, you damned dirty ape."

FILM:
. . . .

YEAR:
. . . .

ACTOR:
. . . .

SILHOUETTES

GIVE EACH COUNTRY ITS CORRESPONDING NAME.

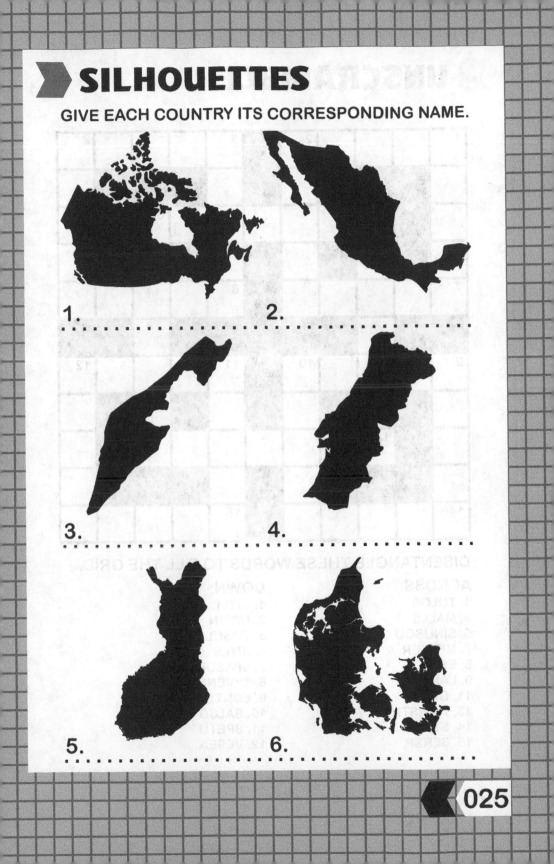

1.

2.

3.

4.

5.

6.

UNSCRAMBLE

SILHOU

GIVE EACH COUNTRY ITS CORRESPONDING NAME.

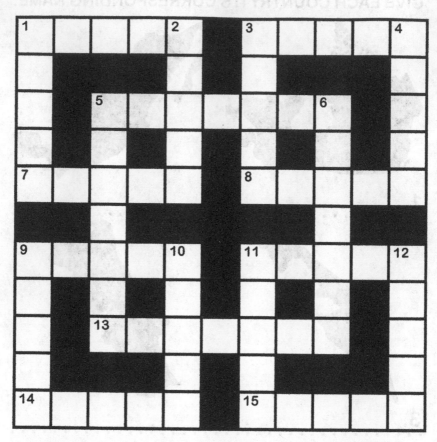

DISENTANGLE THESE WORDS TO FILL THE GRID.

ACROSS:
1. TULOS
3. MALLS
5. SINUSOU
7. MESTER
8. ESILV
9. LANGS
11. GESIN
13. WARSTHY
14. STRUS
15. SERSP.

DOWN:
1. CITLI
2. USSIN
3. TOSOL
4. SITLS
5. SPASURS
6. TYVENSE
9. ECNTS
10. SALSG
11. SPETU
12. VESEA.

▶ TRIVIA

FAMOUS PEOPLE FROM THE PAST.

1.

323BC▶ Founded around twenty cities that bore his name. When he died, his empire was the largest of its time.

2.

161 ▶ A renowned philosopher, he was also known as the last of the Five Good Emperors.

3.

1025 ▶ Regarded as one of the most significant polymaths of his era, he wrote a summary of all the medical knowledge of his time.

4.

1559 ▶ As a ruler, she created an era of peace and prosperity which ushered England as a major world power.

5.

1885 ▶ An English novelist and Victorian writer of African frontier adventure novels.

6.

1904 ▶ Earned a bachelor of arts degree, and went on to become an author and activist, despite being deaf and blind.

7.

1928 ▶ With his brother Roy, he co-founded one of the best-known motion-picture production companies in the world.

8.

1954 ▶ Awarded the Nobel Prize for Literature, he had a sparse narrative style, which had a strong influence on 20th-century fiction.

DEFINITION SEARCH

```
S F A L S E W B M
O L S N A P I U V
A W A R D T D L X
R B T P P E E L M
G A Z E T E K E O
U T L A N C H L N
E S E K O T H E E
Z R U R A L S S Y
T Y P E M M I S S
```

- Quarrel.
- Prize.
- Forbids.
- Male bovine.
- Untrue.
- Stare.
- Leg joint.
- Deceased.
- Fewer.
- Bypass.
- Exchange medium.
- Point.
- Skin removal.
- Solid mineral.
- Countryside.
- Hit with palm.
- Rested.
- Break.
- Portable shelters.
- Word.
- Archaic you.
- Objective case of "they".
- Cured.
- Font.
- Broad.

▶ RIDDLES

DO YOU REMEMBER THE ANSWERS TO THESE?

"Streets, but no pavement.
Cities, but no buildings.
Forests, yet no trees.
Rivers, yet no water."

WHAT IS IT?

. . . .

"Iron roof, glass walls,
burns and burns,
and never falls."

WHAT IS IT?

. . . .

"Goes on four legs in the
morning, on two at midday,
upon three in the evening."

WHAT IS IT?

. . . .

▶ MATCHMAKER

DRAW A LINE TO CONNECT ANOTHER 10 PRESIDENTS OF THE UNITED STATES TO THE YEARS THEY SPENT IN OFFICE.

21. 1881-1885 · · · · · · · · · · Chester A. Arthur

22. 1885-1889   William H. Taft

23. 1889-1893   Stephen G. Cleveland

24. 1893-1897   Warren G. Harding

25. 1897-1901   Woodrow Wilson

26. 1901-1909   William McKinley

27. 1909-1913   Benjamin Harrison

28. 1913-1921   Calvin Coolidge

29. 1921-1923   Theodore Roosevelt

30. 1923-1929   Stephen G. Cleveland

CROSSWORD

¹	²	³	█	⁴	⁵	⁶	⁷	█
⁸			█	⁹				¹⁰
¹¹			¹²			█	¹³	
█		¹⁴			█	¹⁵		
¹⁶	¹⁷			█	¹⁸			
¹⁹			█	²⁰			█	█
²¹		█	²²			█	²³	²⁴
²⁵		²⁶		█	█	²⁷		
█	²⁸				█	²⁹		

ACROSS:
1. Unique ideology.
4. The seven—
8. Grassy land.
9. Caffè—.
11. Surgical blade.
13. Before noon.
14. Pull along.
15. Snow sport.
16. Back end.
18. Sharpen.
19. Matured.
20. Saturday (abbr.).
21. 3.14
22. Heterodoxy.
25. Person who skis.
27. Determining word.
28. Sicilian volcano.
29. Allow.

DOWN:
1. Unwell.
2. Body of water.
3. Predatory insect.
4. Turn violently.
5. Ingest.
6. Location.
7. Wooden post.
10. Discharge.
12. Colonel (abbr.).
15. Small Jewish town.
16. At most.
17. Identical.
18. Armed conflict.
20. Serum (pl)
22. Female fowl.
23. Female pron.
24. So far.
26. A.K.A. Pennywise.

WORDSEARCH

```
C S E A E L E P H A N T R
A H L S E A L I O N Q A Y
P B L U E W H A L E E T S
Y W Q U Q Y K U S B A I W
B O W I E K E G R C Q T L
A Z Y Q Y E E A R V X P Y
R Q R K T F L O C P N M K
A L S A F O E R Q L O A C
G B N A P S W H Y K Z M T
R A R K O D I A K B E A R
M I U O F P B I S O N R A
G K M R H I N O C E R O S
H I P P O P O T A M U S F
```

FIND 14 LARGE MAMMALS AND WRITE THEM BELOW:

....
....
....
....
....
....

CAN YOU THINK OF ANY OTHERS?

....
....

WORDOKU

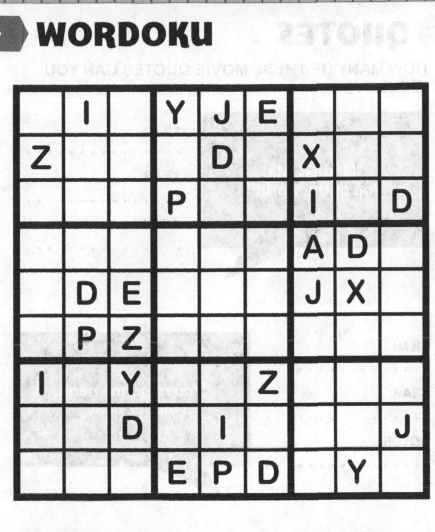

FILL EVERY ROW, COLUMN, AND 3X3 SECTOR,
USING EACH GIVEN LETTER ONLY ONCE!

QUOTES

HOW MANY OF THESE MOVIE QUOTES CAN YOU IDENTIFY?

"Made it, Ma! Top of the world!"

FILM:
. . . .

YEAR:
. . . .

ACTOR:
. . . .

FILM:
. . . .

YEAR:
. . . .

ACTOR:
. . . .

"You're gonna need a bigger boat."

"If you build it, he will come."

FILM:
. . . .

YEAR:
. . . .

ACTOR:
. . . .

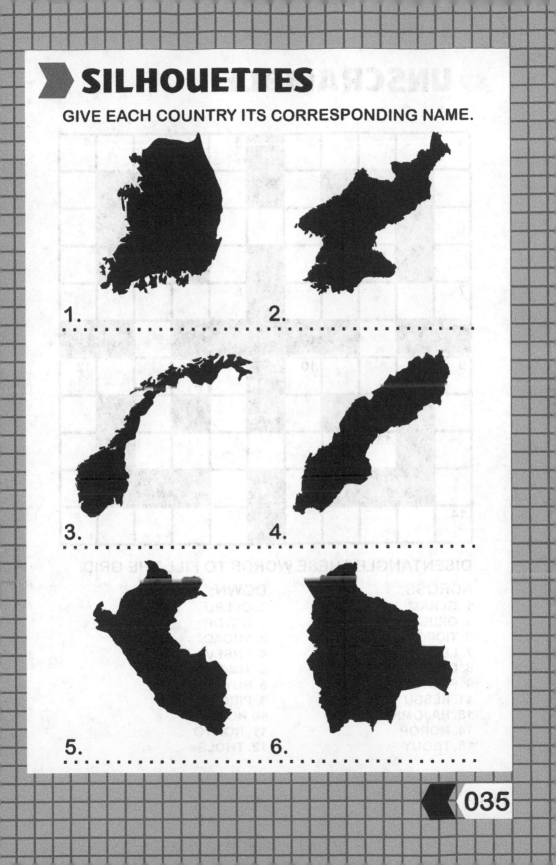

▶ SILHOUETTES

GIVE EACH COUNTRY ITS CORRESPONDING NAME.

1.

2.

3.

4.

5.

6.

▶ UNSCRAMBLE

SILHOU

GIVE EACH COUNTRY ITS CORRESPONDING NAME.

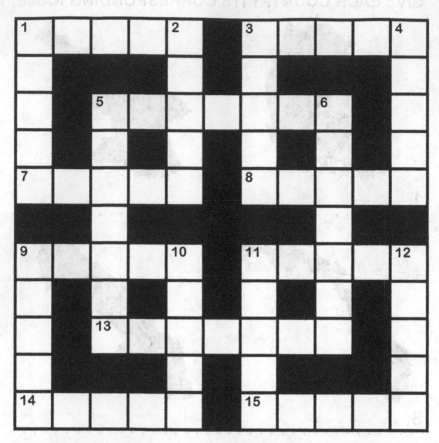

DISENTANGLE THESE WORDS TO FILL THE GRID.

ACROSS:
1. GERAM
3. ORUSY
5. TIOPCAL
7. LERIT
8. DONAD
9. FOMYC
11. RESBU
13. HAJOMNG
14. MOROP
15. THOUY

DOWN:
1. GELRU
2. ORTOR
3. YUCAC
4. ENSEV
5. TIMOPUM
6. BUYALDG
9. PIRCH
10. HOAOY
11. ROMYO
12. THOLS

FAMOUS PEOPLE FROM THE PAST.

1.

1761 ► Showing prodigious musical ability, he composed from the age of five and performed before royalty.

2.

1781 ► Believed that reason is the source of morality, and that aesthetics arise from a faculty of disinterested judgment.

3.

1797 ► Was the first President to belong to a political party—the Federalists.

4.

1837 ► Her reign saw great cultural expansion and advances in industry, science, and communications.

5.

1919 ► One of the most influential filmmakers in history, he worked in close partnership with his wife.

6.

1934 ► Her acting career spanned over six decades, during which time she was honored with four Oscars.

7.

1939 ► Famous for his inspiring speeches and for his refusal to give in, even when things were dire, he successfully lead the UK through World War Two.

8.

1950 ► Created a famous newspaper comic strip about a gang of kids and a beagle.

DEFINITION SEARCH

```
W I R E O W E V E
T H I E F L I O N
S H R L D O Y C R
G R A I N S E A M
B R N N E E L L O
O Q G C O O L S M
T H I P S F M L E
H M E A T G A I N
T H U M B C W T T
```

- Two together.
- Peaceful.
- Aplomb.
- Profit.
- Cereals.
- Wild rose fruits.
- Glazes.
- Lazy.
- Large African feline.
- Be deprived of.
- Flesh.
- Rodents.
- Little while.
- Exclude.
- Using speech.
- Chimed.
- Communists (slang).
- Narrow opening.
- Related to the sun.
- Introduces comparison.
- Burglar.
- First digit.
- We have (contr.).
- Metal filament.
- Shout.

PROVERBS

DO YOU REMEMBER THE MEANINGS OF THESE?

"The grass is always greener on the other side of the fence."

WHAT DOES IT MEAN?

. . . .
. . . .
. . . .
. . . .
. . . .

WHAT DOES IT MEAN?

. . . .
. . . .
. . . .
. . . .
. . . .

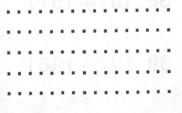

"Strike while the iron is hot."

"Don't judge a book by its cover."

WHAT DOES IT MEAN?

. . . .
. . . .
. . . .
. . . .

▶ MATCHMAKER

DRAW A LINE TO CONNECT 10 MORE PRESIDENTS OF
THE UNITED STATES TO THE YEARS THEY SPENT
IN OFFICE.

31. 1929-1933   Richard M. Nixon

32. 1933-1945   Lyndon B. Johnson

33. 1945-1953   Harry S. Truman

34. 1953-1961   Franklin D. Roosevelt

35. 1961-1963   John F. Kennedy

36. 1963-1969   Gerald R. Ford

37. 1969-1974   Herbert C. Hoover

38. 1974-1977   James E. Carter, Jr.

39. 1977-1981   Dwight D. Eisenhower

40. 1981-1989   Ronald W. Reagan

CROSSWORD

ACROSS:
1. Bitterly regret.
4. Tavern.
8. Culinary herb.
11. Like.
13. Japanese hostess.
14. Malnourished.
16. Sink valve.
17. Breeze.
18. Pastor (abbr.).
19. Tack.
20. Where concubines live.
22. Aligned (alt).
24. Hence.
25. Nightshade.
27. Animal lair.
28. Loneliest number.

DOWN:
2. Higher.
3. Enthusiastic.
4. 23rd letter (Greek).
5. Irish overcoat.
6. Acquits.
7. 19th letter (Greek).
9. Ruby—.
10. Chatter.
12. Moved slowly.
15. Limited.
18. Transmits broadcasts.
19. —smear.
20. Female fowl.
21. Bovine sound.
23. Church sister.
26. Analog (abbr.).

WORDSEARCH

```
T R O B I N S O N C R U S O E
J H U N C L E T O M C A B I N
W A R O F T H E W O R L D S E
B T R E A S U R E I S L A N D
S Q J R E W H I T E F A N G J
S P M Q R M F E O S P I D B U
W N E L D K U W I T K V P G N
D R K P N N P S F L M A B N G
X S B N E Q K I K P L N U B L
N A O D Y S S E Y E B H L I E
F Z L S E O A J X A T O R R B
J A M O B Y D I C K M E X Z O
W G R E A T G A T S B Y E P O
M T H E G O O D E A R T H R K
G R A P E S O F W R A T H Q S
```

FIND 14 CLASSIC BOOKS AND WRITE THEM BELOW:

. . . .
. . . .
. . . .
. . . .
. . . .
. . . .
. . . .

CAN YOU THINK OF ANY OTHERS?

. . . .
. . . .

▶ WORDOKU

FILL EVERY ROW, COLUMN, AND 3X3 SECTOR,
USING EACH GIVEN LETTER ONLY ONCE!

QUOTES

HOW MANY OF THESE MOVIE QUOTES CAN YOU IDENTIFY?

"Fasten your seatbelts. It's going to be a bumpy night."

FILM:
. . . .

YEAR:
. . . .

ACTOR:
. . . .

FILM:
. . . .

YEAR:
. . . .

ACTOR:
. . . .

"What we've got here is failure to communicate."

"No wire hangers, ever!"

FILM:
. . . .

YEAR:
. . . .

ACTOR:
. . . .

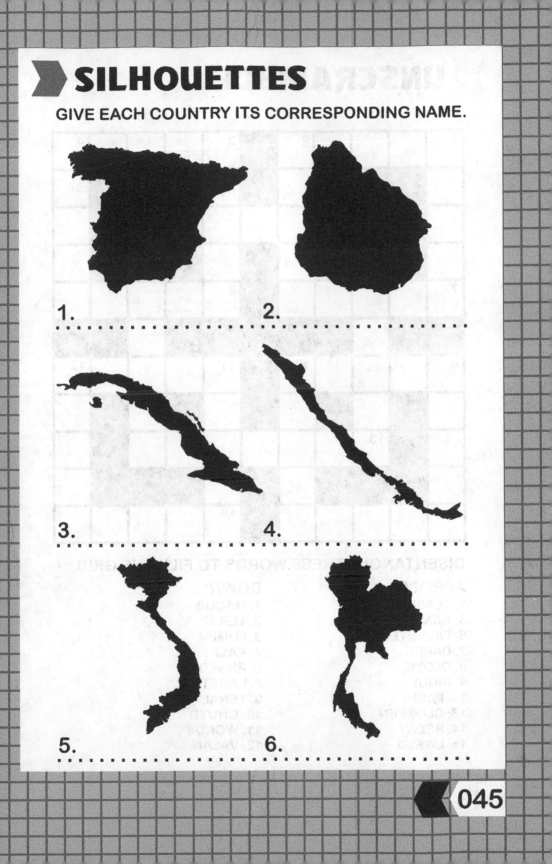

► SILHOUETTES
GIVE EACH COUNTRY ITS CORRESPONDING NAME.

1.

2.

3.

4.

5.

6.

► UNSCRAMBLE

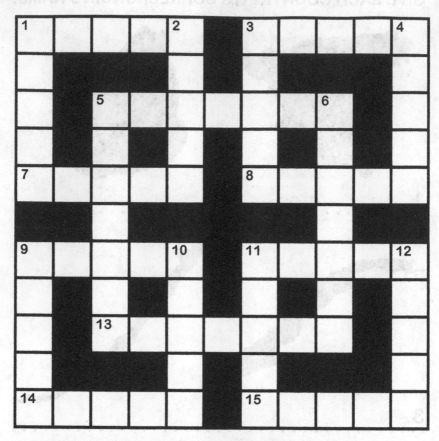

DISENTANGLE THESE WORDS TO FILL THE GRID.

ACROSS:
1. TOMPS
3. GILVI
5. PAULETE
7. DAREC
8. OLDYM
9. RIDUL
11. PASIN
13. CLOSEEN
14. REDAY
15. LWELD.

DOWN:
1. MACUS
2. TERAP
3. LUMEV
4. EALFY
5. ENSEDOR
6. LAGETIL
9. YERAL
10. CHUYD
11. WORDS
12. VALAN.

▶ TRIVIA

FAMOUS PEOPLE FROM THE PAST.

1.

1800 ▶ Commissioned by Napoleon to design the first practical submarine in history.

2.

1867 ▶ Registered 355 patents, including dynamite!

3.

1872 ▶ Signed into law an Act of Congress that established Yellowstone National Park, the nation's first National Park.

4.

1932 ▶ Wrote a series of novels about her homesteading childhood in Wisconsin and Kansas.

5.

1939 ▶ One of the most important and influential film directors, he frequently used long-shots, featuring vast landscapes.

6.

1951 ▶ Created a famous daily cartoon about a mischievous five-year-old kid.

7.

1954 ▶ Won eleven Grammy Awards, an Academy Award for Best Supporting Actor, and the Presidential Medal of Freedom.

8.

1955 ▶ By refusing to give up her seat to a white man, she helped initiate the civil rights movement in the United States.

◗ DEFINITION SEARCH

```
U R C H I N S V E
S B E G E G J I V
C O Y P U E A D W
A R I L I A R E S
A N S R E N R O O
S E E Z S G E S U
H W A X Y H D D R
Y R M X I M O W S
P E A C H T R E E
```

- Greek god of war.
- Exterior seed covering.
- Pale grayish.
- Carried.
- Nutria.
- 4ᵗʰ largest Great Lake.
- Way out.
- Wild cherry.
- Increased.
- Drought-resistant pea.
- Jolted.
- Cuts down.
- Belonging to us.
- Fruit tree.
- Destroy.
- Felt unhappy.
- Junction.
- Foot covering.
- Bullets (slang).
- Long-range shooter.
- Spiny sea creature.
- Analog recordings.
- Very pale

PROVERBS

DO YOU REMEMBER THE MEANINGS OF THESE?

"Too many cooks spoil the broth."

WHAT DOES IT MEAN?

. . . .
. . . .
. . . .
. . . .
. . . .
. . . .

WHAT DOES IT MEAN?

. . . .
. . . .
. . . .
. . . .
. . . .
. . . .

"You can't have your cake and eat it too."

"When in Rome, do as the Romans do."

WHAT DOES IT MEAN?

. . . .
. . . .
. . . .
. . . .
. . . .
. . . .

MATCHMAKER

WHICH TWO ARE PERFECTLY ALIKE?

1.
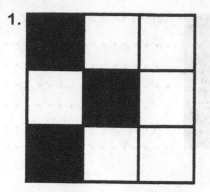

2.

3.
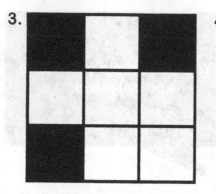

4.

5.

6.
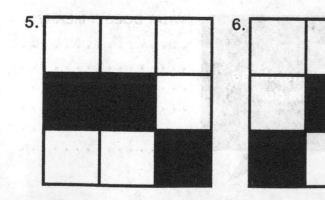

CROSSWORD

ACROSS:
1. Twitch.
4. Lettuce variety.
7. Crafted.
9. To be.
10. Ancient string instrument.
12. Body of water.
13. Vow.
15. Italy (abbr.).
16. Addition result.
17. Hello.
18. Horn sound.
20. Balanced.
21. Uproar.
23. I.
24. Result of loud noise.
26. Chilly.
27. Baton

DOWN:
1. Red fruit for salads.
2. Instant Message (abbr.).
3. Heavenly.
4. Measures pressure.
5. Notion.
6. Beryllium (abbr.).
7. Rock salt.
8. Belonging to me.
11. Gleamed.
14. Given a specific characteristic.
19. Cookie brand.
22. Indicates bond.
24. Perform an action.
25. Negative response.

WORDSEARCH

```
L G E D S A M N A U Q B X
I A L O J C G O C K A K A
B R T C P C E F O Q D H R
R D K T J O P O C T W R C
A E I O D U C Q S X E D H
R N N R V N V I Z H T I I
I E L G V T L U C A I D T
A R C K I A Q A F R G R E
N H Q L N N E Q G T B I C
L N I R E T E Y D I A V T
A G U W S R P E O S K E A
T O Z M U X K R R T E R P
J C A R P E N T E R R M W
```

FIND 14 JOBS AND WRITE THEM BELOW:

....
....
....
....
....
....

CAN YOU THINK OF ANY OTHERS?

....
....

WORDOKU

FILL EVERY ROW, COLUMN, AND 3X3 SECTOR,
USING EACH GIVEN LETTER ONLY ONCE!

▶ QUOTES

HOW MANY OF THESE MOVIE QUOTES CAN YOU IDENTIFY?

"Listen to them. Children of the night! What music they make."

FILM:
. . . .

YEAR:
. . . .

ACTOR:
. . . .

FILM:
. . . .

YEAR:
. . . .

ACTOR:
. . . .

"Toga! Toga!"

"Carpe diem. Seize the day, boys. Make your lives extraordinary."

FILM:
. . . .

YEAR:
. . . .

ACTOR:
. . . .

► SILHOUETTES

GIVE EACH STATE ITS CORRESPONDING NAME.

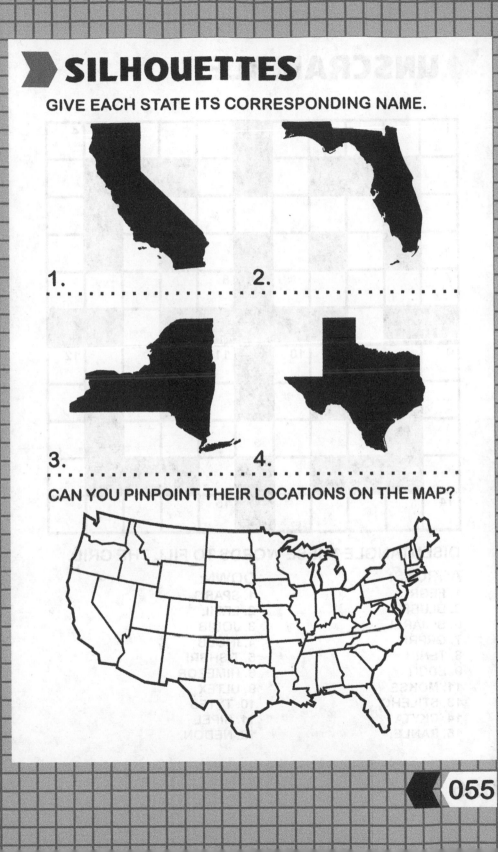

1. ....

2. ....

3. ....

4. ....

CAN YOU PINPOINT THEIR LOCATIONS ON THE MAP?

► UNSCRAMBLE

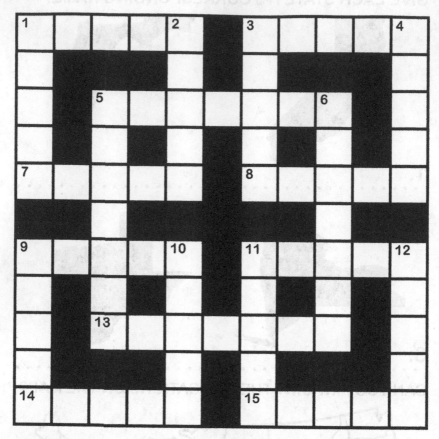

DISENTANGLE THESE WORDS TO FILL THE GRID.

ACROSS:
1. FEGRI
3. BLUBR
5. BLJAREL
7. ORPRI
8. TENIU
9. EDCIT
11. MOKSE
13. STILEHO
14. CKYTA
15. RANLE.

DOWN:
1. SPARG
2. ERFIL
3. JOUIB
4. INGEB
5. TISHBRI
6. HIMEZOR
9. ULTEX
10. TYTES
11. SIPEL
12. NEDON.

▶ TRIVIA

FAMOUS PEOPLE FROM THE PAST.

1.

1783 ▶ Invented the hot-air balloon, an important step in the development of aeronautics.

2.

1821 ▶ Discovered electromagnetic rotations, the principle behind the electric motor.

3.

1851 ▶ Wrote novels, short-stories, and poems, including his masterpiece, Moby Dick.

4.

1928 ▶ An aviation pioneer and author, she was the first female aviator to fly solo across the Atlantic Ocean.

5.

1936 ▶ While never earning more than a high-school diploma, he is considered the father of modern rocketry.

6.

1938 ▶ Directed and narrated the 1938 radio adaptation of The War of the Worlds.

7.

1941 ▶ Alongside writer Joe Simon, he co-created the comic book character "Captain America."

8.

1959 ▶ Created and was in full creative control over classic TV show The Twilight Zone.

DEFINITION SEARCH

```
L A Z D R O F Y L E
A C E D O E Y H N G
R H O V E L L E N D
C O N D U C E I R F
X C E E R T S R C U
P C S S T E W S S S
T G N I K S G R B S
R E M A D E A O H E
P E R U S E G E Q S
I D L E D H A J P F
```

- Did very well.
- Surrender.
- Bring about.
- Male ducks.
- Remnant.
- Hearing organs.
- Radiate.
- Frets.
- Demented.
- Contribute.
- A lot of.
- Inheritors.
- Squalid dwelling.
- Vegetated.
- Grant.
- Bed fabric.
- In singles.
- Hearing in court.
- Drafts.
- Inspect.
- Sacred artifacts.
- Made again.
- Masses of fish eggs.
- Chant.
- Brood.
- Adolescent.

▶ PROVERBS

DO YOU REMEMBER THE MEANINGS OF THESE?

"Many hands make
light work."

WHAT DOES IT MEAN?

· · · · · · · · · · · · · · ·
· · · · · · · · · · · · · · ·
· · · · · · · · · · · · · · ·
· · · · · · · · · · · · · · ·
· · · · · · · · · · · · · · ·
· · · · · · · · · · · · · · ·

WHAT DOES IT MEAN?

· · · · · · · · · · · · · · ·
· · · · · · · · · · · · · · ·
· · · · · · · · · · · · · · ·
· · · · · · · · · · · · · · ·
· · · · · · · · · · · · · · ·
· · · · · · · · · · · · · · ·

"Don't cross the bridge
until you come to it."

"Honesty is the
best policy."

WHAT DOES IT MEAN?

· · · · · · · · · · · · · · ·
· · · · · · · · · · · · · · ·
· · · · · · · · · · · · · · ·
· · · · · · · · · · · · · · ·
· · · · · · · · · · · · · · ·
· · · · · · · · · · · · · · ·

MATCHMAKER

WHICH TWO ARE PERFECTLY ALIKE?

1.
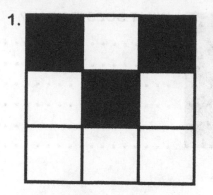

2.

3.
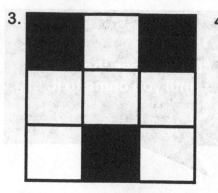

4.
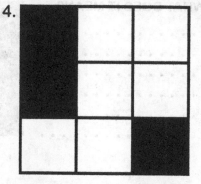

5.

6.

CROSSWORD

	1	2	3		4	5		
6		7		8				9
10	11						12	
13					14			
			15					
16		17			18	19		20
21				22				
		23						
	24				25			

ACROSS:
1. Gene carrier.
4. To consume.
7. Fatuous.
10. Twin hulled boat.
13. Repose.
14. Asian starling.
15. Repent.
16. Disco dancing.
18. Pathway.
21. Lacking capacity.
23. Person sentenced to life.
24. Varnish (abbr.).
25. Coloring pigment.

DOWN:
2. Lice eggs.
3. Doesn't need air.
4. Enamel coated.
5. Ethereal.
6. Expert.
8. Americium (abbr.).
9. Upward prefix.
11. Moses' brother.
12. Concerning (prep.).
16. —rummy.
17. Celebration.
19. Greceful movement.
20. Visual organ.
22. Kipling's poem.

WORDSEARCH

```
F B B Y E N I S E I Y N M
R O R M M A C K E N Z I E
I I A A O K X C N D L Q K
N D O O H X F W I U E X O
M G B D K M V L G S N F N
U C M N E W A N E Q A A G
R O I O O L O P R E K M M
R N T B L Z A A U N A U Y
A G R L A R N P K T H R E
Y O S M N E I U L U R Z L
S H A T T A L A R A B A L
P A R A N A E O D U T S O
Y A N G T Z E J G E U A W
```

FIND 18 OF THE WORLD'S GREATEST RIVERS:

....
....
....
....
....
....
....

CAN YOU THINK OF ANY OTHERS?

....

WORDOKU

FILL EVERY ROW, COLUMN, AND 3X3 SECTOR,
USING EACH GIVEN LETTER ONLY ONCE!

►► QUOTES

HOW MANY OF THESE MOVIE QUOTES CAN YOU IDENTIFY?

"A boy's best friend is his mother."

FILM:
. . . .

YEAR:
. . . .

ACTOR:
. . . .

FILM:
. . . .

YEAR:
. . . .

ACTOR:
. . . .

"You've got to ask yourself one question: 'Do I feel lucky?' Well, do ya, punk?"

"Show me the money!"

FILM:
. . . .

YEAR:
. . . .

ACTOR:
. . . .

▶ SILHOUETTES

GIVE EACH STATE ITS CORRESPONDING NAME.

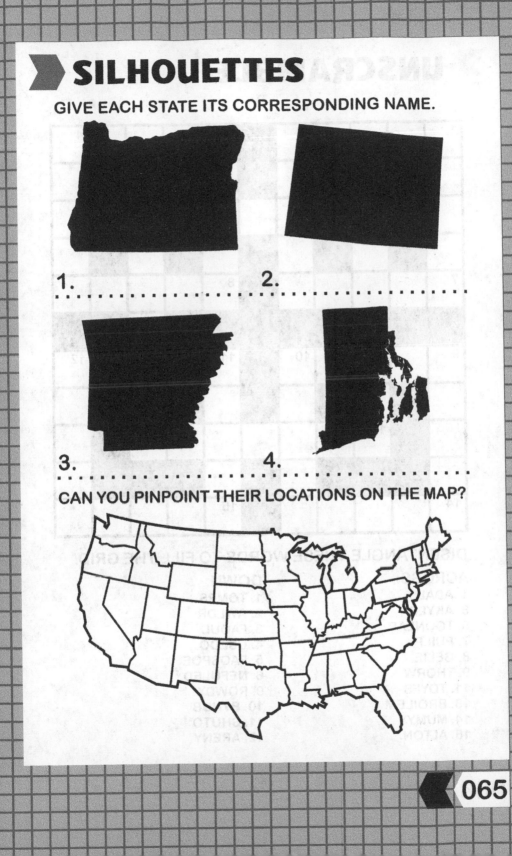

1.

2.

3.

4.

CAN YOU PINPOINT THEIR LOCATIONS ON THE MAP?

▶ UNSCRAMBLE

DISENTANGLE THESE WORDS TO FILL THE GRID.

ACROSS:
1. ADALS
3. AKYLD
5. TOONLAP
7. PUILP
8. GELIE
9. THORW
11. TOYFS
13. BROILEM
14. MUMYY
15. ALTON.

DOWN:
1. TOMPS
2. AWLDR
3. FAOUL
4. USEDO
5. PAOSPOE
6. NEFULED
9. ROWDY
10. BYHUB
11. SHUTO
12. ARENY

▶ TRIVIA

FAMOUS PEOPLE FROM THE PAST.

1.

1767 ▶ Explored and settled what is now Kentucky, but reportedly never wore a coonskin cap while doing so.

2.

1821 ▶ One of America's earliest practitioners of the short story, and considered the inventor of the detective fiction genre.

3.

1881 ▶ A hospital nurse during the Civil War, she founded the American Red Cross.

4.

1918 ▶ His newspaper cartoon featuring odd facts from around the world would branch out into books, radio, and television.

5.

1948 ▶ Founded the State of Israel, and became its first Prime Minister.

6.

1955 ▶ Discovered and developed one of the first successful polio vaccines, which he purposefully did not patent.

7.

1977 ▶ Despite a troubled production, his successful <u>Star Wars</u> film became a global cultural phenomenon.

8.

1981 ▶ Starting out in radio, film, and television, he would launch a political career that would see him become America's 40th President.

DEFINITION SEARCH

```
G A U G E S N H G K
C Q T F M R P E C K
É T U I A B É A H O
L O R E N U Y T E N
A P N E Q O X R S U
Y T A S V Y N A T D
M S I N E I R S S G
A R E E D T S H O E
N O V A T A D E A D
Y P B P A B E S O M
```

- Broom made with twigs.
- Floating navigation mark.
- Caskets.
- Lifeless.
- Be paid.
- Delegate.
- Ornamental case for needles.
- Imitation.
- Measure.
- Skin eruption due to heat.
- Privy to.
- Non-professional.
- Sophia—.
- —tide.
- Suddenly bright star.
- Poked.
- Beginning.
- Chooses.
- Large Asian mammal.
- —Peck.
- Purses the lips.
- Amend.
- Bawdy.
- Footwear.
- Reverse direction.
- Chatter.

PROVERBS

DO YOU REMEMBER THE MEANINGS OF THESE?

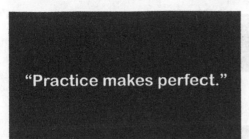

"Practice makes perfect."

WHAT DOES IT MEAN?

. . . .
. . . .
. . . .
. . . .
. . . .
. . . .

WHAT DOES IT MEAN?

. . . .
. . . .
. . . .
. . . .
. . . .
. . . .

"Where there's a will, there's a way."

WHAT DOES IT MEAN?

. . . .
. . . .
. . . .
. . . .
. . . .

"Look before you leap."

MATCHMAKER

WHICH TWO ARE PERFECTLY ALIKE?

1.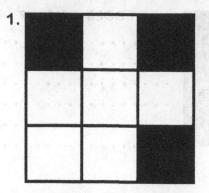

2.

3.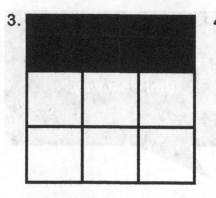

4.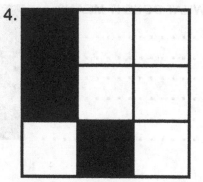

5.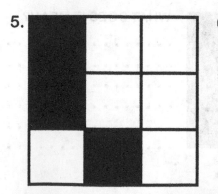

6.

CROSSWORD

ACROSS:
1. Mindless.
8. Emerged.
12. Thermometer (abbr.).
14. Roman copper coin.
15. Earlier.
17. In use.
18. Swine.
19. Entertaining.
20. Helium (abbr.).
21. Imp.
23. Function preposition.
25. Cinder.
27. Elected Regional Assembly (abbr.).
28. Treatise.
31. Trodden.

DOWN:
2. Used to row.
3. Otherwise.
4. Lengthy.
5. Isaiah.
6. Lay.
7. Salt water expanse.
9. Tennessee.
11. Embers.
13. None among thieves.
15. Long time.
16. Away.
20. Headwear.
22. Hindmost.
24. A long way.
26. Female pron.
27. Watch closely.
29. Extremely.
30. —&T.

WORDSEARCH

```
R E Y K J A V I K M X
H E L S I N K I C E Y
L S E O U L Z N O X A
M O S C O W I R P I M
P T G I L L G O E C S
R O L B B N Y M N O T
A K P U I F P E H C E
G Y D J Q S A C A I R
U O I C A I R O G T D
E E M A D R I D E Y A
B E R L I N S K N K M
```

FIND 16 OF THE WORLD'S CAPITALS:

....
....
....
....
....
....
....

CAN YOU THINK OF ANY OTHERS?

....
....

▶ WORDOKU

K			I			T	W	
	T	W					S	
			A			R		K
	R	T	K					N
I				W	M	A		
W		N			A			
	T					W	I	
	I	M			T			A

FILL EVERY ROW, COLUMN, AND 3X3 SECTOR, USING EACH GIVEN LETTER ONLY ONCE!

QUOTES

HOW MANY OF THESE MOVIE QUOTES CAN YOU IDENTIFY?

"I'm walking here! I'm walking here!"

FILM:
. . . .
YEAR:
. . . .
ACTOR:
. . . .

FILM:
. . . .
YEAR:
. . . .
ACTOR:
. . . .

"I am serious… and don't call me Shirley."

"Somebody stop me!"

FILM:
. . . .
YEAR:
. . . .
ACTOR:
. . . .

SILHOUETTES

GIVE EACH STATE ITS CORRESPONDING NAME.

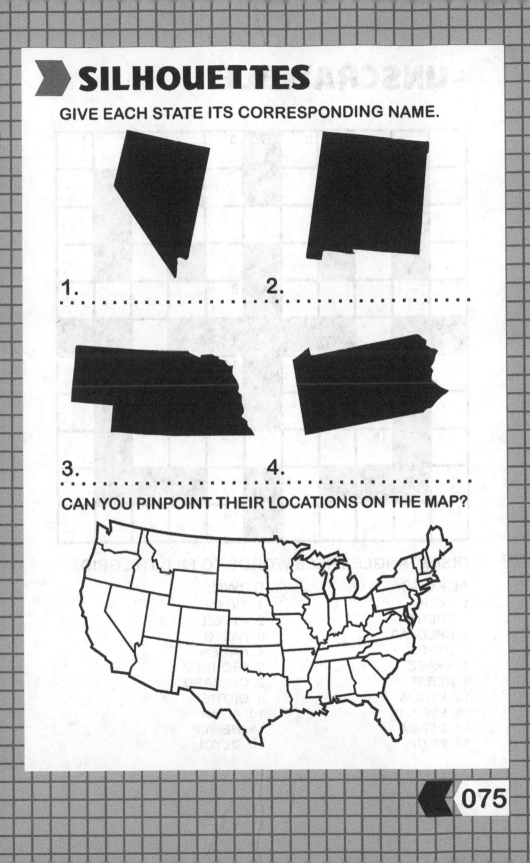

1.

2.

3.

4.

CAN YOU PINPOINT THEIR LOCATIONS ON THE MAP?

⏵ UNSCRAMBLE

DISENTANGLE THESE WORDS TO FILL THE GRID.

ACROSS:
1. AOUDI
3. THENT
5. CPEDLAP
7. UTECH
8. BRAEZ
9. KERAT
11. KYACW
13. EVEYEIL
14. DEEMA
15. PILUP

DOWN:
1. TICAN
2. ATEOR
3. PAZTO
4. NAHEN
5. LECHUCK
6. CLEBAED
9. ORTHE
10. AITAR
11. HEWLP
12. DEYOL

FAMOUS PEOPLE FROM THE PAST.

1.
....

1804 ▶ Despite a modest upbringing, he built a large empire that ruled over continental Europe before its final collapse in 1815.

2.
....

1814 ▶ Was the chief American negotiator, reaching a peace treaty that would end the War of 1812.

3.
....

1841 ▶ A professional violinist born in New York, he was kidnapped and sold into slavery, regaining his freedom twelve years later.

4.
....

1918 ▶ Found inspiration for his prints, paintings, and drawings in the Alaskan wilderness.

5.
....

1927 ▶ Founded the book packaging company which originally produced the <u>Hardy Boys</u> and <u>Nancy Drew</u> book series.

6.
....

1935 ▶ Created and retained all rights to her cartoon character "Little Lulu," becoming a licensing pioneer.

7.
....

1985 ▶ As the seventh and last leader of the Soviet Union, his domestic reforms and nuclear disarmament deals helped end the Cold War.

8.
....

1993 ▶ Her eclectic, poetic prose earned her the Nobel Prize for Literature in 1993.

```
S H O N E Y W Q A K K
I N T O A E A T S E O
G S S R H A L F T E E
N A X E T R M L R P I
I A L P E S C O O E M
F I E L D S C C N R A
I R R U Y O G A O G S
C V E O M P K L M T T
A A Q G B R U S E L L
N S C L U E S B R V D
T E D D Y M U S T F
```

- Friend.
- Amid.
- Students of celestial objects.
- Wagers.
- Traces.
- Crawled.
- Nourishes.
- Meadows.
- 1/2
- Inside.
- Guardian.
- From a particular area.
- Spar.
- Needs to.
- The hunted.
- Bars.
- Kaftan.
- Catches sight of.
- Trade.
- Glowed.
- Important.
- —bear.
- Flowers container.
- Short wavelength raditation.
- Revolutions around the sun.
- Hindu discipline.

▶ PROVERBS

DO YOU REMEMBER THE MEANINGS OF THESE?

"Beggars can't be choosers."

WHAT DOES IT MEAN?

. . . .
. . . .
. . . .
. . . .
. . . .
. . . .

WHAT DOES IT MEAN?

. . . .
. . . .
. . . .
. . . .
. . . .
. . . .

"Don't make a mountain out of a molehill."

"An apple a day keeps the doctor away."

WHAT DOES IT MEAN?

. . . .
. . . .
. . . .
. . . .
. . . .
. . . .

WHICH TWO ARE PERFECTLY ALIKE?

1.
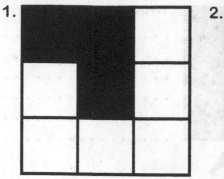

2.

3.

4.

5.
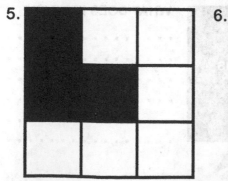

6.

CROSSWORD

ACROSS:
1. Computer—.
7. Change.
8. Region.
10. Guided.
11. Bigger than sea.
12. Ante Meridiem (abbr.).
13. Etchings.
14. Extremely (abbr.).
15. Air Traffic (abbr.).
16. Friendly.
19. —are the World.
20. Flattens.
21. Knight's title.
22. Wagon.
23. Points.
24. Teachings.

DOWN:
1. Written in verse.
2. Dispose.
3. —and on.
4. Ethnic.
5. Not be (contr.).
6. Edible muscle.
7. Vintage.
9. Solutions.
11. Oregon (abbr.).
13. Dots.
14. Grade.
17. Viva Voce.
18. —soon as.
19. Sagacity.
21. Male offspring.
23. —, Re, Mi.

WORDSEARCH

```
R A N U N C U L U S Y
Q P C X F V I O L E T
M S S S O R C H I D C
A U T K T V Z A L U A
R N A P C A I A Y X R
I F R C R N T S Y R N
G L G T N O N I J O A
O O A I U A T E C S T
L W Z N P L W E H E I
D E E S O L I D A G O
R R R B P O M P O N N
```

FIND 16 BEAUTIFUL FLOWER NAMES:

....
....
....
....
....
....
....

CAN YOU THINK OF ANY OTHERS?

....
....

WORDOKU

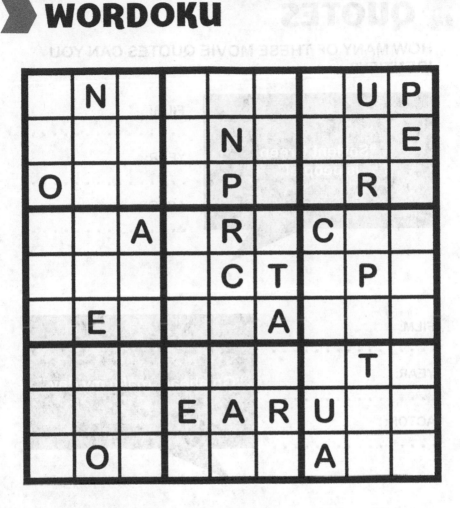

FILL EVERY ROW, COLUMN, AND 3X3 SECTOR, USING EACH GIVEN LETTER ONLY ONCE!

QUOTES

HOW MANY OF THESE MOVIE QUOTES CAN YOU IDENTIFY?

"Soylent Green is people!"

FILM:
. . . .

YEAR:
. . . .

ACTOR:
. . . .

FILM:
. . . .

YEAR:
. . . .

ACTOR:
. . . .

"Go ahead, make my day."

"I'm Batman."

FILM:
. . . .

YEAR:
. . . .

ACTOR:
. . . .

SILHOUETTES

GIVE EACH STATE ITS CORRESPONDING NAME.

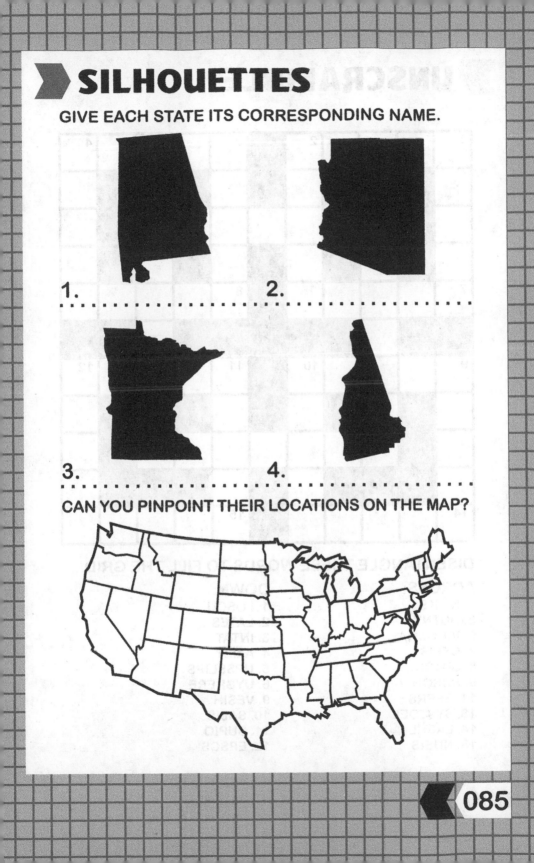

1.

2.

3.

4.

CAN YOU PINPOINT THEIR LOCATIONS ON THE MAP?

UNSCRAMBLE

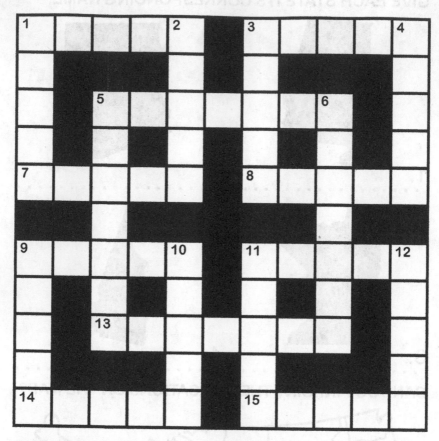

DISENTANGLE THESE WORDS TO FILL THE GRID.

ACROSS:
1. NILKS
3. NUTNY
5. VINGSHA
7. CEPIS
8. SUTRS
9. RUSOH
11. SEPRS
13. SYSTOEL
14. LASHL
15. NUSIS

DOWN:
1. LOSCU
2. LATES
3. INTAT
4. AXISY
5. UPSSLIPS
6. UYGRERE
9. VESIH
10. SALIS
11. SUPIO
12. EPSCS

▶ TRIVIA

FAMOUS PEOPLE FROM THE PAST.

1.

1800 ▶ Achieved Britain's greatest naval victory at the Battle of Trafalgar, but was killed in action.

2.

1868 ▶ The publication of his <u>Ragged Dick</u> novel established his domination over the young adult books market.

3.

1901 ▶ At a Paris show his paintings become a sensation... eleven years after his death.

4.

1921 ▶ Arose to head of the BOI, later renamed FBI, and remained as such until his death in 1972.

5.

1933 ▶ As President for more than two terms, he led the United States through the Great Depression and World War II.

6.

1962 ▶ Won the Oscar for Best Actor for his performance as Atticus Finch in the 1962 film <u>To Kill a Mockingbird</u>.

7.

1979 ▶ The first female head of government in Europe, she led her country successfully through the Falklands War of 1982.

8.

1982 ▶ His successful <u>E.T.</u> film was based on an imaginary friend he created after his parents' divorce.

DEFINITION SEARCH

```
U P D A T I N G T E A R
R P N W E X H A R M A M
D L B W S C Y N I B X A
U N S A Y S O G M I L L
V R G K C G V S X T E E
T O U W O H T N S T S S
R A Y S P R O S P E R R
O D I T H E F T I R L L
M I R A A E N Y K I O O
P E A N N E S X Y N O
F I N I T U D E Z G K
```

- Long period of time.
- Spindle.
- Johann Sebastian—.
- Souring.
- Quality of being finite.
- Bands.
- Damage.
- Originally Persia.
- Equiangular polygon.
- Gaze.
- Cetus constellation star.
- Ancient Greek hymn.
- Do well.
- Band equipment personnel.
- Hurries.
- Jagged.
- Sings "Mr. Roboto".
- Lickspittle.
- Canvas domicile.
- Robbery.
- Cut.
- Trudge.
- Forearm bone.
- Retracts words.
- Renovating.
- Language of Pakistan.

PROVERBS

DO YOU REMEMBER THE MEANINGS OF THESE?

"The early bird catches the worm."

WHAT DOES IT MEAN?

. . . .
. . . .
. . . .
. . . .
. . . .
. . . .

WHAT DOES IT MEAN?

. . . .
. . . .
. . . .
. . . .
. . . .
. . . .

"Better late than never."

"The cat is out of the bag."

WHAT DOES IT MEAN?

. . . .
. . . .
. . . .
. . . .
. . . .
. . . .

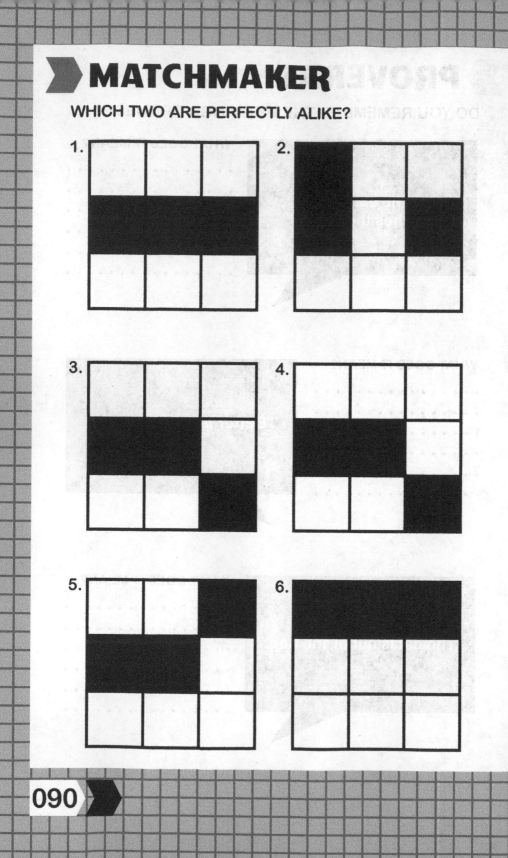

MATCHMAKER

WHICH TWO ARE PERFECTLY ALIKE?

CROSSWORD

1		**2**			**3**	**4**	**5**	**6**
	■		■		**7**			
8	**9**	■	**10**					
11		■		■		■	■	■
12				■	**13**		**14**	**15**
■	■			■			**16**	
17	**18**	**19**					**20**	
21				■		**22**	■	
23				■	**24**			

ACROSS:
1. Temporary support.
3. Not many (2 words).
7. Frost on objects.
8. Motion in direction.
10. False.
11. Conditional clause.
12. Ear-related.
13. Undemanding.
16. Hawaii (abbr.).
17. Enroll.
20. — Man.
21. Classic toy.
23. Paradise
24. Give food.

DOWN:
1. Veranda.
2. Powered up.
3. Most artistic.
4. Coniferous tree.
5. Big flightless bird.
6. Tiny.
9. Archaic "often".
10. Anointment.
14. Call for silence.
15. Surrender.
17. To view something.
18. Movement showing approval.
19. Caustic solution.
22. Engineer's degree (abbr.).

WORDSEARCH

```
J  V  H  A  M  I  L  T  O  N  Z
H  E  F  W  B  U  R  R  O  W  F
A  V  F  R  R  M  P  T  H  I  S
N  N  M  F  A  O  G  E  O  H  H
C  H  A  S  E  N  D  S  N  E  E
O  H  D  M  I  R  K  N  G  N  R
C  E  I  H  G  O  S  L  E  R  M
K  U  S  K  O  E  V  O  I  Y  A
C  A  O  R  U  S  H  D  N  N  N
W  M  N  P  D  A  D  A  M  S  V
M  O  R  R  I  S  P  Z  P  B  F
```

FIND 16 OF AMERICA'S FOUNDING FATHERS:

....
....
....
....
....
....
....

CAN YOU THINK OF ANY OTHERS?

....
....

WORDOKU

					O	E		
	N			E				R
	E		U	D		P		J
P				R		D		N
J		R		A				U
O		D		J	E		R	
E				P			A	
		N	R					

**FILL EVERY ROW, COLUMN, AND 3X3 SECTOR,
USING EACH GIVEN LETTER ONLY ONCE!**

▶ QUOTES

HOW MANY OF THESE MOVIE QUOTES CAN YOU IDENTIFY?

"You know how to whistle, don't you, Steve? You just put your lips together and blow."

FILM:
. . . .

YEAR:
. . . .

ACTOR:
. . . .

FILM:
. . . .

YEAR:
. . . .

ACTOR:
. . . .

"Ray, when someone asks you if you're a god, you say 'YES'! "

"I'm king of the world!"

FILM:
. . . .

YEAR:
. . . .

ACTOR:
. . . .

▶ SILHOUETTES

GIVE EACH STATE ITS CORRESPONDING NAME.

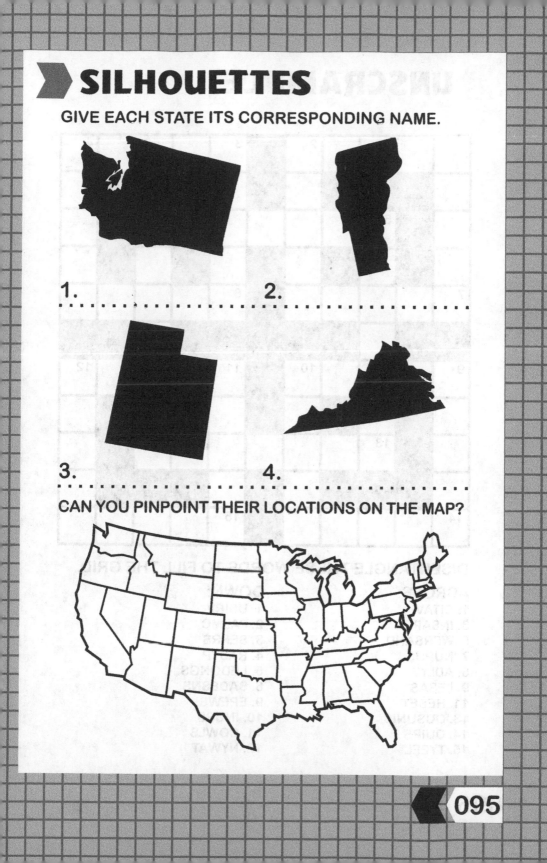

1. ....

2. ....

3. ....

4. ....

CAN YOU PINPOINT THEIR LOCATIONS ON THE MAP?

►UNSCRAMBLE

DISENTANGLE THESE WORDS TO FILL THE GRID.

ACROSS:
1. CITAV
3. INSAP
5. WERSARD
7. NUPUS
8. ADLYS
9. LESAS
11. HESET
13. OUSUNIS
14. OUIPS
15. TYEFL

DOWN:
1. USIRV
2. PALMC
3. SEPRS
4. RASYP
5. LEDONGS
6. SADESNS
9. EPEWS
10. INUSS
11. COWLS
12. NYWAT

096 ►

▶ TRIVIA

FAMOUS PEOPLE FROM THE PAST.

1.

1815 ▶ After the Library of Congress was destroyed by the British in 1814 he offered his personal library as a replacement.

2.

1818 ▶ Helped organize and lead the navies of Chile and Brazil during their wars of independence through the 1820s.

3.

1888 ▶ Designed the alternating-current (AC) electric system, which is the predominant electrical system still in use today.

4.

1916 ▶ Submitted his first successful cover painting to <u>The Sunday Post</u>, becoming America's foremost illustrator of the 20th-century.

5.

1956 ▶ Became Princess of Monaco after marrying Prince Rainier III.

6.

1963 ▶ Delivered his famous "I Have a Dream" speech at the March on Washington.

7.

1966 ▶ Formally established the nonfiction novel genre with his true crime novel, <u>In Cold Blood</u>.

8.

1982 ▶ Released from prison in 1990, he became South Africa's head of state in 1994.

DEFINITION SEARCH

```
L F S G P D S Y N Y O
O Z S T J K T G O L I
U W P L A J N A O U N
D E M O V I E S M U R
K N L Q N M R L T E G
R B W I E E E S C J R
P U A T H A N N W E A
N R S G R T A O G S I
T E N S D C H U D H N
M I I C E S I E N O S
W W C A M U S E E T R
```

- Entertain.
- Sister of father or mother.
- Malignancy.
- Cereals.
- Belonging to her.
- Freezes.
- Holy Land.
- Held on to.
- Noisy.
- Films.
- Acorn-bearing trees.
- Smell.
- Downpour.
- Hit.
- Exhibit.
- Han—.
- Set of steps.
- Peduncle.
- Stupefy.
- Domesticated.
- Machine for nerve stimulation.
- Introduces comparison.
- Objective case of "thou".
- Instruct.
- Birds' forelimb.
- Belonging to you.

PROVERBS

DO YOU REMEMBER THE MEANINGS OF THESE?

"Two wrongs don't make a right."

WHAT DOES IT MEAN?

. . . .
. . . .
. . . .
. . . .
. . . .
. . . .

WHAT DOES IT MEAN?

. . . .
. . . .
. . . .
. . . .
. . . .
. . . .

"Always put your best foot forward."

"Rome wasn't built in a day."

WHAT DOES IT MEAN?

. . . .
. . . .
. . . .
. . . .
. . . .
. . . .

MATCHMAKER

WHICH TWO ARE PERFECTLY ALIKE?

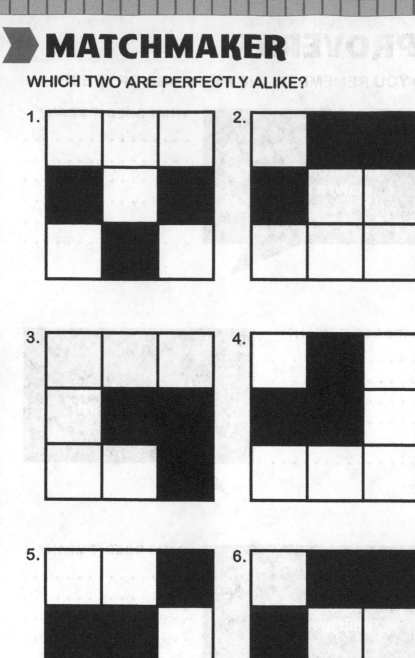

1. 2.

3. 4.

5. 6.

CROSSWORD

ACROSS:

1. Swindle.
5. Speech defect.
9. Beer sans hops.
10. The likes of.
12. Radioactive gas.
14. Rippled silk.
16. Ireland.
17. Better—than out.
18. Drag.
19. Sung poem.
20. Giant in Norse mythology.
21. Highest.
22. Arise.
24. Tricky.
27. To travel.
28. Snow sport.
30. Ingested.
31. —and fro.
32. Appeal.
33. Item.
35. Smear.
36. Scrape by.
37. Parabola.
38. Castrated bulls.
39. Gathers leaves.

DOWN:

2. Small team.
3. Succulent plant.
4. Males.
5. Highlight.
6. UN labor org. (abbr.).
7. Expertise.
8. Predestine.
11. Broker.
13. Assist.
15. Furrow.
17. Adult insect.
20. King's novel.
21. Advert (abbr.).
22. To a great extent.
23. Number (abbr.).
25. Belongs to "it".
26. Castrate.
28. Smooth.
29. Barbie's BF.
31. Adolescent.
32. Beside prefix.
34. —lele.
35. Road coating.

▶ WORDSEARCH

```
B R U N E I B V B A H R A I N
B E L G I U M U O B R A Z I L
U D L Y B A N G L A D E S H D
R A F I B R X Y I G S R G A D
K D U U Z O Y S V O A W U A P
I A R S I E U I I J Y R N I I
N A L A T R M A A V N I I D D
A E O G A R A B H U T A N A B
F A K L E L A I A N R U A T O
A P E V O R Q L E L R B R A S
S B E G V I I G I U B N M A N
O A N D O R R A B A N A E I I
E A F G H A N I S T A N N D A
B O T S W A N A A J C E I I Z
A Z E R B A I J A N B Q A K A
```

FIND 25 COUNTRIES STARTING WITH A AND B:

....
....
....
....
....
....
....
....
....
....
....
....
....
....

WORDOKU

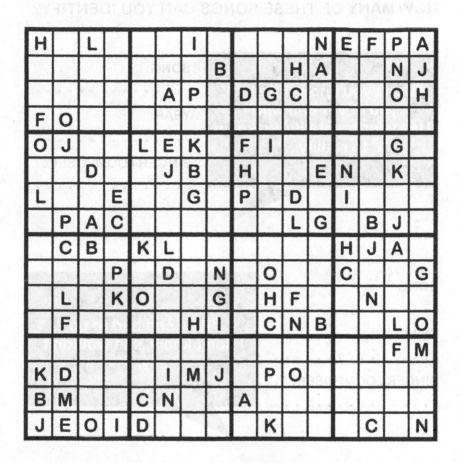

FILL EVERY ROW, COLUMN, AND 4X4 SECTOR,
USING EACH GIVEN LETTER ONLY ONCE!

▶ QUOTES

HOW MANY OF THESE SONGS CAN YOU IDENTIFY?

"Don't you know little fool,
you never can win?
Use your mentality, wake up
to reality..."

SONG:

. . . .

YEAR:

. . . .

SINGER / COMPOSER:

. . . .

SONG:

. . . .

YEAR:

. . . .

SINGER / COMPOSER:

. . . .

"Why she had to go
I don't know, she wouldn't
say..."

"You got to know when to
hold 'em, know when to fold
'em / Know when to walk
away and know when to
run..."

SONG:

. . . .

YEAR:

. . . .

SINGER / COMPOSER:

. . . .

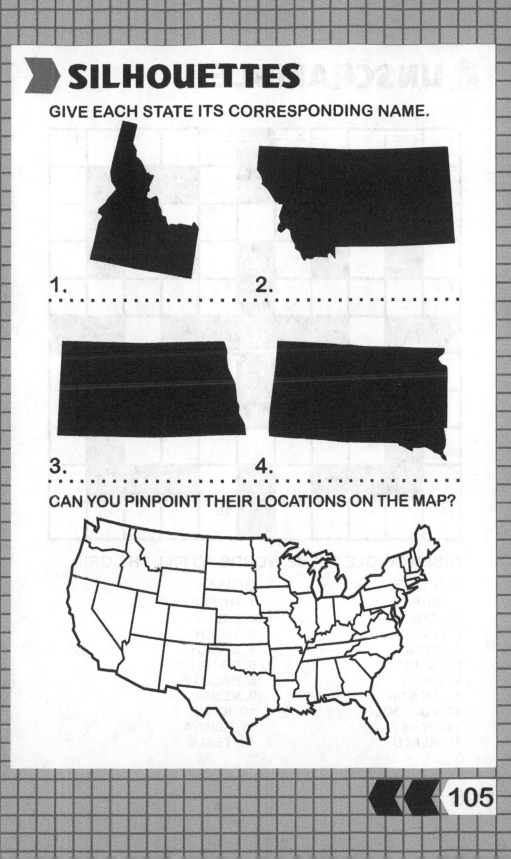

SILHOUETTES

GIVE EACH STATE ITS CORRESPONDING NAME.

1.

2.

3.

4.

CAN YOU PINPOINT THEIR LOCATIONS ON THE MAP?

▶▶ UNSCRAMBLE

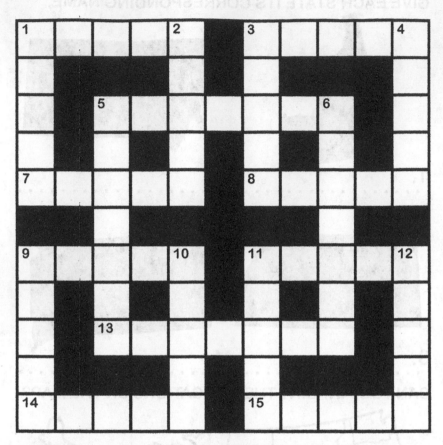

DISENTANGLE THESE WORDS TO FILL THE GRID.

ACROSS:
1. GRUNW
3. ACHET
5. LEWLILO
7. XYROP
8. TCHUH
9. TUZLK
11. SEWOR
13. FULEDOL
14. OCHEP
15. REBLU

DOWN:
1. HWELP
2. LULYG
3. TETEH
4. SHARH
5. ROTUNDO
6. RALLITE
9. VENAK
10. ICHZL
11. FERWA
12. TEALE

▶ TRIVIA

FAMOUS PEOPLE FROM THE PAST.

1.
....
1775 ▶ Devised a system of lanterns to warn the minutemen of a British invasion

2.
....
1858 ▶ Patented the first US sewing machine to stitch buttonholes.

3.
....
1898 ▶ Announced the discovery of two new elements, radium and polonium.

4.
....
1921 ▶ Received the Nobel Prize in Physics "for his services to theoretical physics, and especially for his discovery of the law of the photoelectric effect."

5.
....
1942 ▶ Awarded first ever gold record for selling a million copies of "Chattanooga Choo Choo."

6.
....
1969 ▶ Became the first person to walk on the surface of the Moon.

7.
....
1978 ▶ Was the first human to be conceived in a petri dish and then implanted as a two-and-a-half-day-old embryo.

8.
....
1985 ▶ Scored his 400th career NHL goal and added two assists in a 5-4 Oilers' win over the Sabres in Buffalo.

▶ DEFINITION SEARCH

```
E B I O S L T V K Y E G U
M U D S U K J T H Y P W Q
P S A A C B E T A K E N Z
L Y H K E P R O Q G Y S L
O F O R M A L Z S J A B S
Y P U I E H O O R I G I N
S P L Y S R W A M L R Q N
J G Z A I I L F C J I S S
K V E S S A Y I S T S M A
T M N T L H C L E W S I E
K U L Q A J E L C Z C T I
D O R I O T S S T G X H V
M E L O D I O U S N E S S
```

- Pretends.
- Once more.
- Winglike.
- Cinders.
- Basic software.
- Occupied.
- Hammock riggings.
- Mayflies.
- Soil-like.
- Vomit.
- Gives work to.
- Writes essays.
- Traditional.
- Gain access to.
- Tug.
- ID.
- Small island.
- Prods.
- Green citrus.
- Clingy mollusc.
- Low-born.
- Harmonious quality.
- Sheds feathers.
- Soils with mud.
- Genesis.
- Revolts.
- Cults.
- Gentlemen.
- Metal workers.
- Kidnaped.

PROVERBS

DO YOU REMEMBER THE MEANINGS OF THESE?

"Better safe than sorry."

WHAT DOES IT MEAN?

. . . .
. . . .
. . . .
. . . .
. . . .
. . . .

WHAT DOES IT MEAN?

. . . .
. . . .
. . . .
. . . .
. . . .
. . . .

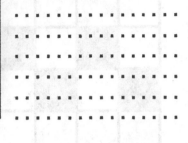

"Don't bite the hand that feeds you."

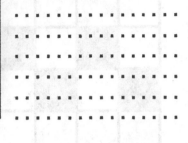

"The squeaky wheel gets the grease."

WHAT DOES IT MEAN?

. . . .
. . . .
. . . .
. . . .
. . . .

MATCHMAKER

WHICH TWO ARE PERFECTLY ALIKE?

1.
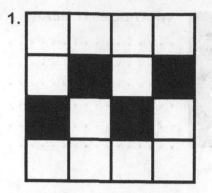

2.

3.
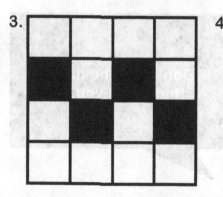

4.

5.
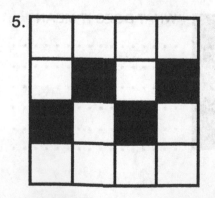

6.
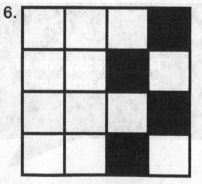

CROSSWORD

ACROSS:
1. Egypt peninsula.
6. Out of date.
8. Similar age.
10. Asylum.
11. 20th studio album by Ray Stevens.
13. Mom.
14. South African party.
15. —apple a day.
16. Social insect.
18. —Hughes.
21. Highway.
23. EU currency.
24. Stupidity.
26. Dijon drink.
27. —day like today.
28. Aboriginal.
31. Like.
32. Supported by.
33. Drainage.
36. Harder.
37. Polyester resin.
38. Praise.

DOWN:
1. Italian microstate.
2. First dinosaur.
3. Charges-free.
4. Ottoman title.
5. Magnetic metal.
6. Secretion.
7. Primate.
9. Pain exclamation.
11. Unions.
12. Backers.
17. Thailand's people.
19. —the people.
20. North seabird.
22. —not disturb.
25. Gape.
29. The BBC.
30. —Roberts.
33. Utter.
34. Obliterate.
35. Bitter malt.

```
M A C O L O M B I A T C E N
S I N C Z E C H I A K D Q A
J C S J T C S D F B E T I D
S A L V A D O R O R I T I T
B N T U M B N S I R A D B K
N A D D M Q U O T O N N M T
D D Y A J R V D R A A H C D
M A C F P I H C L I R Q H E
H D O Y D F B N N H C I M N
G B C E T H I O P I A V C M
M Y T O N F T J U C H I N A
V O G V N S X X I T N D B R
C H I L E G Y P T S I U W K
W C A M E R O O N Q C H A D
```

FIND 23 COUNTRIES STARTING WITH C, D, E, AND F:

....
....
....
....
....
....
....
....
....
....

WORDOKU

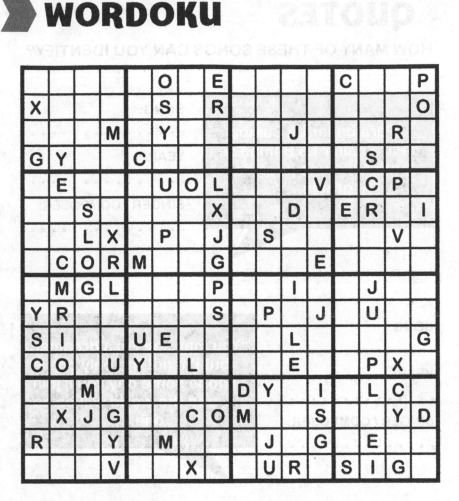

FILL EVERY ROW, COLUMN, AND 4X4 SECTOR,
USING EACH GIVEN LETTER ONLY ONCE!

QUOTES

HOW MANY OF THESE SONGS CAN YOU IDENTIFY?

"Para bailar La Bamba / Para bailar La Bamba se necesita una poca de gracia…"

SONG:
. . . .

YEAR:
. . . .

SINGER / COMPOSER:
. . . .

SONG:
. . . .

YEAR:
. . . .

SINGER / COMPOSER:
. . . .

"You may say I'm a dreamer, but I'm not the only one / I hope some day you'll join us, and the world will be as one…"

"Scaramouche, Scaramouche, will you do the Fandango? Thunderbolt and lightning, very, very frightning…"

SONG:
. . . .

YEAR:
. . . .

SINGER / COMPOSER:
. . . .

⏵ SILHOUETTES

GIVE EACH STATE ITS CORRESPONDING NAME.

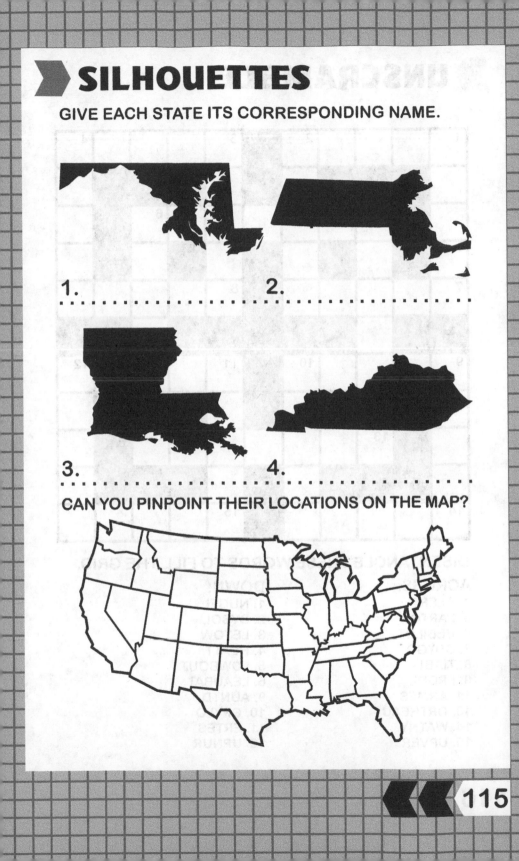

1. . . . .

2. . . . .

3. . . . .

4. . . . .

CAN YOU PINPOINT THEIR LOCATIONS ON THE MAP?

UNSCRAMBLE

DISENTANGLE THESE WORDS TO FILL THE GRID.

ACROSS:
1. ALERF
3. PARTO
5. BEBILOT
7. ODYGO
8. TIABI
9. LRODL
11. ARMES
13. ORTHEAU
14. WATNY
15. UPVER

DOWN:
1. NUGFL
2. BYBOL
3. LETOW
4. HEATT
5. LOWBOUT
6. LEAUBAT
9. AUNTD
10. OPYLO
11. ERTES
12. UPNUR

116

▶ TRIVIA

FAMOUS PEOPLE FROM THE PAST.

1.

1854 ▶ Sailed frigate "Susquehanna" into Tokyo Bay, forcing Japan open to Western trade.

2.

1872 ▶ Patented the "failsafe" automatic railway air brake, which would save many lives.

3.

1883 ▶ Opened the first "Buffalo Bill's Wild West Show" in Omaha, Nebraska.

4.

1928 ▶ Patented an innovation that used a loop instead of a knot around the yo-yo axle, allowing it new tricks such as the ability to "sleep."

5.

1936 ▶ Abdicated the throne of England after 325 days to marry American commoner Wallis Simpson.

6.

1957 ▶ Purchased a mansion in Memphis, Tennessee and called it "Graceland."

7.

1975 ▶ Together with Paul Allen, he developed and released the Altair 8800 microcomputer.

8.

1983 ▶ Created and produced one of HBO's first original shows, <u>Fraggle Rock</u>, which would run until 1987.

```
C B R L B R V S O M P H I
E U R O W E R I R J E R D
V L T D F N T D I U E W I
A B Q T R A W E G M V Y O
L U S O H M O T I V E S M
U L M M D E R A N G E D A
A U F R C O M B A T A N T
T L F O R T E U L M G A I
E B W W L U D P S N E W C
P E R A M B U L A T I N G
O P E N Y E W T U N A S T
S L A V E S O U R L Y R V
H Q B P T A L I B A N L D
```

- Invariably.
- Catkin.
- Stiff bristles.
- White wine.
- Passerine songbird.
- Serviceman.
- Hack it (three words).
- Mad.
- Assess.
- Speciality.
- Relating to idiom.
- Loyal.
- Mangler.
- Reasons.
- Accessible.
- Prototypes.
- Annoy.
- Walking around.
- Chic.
- Give new name.
- Mountain ash.
- Person who rows.
- Serfs.
- Unpleasantly.
- Afghan militia.
- Strong flavor.
- Hollow cylinders.
- Neoplasm.
- <u>Thunnus albacares</u> (pl.).
- Insinuated.

PROVERBS

DO YOU REMEMBER THE MEANINGS OF THESE?

"Don't bite off more than you can chew."

WHAT DOES IT MEAN?

. . . .
. . . .
. . . .
. . . .
. . . .
. . . .

WHAT DOES IT MEAN?

. . . .
. . . .
. . . .
. . . .
. . . .
. . . .

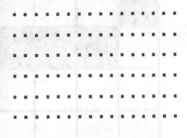

"You made your bed, now you have to lie in it."

"Action speaks louder than words."

WHAT DOES IT MEAN?

. . . .
. . . .
. . . .
. . . .
. . . .
. . . .

MATCHMAKER

WHICH TWO ARE PERFECTLY ALIKE?

1.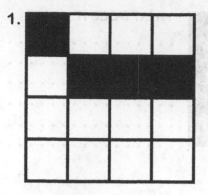

2.

3.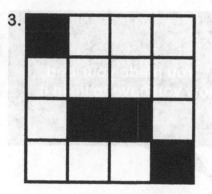

4.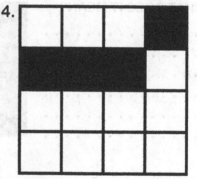

5.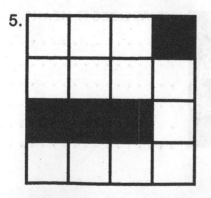

6.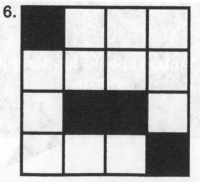

▶ CROSSWORD

ACROSS:
1. Rolling—.
5. Arab Republic.
10. Mexican dish.
11. Promotes.
12. Exposed.
13. Actress (two words).
15. Prepare.
16. Web address.
17. Deep hole.
18. Ashes vase.
19. Ovum.
21. —American in Paris.
22. Mound.
23. Morning time.
24. Hankering.
25. Strive.
26. Burmese currency.
27. Age.
28. Inkling.
29. Refugee.
32. Flower necklace.
33. Darkness.
34. Disaster.
35. Tooth set.
36. Belief in God.

DOWN:
1. Freeze.
2. Bull related.
3. 8 musicians.
4. Nitric oxide (abbr.).
5. Severely.
6. Wailing cry.
7. Remorse.
8. IT Support (abbr.).
9. Blurry vision.
14. Polar lights.
18. Fabrication.
20. Carefree attitude.
26. Mushroom cap.
27. Authentic.
30. Strive.
31. Era.
34. Maine (abbr.).

WORDSEARCH

```
G H A N A H H E G H N J O A
O J O R D A N U I U U K L Z
I C A N P N X H N X I A G T
T N V P D T C V P G M N K T
A V D F A U R J F E A K E K
L C I O P N R J T R J R N A
Y G R E N A D A H M N S Y Z
A U A D L E U M S A G V A A
A Y Q B K G S A R N L A R K
A A U H O U J I T Y I N L H
Q N Z A Y N W C A D Q P O S
S A J I C E L A N D Q T K T
O G M T F R Z I I J Y P W A
M R O I S R A E L T L I R N
```

FIND 23 COUNTRIES STARTING WITH G, H, I, J, AND K:

....
....
....
....
....
....
....
....
....

WORDOKU

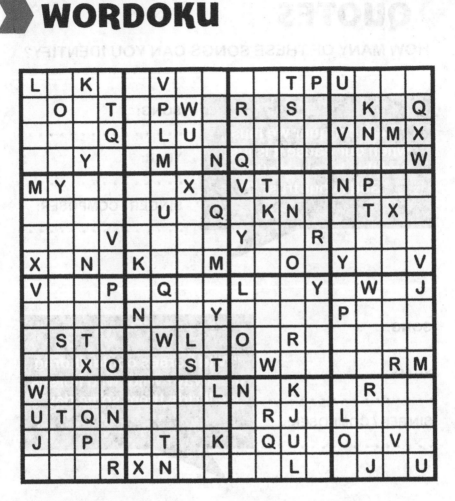

FILL EVERY ROW, COLUMN, AND 4X4 SECTOR, USING EACH GIVEN LETTER ONLY ONCE!

QUOTES

HOW MANY OF THESE SONGS CAN YOU IDENTIFY?

"Then conquer we must, when our cause it is just, and this be our motto: 'In God is our trust.'"

SONG:
. . . .

YEAR:
. . . .

SINGER / COMPOSER:
. . . .

SONG:
. . . .

YEAR:
. . . .

SINGER / COMPOSER:
. . . .

"Wild horses couldn't drag me away / Wild, wild horses we'll ride them some day."

"Who let the dogs out? Who, who, who, who, who?"

SONG:
. . . .

YEAR:
. . . .

SINGER / COMPOSER:
. . . .

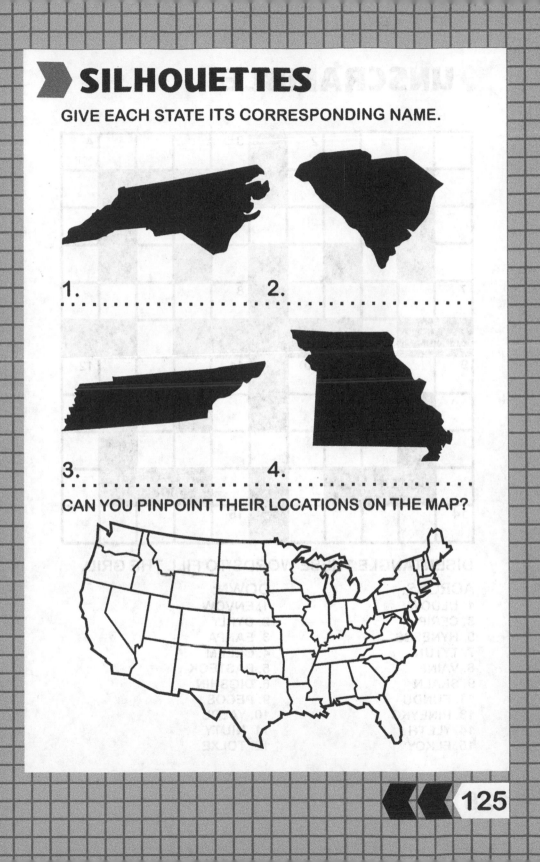

SILHOUETTES

GIVE EACH STATE ITS CORRESPONDING NAME.

1.

2.

3.

4.

CAN YOU PINPOINT THEIR LOCATIONS ON THE MAP?

▶▶ UNSCRAMBLE

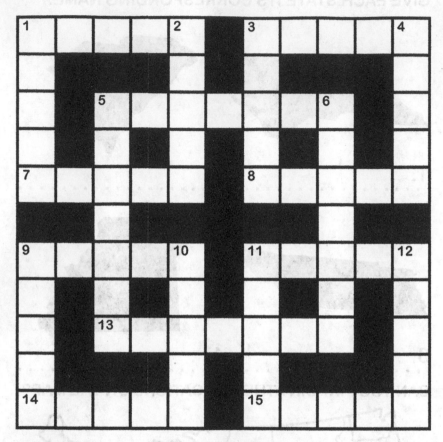

DISENTANGLE THESE WORDS TO FILL THE GRID.

ACROSS:
1. ULDOW
3. CERIP
5. HYNESSS
7. TYTUN
8. VAINE
9. SRALN
11. EUNDU
13. RINEYKG
14. YLETH
15. ELKOY

DOWN:
1. ENVOW
2. DYRLY
3. EANPA
4. CEEEM
5. BASTECK
6. DIGSHIN
9. PECOS
10. YALOL
11. NIUTY
12. TOLXE

► TRIVIA

FAMOUS PEOPLE FROM THE PAST.

1.

1896 ► On Jan.1st, he announced his discovery of X-rays.

2.

1899 ► Published his discovery of two different kinds of radiation (Alpha and Beta Particles)

3.

1913 ► Established the Federal Reserve System, the central banking system of the United States.

4.

1953 ► During his two-term presidency, he continued and even expanded all the major New Deal programs still in use.

5.

1968 ► First published his pseudo-scientific best-seller <u>Chariots of the Gods?</u> in Germany.

6.

1973 ► Despite a failed appearance on <u>The Tonight Show Starring Johnny Carson</u>, he became a celebrated spoon-bending psychic.

7.

1974 ► Published his first horror novel, a story about a bullied girl who uses telekinesis to exact revenge on her tormentors.

8.

1984 ► His "1984" Apple Macintosh computer commercial was aired during the third quarter of Super Bowl XVIII.

DEFINITION SEARCH

```
O D S E E M A R S U P I A
L E I O S P T O W N B W S
C A Y S Z W A T S C I U B
H D R M A G U C S O L D E
I E G O O F F M I M L R L
L N P S O A F D B F Y A A
D I U E A M I E S O I J R
I N E P W R I R C R L E U
S G B G O O I E S T W A S
H I L L I N E S S A I L S
M C O E R C I O N B C O R
S Q S E P L L G T L N U N
U P A N G R A M A Y A S G
```

- Lung alveolus.
- Formerly Byelorussia.
- Pot for boiling water.
- Boleadoras (Eng.).
- Immature.
- Intimidation.
- Numbing.
- Estrangement.
- Chewer.
- Explode.
- Most viscous.
- Hilly.
- Distrustful.

- Astray.
- Kangaroo pouches.
- Yucatan indigenous.
- Gradually assimilating.
- Placates.
- Sentence w. all alphabet.
- Hopi peoples.
- Roommates.
- Indian garment.
- Appear.
- Sibling (abbr.).
- Sun-powered.
- Village.

- It was (contr.).
- Protuberance.
- Uneasily.
- Buddhist monasteries.

PROVERBS

DO YOU REMEMBER THE MEANINGS OF THESE?

"It takes two to tango."

WHAT DOES IT MEAN?

. . . .
. . . .
. . . .
. . . .
. . . .
. . . .
. . . .

WHAT DOES IT MEAN?

. . . .
. . . .
. . . .
. . . .
. . . .
. . . .

"Don't count your chickens before they hatch."

"It's no use crying over spilled milk."

WHAT DOES IT MEAN?

. . . .
. . . .
. . . .
. . . .
. . . .
. . . .

MATCHMAKER

WHICH TWO ARE PERFECTLY ALIKE?

1.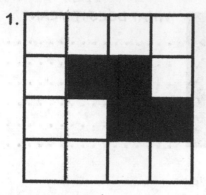

2.

3.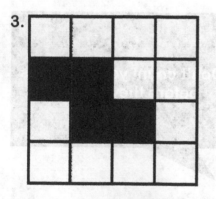

4.

5.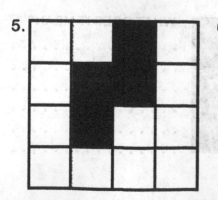

6.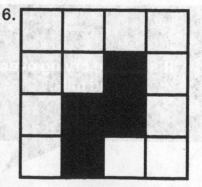

CROSSWORD

ACROSS:
1. Segment.
4. Achievement.
8. Spiced stew (Spanish).
9. Conversation.
11. Welcoming.
12. Green.
13. Turkish currency.
14. —arm and leg.
15. Normalize.
20. Frozen water.
21. Tea container.
22. Code solver.
27. Oregon (abbr.).
28. Escape.
29. Nappy.
33. Weaken.
34. Calm.
35. —Blyton.
36. Borrow.
37. Strongly suggest.

DOWN:
1. Braid.
2. Bombing (2 words).
3. Affair.
4. Flipper.
5. Hearing organ.
6. Muhammad—.
7. Yellow stone.
8. Nocturnal birds.
9. Russian assembly.
10. —Wilder.
16. Debutante (abbr.).
17. French street.
18. Recruiter.
19. Notion.
22. Large sea fish.
23. Bay window.
24. Unusual.
25. Sinister.
26. Slender grass.
30. Egypt (abbr.).
31. Writing tool.
32. Conclusion.

WORDSEARCH

```
L M M A L A Y S I A M B I V L
J N A A M O N T E N E G R O X
S Z R C L I B E R I A A O Z C
N L T Q A T L I P L Y M L L M
E L I T H U A N I A K O E K N
W S N B W X O P W H L Z B M I
Z H I J Y C S R N A R A A A C
E B Q T I A O X I A Q M N U A
A U U X Z N K R M Y M B O R R
L I E C H T E N S T E I N I A
A M A D A G A S C A R Q B T G
N H Q B I Y A S Y H G U Z I U
D R M N M O R O C C O E M U A
A P D N E T H E R L A N D S N
H J M C K B P I N V J D C A O
```

FIND 24 COUNTRIES STARTING WITH L, M, AND N:

....
....
....
....
....
....
....
....
....
....

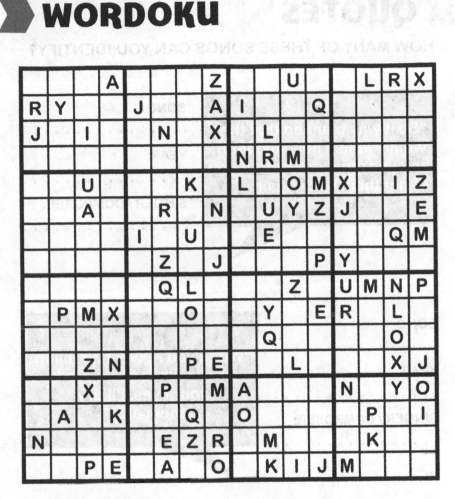

		A			Z			U			L	R	X
R	Y			J		A		I			Q		
J		I			N		X		L				
						N	R	M					
	U				K		L		O	M	X		I	Z
	A			R		N		U	Y	Z	J			E
		I		U			E			P	Y		Q	M
		Z			J				P	Y				
		Q	L				Z		U	M	N	P
P	M	X		O			Y		E	R		L
						Q					O	
Z	N			P	E			L			X	J
X		P		M	A			N		Y	O
A		K		Q		O				P		I
N			E	Z	R		M			K
	P	E		A		O		K	I	J	M

FILL EVERY ROW, COLUMN, AND 4X4 SECTOR, USING EACH GIVEN LETTER ONLY ONCE!

QUOTES

HOW MANY OF THESE SONGS CAN YOU IDENTIFY?

"So it was planned that they would vanish now and then, and you must pay before you get them back again..."

SONG:

. . . .

YEAR:

. . . .

SINGER / COMPOSER:

. . . .

SONG:

. . . .

YEAR:

. . . .

SINGER / COMPOSER:

. . . .

"When you're weary, feeling small / When tears are in your eyes, I'll dry them all..."

"I'm ten years burning down the road / Nowhere to run ain't got nowhere to go..."

SONG:

. . . .

YEAR:

. . . .

SINGER / COMPOSER:

. . . .

SILHOUETTES

GIVE EACH STATE ITS CORRESPONDING NAME.

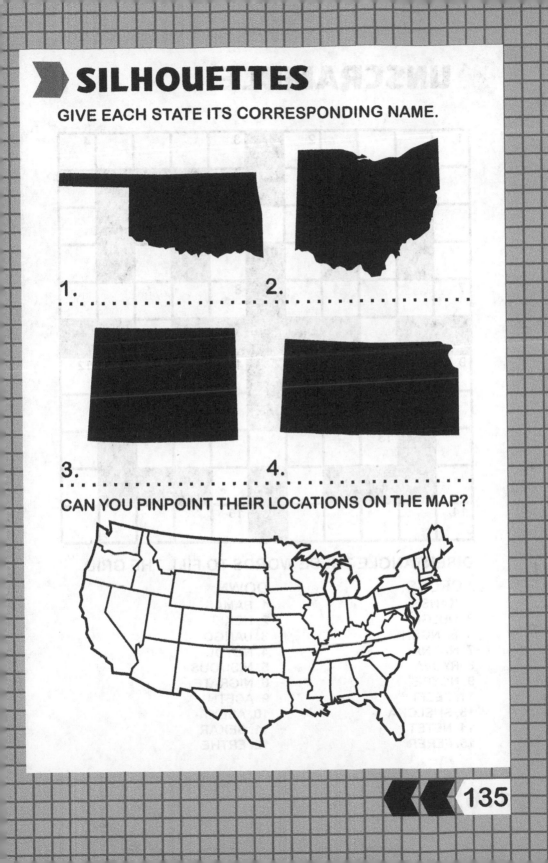

1.

2.

3.

4.

CAN YOU PINPOINT THEIR LOCATIONS ON THE MAP?

⟫ UNSCRAMBLE

DISENTANGLE THESE WORDS TO FILL THE GRID.

ACROSS:
1. KANSH
3. OULGH
5. BANGSHE
7. NULNA
8. RYOVA
9. NOYBE
11. SEZEI
13. SHELCKA
14. NETET
15. FERER

DOWN:
1. BAMAS
2. NEKEL
3. UANGO
4. NOYOL
5. NISUOUS
6. NIGRATE
9. ACETN
10. ASEYT
11. SEKAR
12. ERTHE

▶ TRIVIA

FAMOUS PEOPLE FROM THE PAST.

1.

1495 ▶ Started painting his famous mural, "The Last Supper," in Milan.

2.

1520 ▶ Found a strait to the Pacific, which would later be named after him.

3.

1759 ▶ Published <u>Candide</u>, a scathing satire of Leibniz philosophical optimism.

4.

1898 ▶ Obtained the patent for his internal combustion engine.

5.

1919 ▶ Beat champion Jess Willard in Toledo, Ohio, for world heavyweight championship

6.

1927 ▶ At age 25 he successfully made the first solo transatlantic plane flight between New York and Paris.

7.

1959 ▶ Released his last hit, "It Doesn't Matter Anymore," 29 days before his death.

8.

1974 ▶ Bought the San Diego Padres baseball team for 12 million dollars.

DEFINITION SEARCH

```
U M C Z M C A M C F I U O
S U M N E R S C O P E R F
S C U R R I L O U S L Y N
I C L J N P R S A M T O P
S A Y I G P T R W H E T U
A L B G R L R N L H E N T
L L N A O E R U C B N N R
A A P M T S P T H E A T E
P S M E W M U H L K G E F
I M P E A C H A B L E A I
T R A N S L I T E R A T E
Y O B E G U N P I C K S D
S V F Y Y H U F D T W H B
```

- Awareness.
- Lack of melanin.
- Glass capsule.
- Undergone.
- Arum plants.
- Horse dealer.
- Immobilizes.
- Shield.
- Pastime.
- Unpleasant.
- Liable to be accused.
- Immanuel—.
- Disabled.
- Sheds.
- Ring loudly.
- Sympathy.
- Decomposed.
- Upper covering.
- Abusively.
- Mexican agave.
- Charles—.
- Nipples.
- Adolescent.
- Earths (Latin).
- This or—.
- Mother of Helios.
- Convert to a different Alphabet.
- —the Night Before Christmas.
- Undo sewing.
- Hone.

▶ PROVERBS

DO YOU REMEMBER THE MEANINGS OF THESE?

"Don't put all your eggs in one basket."

WHAT DOES IT MEAN?

. . . .
. . . .
. . . .
. . . .
. . . .
. . . .

WHAT DOES IT MEAN?

. . . .
. . . .
. . . .
. . . .
. . . .
. . . .

"People in glass houses shouldn't throw stones."

"A rolling stone gathers no moss."

WHAT DOES IT MEAN?

. . . .
. . . .
. . . .
. . . .
. . . .

MATCHMAKER

WHICH TWO ARE PERFECTLY ALIKE?

1.

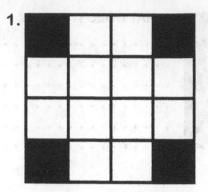

2.

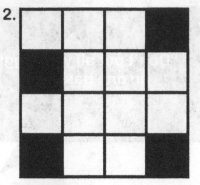

3.

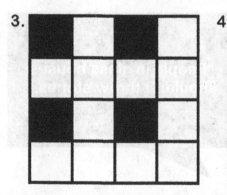

4.

5.

6.

CROSSWORD

Crossword grid with numbered cells: 1-10 across top row, 11, 12, 13, 14, 15, 16, 17, 18, 19, 20, 21, 22, 23, 24, 25, 26, 27, 28, 29, 30, 31, 32, 33, 34, 35, 36, 37.

ACROSS:
1. Consign to misery.
8. Seed vessel.
11. Trailblazer.
12. Black cuckoo.
13. More unpunctual.
14. Green seed.
15. Unequaled.
17. —Maria.
19. Lit by the stars.
20. Horoscope.
23. Minute bug.
24. Turn to bone.
26. Highest card.
27. Cowboys.
30. Heretofore.
31. Combination.
34. Corben's comic.
35. Mosaic tile.
36. —to Joy.
37. Went in.

DOWN:
1. Able.
2. Federal agency.
3. Foundation.
4. Unfasten.
5. Check or guide.
6. Oozes.
7. Corrected errors.
8. Wallpaper decorator.
9. Dreams related.
10. Undergo dialysis (UK).
16. Thump.
17. Palta (Spanish).
18. Facial appearance (adj.).
21. Intestinal tract (abbr.).
22. Recently (two words).
25. Tip of Arabia.
28. Gaff
29. In addition.
32. Plural "be".
33. Humor magazine.

WORDSEARCH

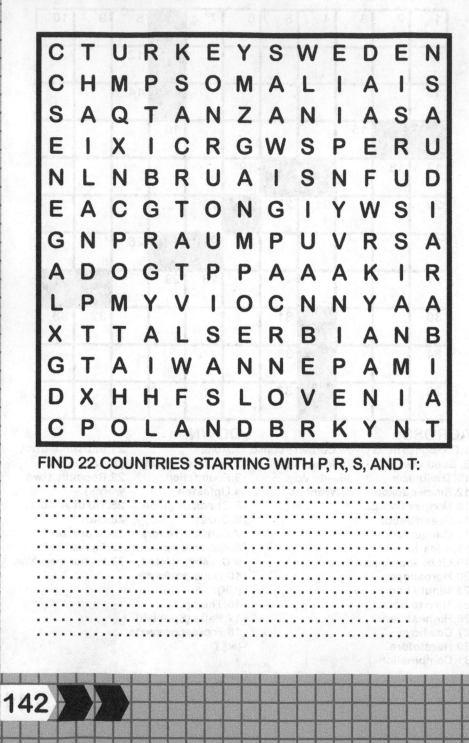

```
C T U R K E Y S W E D E N
C H M P S O M A L I A I S
S A Q T A N Z A N I A S A
E I X I C R G W S P E R U
N L N B R U A I S N F U D
E A C G T O N G I Y W S I
G N P R A U M P U V R S A
A D O G T P P A A A K I R
L P M Y V I O C N N Y A A
X T T A L S E R B I A N B
G T A I W A N N E P A M I
D X H H F S L O V E N I A
C P O L A N D B R K Y N T
```

FIND 22 COUNTRIES STARTING WITH P, R, S, AND T:

....
....
....
....
....
....
....
....
....

WORDOKU

FILL EVERY ROW, COLUMN, AND 4X4 SECTOR, USING EACH GIVEN LETTER ONLY ONCE!

◀ QUOTES

HOW MANY OF THESE SONGS CAN YOU IDENTIFY?

"Southern trees bear
strange fruit,
blood on the leaves and
blood at the root..."

SONG:

. . . .

YEAR:

. . . .

SINGER / COMPOSER:

. . . .

SONG:

. . . .

YEAR:

. . . .

SINGER / COMPOSER:

. . . .

"My little baby sister can do
it with me / It's easier than
learning your A-B-C..."

"Don't go 'round tonight
/ It's bound to take your life
/ There's a bad moon on the
rise..."

SONG:

. . . .

YEAR:

. . . .

SINGER / COMPOSER:

. . . .

144 ▶▶

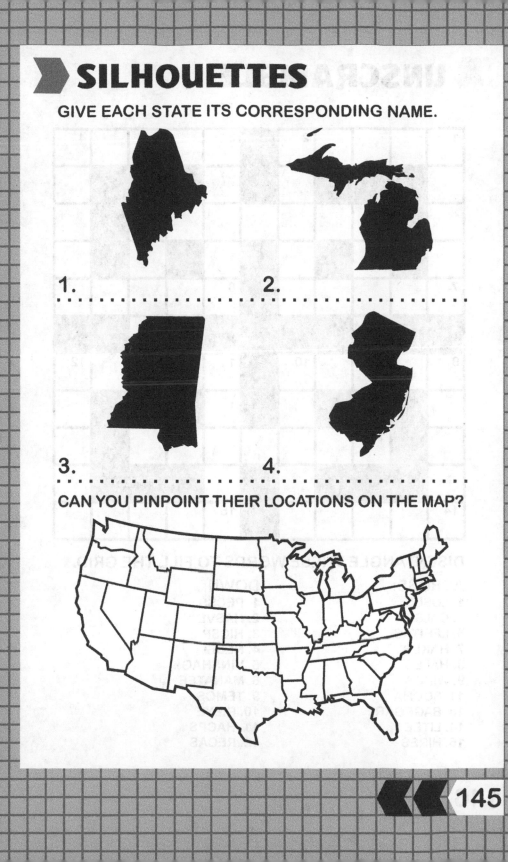

SILHOUETTES

GIVE EACH STATE ITS CORRESPONDING NAME.

1.

2.

3.

4.

CAN YOU PINPOINT THEIR LOCATIONS ON THE MAP?

► UNSCRAMBLE

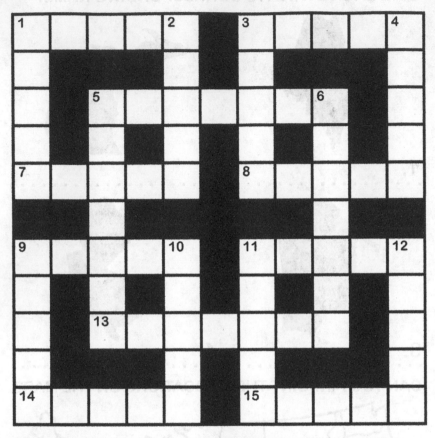

DISENTANGLE THESE WORDS TO FILL THE GRID.

ACROSS:
1. LOSUS
3. CALSS
5. LEBITAS
7. HAKES
8. HALES
9. WINES
11. SOCHA
13. BAGEGAR
14. LITEE
15. HIRES

DOWN:
1. PECSS
2. HASVE
3. HICSP
4. NESEI
5. VINSHAG
6. MANATEE
9. TEMOS
10. RIEYE
11. HACPS
12. RECAS

► TRIVIA

FAMOUS PEOPLE FROM THE PAST.

1.

1861 ▶ Shot and killed David McCanles, possibly in self-defense.

2.

1894 ▶ Became the new Tsar of Russia after his father, Alexander III, died.

3.

1902 ▶ Was an empress who issued an anti-foot-binding edict.

4.

1914 ▶ Signed to play minor league baseball for the Baltimore Orioles.

5.

1940 ▶ Debuted his most commercially successful film, <u>The Great Dictator</u>.

6.

1945 ▶ Began to oversee the occupation of Japan by American forces from a small office in the Dai Ichi Life Insurance Building.

7.

1968 ▶ Around midnight, on June 5th he was shot and died the next day.

8.

1983 ▶ His hit TV show, <u>The A-Team</u>, premiered on NBC.

▶ DEFINITION SEARCH

```
U E T R S I S E C E D E S
S H O E I N G H K T I T L
H E L J P D R O O P S P I
E A R U B E J R S I T S G
R R A V E N E R G N I W H
E T B E I T M O O N L I T
C F A N J C L R E L L M I
O A S E O O E S A G A S N
R I S S T T U M U L T S G
D L W C N B R N E V I L S
E U O E A E Y X C N O V M
D R O N H V I O L E N C E
P E D T S U M M O N S E D
```

- Mistreat.
- American lime tree.
- Purification.
- Dangles.
- Intestine (Greek).
- Wrongdoings.
- Cardiac arrest (2 words).
- Terrors.
- Notch.
- Minority jest.
- Jolt.
- Lit by the moon.
- Rectum specialists.
- Lung rattlings.
- Plunderer.
- Kept record.
- Invigorating.
- Epic chronicles.
- Separates itself.
- Soldiers.
- Fitting horse with shoe.
- Disrespecting.
- Call for.
- Moves through water.
- Native American tent.
- Heated.
- Racket.
- Escort.
- Brutality.

PROVERBS

DO YOU REMEMBER THE MEANINGS OF THESE?

"First things first."

WHAT DOES IT MEAN?

. . . .
. . . .
. . . .
. . . .
. . . .
. . . .

WHAT DOES IT MEAN?

. . . .
. . . .
. . . .
. . . .
. . . .
. . . .

"Still waters run deep."

"If it ain't broke,
don't fix it."

WHAT DOES IT MEAN?

. . . .
. . . .
. . . .
. . . .
. . . .
. . . .

MATCHMAKER

WHICH TWO ARE PERFECTLY ALIKE?

1.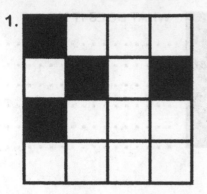

2.

3.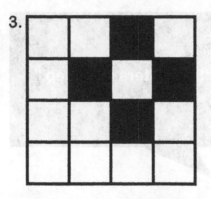

4.

5.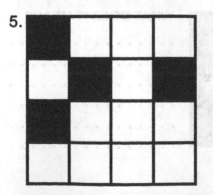

6.

CROSSWORD

ACROSS:
1. Fall asleep (2 words).
7. Amplifier.
11. Sir Lawrence—.
12. Natural deposit.
13. Tumults.
14. Mollusk.
15. At a distance.
16. Thin.
18. Dunk.
19. Covered in weeds.
20. Near.
22. Wealthy.
25. Day-to-day.
27. Lubricant.
29. Italian square.
31. Indolent.
32. Routine.
33. Fastened seat.
35. In debt.
36. Lapidarist.
37. Prepared.
38. Medicine.

DOWN:
1. Itinerant.
2. Alkene.
3. Ruined
4. Finished.
5. Archaic "disgust".
6. Horizontal stripe.
8. Pamper.
9. Idiot (British).
10. Male seed.
14. Ghana currency.
17. Extremely.
19. Move quickly.
21. Stare.
23. Heaped.
24. Memory chip.
26. Light beam.
28. Cautious.
30. IA.
31. Ditto.
34. Amazement.

WORDSEARCH

```
B M N E W M A R K E T Z I
R C T G Z T S P A D E S S
I E W B S Y H R I B R T O
D L E A N O B E U Q M C L
G I N C A D L G A M U O O
E A T C P N A I L R M E D
C D Y A S F C M T J T Y T
H A O R P O K E R A M S S
V B N A I B J N Z G I H E
V R E T D U A T K H S R V
P A T I E N C E W I E F E
K G P H R K K K H F O R E N
D V V J J O S T R E E T S
```

FIND 26 POPULAR CARD GAMES:

. . . .
. . . .
. . . .
. . . .
. . . .
. . . .
. . . .
. . . .
. . . .
. . . .
. . . .

▶ WORDOKU

QUOTES
HOW MANY OF THESE SONGS CAN YOU IDENTIFY?

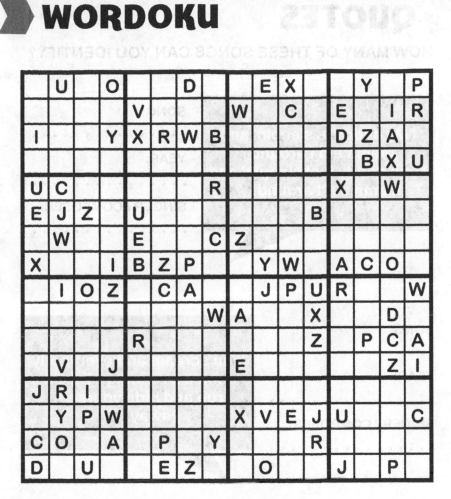

FILL EVERY ROW, COLUMN, AND 4X4 SECTOR,
USING EACH GIVEN LETTER ONLY ONCE!

QUOTES

HOW MANY OF THESE SONGS CAN YOU IDENTIFY?

"My daddy is sleepin' and mama ain't around /
Yeah daddy just sleepin' and mama ain't around..."

SONG:
. . . .

YEAR:
. . . .

SINGER / COMPOSER:
. . . .

SONG:
. . . .

YEAR:
. . . .

SINGER / COMPOSER:
. . . .

"You scream and everybody comes a running / Take a run and hide yourself away..."

"Got the feel for the wheel, keep the moving parts clean..."

SONG:
. . . .

YEAR:
. . . .

SINGER / COMPOSER:
. . . .

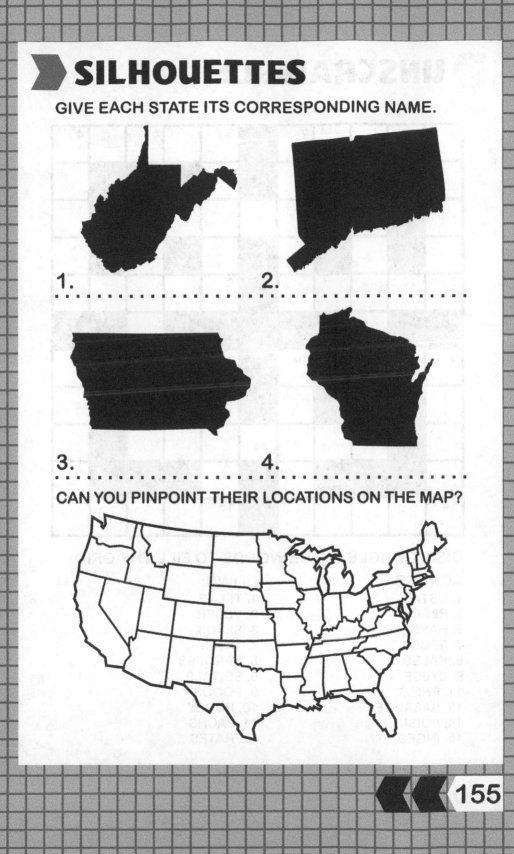

SILHOUETTES

GIVE EACH STATE ITS CORRESPONDING NAME.

1.

2.

3.

4.

CAN YOU PINPOINT THEIR LOCATIONS ON THE MAP?

▶ UNSCRAMBLE

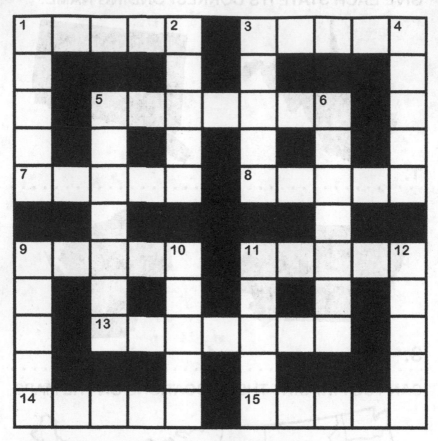

DISENTANGLE THESE WORDS TO FILL THE GRID.

ACROSS:
1. USTAL
3. RESCS
5. HAPSERP
7. PECOS
8. KALES
9. DYESE
11. PHICS
13. SASAUGE
14. POISU
15. INGES

DOWN:
1. TELAS
2. VESER
3. SLACS
4. TATES
5. SPROFES
6. SBITALE
9. POCOS
10. RUSOY
11. PACHS
12. RATES

▶ TRIVIA

FAMOUS PEOPLE FROM THE PAST.

1.

....

1841 ▶ Became the first white man to be granted the title of Rajah of Sarawak (Borneo).

2.

....

1886 ▶ Published his novel, <u>The Strange Case of Dr Jekyll and Mr Hyde</u>.

3.

....

1904 ▶ His opera <u>Madama Butterfly</u> premiered in Milan.

4.

....

1924 ▶ Renamed the Computing-Tabulating-Recording Company (CTR) as International Business Machines (IBM).

5.

....

1947 ▶ Presented his first influential "haute couture" collection, named the "New Look."

6.

....

1963 ▶ Together with artist Bruno Premiani, he created the <u>Doom Patrol</u> comic book.

7.

....

1971 ▶ Released his famous single about police brutality, "What's Going On."

8.

....

1982 ▶ Bit the head off a bat on stage in Des Moines, Iowa.

◥ DEFINITION SEARCH

```
M E S S A G E S A T E S H
J X G W P C M Y R R H U L
A O C D P E A O U T C R Y
C G E I R S M L N V F C H
K A M V O A P P I P R E P
K M B I X G J U T X A A A
N I A S I S A A E I M S R
I C R I M P Y L D D E E E
F A G O A B D L V I U S N
I U O N T D U O M A P H T
N R I V I C H Y R W N P S
G A N R O J T P I I L I X
A L G I N S I T U N C Z C
```

- Algae substance.
- Metal combination.
- Cast down.
- Estimate.
- Related to hearing.
- Buying shares back.
- Sepals whorl.
- Frizzly.
- To break up.
- Classical Greek dialect.
- Banning.
- Most empty.
- Married to a foreigner.
- Setup (two words).
- Involving electricity.
- Leaving.
- Iron plate for cooking.
- Brushes.
- In position (Latin).
- Bending one's body.
- Dispatches.
- Fragrant gum resin.
- Scandal.
- Father or mother.
- Conditions.
- Spouted .
- Hampers.
- Consoles.
- Jointed.
- Pétain's France.

PROVERBS

DO YOU REMEMBER THE MEANINGS OF THESE?

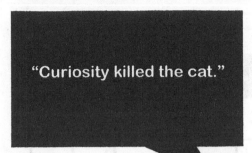

"Curiosity killed the cat."

WHAT DOES IT MEAN?

. . . .
. . . .
. . . .
. . . .
. . . .
. . . .

WHAT DOES IT MEAN?

. . . .
. . . .
. . . .
. . . .
. . . .
. . . .

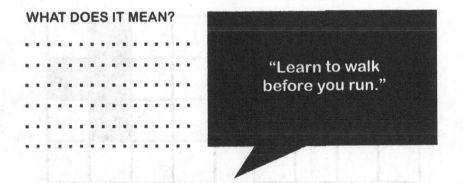

"Learn to walk
before you run."

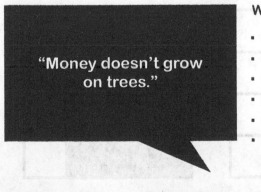

"Money doesn't grow
on trees."

WHAT DOES IT MEAN?

. . . .
. . . .
. . . .
. . . .
. . . .
. . . .

▶ MATCHMAKER

WHICH TWO ARE PERFECTLY ALIKE?

1.
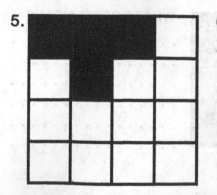

2.

3.
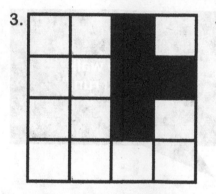

4.
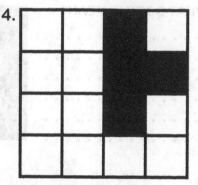

5.
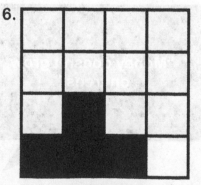

6.

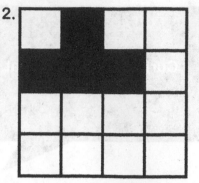

► CROSSWORD

ACROSS:
1. Sound charact.
9. Works of art.
10. Scythes.
12. More polite.
13. Feline.
14. Iranian currency.
15. Leak.
16. Malaysian currency.
17. Praise.
20. Audibly.
21. Salacious.
24. Telephone (abbr.).
27. Lure.
28. Steep hillside.
29. Tide retreat.
30. Break off.
33. To fluctuate
35. Blackbirds.
36. Smell-related.

DOWN:
1. Eagle's nest.
2. From Cuba.
3. Elliptical.
4. Vase.
5. Look.
6. Intramuscular (abbr.).
7. Chocolate powder.
8. From Swaziland.
9. One Union of Regional Staff (abbr.).
11. Stalk.
15. Elderly.
17. Bitter beer.
18. Convention (abbr.).
19. Signal.
20. Performance.
21. Heed.
22. Indian male title.
23. Prophetess.
24. More accurate.
25. Premature.
26. Laser Engineered Net Shaping (abbr.).
28. Stupid man.
31. Doctor.
32. Stick out.
34. Belonging to.

WORDSEARCH

```
Y G D F I T Z G E R A L D
J O O Z R B D R Z R N O I
S G Y L D R C E G O X V C
T O L S T O I E F Q V E K
E L E W S N T N P O N C E
N T D I M T W E K R E R N
D K W F T E E F E M G A S
H I I T Q O L V M Y M F T
A P L I W D L V E T D T O
L L D U M A S K I N G Z K
B I E R C E I H I L S P E
H N U D S K W N Y E L O R
N G Q V S P I L L A N E N
```

FIND 26 FAMOUS AUTHORS:

....
....
....
....
....
....
....
....
....
....

WORDOKU

	P		A		R	L	K	C	S		V	H	I
Z	K	H	L		T		P					S	
E	C	R	V			T		H		P	K		
			I		Z			E			T	R	
Z		S		V	O	A							P
	K		E	F		O					A		
F	I		H	Z				T		O			
	C	F	I		A		E		S		Z		
S		O		R		V		Z	P	A			
T		P				L	K		E		R		
I			O		M	R		S					
A				H	M	E		F		S			
V	H		E		K		T						
	A	T		P		V			M	C	I	F	
C			A		P			O	K	R	T		
O	K	L	M	T	R	F	S		C		H		

FILL EVERY ROW, COLUMN, AND 4X4 SECTOR, USING EACH GIVEN LETTER ONLY ONCE!

163

▶ QUOTES

HOW MANY OF THESE SONGS CAN YOU IDENTIFY?

"And it's magic if the music is groovy / It makes you feel happy like an old-time movie..."

SONG:
. . . .

YEAR:
. . . .

SINGER / COMPOSER:
. . . .

SONG:
. . . .

YEAR:
. . . .

SINGER / COMPOSER:
. . . .

"Oh Mama, I'm in fear for my life from the long arm of the law..."

"And I, I don't need no life preserver / I don't need no one to hose me down..."

SONG:
. . . .

YEAR:
. . . .

SINGER / COMPOSER:
. . . .

SILHOUETTES

GIVE EACH STATE ITS CORRESPONDING NAME.

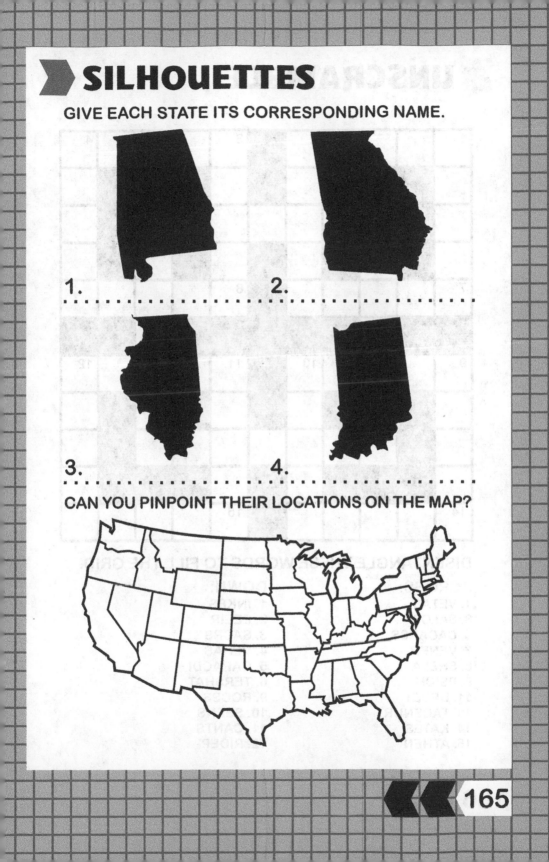

1.

2.

3.

4.

CAN YOU PINPOINT THEIR LOCATIONS ON THE MAP?

►UNSCRAMBLE

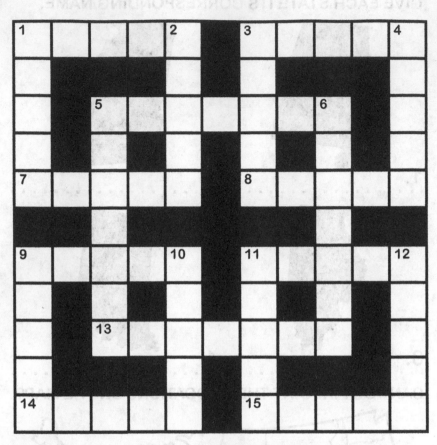

DISENTANGLE THESE WORDS TO FILL THE GRID.

ACROSS:
1. VETAS
3. SALCS
5. CACARSS
7. VENER
8. SHELA
9. PSICH
11. UPSET
13. TACENUR
14. KATES
15. ATHEN

DOWN:
1. INKES
2. EEEIR
3. SACRS
4. VEHAS
5. CARACDI
6. TERSHAT
9. ROCSS
10. SEENS
11. CANTS
12. RIDEP

FAMOUS PEOPLE FROM THE PAST.

1.

1859 ❯ Dedicating his life to the education of disadvantaged youth, he founded the Salesian Society.

2.

1876 ❯ Finished his famous <u>Swan Lake</u> ballet.

3.

1901 ❯ Nine years after leading the creation of the General Electric Company, he organized the US Steel Corporation.

4.

1916 ❯ Won his first aerial combat near Cambrai, France, becoming known as the "Red Baron."

5.

1949 ❯ Announced evidence of the USSR's 1st nuclear device detonation.

6.

1952 ❯ Starred in <u>High Noon</u>, an American Western film directed by Fred Zinnemann.

7.

1961 ❯ Became the first person to orbit Earth aboard the Vostok 1.

8.

1962 ❯ Became the first American to orbit Earth aboard the Friendship 7.

DEFINITION SEARCH

```
E L F I S H M T E R S E R
R F A T T Y O E P E F H Y
R K L O G M N R N R C S A
E U O D A N I P P R O I B
D M E O U A T S A B R A A
S S S R T R O I K A A F S
A S L K O Y R C M N N L T
B E A Y M T L H V D G I E
O A V I A T I O N I L N R
T R S M T W Z R O T A T E
E I U O I T A E C R I S P
U N L O C K R A R Y S C Y
R G L A S E D N U D N I K
```

- Succulent plants.
- Keep guns cocked.
- Aircraft operation.
- Robbery.
- Keep meat moist.
- Alto oboe (2 words).
- Crunchy.
- Awkward.
- Related to elves.
- Mistaken.
- Greasy.
- Chert rocks.
- Book of hymns.
- Cut with a laser.
- Plural for "mare".
- Female head of tribe.
- Invasive lizard (2 w.).
- Pestering person.
- Indonesian boat.
- Go around.
- Disruptor.
- Scorching.
- Grassy.
- Slavic people (plural).
- Creamy.
- Related to dancing.
- More abrupt.
- Triumvirate.
- Unbolt.

PROVERBS

DO YOU REMEMBER THE MEANINGS OF THESE?

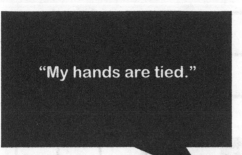

"My hands are tied."

WHAT DOES IT MEAN?

· · · · · · · · · · · · · · ·
· · · · · · · · · · · · · · ·
· · · · · · · · · · · · · · ·
· · · · · · · · · · · · · · ·
· · · · · · · · · · · · · · ·
· · · · · · · · · · · · · · ·

WHAT DOES IT MEAN?

· · · · · · · · · · · · · · ·
· · · · · · · · · · · · · · ·
· · · · · · · · · · · · · · ·
· · · · · · · · · · · · · · ·
· · · · · · · · · · · · · · ·
· · · · · · · · · · · · · · ·

"It's the tip of the iceberg."

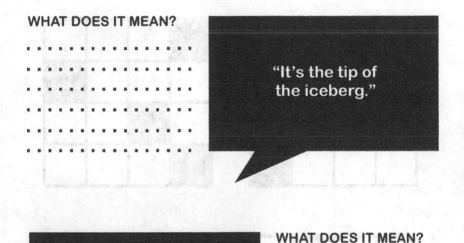

"No news is good news."

WHAT DOES IT MEAN?

· · · · · · · · · · · · · · ·
· · · · · · · · · · · · · · ·
· · · · · · · · · · · · · · ·
· · · · · · · · · · · · · · ·
· · · · · · · · · · · · · · ·
· · · · · · · · · · · · · · ·

MATCHMAKER

WHICH TWO ARE PERFECTLY ALIKE?

1.
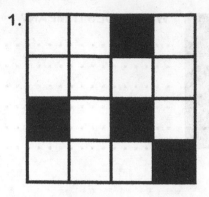

2.

3.

4.
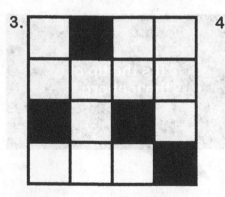

5.
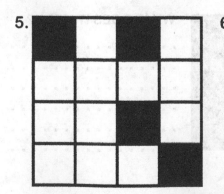

6.

CROSSWORD

¹	²	³	⁴	⁵	⁶	⁷	⁸	⁹	¹⁰	

ACROSS:

1. Alcoholic.
11. Valence of three.
13. Equipment Restraint Area (abbr.).
14. Save Our Sailors (abbr.).
16. Little devil.
18. Laos natives.
20. Before.
22. Deprivation.
23. Ugly woman.
24. "What's up, —?"
25. Metal machining piece.
26. Metal container.
27. Reverberation.
28. Hollow bread.
29. Which person.
30. Thin gravy.
32. Be able.
33. —Wan Kenobi.
35. Pacific Sea bream.
37. Musical slides.
40. Autopsies.

DOWN:

2. Information Tech. (abbr.).
3. Pre-K schools.
4. Baronet title.
5. Egg shaped.
6. Mom.
7. Additionally.
8. New (Greek).
9. Insect killer.
10. Astatine (abbr.).
12. Fungal coatings.
15. Ruling.
17. Beg.
19. Goodbye.
21. Yogurt side dish.
30. Body (Arabic).
31. Leading role.
34. Small portion.
36. Atom—.
37. General order (abbr.).
38. Peter Gabriel's 5ᵗʰ studio album.
39. Investment Mgmt. (abbr.).

WORDSEARCH

```
H E R A C L E S O A V J R
E X V T P J D H A D E S Q
R P U H P H U V E E N F Z
M O L E A L R N N Q U T Z
E S C N I E U O O E S X D
S E A A N T H T D S V I O
L I N I P P A N O I P H D
D D M E E M A R S U T Z Y
B O N S J H E R C U L E S
U N R H E P H A E S T U S
C E N W E U L Y S S E S E
P P M M E R C U R Y R U U
A Q Z L Z B A R T E M I S
```

FIND 25 GREEK AND ROMAN DEITIES AND HEROES:

WORDOKU

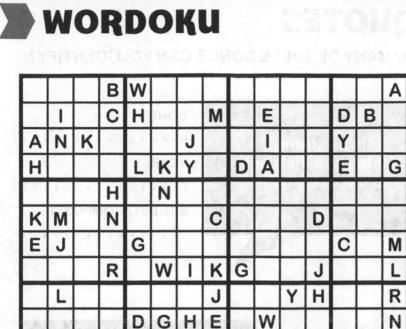

FILL EVERY ROW, COLUMN, AND 4X4 SECTOR,
USING EACH GIVEN LETTER ONLY ONCE!

QUOTES

HOW MANY OF THESE SONGS CAN YOU IDENTIFY?

"Is he strong?
Listen bud, he's got
radioactive blood..."

SONG:

. . . .

YEAR:

. . . .

SINGER / COMPOSER:

. . . .

SONG:

. . . .

YEAR:

. . . .

SINGER / COMPOSER:

. . . .

"In your satin tights /
Fighting for your rights /
And the old Red, White,
and Blue..."

"Believe it or not, I'm walking
on air / I never thought I
could feel so free..."

SONG:

. . . .

YEAR:

. . . .

SINGER / COMPOSER:

. . . .

MAZE

FIND A STRAIGHT PATH THAT FOLLOWS THIS
PATTERN: ▢■▢■ , HORIZONTAL OR VERTICAL
(NEVER DIAGONAL!), FROM THE TOP CHEVRON TO
THE CHEVRON AT THE BOTTOM OF THE GRID.

► UNSCRAMBLE

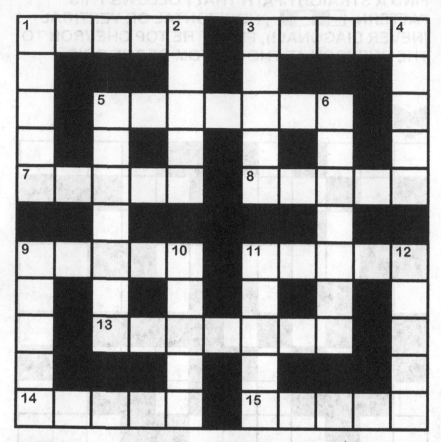

DISENTANGLE THESE WORDS TO FILL THE GRID.

ACROSS:
1. CHAIT
3. LAYIN
5. FIRMCON
7. DEARR
8. INMTY
9. RUTTS
11. LAVAR
13. CENTASN
14. TYNAS
15. THOYU

DOWN:
1. DIAVO
2. HORNO
3. MODII
4. MUMYY
5. CHONREV
6. MIETNAR
9. INTES
10. TYTAS
11. ERYEL
12. SHAWA

▶ TRIVIA

FAMOUS PEOPLE FROM THE PAST.

1.

1973 ▶ After giving his last speech, while under siege during a military coup, he shot himself.

2.

1975 ▶ A pioneering female comedian, she got a star on the Hollywood Walk of Fame.

3.

1977 ▶ While still at the university, he got his first radio broadcasting job at WRNW, in Briarcliff Manor, NY.

4.

1979 ▶ Originally from Uruguay, he got his first job in US comics, inking <u>Marvel Team-Up</u> #88 for Marvel Comics.

5.

1981 ▶ Announced his engagement to Lady Diana Spencer.

6.

1986 ▶ Scored his 34,000th career point during 124-102 Los Angeles Lakers win over the Indiana Pacers.

7.

1989 ▶ Beat "Macho Man" Savage at the WrestleMania V event.

8.

1993 ▶ Became the first African American woman to recite a poem at the inauguration of a US President.

DEFINITION SEARCH

```
D U F U S C N Y C L A N G
H U L K S O O W R A S S E
T R I P S N R E A V O G Y
Z G G A H T T E N U R E S
H I H N A E H W K Y W D E
E B T G M M A M A Y E R R
L I D O M P M R B A L E S
M N E L E L E A S E L S B
H G C I R A R S I E I S A
O M K N E T I L N L A E R
L A S E R O C I T I N R N
T E L E G R A P H I S T S
Z W I N K S N S E F Y G T
```

- Anise flavored spirits.
- Bundles.
- Sheds.
- Metallic sound.
- Observers.
- Turn handle.
- Woman's attire.
- Chest of drawers.
- Stupid person.
- Artist canvases.
- Cockpits (2 words).
- Geometry specialist.
- Hot springs.
- Taunting.
- Person who hammers.
- Listens.
- Funerary vehicle.
- Hermann Von—.
- Heavyweights.
- Intense beam of light.
- Metro Goldwyn—.
- Native of North America (two words).
- Totalitarian setting.
- Scaly mammal.
- Small paper notes.
- Telegraph operators.
- Possessions.
- Stumbles.
- Flutters.
- Marine fish.

PROVERBS

DO YOU REMEMBER THE MEANINGS OF THESE?

"Out of sight,
out of mind."

WHAT DOES IT MEAN?

· · · · · · · · · · · · · · · ·
· · · · · · · · · · · · · · · ·
· · · · · · · · · · · · · · · ·
· · · · · · · · · · · · · · · ·
· · · · · · · · · · · · · · · ·
· · · · · · · · · · · · · · · ·

WHAT DOES IT MEAN?

· · · · · · · · · · · · · · · ·
· · · · · · · · · · · · · · · ·
· · · · · · · · · · · · · · · ·
· · · · · · · · · · · · · · · ·
· · · · · · · · · · · · · · · ·
· · · · · · · · · · · · · · · ·

"If you scratch my back,
I'll scratch yours."

"Ignorance is bliss."

WHAT DOES IT MEAN?

· · · · · · · · · · · · · · · ·
· · · · · · · · · · · · · · · ·
· · · · · · · · · · · · · · · ·
· · · · · · · · · · · · · · · ·
· · · · · · · · · · · · · · · ·

MATCHMAKER

WHICH TWO ARE PERFECTLY ALIKE?

1.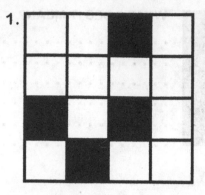

2.

3.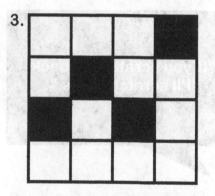

4.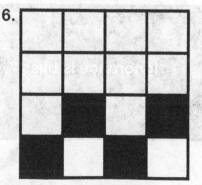

5.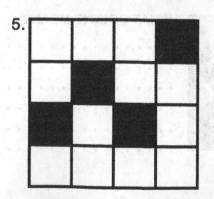

6.

CROSSWORD

ACROSS:
1. Ottoman title.
5. Payments.
9. Tropical mollusk.
10. Assign.
12. Retirement acct. (abbr.).
13. Metrical feet.
14. To open (archaic).
15. Automobiles.
17. Unprepared.
20. Ointment.
22. Bewitched.
25. Metropolis.
26. Live and obstruct (abbr.).
27. Rn86.
30. Donkey.
31. Pleasant Island.
32. Insert.
34. Piping.
35. Highest quality.

DOWN:
1. Gold (Latin).
2. Seize.
3. Her Excellency (abbr.).
4. Cleaver.
5. Justice (two words).
6. Tissue protein.
7. <u>Ulmus</u> tree.
8. Whimper.
9. Calf-length skirt.
11. Russian king.
15. Persist.
16. Lower cost.
18. Resentments.
19. Release grip.
21. Morning (abbr.).
23. Mitigates.
24. Do (archaic).
28. Exclaim surprise.
29. Duet.
32. Interstitial tissue (abbr.).
33. Doctor—.

WORDSEARCH

```
X Q J H A L L E Y S C O M E T
R B U R E W A H U B B L E P M
A L P H A C E N T A U R I L E
D A I D T D A R K M A T T E R
I C T T O R I O N V B A T I C
O K E Y U G T L O M E I M A U
T H R N A A G N S N R N V D R
E O P E M L R R P O H G U E Y
L L N P P E K L E D M A R S T
E E Q T P S A T E L L I T E E
S A T U R N E B U L A A N T O
C D S N A M I L K Y W A Y I W
O M C E Y S P W G A L A X Y N
P L U T O Z A Q U P V B J L S
E S L A S T E R O I D Y J M U
```

FIND 26 TERMS AND NAMES RELATED TO ASTRONOMY:

....
....
....
....
....
....
....
....
....
....
....

WORDOKU

					O	G					A		P		S
R		T	O			K	C	L							V
		L		P		Q					U		J		
	U		W		R	S		O	K	P		N			
S	Q	R	A			C	L		V						
G				P	S			K		L	U	Q			
	U	P				N	T			G					
O			U		K			G	R	J		T			
P		L	K	W			N		J			G			
	O				V	U			T	A					
V	R	S		G				O	K						N
			K		R	U						O	W	S	P
	W			O	A	R			J	T		P		V	
	T		J			G				W		L			
N					T	Q	A					W	S		R
Q		O		K					S	P					

FILL EVERY ROW, COLUMN, AND 4X4 SECTOR, USING EACH GIVEN LETTER ONLY ONCE!

QUOTES

HOW MANY OF THESE SONGS CAN YOU IDENTIFY?

"From the town of Bedrock / They're a page right out of history…"

SONG:
. . . .

YEAR:
. . . .

SINGER / COMPOSER:
. . . .

SONG:
. . . .

YEAR:
. . . .

SINGER / COMPOSER:
. . . .

"You are my candy girl / And you've got me wanting you…"

"D-d-d-danger! Watch behind you! There's a stranger out to find you / What to do, just grab on to some…"

SONG:
. . . .

YEAR:
. . . .

SINGER / COMPOSER:
. . . .

MAZE

FIND A STRAIGHT PATH THAT FOLLOWS THIS PATTERN: ▢■▢■ , HORIZONTAL OR VERTICAL (NEVER DIAGONAL!), FROM THE TOP CHEVRON TO THE CHEVRON AT THE BOTTOM OF THE GRID.

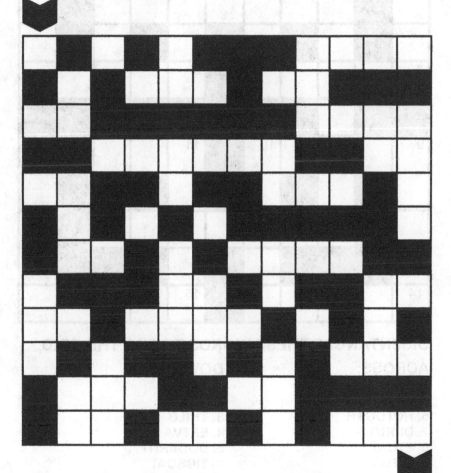

⏵ UNSCRAMBLE

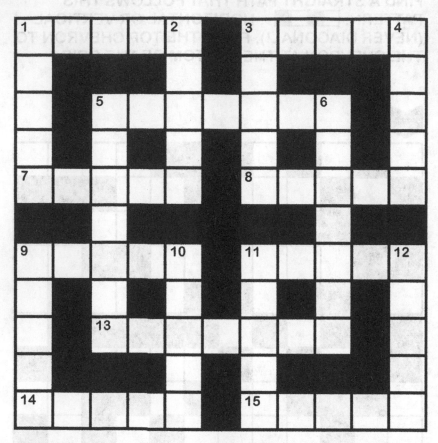

DISENTANGLE THESE WORDS TO FILL THE GRID.

ACROSS:
1. PUCRO
3. MALLA
5. HOTUGTH
7. DIDRO
8. ETCAT
9. DIELO
11. KRISH
13. LUNEUCS
14. DEXIO
15. TRAXE

DOWN:
1. RECED
2. ROPUD
3. THILG
4. ERTVA
5. DODERNT
6. TICSCAT
9. DUOTO
10. EEECM
11. DEWES
12. REKOA

▶ TRIVIA

FAMOUS PEOPLE FROM THE PAST.

1.
....

1954 ▶ Recorded "Rock Around the Clock" at DECCA Records, which would go on to become a 1950s youth anthem.

2.
....

1958 ▶ Completed the first overland crossing of Antarctica as part of the Commonwealth Trans-Antarctic Expedition.

3.
....

1965 ▶ The debut of TV comedy, <u>Get Smart</u>, made him famous worldwide.

4.
....

1966 ▶ Published her novel, <u>Valley of Dolls</u>, which, despite poor reviews, became one of the best-selling novels of all time.

5.
....

1970 ▶ After deposing King Idris, he was proclaimed premier of Libya and would stay in power until 2011.

6.
....

1975 ▶ Together with brothers Robin and Maurice, he created the <u>Saturday Night Fever</u> film soundtrack.

7.
....

1978 ▶ Led 918 members of his cult to commit suicide in Jonestown, Guyana.

8.
....

1983 ▶ Published <u>The Colour of Magic</u>, the first book in the "Discworld" series of fantasy novels.

DEFINITION SEARCH

```
C R V E S C S T L K H I N
F O E H M R O R D T H P A
U I N S O A R U A Y A A R
B L T D O N G E F L Y I K
W M E C T E H R A V E L S
C A R C H D U C H E S S N
U N J U S T M N D I R S A
B R A I N S T E M A T H K
U N S E R V I C E A B L E
U Q S E W R A W C S N O O
W E L Y R B A G H D A D I
R I T U A L I S M I C Y L
T E H E E B I R D C A G E
```

- Archduke's wife.
- Early sonar.
- Capital of Iraq.
- Large felines.
- Coop.
- Brain central nerve.
- Stretched.
- Polecat.
- 19th president.
- Moor.
- Rushed.
- Federal informants.
- Oil company worker.
- Buckets.
- Rattlings.
- Complicates.
- Begrudge.
- Fixed behavior.
- Velvety.
- Liniment.
- Grain cereal.
- Giggle.
- Masonic doorkeeper.
- Not false.
- Covered in grass.
- Biased.
- Deprive of courage.
- Malfunctioning.
- Abdomen.
- Erodes.

PROVERBS

DO YOU REMEMBER THE MEANINGS OF THESE?

"Easy come, easy go."

WHAT DOES IT MEAN?

. . . .
. . . .
. . . .
. . . .
. . . .
. . . .

WHAT DOES IT MEAN?

. . . .
. . . .
. . . .
. . . .
. . . .
. . . .

"The forbidden fruit is always the sweetest."

"Every cloud has a silver lining."

WHAT DOES IT MEAN?

. . . .
. . . .
. . . .
. . . .
. . . .

MATCHMAKER

WHICH TWO ARE PERFECTLY ALIKE?

1.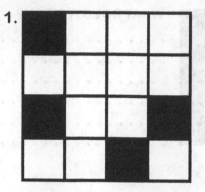

2.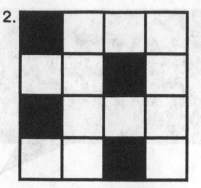

3.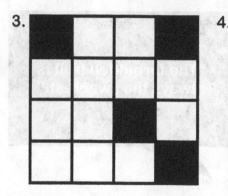

4.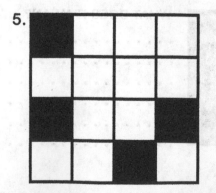

5.

6.

CROSSWORD

ACROSS:
1. "S" curve.
5. Toboggan.
9. Break down.
11. Slap.
13. Number 9 in a list.
15. Charged atom.
16. International Atomic Time (abbr.)
17. Apartment (abbr.).
18. Thug.
19. Shoulder piece.
21. Pale.
24. Ronald's nickname.
25. Single.
26. Sneak.
28. Mix again.
30. Broadcast time.
31. Second-hand.
32. Manure.

DOWN:
2. Auliropoda (2 words).
3. Etcetera (abbr.).
4. Horror expression.
5. Caught line drive.
6. Israeli machine gun.
7. Ladies.
8. Largest continent.
10. Impulse.
12. Swab.
14. Greek "T".
18. Spear with axe.
19. Gaelic language.
20. Hawaii taro dish.
22. Automatic Number Identification (abbr.).
23. Upcoming.
27. Recline.
28. Cleanse.
29. Aussie ostrich.

```
P F L I N T S T O N E S O D S X
P M X J S W H H A P P Y D A Y S
T S T A R T R E K D L G Z U L G
W I I K G B R E A K I N G B A D
Q F G E T S M A R T A Y K D W W
Q R F K A P S R H N E H B I A G
H I G H W A Y T O H E A V E N E
M V F A T A L B E R T W M C D I
S F A N T A S Y I S L A N D O U
K O J A K N I G H T R I D E R S
D B A T M A N S D F R I E N D S
A Q S I M P S O N S X F R Z E D
L O V E B O A T M G A I A O R W
L I F E O N M A R S S V R C K W
A G I N C R E D I B L E H U L K
S A N F O R D A N D S O N E Q D
```

FIND 24 CLASSIC TV SHOWS:

....
....
....
....
....
....
....
....
....
....
....

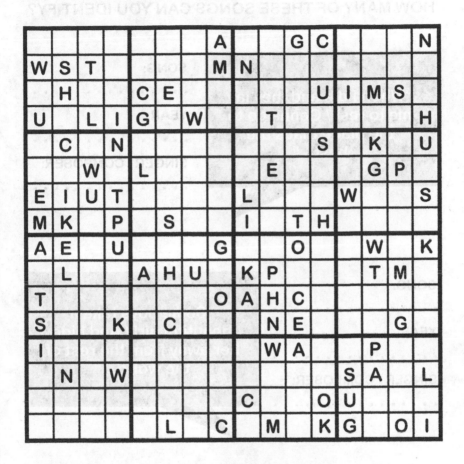

FILL EVERY ROW, COLUMN, AND 4X4 SECTOR, USING EACH GIVEN LETTER ONLY ONCE!

QUOTES

HOW MANY OF THESE SONGS CAN YOU IDENTIFY?

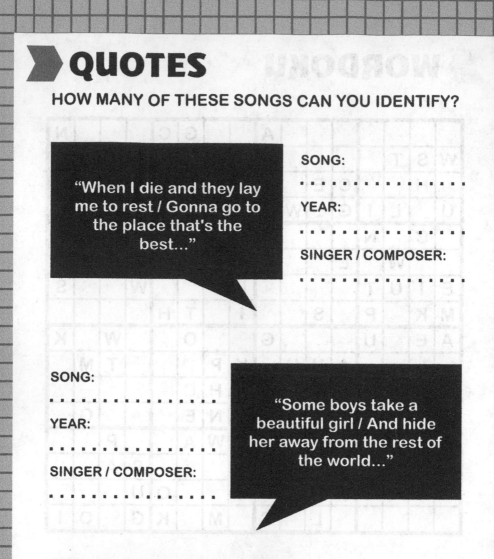

"When I die and they lay me to rest / Gonna go to the place that's the best..."

SONG:
. . . .

YEAR:
. . . .

SINGER / COMPOSER:
. . . .

SONG:
. . . .

YEAR:
. . . .

SINGER / COMPOSER:
. . . .

"Some boys take a beautiful girl / And hide her away from the rest of the world..."

"Your hair's a mess, you better put on a dress / And get your feet back on the ground..."

SONG:
. . . .

YEAR:
. . . .

SINGER / COMPOSER:
. . . .

◗ MAZE

FIND A STRAIGHT PATH THAT FOLLOWS THIS PATTERN: □■□■ , HORIZONTAL OR VERTICAL (NEVER DIAGONAL!), FROM THE TOP CHEVRON TO THE CHEVRON AT THE BOTTOM OF THE GRID.

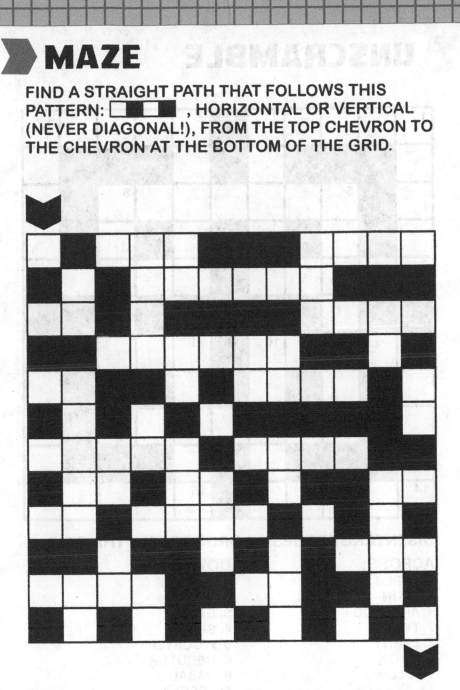

UNSCRAMBLE

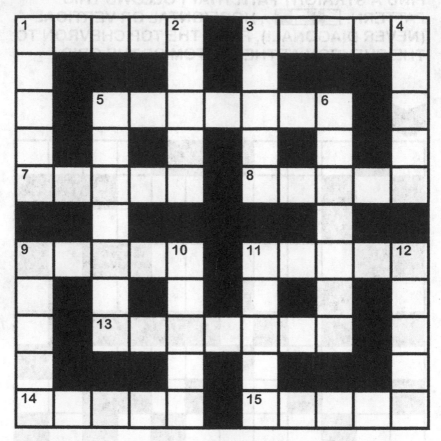

DISENTANGLE THESE WORDS TO FILL THE GRID.

ACROSS:
1. TOPES
3. TATIN
5. ARSENCO
7. TYLES
8. SARNY
9. CITOS
11. PLUMC
13. RILEFEB
14. DEUSO
15. PLIMY

DOWN:
1. MOSROP
2. TERAO
3. ETSYT
4. SEXUN
5. WOCRYLF
6. NERUTUR
9. DASAL
10. CEBLA
11. ILICH
12. MYPYG.

▶ TRIVIA

FAMOUS PEOPLE FROM THE PAST.

1.

1513 ▶ Reached Florida and claimed it for Spain.

2.

1631 ▶ Was elected first Governor of the Massachusetts Bay Colony.

3.

1774 ▶ Delivered the fourth annual Massacre Day oration, denouncing the presence of British troops in Boston.

4.

1853 ▶ Patented his condensed milk invention, which allowed milk to be kept without refrigeration for the first time.

5.

1937 ▶ Won the Pulitzer Prize for her novel, Gone With the Wind.

6.

1958 ▶ Published his best-selling historical novel about the founding of the State of Israel, Exodus.

7.

1980 ▶ His PBS series, Cosmos: A Personal Voyage, premiered, becoming a hit worldwide.

8.

1981 ▶ A Hanna-Barbera animated cartoon based on his Belgian comic strip, The Smurfs, became a sensation in America.

DEFINITION SEARCH

```
O M D E P R E P P E D E M
D T V G E U Q P G F O T B
I A P V M X M N X Q M T U
S W A G E S U M P X E A F
D H R S M O O C H S C O Y
A N T I L O G A R I T H M
I O Y G U N R O T I S G K
N H T I M E C A P S U L E
I H A P P L A U D A B L E
N U G O S W E A R I N A T
G E R M I N A T E D D T M
P O S S I B I L I T I E S
B R O O M S E R A P H I C
```

- Logarithm number.
- Express approval.
- Praiseworthy.
- Used to sweep.
- Girdle.
- December (abbr.).
- Deriding.
- Sprouted.
- Firearm.
- Babble.
- Tint.
- It would (contr.).
- Sitting room.
- Chunks.
- Master of Business Administration (abbr.).
- Nobelium (abbr.).
- Lex Luthor's sidekick.
- Shindig.
- Leg prosthesis.
- Brad—.
- Probability.
- Ready.
- Lassoist.
- Keep.
- Sublime.
- Scale Index Base (abbr.).
- Kiss.
- Metal taperer.
- Induct (two words).
- Historic cache.

PROVERBS

DO YOU REMEMBER THE MEANINGS OF THESE?

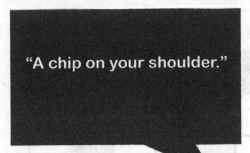
"A chip on your shoulder."

WHAT DOES IT MEAN?

. . . .
. . . .
. . . .
. . . .
. . . .
. . . .

WHAT DOES IT MEAN?

. . . .
. . . .
. . . .
. . . .
. . . .
. . . .

"A drop in the bucket."

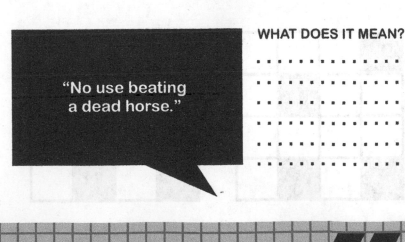
"No use beating
a dead horse."

WHAT DOES IT MEAN?

. . . .
. . . .
. . . .
. . . .
. . . .
. . . .

MATCHMAKER

WHICH TWO ARE PERFECTLY ALIKE?

1.
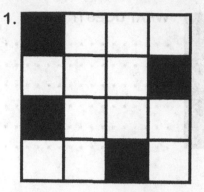

2.
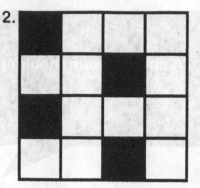

3.
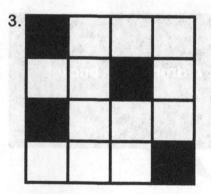

4.

5.
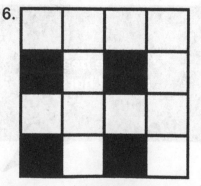

6.

CROSSWORD

ACROSS:
1. Peasant.
6. Vomits.
11. Dreamier.
13. Armed robbers.
15. Spontaneous.
17. Specific gravity (2 w.).
18. Correct.
19. Senior.
20. Asian weight.
21. Positioned.
23. Cunning.
24. Nicknamed "Highpockets."
25. Fragant conifer.
27. Horse-looking.
28. Boaster.
29. Locomotive.
32. Tides.
36. Appears.
37. Joan of—.
39. Relent.
41. Luggage.
42. Chairman.
43. Crack.
44. Particle viewer.
49. The (2 words).
50. Impertinently.
51. Reins.
52. Pocket container.
53. Mountain nymph.

DOWN:
1. Funny.
2. Greek soldier.
3. Not classified.
4. Tumult.
5. —Strauss & Co.
6. Angry mood.
7. Similar.
8. Male chicken.
9. Roof ornament.
10. Dignified.
11. Swaps.
12. Tears.
13. Father.
14. Artfully.
16. Horse auction (2 w.).
22. "Garfield" creator.
24. North & South—.
26. Darted.
27. Health Environment and Negotiation (abbr.).
29. Infusion leaves (2 w.).
30. Relaxed.
31. U.S. of —.
33. Cut off.
34. Wheat pudding.
35. Attached.
36. Moves along swiftly.
37. Friendship.
38. Anthozoa colony.
40. Fencing swords.
45. Aniseed (abbr.).
46. Goes w/ 47.
47. Sandwich cookie.
48. Luminous body.

WORDSEARCH

```
J E F F F O X W O R T H Y P P N N
O O C D O N A L D T R U M P D O M
A P S E L E N A R D F E R G I E I
N H R S T O M B R A D Y R D D N A
R I P I S L T E U N X O E D D K H
I L E U N T H R T I L N M K Y S A
V J T P J C O V H E I D I K L U M
E A E A E O E N W L V K K Y D C M
R C R U R L I B E R A C E J E A T
S K J L R I E C S A N D T U A R O
B S E S Y N C J T D K W Y D N L N
M O N I G P B A H C A E S G M R Y
J N N M A O B Y E L T L O E A O B
T Q I O R W K L I I R V N J R G L
U M N N C E I E M F U I C U T U A
Y M G X I L N N E F M R I D I E I
W W S E A L G O R E P A A Y N L R
```

FIND 36 FAMOUS PEOPLE AND CELEBRITIES:

....
....
....
....
....
....
....
....
....
....
....
....

WORDOKU

	J		D				I	Q	F		N			L				T	
H				T			O					D			J				
		N	O	D	B		T	H	G		Q	E			S				
K				M	P	J	S		F						I	C			
	P	B	H			K	Q			T		C		L					
O	E	K	F				M	A				C	Q		H				
A		C	J			L	H	P		F			M	T	R				
		G	R	C		J		K	I			O	F			B			
S	Q		F		H		O	R	P	L			D	T		K	A		
E		A		N			G	R	Q		H	B	P				E		
	G	F	K		M	P	O					I			C		E		
P	C		I	E		D	A	T	J		G		H		F		N		
C		J	N		G	I		F		P	B	A							
M	P	K		D		S	N	I				G	E			O			
I		B	Q			T	D					K	J	N	C				
	A	M		H		N	E		T	S	P								
D	G				R		E	T	L	A					H				
	E		P	A		D	M	O		S	F	K	R						
	I		S				C			D			F						
A		C		L	K	D	R			G		O							

FILL EVERY ROW, COLUMN, AND 5X4 SECTOR,
USING EACH GIVEN LETTER ONLY ONCE!

⏵ MAZE

FIND A STRAIGHT PATH THAT FOLLOWS THIS
PATTERN: ⬜⬛⬜⬛ , HORIZONTAL OR VERTICAL
(NEVER DIAGONAL!), FROM THE TOP CHEVRON TO
THE CHEVRON AT THE BOTTOM OF THE GRID.

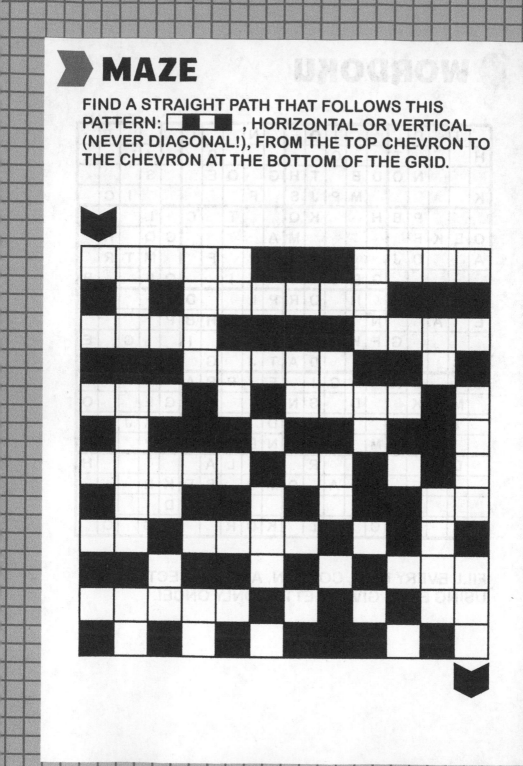

HOW MANY OF THESE FAMOUS TV LINES CAN YOU IDENTIFY?

"Live long and prosper."

SHOW:
. . . .

YEAR:
. . . .

"I don't wanna be the one."

SHOW:
. . . .

YEAR:
. . . .

"Suit up!"

SHOW:
. . . .

YEAR:
. . . .

WORDFILL

WHICH 3-LETTER COMBINATIONS ON THE LEFT DO YOU NEED TO COMPLETE THE 9-LETTER WORDS ON THE RIGHT?

IST	I	D	E				C	A	L
NES	C	H	O				A	T	E
IST	C	H	R				M	A	S
TRA	B	E	A				F	U	L
EGU	H	A	P				E	S	S
EBR	W	E	D				D	A	Y
CUL	C	H	A				N	G	E
NTI	A	D	V				U	R	E
SON	I	M	P				A	N	T
PIN	C	O	N				A	N	T
GER	C	H	R				I	A	N
UTI	D	A	N				O	U	S
ORT	M	A	S				I	N	E
ENT	C	E	L				A	T	E
LLE	A	U	S				L	I	A
COL	I	R	R				L	A	R

206

FAMOUS PEOPLE FROM THE PAST.

1.
....

1915 ► Published his novella <u>Die Verwandlung</u>
(<u>The Metamorphosis</u>).

2.
....

1931 ► Considered the father of modern organized
crime in the US for reorganizing the old
Cosa Nostra into The Commission.

3.
....

1945 ► The first Hollywood star in uniform during
WWII; as a pilot he led several combat
bombing missions, and was promoted to
full colonel.

4.
....

1959 ► Buried in his "Clark Kent" outfit after an
apparent suicide.

5.
....

1966 ► Never stopped fighting for his innocence,
while spending almost twenty years in
prison for a crime he didn't commit.

6.
....

1975 ► Patented his "Magic Cube," later to be
known as a Rubik's Cube

7.
....

1985 ► Beating Anatoly Karpov, he became the
youngest ever (22) world champion of
chess.

8.
....

1987 ► Issued US patent US4704583 for the laser,
after a 30-year battle to be credited as its
inventor.

```
C L A S P I N G T L R O C S S
J U N C O S N O W E D N L S S
J P W P R I N C E A L B E R T
A T E A F E U L A F T N A I S
N O Z F V G K N V S E E R N U
A C I A R C U G E V R E E C P
C R H W E A K D I R R D Y U E
O A G H F S L T A U N C E D R
N F D A R E I N G I X T D E B
D L G D A S I I L D O H F S A
A E B U I E F F E R E N T T E
M E N U N S H S W E E P I N G
Z I Q T O I L E T O F F Y P E
U N I C Y C L E S Y S P U P A
I G R A N D I O S I T Y W B N
```

- Greek Mediterranean.
- Water boa.
- Sedge-fly.
- Investigation.
- Clutching.
- No-nonsense.
- Slavic kings.
- Indentation (abbr.).
- Conducted outwards.
- Firstborn.
- Calculation expert.
- Escaping.
- Impressive quality.
- Disadvantaged.
- Interrupt.
- Overdue.
- Middle ear bones.
- Curiousness.
- Brown songbird.
- Fronds.
- Lime trees.
- Large mammals.
- Saskatchewan city (2 w.).
- Hold back.
- Play riffs.
- Snow (past tense).
- Outstanding.
- Broad.
- Sugar and butter sweet.
- Water Closet.
- Single wheel bikes.
- Until.
- Puny.
- Entwine.
- Reported.

SPEECHES

CAN YOU COMPLETE THESE?

"We are not interested in the possibilities of…"

WHAT:
. . . .
. . . .
. . . .

WHO:
. . . .
. . . .

WHAT:
. . . .
. . . .
. . . .

WHO:
. . . .
. . . .

"We shall defend our island, whatever the cost may be, we shall fight on the…"

"Mr. Gorbachev, open this gate! Mr. Gorbachev, tear…"

WHAT:
. . . .
. . . .
. . . .

WHO:
. . . .
. . . .

▶ MATCHMAKER

WHICH TWO ARE PERFECTLY ALIKE?

1.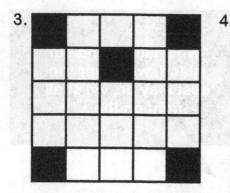

2.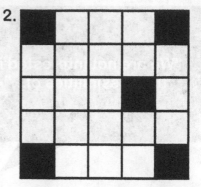

3.

4.

5.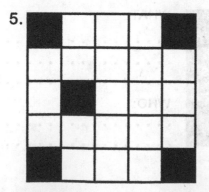

6.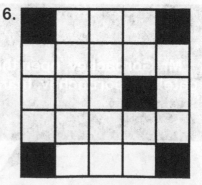

CROSSWORD

ACROSS:
1. Thomas—.
4. Health club.
7. Drinks slowly.
11. Gatherings.
15. Free from ice.
16. Adopted child.
17. Auks.
18. Painting medium.
19. Blackthorn fruits.
20. Frozen.
22. Liquefies.
23. Marshal—.
24. Neither.
25. It will (contr.).
26. Argot.
28. Dissertation.
29. Slippery.
30. Alan—.
33. Burst.
37. After pizzicato.
38. Belonging to male.
40. Again.
41. Sorrow.
42. Fuss.
43. Indian tent.
45. Erode (2 words).
47. Flown.
49. Small sailboat.
50. Rampaging.
51. Parodies.
52. Indefinitely (2w.).
53. Lysergic acid (abbr.).
54. Born as.

DOWN:
1. Conceals.
2. Three-leaved.
3. Fine silk.
4. Croutons.
5. Kneecap.
6. Vigilantly.
7. Drinks.
8. POW.
9. Even.
10. Glue.
11. Debaucher.
12. Elegy.
13. Condolence.
14. Oceans.
21. Gel.
27. —whiz!
28. Skimp on.
30. —Arts.
31. Positions.
32. Sea nymph.
34. Not eaten.
35. Amino chain.
36. Maid (archaic).
38. —Valley.
39. Rises high.
41. Openings.
44. Fringe.
46. Master.
48. Seven (Roman).

▶ **WORDSEARCH**

```
H Y N O N S E Q U I T U R U T
L B A J X I G T M J P Y Y X V
K B E E Q B X I C F O H M J F
M S X J C I R C A E S U K Q F
K R L S A D L I B O T I L U Y
V X I Y M E P Z A I S E C O F
Z E B T P M D K N B C T R V K
G V R H Y W E I N Z R A J A P
F W I S X R F X O R I L V D K
X Q S A U N A P D B P D U I V
A S W J I S C O O W T K U S P
U M E D N D T L M Q U P I V J
W D A K D Q O E I Y M Y O S G
P J C P E R C E N T D E R Y Y
H N C A R P E D I E M T C B E
```

**FIND 18 COMMON USAGE LATIN PHRASES AND WORDS.
CAN YOU THINK OF ANY OTHERS?**

. . . .
. . . .
. . . .
. . . .
. . . .
. . . .
. . . .
. . . .

WORDOKU

FILL EVERY ROW, COLUMN, AND 5X4 SECTOR, USING EACH GIVEN LETTER ONLY ONCE!

MAZE

FIND A STRAIGHT PATH THAT FOLLOWS THIS PATTERN:  , HORIZONTAL OR VERTICAL (NEVER DIAGONAL!), FROM THE TOP CHEVRON TO THE CHEVRON AT THE BOTTOM OF THE GRID.

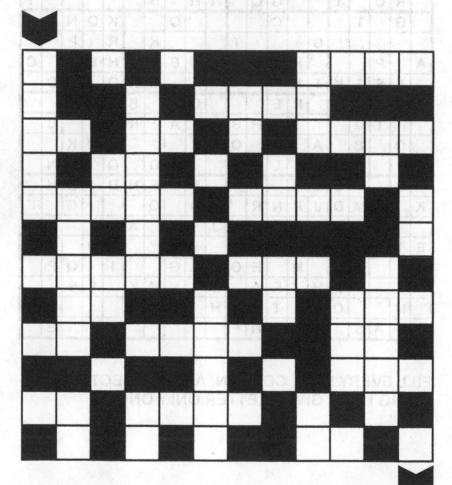

HOW MANY OF THESE FAMOUS TV LINES CAN YOU IDENTIFY?

"I can get along with just about anybody.
Just might have to bust him in the mouth to do it."

SHOW:
. . . .

YEAR:
. . . .

SHOW:
. . . .

YEAR:
. . . .

"A gesture which becomes less significant with each passing year."

"This is an environment of welcoming, and you should just get the hell outta here."

SHOW:
. . . .

YEAR:
. . . .

WORDFILL

WHICH 3-LETTER COMBINATIONS ON THE LEFT DO YOU NEED TO COMPLETE THE 9-LETTER WORDS ON THE RIGHT?

WLE	S	O	M				I	N	G
LOW	K	N	O				D	G	E
LUT	P	O	L				I	O	N
ECT	P	R	E				E	N	T
RET	W	R	E				I	N	G
ENT	P	I	N				P	L	E
GRU	A	D	J				I	V	E
ETH	S	E	C				A	R	Y
ULA	U	N	D				N	E	D
MUN	H	A	L				E	E	N
STL	A	M	B				N	C	E
IGA	A	L	L				T	O	R
EAP	S	E	V				E	E	N
EFI	A	F	F				I	O	N
ECT	C	O	N				E	N	T
SID	C	O	M				I	T	Y

FAMOUS PEOPLE FROM THE PAST.

1.

1959 ▶ Got his first big acting break playing Ben Frazer on the <u>Riverboat</u> TV series.

2.

1960 ▶ Published his first "Matt Helm" novel, <u>Death of a Citizen</u>, which would become a popular series of action-comedy films starring Dean Martin.

3.

1961 ▶ Became the first black singer to perform at the Bayreuth Festival, Germany, earning 42 curtain calls.

4.

1965 ▶ Got booed off the Newport Folk Festival stage after performing three songs with an electric guitar.

5.

1968 ▶ Barely survived being shot by a radical feminist.

6.

1980 ▶ Pitched his "Nature's Way" cartoon to the <u>San Francisco Chronicle</u>, which published it as <u>The Far Side</u>.

7.

1984 ▶ Wrote the pilot for a new TV show, <u>Highway to Heaven</u>, which he would also star in and produce.

8.

1989 ▶ Began writing the <u>Sandman</u> comic book series which would catapult him to stardom.

DEFINITION SEARCH

```
W A T E R T A B L E E R E R D
B C W V E D F U L L F A C E A
O K H M E Q S M B A O E H O M
O H L I E T V A M F U C Q I U
R E C O N S T R U C T I N G P
H M A T R I C U L A T I O N S
J S H Y V U N P L U M B E D Q
M I N E R S F G I E I H M P V
C O N V E N T I O N A L I T Y
Q I H M I C S B N L F Y T E I
X Y U L E L O G S P G I S U Z
R C C S O V G R U E S O M E R
S H K O W A D E P I L A T E L
I S P O W C W A V Y R X R H B
A S U R F O K J A C K A S S A
```

- Queries.
- Cutting backbone meat.
- Conventional practice.
- Corporation (abbr.).
- Pack.
- Obstruct.
- Evening (contr.).
- Effuses.
- Facing directly (2 words).
- Calvary.
- More repugnant.
- Protective hat.
- Edges.
- Throw.
- Inescapable.
- Stupid person.
- Fastened.
- College examination.
- Mine laborers.
- Vertical window bars.
- Double reed instrument.
- Be in debt.
- Rebuilding.
- Rabble.
- Timid.
- Tape cylinders.
- Sea foam.
- Flying saucer.
- Unexplored.
- Veteran (abbr.).
- Call in on.
- Wallow.
- Level below river bed.
- Christmas firewood.

► SPEECHES

CAN YOU COMPLETE THESE?

"Those who refuse to learn from history are…"

WHAT:
. . . .
. . . .
. . . .
WHO:
. . . .
. . . .

WHAT:
. . . .
. . . .
. . . .
WHO:
. . . .
. . . .

"The only thing we have to fear is…"

"Revolution is not a dinner party, not an essay, nor a painting, nor…"

WHAT:
. . . .
. . . .
. . . .
WHO:
. . . .
. . . .

MATCHMAKER

WHICH TWO ARE PERFECTLY ALIKE?

1.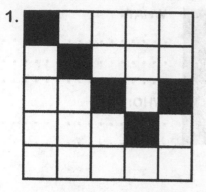

2.

3.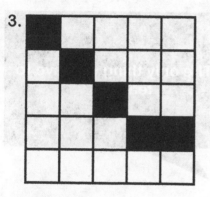

4.

5.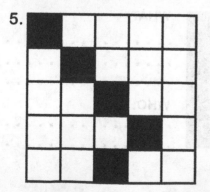

6.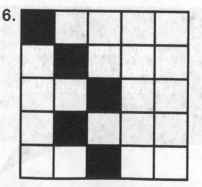

CROSSWORD

ACROSS:
1. Bearded man.
6. Like a "T".
13. Farewell (French).
14. Protuberance.
15. Loose stitching.
16. Cover w/ papillae.
17. Mimic.
18. Eastern Asia.
19. Yes.
20. Small red fruit.
22. Female horse.
23. Whispers.
24. Toxic protein.
25. Sow again.
26. Tests flavor.
27. Humble.
28. Expresses.
29. Grieves.
30. Felt.
31. Assign.
32. Mangelwurzel (abbr.).
33. Noticed.
34. Spirit of a place (2 words).
38. Do something.
39. Poisonous gas.
40. So be it.
41. Lute players.
43. Alongside.
44. Random.
45. Anxious.
46. Sextets.
47. Amplifies EM waves (abbr.).

DOWN:
1. Small cakes.
2. Adjust.
3. Vertical pipe.
4. Shape w/ 4 sides.
5. Tone.
6. Reduces.
7. Covered w/ spines.
8. Sword handle.
9. The whole of.
10. Pretended.
11. Restaurants.
12. Intensifies.
14. Put w/ another.
16. Set in advance.
18. Preoccupy.
21. European bison.
22. Collection.
24. Puts higher.
25. Gambling spinners.
26. Language.
27. Small particle.
28. Toxic elements.
29. Spicy pastes.
30. Lucidity.
32. Messieurs (abbr.).
34. African storyteller.
35. Prophecies.
36. Burn incense.
37. Bury.
39. Poker stake.
42. Consume.
43. Teller machine.

```
C A T C H M E I F Y O U C A N
C A S A B L A N C A Y M B O U
A X A R A L U D N S U B I D E
S A R R C O L Z C G B R G G Z
I M M I H E W A A O N U M B N
N A A E E A A N S O Z C O R M
O D G D L W C N T D I E M A B
R E E G O I L I A A B A M V Y
O U D T R W E E W S A L A E Z
Y S D K P M O H A I T M S H Q
A Q O B A T P A Y T M I H E C
L X N L R C A L W G A G O A H
E A B S T C T L B E N H U R D
M I I B Y C R F I T E T S T L
C H O C O L A T G S Q Y E S F
```

FIND 20 CLASSIC MOVIES STARTING WITH A, B, AND C.
CAN YOU THINK OF ANY OTHERS?

....
....
....
....
....
....
....
....

WORDOKU

	A	J	I		G	O			P	L		Q	B	E					
K		T					A		F		S			P	Q	M			
	M		H		Q	P		D	G					K	F	J			
N		P		B			R	J				C				T	O		
	O	F		A	I	Q		C							P				
	B	K			R		T	N		D			L	Q				H	
	L			K		D		N		T	M	R	F			C	I		
					L			P	F			I			A		R	K	
				P			D	O	I	H	K	M			F	N	A		
A			R	M	C		T		L		S								
				R			O		B			F	E	Q			L		
S	K	L		E	F	B	I	Q	T			N							
L	O		E		J			H	R		F								
I	Q		S	D	M	A			E		G		K			J			
T		C	A			Q		E	J			H			R	P			
B						G			T	I	Q		H	L					
A	E				O			G	L			H			J		Q		
	O	D	Q				K	F		M	E			P		I			
	J	C	M			S		E		A						B		D	
		F	T	R		J	A			B	O		K	M	G				

FILL EVERY ROW, COLUMN, AND 5X4 SECTOR, USING EACH GIVEN LETTER ONLY ONCE!

MAZE

FIND A STRAIGHT PATH THAT FOLLOWS THIS PATTERN: ▢■▢■ , HORIZONTAL OR VERTICAL (NEVER DIAGONAL!), FROM THE TOP CHEVRON TO THE CHEVRON AT THE BOTTOM OF THE GRID.

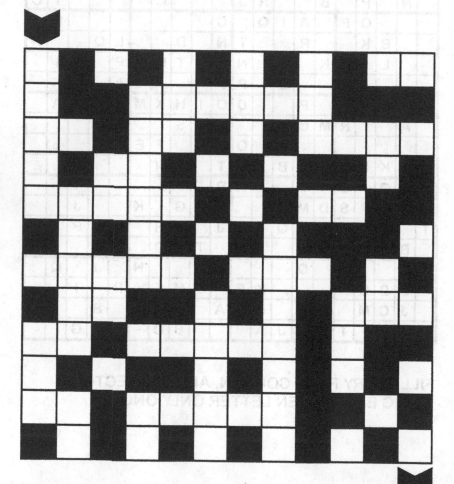

HOW MANY OF THESE FAMOUS TV LINES CAN YOU IDENTIFY?

"There are certain rules about a war, and rule number one is that young men die. And rule number two is that doctors can't change rule number one."

SHOW:
. . . .

YEAR:
. . . .

SHOW:
. . . .

YEAR:
. . . .

"Whacked? Phoebe, you've been in New York way too long."

"A guy opens his door and gets shot, and you think that of me? No! I am the one who knocks!"

SHOW:
. . . .

YEAR:
. . . .

WORDFILL

WHICH 3-LETTER COMBINATIONS ON THE LEFT DO YOU NEED TO COMPLETE THE 9-LETTER WORDS ON THE RIGHT?

ETA	D	I	F				E	N	T
RIT	V	E	G				B	L	E
INN	I	N	F				N	C	E
COD	S	T	R				U	R	E
ISI	I	N	V				B	L	E
LEV	W	O	N				F	U	L
HER	P	A	C				I	N	G
FER	P	R	O				I	N	G
UND	N	U	T				I	O	N
DER	C	R	O				I	L	E
INL	E	D	U				I	O	N
UCT	A	B	O				I	N	G
CAT	B	E	G				I	N	G
KAG	B	R	A				E	S	S
VOK	B	O	U				A	R	D
LUE	W	I	T				I	N	G

226

▶ TRIVIA

FAMOUS PEOPLE FROM THE PAST.

1. ....

1386 ▶ Began writing his magnum opus, which would popularize the use of English vernacular language in mainstream British literature, as opposed to French or Latin.

2. ....

1879 ▶ Signed a formal agreement to edit the <u>Oxford English Dictionary</u>.

3. ....

1931 ▶ His comic strip about a plainclothes police detective named Tracy made its debut in the <u>Detroit Mirror</u> newspaper.

4. ....

1952 ▶ Became boxing World Heavyweight Champion and kept the title until his retirement in 1956.

5. ....

1971 ▶ Successfully hijacked a Boeing 727 flight, extorted $200,000 in ransom, and parachuted out of the plane, disappearing forever.

6. ....

1974 ▶ Released the first commercial version of his <u>Dungeons & Dragons</u> board game.

7. ....

1983 ▶ Won a Grammy for his hit song "Rockit," which was widely considered to be the first jazz hip-hop anthem.

8. ....

2015 ▶ Became the longest-reigning British monarch on September 9th.

DEFINITION SEARCH

```
R K Z B D F X K L Y J B A C T
C A R A T L S P Q V O H O I
K C E X P E D I T I O N S N J
C H X F L E A M A R K E T S U
T U M F A R E D L I N E R E D
T M I S P R O N O U N C I N G
X S S Q U A R E D E A L P G E
O O T T A W A H U T U U E I S
W N I F R E S H M A N B D R H
L U T H E R A Y P E M R Q D I
V O L U M E T R I C A L L Y P
B R I E F E D J N Y N N F L U
M O N O T Y P E G O N M S B N
H X G O D S P E E D E R U S K
S B J Z V V M E J P D Z X M C
```

- Informed.
- Gemstone weight.
- Disadvantages.
- Throwing away.
- Sand mounds.
- Surround.
- Epoch.
- Voyages.
- A long way.
- Secondhand markets.
- Jeer.
- 1st year student.
- Traveler good wish.

- Bantu tribes.
- Chinese idol.
- Judge appointment.
- German theologian.
- Resources.
- Pronouncing incorrectly.
- Wrongly giving title.
- Single print.
- Canada's capital.
- Thug.
- Son of Kaemsekhem.
- Beam.
- Cancel.

- Twice-baked bread.
- Male offspring.
- Fair transaction.
- Banded.
- Not needing a crew.
- Based on volume.
- Jamaican criminal.

▶ SPEECHES

CAN YOU COMPLETE THESE?

"You must not fight too often with one enemy, or..."

WHAT:

. . . .
. . . .
. . . .

WHO:

. . . .
. . . .

WHAT:

. . . .
. . . .
. . . .

WHO:

. . . .
. . . .

"It is not the critic who counts; not the man who points out how the strong man stumbles..."

"Ask not what your country can do for you..."

WHAT:

. . . .
. . . .
. . . .

WHO:

. . . .
. . . .

MATCHMAKER

WHICH TWO ARE PERFECTLY ALIKE?

1.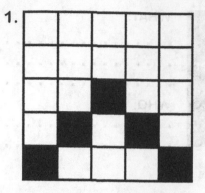

2.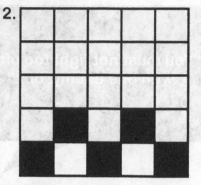

3.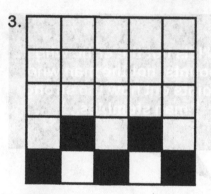

4.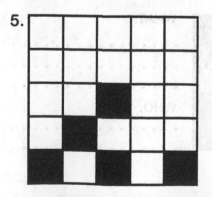

5.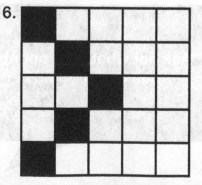

6.

CROSSWORD

ACROSS:

1. Amusing.
8. Cashew tree.
13. Buttercup plant.
14. "Sweet potato".
16. Postponement.
17. Ferret.
18. Barley waters.
19. Increase.
20. Ireland.
21. No.
22. Killer cetacean.
23. Tendon.
25. —of clay.
27. Contempt noise.
28. CA.
31. EM units (abbr.).
32. Balcony.
33. —Ra.
36. Current (2 words).
40. —dynasty.
41. Pour out.
42. Reddish-brown.
44. Vast sand area.
45. Parent-Teacher Assoc. (abbr.).
46. Fixed charges.
47. Ever-changing.
49. Fills again.
52. Bombing (2 w.).
53. Environmental destruction.
54. Respects.
55. Hook-billed birds.
56. Squirrel nests.
57. Staggers.

DOWN:

1. Cards (French).
2. Dreams-related.
3. Sicily's 3rd city.
4. Choose a jury.
5. Mint.
6. Player stake.
7. Wine sediment.
8. Quip.
9. Carbamide.
10. Germ.
11. Rearrangement.
12. Acacia extract.
14. Without limit (2w.).
15. Inclination.
24. Crybaby.
25. Racket stroke.
26. Rub out.
29. Emergency care.
30. Art branches.
33. Sam ...
34. Hunting hound.
35. Eat ravenously.
37. Shortfall.
38. Similar to ape.
39. Gainer.
43. Evaluate.
45. Pyrus communis.
48. Platter.
49. Lie down.
50. Repeat.
51. Garrison.

WORDSEARCH

```
D E N T R A P M E N T D H E N A L
F R T K F R E A K Y F R I D A Y F
O I I M F F A D L Z C B O P D K A
R N D V A L T D F N G W Y X E P T
R B A D I E I G H T B E L O W E H
E R R R L N N M Z Y S P X C E A E
S O E A J E G F R A C T U R E R R
T K D G Y E R M A V Y G H P A T O
G O E O N A A O I C L C E I J H F
U V V N Y S O S N S E C B U Q Q T
M I I H W T U N R T S O M H I U H
P C L E F O L Z H J H D F I C A E
P H X A B F J R M T O E A F Q K B
M G S R N E B A E A S Y R I D E R
O M P T Q D R Z H I V A G O S N I
F G Z A N E G H T X S C O Y O Y D
D J F R E N C H K I S S J C B F E
```

**FIND 20 CLASSIC MOVIES STARTING WITH D, E, AND F.
CAN YOU THINK OF ANY OTHERS?**

WORDOKU

	S		W		R		M		X	Y			I	N				K	
M			I	K		Q	T			W	O		R			N			G
		V			G		I			N		X		P		S	T		
U		Q			S	J	V	P		K	G				M	L			I
R	U		O		T			L	J			G			I	X	Q	N	
N	Z	V	Q					K			H				R			T	
L	H		T	X			G	U		P								J	Y
J	G				S	N				T	W	Q		V	P				
V			G	T	Y		U				Z					H		I	
	Y		U	J				I			S	L	Q						
			X	H	R			U						Y	M		P		
	K		R			J				V			X	G	W				S
		Y	N		R	S	M			O	V						L	Q	
H	L					O		S	I					M	J		R	V	
	W		V			L		Z							I	T	Y	O	
	O		K	R	I		X			T	H		G			S		Z	W
W			S	J			Z	R		L	X	G	O				K		N
		J	M		N		I			R		Y		U		Z			
P			U			G		T	M		K	I			W	L			R
	T			V	W		M	H			P		Z		U		G		

**FILL EVERY ROW, COLUMN, AND 5X4 SECTOR,
USING EACH GIVEN LETTER ONLY ONCE!**

MAZE

FIND A STRAIGHT PATH THAT FOLLOWS THIS
PATTERN: ▢■■▢■ , HORIZONTAL OR VERTICAL
(NEVER DIAGONAL!), FROM THE TOP CHEVRON TO
THE CHEVRON AT THE BOTTOM OF THE GRID.

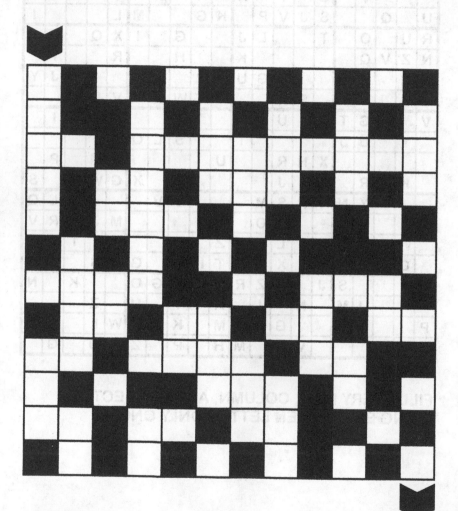

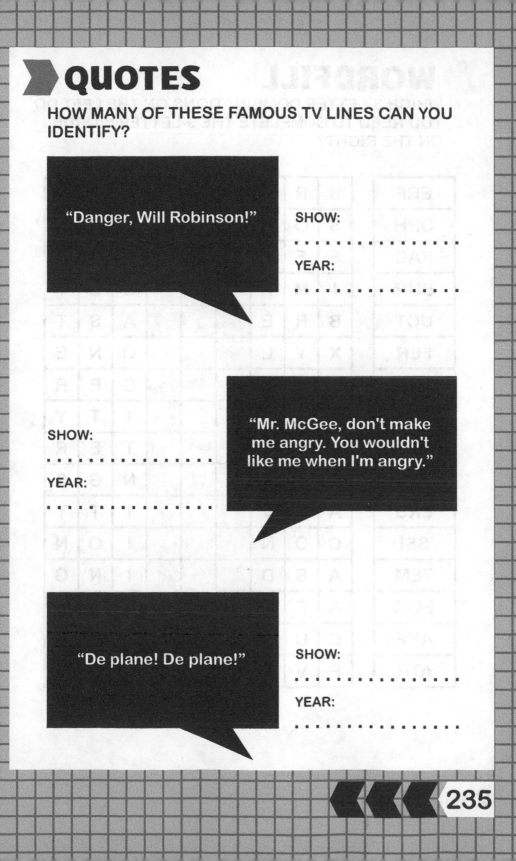

QUOTES

HOW MANY OF THESE FAMOUS TV LINES CAN YOU IDENTIFY?

"Danger, Will Robinson!"

SHOW:
. . . .

YEAR:
. . . .

SHOW:
. . . .

YEAR:
. . . .

"Mr. McGee, don't make me angry. You wouldn't like me when I'm angry."

"De plane! De plane!"

SHOW:
. . . .

YEAR:
. . . .

WORDFILL

WHICH 3-LETTER COMBINATIONS ON THE LEFT DO YOU NEED TO COMPLETE THE 9-LETTER WORDS ON THE RIGHT?

ERF	B	R	E				I	N	G
OPH	S	O	P				O	R	E
RAC	S	E	P				B	E	R
BUR	I	M	P				E	C	T
UCT	B	R	E				A	S	T
FER	X	Y	L				O	N	E
RYB	H	A	M				G	E	R
FUS	I	N	T				I	T	Y
HOM	C	H	A				T	E	R
ERL	B	L	E				N	G	S
ERS	A	D	V				I	T	Y
SSI	C	O	N				I	O	N
TEM	A	B	D				I	N	G
EGR	A	F	T				I	F	E
AKF	S	U	F				I	N	G
ATH	E	V	E				O	D	Y

▶ TRIVIA

FAMOUS PEOPLE FROM THE PAST.

1.

1913 ▶ A famous writer and journalist during his lifetime, he crossed the Mexican border in December, never to be seen again.

2.

1925 ▶ From her uncredited screen debut in <u>The Street of Forgotten Men</u> she became a movie icon on both sides of the Atlantic.

3.

1938 ▶ Nicknamed the "Brown Bomber," he beat German champ Max Schmeling after a brief two minutes and four seconds match.

4.

1941 ▶ The film <u>I Wanted Wings</u> made her a star while still in her teens.

5.

1964 ▶ A sitcom based on his cartoon series for <u>The New Yorker</u> premiered on television.

6.

1966 ▶ Began her modeling career when she was eleven months old!

7.

1971 ▶ Drew his first "Donald Duck" comic for Egmont Publishing in Denmark.

8.

1983 ▶ Signed a five-year contract with Columbia Pictures for 40 million dollars.

DEFINITION SEARCH

```
J G F A C I G J A R M V W E D
P S M A L L S C R E E N L A O
Q S W Q I R G Y S L H G R P M
A V B Q E G G C N T N Z F Q I
R D B L U R M Y D O A J L A C
C R I U E M B E D D I N G M I
H M E N T A L H O S P I T A L
E O A D R P Q D O X Z I G O I
R M A E U Z I O D H D N T A N
W E A R E H A P L O I D Y O G
Q X C C D O G I E S E M G I D
N S C O N G R E G A T I O N S
R O M A N T I C I Z A T I O N
W E S T O E P O T S H E R D T
L O V I N G A R N E T S T E T
```

- Inactiveness.
- Bowman.
- Flocks.
- Legislature.
- Orphaned calves.
- Settling a home.
- Small computer device.
- Scribble.
- Implanting.
- Precious silicate stones.
- Half a chromosome set.
- Stash.
- Information System (abbr).

- Adoring.
- Asylum (2 words).
- Trained to run a mile.
- Small ticks.
- Pottery piece.
- Idealization.
- Regretted.
- Ho Chi Minh City.
- Hesitant.
- Intone.
- Television (2 words).
- Eric—.
- "Let it stand".

- Front veranda.
- Golden-brown skin.
- Layer after primer.
- Unione Zoologica Italiana (abbr.).
- Workplace Economics (abbr.).
- Abrade.
- Where the sun sets.
- Zimbabwean language.
- —zag.

SPEECHES

CAN YOU COMPLETE THESE?

"You and I, gentlemen, have shared the labour and shared the danger…"

WHAT:
. . . .
. . . .
. . . .

WHO:
. . . .
. . . .

WHAT:
. . . .
. . . .
. . . .

WHO:
. . . .
. . . .

"Hear me, my Chiefs! I am tired…"

"But has the last word been said? Must hope disappear? Is defeat final?…"

WHAT:
. . . .
. . . .
. . . .

WHO:
. . . .
. . . .

MATCHMAKER

WHICH TWO ARE PERFECTLY ALIKE?

1.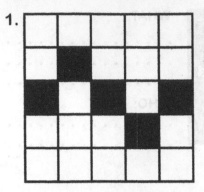

2.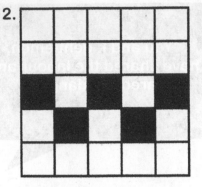

3.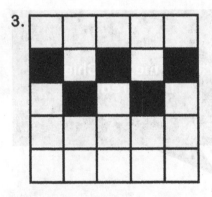

4.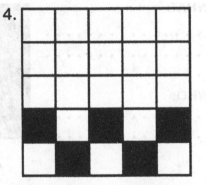

5.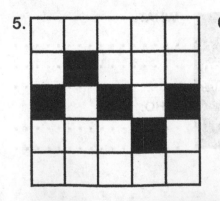

6.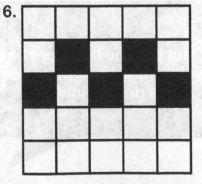

CROSSWORD

ACROSS:
1. Accept eagerly (2 w.).
6. Gives off fumes .
11. Rolls up (2 w.).
13. Small bone.
15. From Israel.
16. Micturate.
17. Cardboard cutout.
18. Get a move on.
19. Dollar fraction.
20. Manner (archaic).
22. Gentlemen.
23. Harmonium.
25. String toy.
26. Shed.
27. Watery fluid.
29. Carcass
31. Wash.
33. Lower edge.
36. Nook.
40. Function as laser.
41. After taxes.
43. Beside.
45. Killer whale.
46. Puree.
47. —Binder.
48. Freight wagon (2 w.).
50. Electrode.
53. Uppermost.
54. Adding color.
55. Surreptitious.
56. Firm (Italian).
57. Dispatches.
58. Hostel.

DOWN:
1. Splendors.
2. Put together.
3. Foot underside.
4. Secondhand.
5. Mewl.
6. Female jury leader.
7. Single element.
8. Plural meniscus.
9. Happiness.
10. Counters.
11. Francisco (abbr.).
12. Devoutness.
13. Bulging eyes.
14. Strained.
21. Paper wasps.
24. Void.
28. Tallest masts.
30. Opera solo song.
32. Excavate.
33. Cyprians.
34. Fugitive.
35. Butcher.
37. Clogged.
38. Joyriding.
39. Agreement.
40. Adaptable space.
42. Greek "th".
44. Ravine.
49. Chilly.
51. Grind.
52. Re: India.

WORDSEARCH

```
T R B M P B S G A N D H I I P V P
L G O S F O R D P A R K N N Z Q A
G O L D F I N G E R M G D S Y I V
L N A K G C C G I L D A E P D H U
A E I N D E P E N D E N C E D A Y
D W O O U S Y H E A T G E C J I Y
I I I S B T U I I H A S N T S R M
A T N A S A G G S G J O T O G S P
T H N R O T K H A O H F P R B P Y
O T E Z A I H L O B S N R C E R T
R H R T K O B A P S U E O L R A A
K E S V L N W N R U T W P O Z Y J
H W P R S Z G D D N G Y O U N L W
Z I A M L E G E N D C O S S N L M
K N C T K B Q R B O Y R A E K V D
J D E O G R E A S E Q K L A X U U
V F Y T E A P P I H O T F U Z Z D
```

FIND 20 CLASSIC MOVIES STARTING WITH G, H, AND I. CAN YOU THINK OF ANY OTHERS?

. . . .
. . . .
. . . .
. . . .
. . . .
. . . .
. . . .
. . . .

P	Y		N		R	T				E		D					Q		A
		O	X			S		B			U	T							Y
B	K			T		Q				Y		C				O	L		
	C	V			U	K	Y			Q				S			W		
		Y								L	X	O	M	N	E		U		
E		A		Q		B	W					C				P	O	V	
D			C					M		P	Q	W	A				L		
N	W	L	V		O			U			Y		T			K	B	Q	
	Y	R		W			P		C	M									
C			P		Y	U			S	W		X	K		T		R	Q	N
Q	T	E		V		X	D		N	Y			L	U		B			P
					M	T		P			N			E	V				
Y	Q	W			X		V			E			B		L	A	P	R	
	B			D	Q	M	E		O				U						S
A	U	T			P					Q	V		K		B				C
X		C	S	R	K	N	T						V						
		B			T			V		N	A	L			O	R			
		O	C			A		D			B		Y				S	K	
T					B	Q			D		W		V	U					
U		D			S		W			Y	E		Q		M	B			

FILL EVERY ROW, COLUMN, AND 5X4 SECTOR, USING EACH GIVEN LETTER ONLY ONCE!

MAZE

FIND A STRAIGHT PATH THAT FOLLOWS THIS PATTERN: ▢■▢■ , HORIZONTAL OR VERTICAL (NEVER DIAGONAL!), FROM THE TOP CHEVRON TO THE CHEVRON AT THE BOTTOM OF THE GRID.

QUOTES

HOW MANY OF THESE FAMOUS TV LINES CAN YOU IDENTIFY?

"Gee, Mrs. Cleaver..."

SHOW:
....

YEAR:
....

"Elizabeth, I'm coming!"

SHOW:
....

YEAR:
....

"I love it when a plan comes together!"

SHOW:
....

YEAR:
....

WORDFILL

WHICH 3-LETTER COMBINATIONS ON THE LEFT DO YOU NEED TO COMPLETE THE 9-LETTER WORDS ON THE RIGHT?

ENT	C	U	R				I	T	Y
PAN	C	E	L				I	T	Y
MSI	D	E	L				O	U	S
HTN	T	U	R				I	S	E
ESS	A	T	T				I	O	N
ATM	C	O	M				I	O	N
GHE	E	L	O				I	O	N
FIC	W	H	I				C	A	L
MIS	D	I	F				U	L	T
ICI	A	G	I				I	O	N
YCL	N	E	C				A	R	Y
QUO	L	I	G				I	N	G
IOS	C	H	E				T	R	Y
TAT	R	E	C				I	N	G
CUT	T	R	E				E	N	T
EBR	S	P	A				T	T	I

▶ TRIVIA

FAMOUS PEOPLE FROM THE PAST.

1.

1869 ▶ Sent to Africa by the <u>New York Herald</u>, to find Dr. Henry Livingstone.

2.

1875 ▶ At fifteen, she won a shooting match against traveling-show marksman Frank E. Butler, whom she later married.

3.

1903 ▶ Made the first controlled, sustained flight of a powered, heavier-than-air aircraft.

4.

1915 ▶ Premiered his controversial, yet groundbreaking film, <u>Birth of a Nation</u>, in Los Angeles.

5.

1918 ▶ Awarded the French Croix de Guerre for his first five victories as an ace pilot.

6.

1920 ▶ Became one of the highest paid actors in Hollywood after signing a contract with Paramount Pictures for $14,000.

7.

1941 ▶ Her MGM contract included a guest pass to The Beverly Hills Hotel where she could swim in the pool every day.

8.

1967 ▶ Recorded and released his classic ballad, "What a Wonderful World."

DEFINITION SEARCH

```
E M B U K F H W A V B G E L W
A W O P Q L U C D X A T Z O O
J F N J P G R O S S N E S S R
O L E R A P T F R O T H Y E T
N A M J J R L L G S U M C R H
A L A S V G E I U U D A O B I
T P R B J M P V E R R U C A E
H A R D H E A R T E D N E S S
A S O I J C E U S C R O O K T
N H W C O N T R I V A N C E S
C E N T E R O F G R A V I T Y
P W A Y Y H Y T C A T R Y S T
L I C K S K L F I R E L I T Z
J H C A M E R A L U C I D A S
Q D I N K R G W H I S K E R S
```

- Advertisements (abbr.).
- Niger-Congo languages.
- Shetland Argus (2 w.).
- Myeloid tissue (2 w.).
- Optical tracing device.
- Center of mass (3 w.).
- Schemes.
- Criminal.
- Copycat.
- Illuminated by fire.
- Foamy.
- Mother Earth (Greek).
- Flagrant quality.
- Callousness.
- Close contest (2 w.).
- Lunge.
- Mock.
- Young kangaroos.
- US cooking apple.
- Salmon.
- Flickers.
- Extinct flightless bird.
- Numbers (abbr.).
- S. American wood sorrel.
- Picture (abbr.).
- Cloister.
- Serbian.
- Show (archaic).
- Certain.
- Romantic rendezvous.
- United States (abbr.).
- Wart.
- Path.
- Hair bristle.
- Most deserving.

SPEECHES

CAN YOU COMPLETE THESE?

"Having now finished the work assigned to me, I retire from..."

WHAT:

. . . .
. . . .
. . . .

WHO:

. . . .
. . . .

WHAT:

. . . .
. . . .
. . . .

WHO:

. . . .
. . . .

"In the democracy which I have envisaged, a democracy established by..."

"In the councils of government, we must guard against..."

WHAT:

. . . .
. . . .
. . . .

WHO:

. . . .
. . . .

▶ **MATCHMAKER**

WHICH TWO ARE PERFECTLY ALIKE?

1.
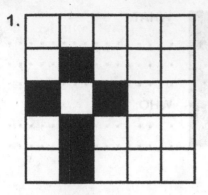

2.
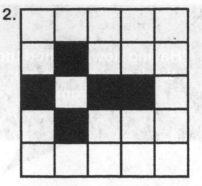

3.
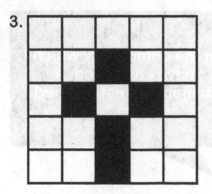

4.
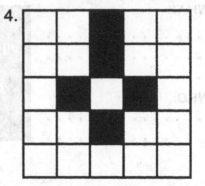

5.
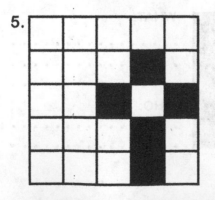

6.
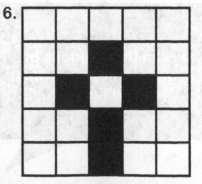

CROSSWORD

ACROSS:

1. Scrutinize.
5. Pinnacle.
9. Electron removal.
12. Wardress.
14. Wanders around (2 w.).
16. Victorian artists.
17. Re: middle line.
18. Endorheic lakes (2 w.).
20. N. Italian city.
21. Saw (Latin).
22. Obtains.
25. Relax.
27. Dangled.
30. C_5H_{11}.
33. Precipitation.
36. King (Semitic).
39. Roams.
42. Pledged to.
45. Recouped.
46. Shape w/ 3 acute angles (2 w.).
48. Digestive cells (2 w.).
49. Puglia.
50. Mesh.
51. Cheek.
52. N. Ireland party (abbr.).

DOWN:

1. Drinking straw.
2. Route.
3. Betting on Poker.
4. Treated w/ nitric acid.
5. Coral reefs.
6. Patrol car.
7. City in central CA.
8. Generates affection.
10. Fanaticism.
11. Enterprise Resource Planning (abbr.).
12. Low volcano crater.
13. Zone.
15. Thicket.
17. Meeting (abbr.).
19. Saturday (abbr.).
23. Therefore.
24. Mill watercourse.
26. Carpenter bees.
28. Public Relations (abbr.).
29. Grimness.
30. Amplifier (abbr.).
31. Shak-shaks.
32. Horseshoe crab.
34. Annoyed.
35. US Navy (abbr.).
37. Fishtail palms.
38. Dusky (Irish).
40. Cheap trimmings.
41. Binds (2 words).
43. Half.
44. Sicilian volcano.
47. Internal rate of return (abbr.).

```
J S R L P P J K N Z Q B M L H V L T J
Y Y K A J J L I Q N J N A P A F O C O
F R R D Y W I S O L Z L U X K X S S E
B J A Y Q S L S E A B K Z S E H T T V
J U M A N J I I K W Z A K C L O I G E
E R E N E C E N A R X R S A R P N G R
R A R D M B S G T E G A I O N O T K S
R S V T H D O J E N I T I Z K S R R U
Y S S H L J F E A C N E B G H J A W S
M I K E E S T S N E H K N J V I N S T
A C R T H S H S D O L I R N L E S W H
G P A R O X E I L F K D Q R W J L N E
U A M A I M F C E A L J A R H E A D V
I R E M N N I A O R Q I L S I H T N O
R K R P O I E S P A L K I L L B I L L
E C I C D D L T O B L C C Q T J O Q C
J O A O E J D E L I P I V K R M N Z A
C L J H N L O I D A L N V N O Z P A N
J E S U S O F N A Z A R E T H J V J O
```

FIND 20 CLASSIC MOVIES STARTING WITH J, K, AND L. CAN YOU THINK OF ANY OTHERS?

. . . .

. . . .

. . . .

. . . .

. . . .

. . . .

. . . .

WORDOKU

```
. . . W I . . D . . | . . Z . . . . . . A
. U T . . . X . . L | N W E . . . . . . I
. . I V . N U . G Z | . M W . . K B D . .
Z . . . . J . A K . | . V L N F X . . . .
---------------------+---------------------
. W E . . J B M L . | . . . . F . . . . T
. A T . Z . . F . E | . U . . . . . M K .
. D M . C T . H . . | N G V . . . . E . Z
N . . . X . L . . E | H B T K . I . . . .
---------------------+---------------------
. . B C I . N U . G | X . . . H . . . D .
E V . A . . D . . . | . B H . N . G K . .
. N U . W . I H . . | . E . . . Z . . C X
. X . . D . . . C J | . U G . A I L . . .
---------------------+---------------------
. . . U . X K D J M | . . N . B . . . . V
B . J . . H L T . . | V . . X M . A U . .
T A . . . E . V . . | F . . . D . L I . .
F . . H . . . . . I | K A L . . W D . . .
---------------------+---------------------
. Z C U E . . I . . | . X J . . T . . . F
J F V . T . E . . N | G . L W . U C . . .
D . . . G . M N Z . | K . . . . H E . . .
H . . . N . . J . . | M E . . . . . . . .
```

FILL EVERY ROW, COLUMN, AND 5X4 SECTOR,
USING EACH GIVEN LETTER ONLY ONCE!

▶ MAZE

FIND A STRAIGHT PATH THAT FOLLOWS THIS PATTERN: ▢■■▢ , HORIZONTAL OR VERTICAL (NEVER DIAGONAL!), FROM THE TOP CHEVRON TO THE CHEVRON AT THE BOTTOM OF THE GRID.

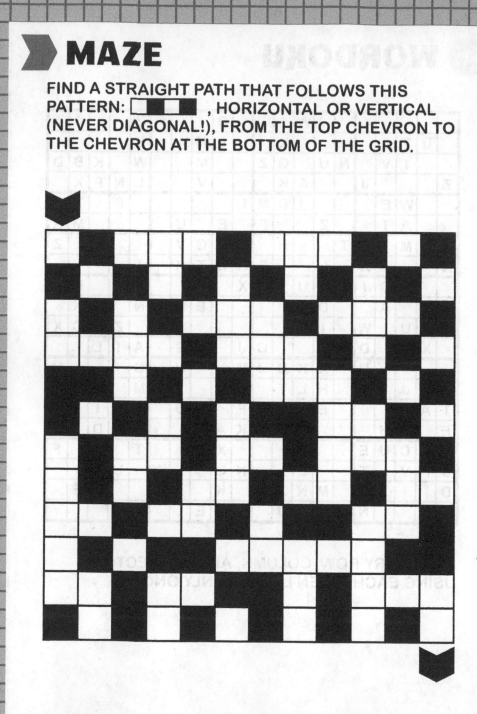

►QUOTES

HOW MANY OF THESE FAMOUS TV LINES CAN YOU IDENTIFY?

"Just one more thing..."

SHOW:
. . . .
YEAR:
. . . .

"If it weren't for you meddling kids!"

SHOW:
. . . .
YEAR:
. . . .

"No soup for you!"

SHOW:
. . . .
YEAR:
. . . .

▶ WORDFILL

WHICH 3-LETTER COMBINATIONS ON THE LEFT DO
YOU NEED TO COMPLETE THE 9-LETTER WORDS
ON THE RIGHT?

RIT	B	I	L				A	R	D
DGL	A	G	R				E	N	T
EPT	T	E	R				O	R	Y
HIB	A	M	E				E	N	T
NES	A	R	C				E	C	T
ERA	F	L	E				I	N	G
EEM	E	C	O				T	E	M
IBB	M	A	G				I	U	M
NGU	T	W	E				E	T	H
NDM	D	E	C				I	O	N
SYS	C	A	R				E	A	N
IAT	G	E	N				T	O	R
LBO	P	E	R				T	E	R
IME	A	M	P				I	A	N
NTI	R	A	D				I	O	N
HIT	O	R	A				T	A	N

▶ TRIVIA

FAMOUS PEOPLE FROM THE PAST.

1.

1887 ▶ Took over management of his father's newspaper, the <u>San Francisco Examiner</u>.

2.

1921 ▶ Starred alongside Gloria Swanson in the film <u>Beyond the Rocks</u>, which was a critical flop.

3.

1929 ▶ Introduced a new character to his <u>Thimble Theatre</u> comic strip: Popeye!

4.

1945 ▶ Recruited and secretly moved to the U.S. under a program called Operation Overcast (later known as Operation Paperclip).

5.

1958 ▶ Patented the modern LEGO brick.

6.

1963 ▶ Created and hosted one of the first cooking shows on American TV, <u>The French Chef</u>.

7.

1975 ▶ Won both an Oscar and a Golden Globe for her arresting performance in <u>One Flew Over the Cuckoo's Nest</u>.

8.

1983 ▶ Starred alongside Desi Arnaz Jr. in the short lived <u>Automan</u> TV show.

▶ DEFINITION SEARCH

```
M L M A C D B Z U Y J L T W F
H C J W R O V N K M S E A S T
D A U A K R R P B R A C E D Z
R U W T R C J S C P W O D P T
B A C C B H L O E R R R C U S
L I O H U A A J D H U U O O C
F W T M Y R C Y T U W E S W P
S A T A E D D K L M T R L H Q
B C O N F E D E R A T I V E K
W I N C A S Q L Q N S D Z L R
X I M R N L O G S U E W U E P
P J O A D N A V E L O B W N M
A O U N E F E P D C O R G I A
R P T K A U R I S T X C U U M
D A H S N R S R I W O J I M A
```

- From the Andes.
- Ate at a restaurant (2 w.).
- Otologist.
- Prize.
- Tub.
- Volume.
- United in confederacy.
- US pit viper.
- Starts.
- More cruel.
- Cauliflower head.
- Reduction.
- Dukedom.
- Sneezeweed.
- Anthropoid.
- Ancient Peruvians.
- Ogasawara island.
- Pitcher.
- Military vehicles.
- Waste to knees.
- Locations (Latin).
- Mother.
- Bellybutton.
- Plantation.
- Paragraph (abbr.).
- One who pins.
- Majority gathering.
- Ran.
- Indian king.
- Flat boat.
- Crept.
- Pains.
- Guard.

SPEECHES

CAN YOU COMPLETE THESE?

"It is this fate,
I solemnly assure you,
that I dread for you..."

WHAT:
. . . .
. . . .
. . . .
WHO:
. . . .
. . . .

WHAT:
. . . .
. . . .
. . . .
WHO:
. . . .
. . . .

"Of course, in one sense,
the first essential for a man
being a good citizen is ..."

"Fans, for the past two
weeks you have been
reading about ..."

WHAT:
. . . .
. . . .
. . . .
WHO:
. . . .
. . . .

MATCHMAKER

WHICH TWO ARE PERFECTLY ALIKE?

1.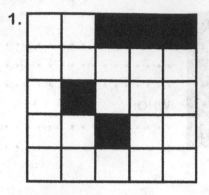

2.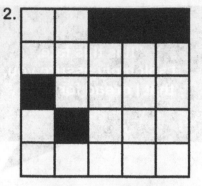

3.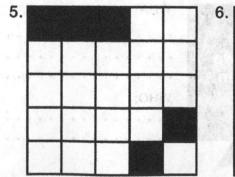

4.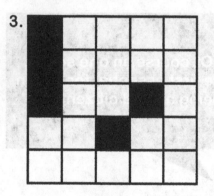

5.

6.

CROSSWORD

1	2	3	4	5	6		7	8	9	10	11	12
13							14					
15							16					
17				18	19			20			21
22				23				24			
25				26				27			
			28								
29	30	31	32		33			34	35	36	37
38					39			40			
41					42			43			
	44		45			46	47			
	48					49				
	50					51				

ACROSS:
1. White rust fungi.
7. Throw upwards.
13. Piety (Latin).
14. Pupal stage.
15. Slight
16. Cunning.
17. Nile god.
18. Italic tribe.
20. Wheat flour.
22. Acerbic.
23. —Dracula.
24. Glass furnace.
25. Yawn.
26. Arawak people.
27. 1337.
28. Dwell (archaic).
29. China currency.
33. Fishing net.
34. Rude person (German).
38. Lacquer box.
39. Curtsy (Filipino).
40. Stalk.
41. Claim.
42. Mixed soil.
43. Power Rangers 15ᵗʰ season (abbr.).
44. Tiny.
46. Pseudofossil.
48. Oil palms.
49. Hedge hole.
50. Danish feature.
51. Tanning agent.

DOWN:
1. Tupi language.
2. Linchpin (abbr.).
3. Alongside.
4. Balance (Maori).
5. Dog mastitis.
6. Bone aneurysm.
7. Ignorance.
8. Peritoneum incision.
9. Galactus' planet.
10. Assault.
11. Occupying seat.
12. Sickle.
17. Ugly old witch.
19. Indian tonic water.
21. Creative process.
29. Yiddish (abbr.).
30. —Airlines.
31. Ancient battle site.
32. Noselite.
34. Spurted.
35. Serous membrane.
36. Made of stone.
37. Small silversides.
45. National Eye Institute (abbr.).
47. Tranquil.

261

► WORDSEARCH

```
U J L M O M H B J M Q R O M L C G
Z X N I R T Y M P L N A U I N Z Y
N I Z S D I N M Y F A I R L A D Y
D A X S I O N H Q C T E M L P S X
Y E P C N C O I I M I M A I O O T
P J E O A E R M A A O D N O L F M
H O U N R A M E J G N K I N E F Y
J U F G Y N A N M N A G N D O I L
U T S E P S R I J O L R H O N C E
B O S N E E A N D L T M A L D E F
H F Q I O L E B T I R I V L Y S T
D A Y A P E U L M A E C A A N P F
F F R L L V S A M I A H N R A A O
L R E I E E N C A J S A A B M C O
H I H T T N S K A A U E J A I E T
S C K Y R T U N Y P R L R B T V D
M A G N U M F O R C E L R Y E W Q
```

FIND 20 CLASSIC MOVIES STARTING WITH M, N, AND O.
CAN YOU THINK OF ANY OTHERS?

. . . .
. . . .
. . . .
. . . .
. . . .
. . . .
. . . .
. . . .
. . . .
. . . .

N				C			K				X	M	D	V			I	Q	
S			K	T		A		C		Q	B	P	N					L	V
	Q	V	B		D				I		L	A							
	L		M		Q	Y	Z	V			T			S	P	C			
		J	S	V	O			M		A	Z				P		Q		
	R	I				A						Q	V		C				
M	D			P		R			T	S		V			K				
	Z			V	I	K		S		D		C	J	N	A		B		M
P		K				N		C						Y	J		M		
	A			R	C			Z				I			Q		L		
	I		S			V			B				Z	X			O		
	J		T	Y				O		D						Z		K	
R		X		A	T	N	L		K		Y		C	P	J			D	
		P			D		R	Q				T		C				X	N
	N		K	S						I						A	P		
	Y		Z			B	M		J			Q	O	I	L				
		Y	O	M			Z			V	S	X	K		R			J	
				T	X		N				R				A	K	C		
	M	R			I	V	J	P		Q			O		D	N			L
	Q	I		A	S	O	K				J			M					Z

FILL EVERY ROW, COLUMN, AND 5X4 SECTOR, USING EACH GIVEN LETTER ONLY ONCE!

MAZE

FIND A STRAIGHT PATH THAT FOLLOWS THIS PATTERN: 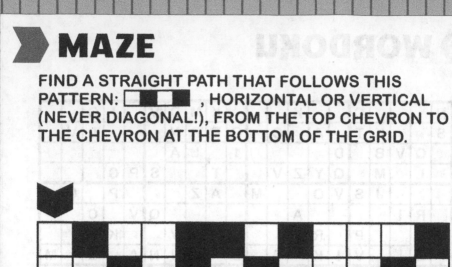, HORIZONTAL OR VERTICAL (NEVER DIAGONAL!), FROM THE TOP CHEVRON TO THE CHEVRON AT THE BOTTOM OF THE GRID.

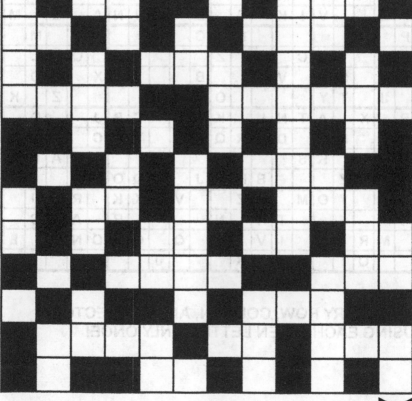

HOW MANY OF THESE FAMOUS TV LINES CAN YOU IDENTIFY?

"Baby, you're the greatest!"

SHOW:
....

YEAR:
....

SHOW:
....

YEAR:
....

"Book 'em, Danno!"

"Gentlemen, we can rebuild him. We have the technology."

SHOW:
....

YEAR:
....

▶ WORDFILL

WHICH 3-LETTER COMBINATIONS ON THE LEFT DO YOU NEED TO COMPLETE THE 9-LETTER WORDS ON THE RIGHT?

HTM	I	N	N				N	C	E
NDA	D	A	N				I	O	N
STA	N	I	G				A	R	E
HOR	C	O	M				I	T	Y
EPT	A	B	U				N	C	E
ECT	D	I	R				I	O	N
MOD	D	I	V				E	N	T
EWO	R	E	F				N	C	E
DEL	S	U	N				W	E	R
REN	A	U	T				I	T	Y
FLO	M	O	U				C	H	E
ERG	I	N	C				T	O	N
OCE	F	I	R				R	K	S
ERE	A	W	A				E	S	S
TEN	H	U	R				A	N	E
RIC	L	I	S				I	N	G

▶ TRIVIA

FAMOUS PEOPLE FROM THE PAST.

1.

1868 ▶ Wrote an account of a fraud he suffered and sold it to the St. Louis <u>Westliche Post</u>, starting a career in journalism.

2.

1879 ▶ Awarded U.S. Patent D11023, for the Statue of Liberty design.

3.

1927 ▶ Starred in the now lost cult horror film, <u>London After Midnight</u>.

4.

1948 ▶ Premiered his most successful musical, <u>Kiss Me, Kate</u>, which earned the first Tony Award for Best Musical.

5.

1955 ▶ Originally a cartoonist, he found success as a children's book author with the publication of <u>Harold and the Purple Crayon</u>.

6.

1963 ▶ Arrested after he published nude shots of Jayne Mansfield in bed with a man.

7.

1970 ▶ Published his classic romantic time travel novel, <u>Time and Again</u>.

8.

1981 ▶ Beat Hana Mandlíková for her third Wimbledon singles title.

```
D A V Y L O C G R K B P T R U
E C L F L H Z A E X I B B N R
N O H I T T E R G D E L I Y G
O T K N W T C B I R R D O C E
T T A E J K H A M N E L T Y D
E O V T G W O G E W L L A N O
D N E O K Y S E N A Y A T F O
M S D O F F L D T S N N I U R
D E A T R Q O I E T H I C D K
T E T H Y U V S D I O F U D E
Z D U C C J A P A N S T C L E
O S N O O K K O J G O Y H E P
M N B M U N I S U D S E R E E
L O D B L W A A D B U M P E R
I K F J D E N L V W L T C B W
```

- —Baba.
- Amalgam.
- Yes (archaic).
- Coffin frame.
- Life in a specific habitat.
- Fender.
- —oil.
- Czechoslovakia national.
- Delicatessen (abbr.).
- Designated.
- Doctor.
- Doorman.
- Moral principle.
- Comb w/ close teeth (2 words).
- Stupefy.
- Trash discarder (2 w.).
- Ornamented.
- Belonging to Japan.
- Kilogram (abbr.).
- Grass plain (Spanish).
- Metropolitan Museum (abbr.).
- Stylish.
- Norway (abbr.).
- Baseball game w/ no hits.
- Strictly organized.
- Depend.
- Soap opera.
- Turn over & spread out.
- The other (archaic).
- Russian edicts.
- Impulse.
- Sanskrit scripture.
- Important.
- Squandering.

SPEECHES

CAN YOU COMPLETE THESE?

"... and if I say again that daily to discourse about virtue, and of those other things about..."

WHAT:

. . . .
. . . .
. . . .

WHO:

. . . .
. . . .

WHAT:

. . . .
. . . .
. . . .

WHO:

. . . .
. . . .

"I believe that man will not merely endure..."

WHAT:

. . . .
. . . .
. . . .

WHO:

. . . .
. . . .

"And like the old soldier of that ballad, I now close..."

▶ MATCHMAKER

WHICH TWO ARE PERFECTLY ALIKE?

1.
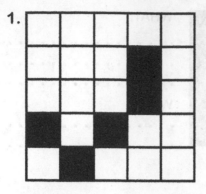

2.
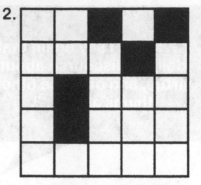

3.
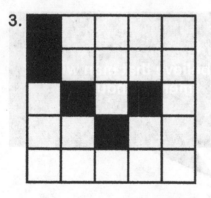

4.

5.
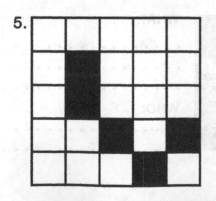

6.
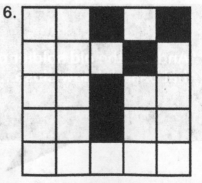

CROSSWORD

ACROSS:
1. Nourishments.
6. Transform.
8. Absolute.
9. Flown.
11. Ladies.
13. Pith helmet.
16. Armed conflict.
17. Fixed durations.
20. Unfasten.
22. Beat violently.
23. Cone tip cut (Latin).
24. Speculate.
25. Jazz drum.
27. Goalkeeper.
28. Slumber.
29. Himself.
31. Buffalo.
32. Monkeys (Spanish).
34. Hard-roofed car.
35. The Holy—.
36. Trend follower (2 w.).
37. Rocky antagonist.

DOWN:
1. Flows easily.
2. Criminal.
3. Turkish empire.
4. Warrior (German).
5. Swellings.
6. Passenger ferry (2 w.).
7. Emotive art style.
10. Gorged.
12. Aircraft post .
13. Clumps.
14. Feathers.
15. Preclude.
17. Palpitation.
18. Remits.
19. Charlie—.
21. Croon.
22. —of war.
26. Insecticide.
29. Terror.
30. Rationale.
32. Enchantment.
33. Reliable.

WORDSEARCH

```
L H X Q W Y P H I L A D E L P H I A P
Y Z F U S P T Y Q U E E N M A R G O T
H E R E V E N G E O F T H E N E R D S
D Y S E M G O D I M C B L O S R A L L
U L B N D G P O S E I D O N L M G L X
R H S O U Y U I W F R T A J A S I R B
O U G F M S Q U O V A D I S B C N Y S
S U S T C U P U L L I P X K Y L G X C
E P N H R E B F P P S R Q F R F B Z A
M R Q E M G D M U W I E U C I Q U J D
A E V A V O P S L Z N T I N N B L N O
R T I M Z T R X P F G T C T T K L O I
Y T R A S M N E F Y A Y K H H X Z G J
S Y A Z C A J M I G R I S S B L H J T
B W G O M R E W C T I N A L M L I N V
A O T N K R J B T D Z P N V X W A X K
B M I S T I E V I C O I D X Q R H C E
Y A M J F E X G O K N N B T S Z I Y K
R N E V V D Q Z N F A K M O L Q Q M S
```

FIND 20 CLASSIC MOVIES STARTING WITH P, Q, AND R.
CAN YOU THINK OF ANY OTHERS?

....
....
....
....
....
....
....
....
....
....

	N			A	P			J		W			L	U					
C		K	P	R		U			V		O		M				D	W	X
U	X	O				J		C	N		D	R				Q			
				X	M		N		K	U	V				Y	R	J		
Q	P	X	M		D			L		V					W			O	
	V			B				J		S	M				C			K	
S	Y		C				X		A	T		L	D			M	Q		V
	R	W			M			V				Y	O	P	U	L			
J					V					O	C		Q	N			A	K	
N				C			B	L		A				V					
		Q			Y		U	W				S						R	
A	M		U	O		Q	K				B								W
	B	T	X	N	K				C			A			U	Q			
Y		Q	W			T	R		O	X		P				L		J	S
	A		J			Q	P		O				R		X				
	U		O				Y		Q			W			D	T	V	M	
		C	A	J			W	K	L		P			V	U				
		N			D	C			M	R		J					W	S	Q
R	T	M			V		X		Q				O		C	K	Y		J
			V	S		O		P			T	N					R		

FILL EVERY ROW, COLUMN, AND 5X4 SECTOR, USING EACH GIVEN LETTER ONLY ONCE!

MAZE

FIND A STRAIGHT PATH THAT FOLLOWS THIS
PATTERN: ⬜⬛⬜⬛ , HORIZONTAL OR VERTICAL
(NEVER DIAGONAL!), FROM THE TOP CHEVRON TO
THE CHEVRON AT THE BOTTOM OF THE GRID.

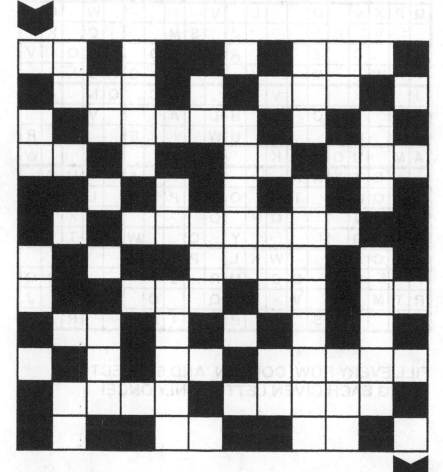

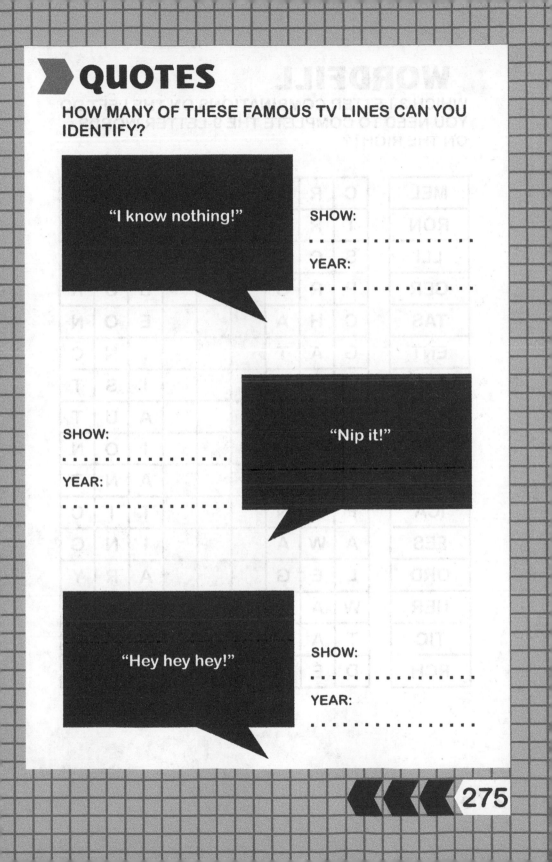

QUOTES

HOW MANY OF THESE FAMOUS TV LINES CAN YOU IDENTIFY?

"I know nothing!"

SHOW:
. . . .

YEAR:
. . . .

"Nip it!"

SHOW:
. . . .

YEAR:
. . . .

"Hey hey hey!"

SHOW:
. . . .

YEAR:
. . . .

WHICH 3-LETTER COMBINATIONS ON THE LEFT DO YOU NEED TO COMPLETE THE 9-LETTER WORDS ON THE RIGHT?

MEL	C	R	I				I	S	M
RON	T	R	A				I	O	N
LLI	S	C	O				I	N	G
GER	P	R	O				S	O	R
TAS	C	H	A				E	O	N
ENT	G	A	T				I	N	G
END	S	C	I				I	S	T
KEN	A	S	T				A	U	T
DIT	A	C	C				I	O	N
ERF	B	R	I				A	N	T
ICA	F	A	N				T	I	C
FES	A	W	A				I	N	G
ORD	L	E	G				A	R	Y
HER	W	A	T				A	L	L
TIC	T	A	N				I	N	E
RCH	D	E	D				T	E	D

▶ TRIVIA

FAMOUS PEOPLE FROM THE PAST.

1.

1925 ▶ Got his first story, "Spear and Fang," published in the July issue of <u>Weird Tales</u> magazine.

2.

1937 ▶ Began studying moviemaking at the Centro Sperimentale di Cinematografia (Rome).

3.

1967 ▶ Illustrated the cover for Jefferson Airplane's third studio album, <u>After Bathing at Baxter's</u>.

4.

1972 ▶ Recognized as the best "tuberider" surfer in the world when he won the Pipeline Masters competition that year.

5.

1979 ▶ Took home the Best Adapted Screenplay Oscar for his film <u>Midnight Express</u>.

6.

1984 ▶ Wrote and directed cult film <u>Red Dawn</u>.

7.

2003 ▶ Elected as the 38th Governor of California, staying in office until 2011.

8.

2007 ▶ Published his autobiography, <u>Strong Man in Hollywood</u>, which sold out in 24 hrs.

DEFINITION SEARCH

```
N W P T B I L I S I C R D P R
L E O N S U B S P A C E I A N
Z D C X O K M S R P C P D B K
K D O F X R U H I O O L O D A
K E A X E M S A T U B A T U Q
B D U Z I C T Y E T O C D C S
P T A R N I S H E S L E E T Y
C L P I N E V A N S K M A E A
B R A N S P O O G C R E C S W
E I L N M Y F C A W H N H L L
R N L D N F W J T C Q T A A B
T L E G I I H H C A I C P S T
H A R R E G N J E A D O L I Z
G I G W I S T G R E O S I E U
G D Y H F O S W F W L T N W W
```

- Kidnap.
- Into conflict.
- Hypersensitivity.
- Moor.
- Hull's lowest portions.
- Plan formal jacket.
- Pieces of grain husk.
- Charlie—.
- Tricks.
- Ball of yarn.
- Computer language.
- Typewriter device (2 words.).
- NW European dog breed.
- Stolen.
- Studded.
- Lion (Spanish).
- Ought to.
- Set of eight.
- Languish.
- Designing.
- Looks petulant.
- Portable stove.
- Substitution cost (2 w.).
- Chaise.
- Wet with sleet.
- Rainbow Brite creatures.
- Mathematical space.
- Besmirches.
- Georgian Republic capital.
- Electric cars.
- Funerary vase.
- Campers.
- Married.
- Apparition.
- Sailing vessel.

SPEECHES

CAN YOU COMPLETE THESE?

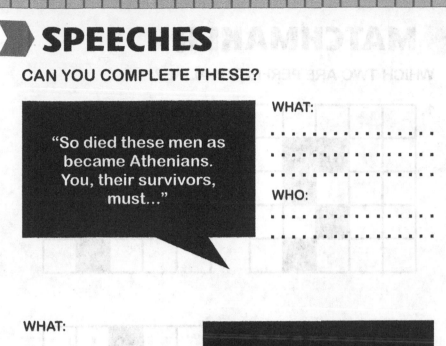

"So died these men as became Athenians. You, their survivors, must…"

WHAT:
. . . .
. . . .
. . . .

WHO:
. . . .
. . . .

WHAT:
. . . .
. . . .
. . . .

WHO:
. . . .
. . . .

"I know not what course others may take; but as for me…"

"With malice toward none, with charity for all, with…"

WHAT:
. . . .
. . . .
. . . .

WHO:
. . . .
. . . .

MATCHMAKER

WHICH TWO ARE PERFECTLY ALIKE?

1.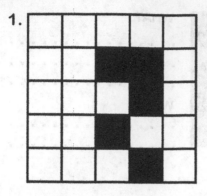

2.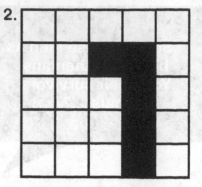

3.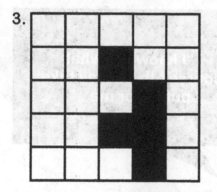

4.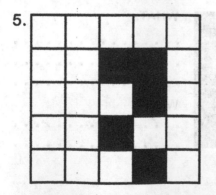

5.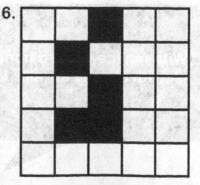

6.

CROSSWORD

ACROSS:

1. Saying in jest.
7. Expressions.
13. One who edits.
14. Coffin.
15. Pierced.
16. Loop.
18. Coca—.
21. New Orleans (abbr.).
22. Indiana (abbr.).
23. Port in NW Portugal.
25. Papyrus (Plural).
27. Animal's foot.
28. Ashen.
29. Not wounded.
32. Removing dishes.
34. Order Form (abbr.).
35. Arsenic (abbr.).
36. Shabby.
38. _Oryza sativa_.
40. Impromptu.
41. Electrical resistance.
45. Jutland people.
49. More tidy.
50. Sell overseas.

DOWN:

1. Rocket launch.
2. _Anno Domini_ (abbr.).
3. Life of—.
4. Iced Tea (abbr.).
5. Not ready.
6. Artificial cave.
7. Polar ice covering.
8. Groove cut.
9. Intl. Security (abbr.).
10. Alright.
11. Maine (abbr.).
12. Obstacle (2w.).
16. Expertise.
17. Not either.
19. Labium.
20. In any manner.
24. Peter—.
26. Turmoil (Japan).
30. Ultra-Fast Optics (abbr.).
31. Flammable wood.
32. Barium sulfate.
33. Pouch.
37. Anger.
39. Eurasian goat.
42. Higher education (abbr.).
43. Master of Arts (abbr.).
44. Anti-tank (abbr.).
46. Pixar film.
47. Toronto (abbr.).
48. Operating room (abbr.).

WORDSEARCH

```
S C H I N D L E R S L I S T H U T
T H I H S O M F S U T O P G U N I
E C K C I Y N Y K P H A I L N D T
E G B I X Q A Z Z E E E R H C E A
L J I K T W V O A R R O M W H R N
M N Q Q E U Q T U M E T P E A G I
A W C D E N T O U A W D A H I R C
G L I D N F H V S N I V A K N O S
N S W Q C O D N P M L S A H E U A
O W O T A R A N T U L A M P D N R
L A U O N G C Q A Z B B O X J D V
I I U O D I K T R U E G R I T K K
A T Q T L V W K C T B I K U A J T
S S B S E E A G M M L O D G Z K E
E Q Z I S N B M G B O O W U Q F I
H S C E N T O F A W O M A N D A O
E A F O X T S T A N D B Y M E M K
```

FIND 20 CLASSIC MOVIES STARTING WITH S, T, AND U.
CAN YOU THINK OF ANY OTHERS?

WORDOKU

T	X		P		S	J	I	Y		Z				D	H			G	E
H	K			Y	D				T							Q			
	Z				F	P			R				Y			B	C	J	I
			E				C	L	G		S	D							A
C			I		K	R	J	F	P			A		Q				Y	T
	T						I	B			Y			P					D
F		Z	Q			L				P						B	A		G
	P	Y	S	R		D	H	X		J		T	Z			L	F		
		Y							Q		R		X			H	D	C
			R	I		D	C			X	L				K	P	Y
X	H	D			B	K		A	E		T	Z					
L	E	J		I		A		H						F			
	D	S			Y	B		I		C	Z	E		K	G	X	L
Y	L	P				X				J				T	I		B
R			B			E		X	P				A		
G	T			J		L		D	S	K	A	B		Y			H
P				X	A		H	F	K			B			
Z	B	H	A		L			R			X	G			C
	S						Y			A	E		H	P
Q	Y		L	G			E		Z	B	P	H		I		X	R

FILL EVERY ROW, COLUMN, AND 5X4 SECTOR,
USING EACH GIVEN LETTER ONLY ONCE!

MAZE

FIND A STRAIGHT PATH THAT FOLLOWS THIS PATTERN: ▢■▢■ , HORIZONTAL OR VERTICAL (NEVER DIAGONAL!), FROM THE TOP CHEVRON TO THE CHEVRON AT THE BOTTOM OF THE GRID.

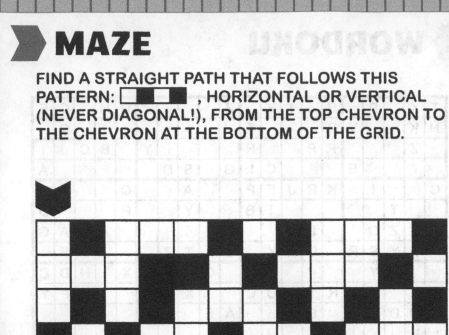

HOW MANY OF THESE FAMOUS TV LINES CAN YOU IDENTIFY?

"This is the city.
I work here.
I carry a badge."

SHOW:
. . . .

YEAR:
. . . .

"Stifle!"

SHOW:
. . . .

YEAR:
. . . .

"Tell me what you don't
like about yourself."

SHOW:
. . . .

YEAR:
. . . .

WORDFILL

WHICH 3-LETTER COMBINATIONS ON THE LEFT DO YOU NEED TO COMPLETE THE 9-LETTER WORDS ON THE RIGHT?

ASU	A	D	M				B	L	E
CTU	J	E	L				I	S	H
LIS	B	A	L				T	I	C
LYF	B	U	T				F	L	Y
RYT	F	O	R				T	E	N
SAT	S	L	E				V	E	R
EPO	T	R	E				R	E	R
INS	S	A	N				A	R	Y
ERT	S	I	G				U	R	E
OPH	S	H	R				I	N	G
IRA	F	A	I				A	L	E
NAT	M	E	C				I	S	M
IEK	S	E	N				I	O	N
HAN	P	E	N				U	L	A
TER	S	A	X				O	N	E
GOT	A	D	V				I	S	E

►TRIVIA

FAMOUS PEOPLE FROM THE PAST.

1.

1780 ► Placed the noose around his own neck to be hanged as a spy.

2.

1792 ► Fought a duel with the Earl of Lauderdale after the Earl impugned his honor in the House of Lords.

3.

1851 ► Upon his death, he left a legacy of more than 550 oil paintings, 2,000 watercolors, and 30,000 works on paper.

4.

1900 ► Began to serialize his novel, <u>Kim</u>, in the pages of <u>McClure's Magazine</u>.

5.

1902 ► Invented the first Air Conditioner for a printer in NYC.

6.

1912 ► Formed the first Girl Guides (Girl Scouts) in Savannah, Georgia.

7.

1920 ► Died a day after being hit in head by Yankees pitcher Carl Mays.

8.

2007 ► Named <u>Time</u> magazine's "Man of the Year".

```
E E N O B B E X R R S B P T H
H G V E A P A P P R O V A L S
L M E G A F L O P E U O S H P
B B H R E D L T O G R V S H Z
A W C F N Z T V O E Z E E A O
C S T E E P E R P N G R R I L
K R C G A B L E B E L B E R A
O Y A R S S E A T R O U T L C
R E N A P R I E R A A R R I O
D B A D C B O M S T T D O N N
E R L A X A G E O I S E C E I
R E S T R I C T I V E N E S S
T A M E S T U N N E L E D S M
R D Z C L E A R H E A D E D A
D O U B L E J E O P A R D Y I
```

- Son of Anchises.
- Consents.
- Isaac—.
- Order out of stock item.
- Decoy.
- BBC (slang).
- Small blister.
- Waterways.
- Alert.
- Ditko's DC superhero.
- Procedural defense.
- Chatter.
- Brags about.

- Arrange in grades.
- Fine lines.
- Quality of being concise.
- Complete failure.
- Overloaded.
- Player who makes a pass.
- Highest deck of ship.
- Overly curious person.
- Fascinated.
- Able to regenerate.
- Imposing limitations.
- Backtrack.
- Made with rye flour (2 w.).

- Barely manage one's existence.
- Atlantic fish (2 w.).
- Acidic.
- More steep.
- Most tame.
- With tunnels.
- Vice President (slang).
- Émile—.

SPEECHES

CAN YOU COMPLETE THESE?

"Blessed are they that mourn: for they…"

WHAT:
. . . .
. . . .
. . . .

WHO:
. . . .
. . . .

WHAT:
. . . .
. . . .
. . . .

WHO:
. . . .
. . . .

"Your high independence only reveals the…"

"This is our hope. This is the faith that I go back to…"

WHAT:
. . . .
. . . .
. . . .

WHO:
. . . .
. . . .

MATCHMAKER

WHICH TWO ARE PERFECTLY ALIKE?

1.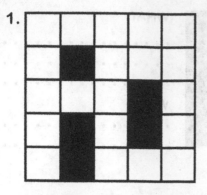

2.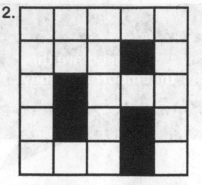

3.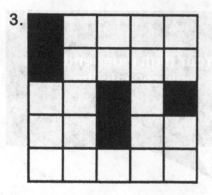

4.

5.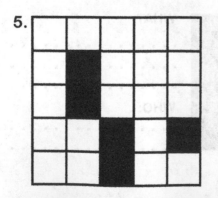

6.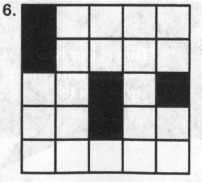

CROSSWORD

ACROSS:
3. Pridae bird.
6. 1st bomber jet.
10. Civil War end site.
11. The note A.
13. Cerium (abbr.).
14. Analog (abbr.).
15. Arkansas (abbr.).
16. Gee up.
17. Tuning fork.
18. Oersted (abbr.).
20. Academic Year (abbr.).
21. Touchdown (abbr.).
22. Selenium (abbr.).
23. Head Office (abbr.).
24. Abdominal (abbr.).
25. Ancient Siberian language.
26. —Manning.
27. Nickel (abbr.).
29. Knockout (abbr.).
30. OK (Uruguay).
31. Delight expression.
32. Promiscuous woman.
36. Farrier (British).
37. Lying helplessly.

DOWN:
1. Savory meat jelly.
2. Powhatan tribes.
3. Miocene marsupial.
4. Rheumatoid arthritis (abbr.).
5. United Press (abbr.).
7. Artificial language.
8. Axe.
9. Too much eyebrows.
12. Inability to feel pleasure.
13. 2nd altar cloth.
19. Quoth the Raven—.
28. Adult female.
32. Training Officer (abbr.).
33. Regarding (abbr.).
34. Pain expression.
35. Georgia (abbr.).

WORDSEARCH

```
Y A N K E E D O O D L E D A N D Y
J O Q V I C T O R V I C T O R I A
W N U Q V I G I L A N T E N Z N T
A E J V Q O E V I D E O D R O M E
L O S V E L L J U D I N K G R A B
K C B T Z G B C N O H H A K T D Y
T I X P S B O E A T D R L A M V E
H P T J P I V T E N D Z P E U A S
E W M Z Q R D E M E O A L Q R N M
L W R P O M R E H A Z R E E U W A
I D R F A T B T S A I D V G L I N
N S V B S H F X V T P L G X J L E
E U V L Y O J I M B O N L J S D A
K G L K R C V S K V U R W S C E V
X A V A M P Y R J O Z S Y R U R I
W H E N H A R R Y M E T S A L L Y
N Y T U M A M A T A M B I E N E X
```

FIND 20 CLASSIC MOVIES STARTING WITH V, W, AND Y.
CAN YOU THINK OF ANY OTHERS?

....
....
....
....
....
....
....
....

WORDOKU

M	A		E		I	L			D		F	B					N		J
		T	B	F			A			I		H			Z	D	E		
G	I			Z		P		X			K			L					F
		F	N				Y		C	G		L		I		P			O
I		L			P				E	O				Z		H		C	
P	F		O	C	X				K		G		E					I	T
						T			A		J			P			N		
		Z	A						T	Y	P	D	J		K		O		
Y		P	X	T	M			H			A					O	D		
	L	A		K	D		N			B			G	M			H	T	
	G	B		Y	F			K		D			N	X		J	L		
	C	H				O			E			I	K	G	M				A
	X	D	I	N	H	M	Z							K	T				
	Y			F			P		X		Z								
K	Z			N		C		Y				O	B	A		H	X		
	O		P		B		F	X		J				C			Y		
F		T		O		N		E	L		B					I	A		
A			E			H			O		F		T				J	D	
	P	G	H		O		A			D			K	E	C				
Z		C			Y	G		E			H	X		F			P	N	

FILL EVERY ROW, COLUMN, AND 5X4 SECTOR,
USING EACH GIVEN LETTER ONLY ONCE!

FIND A STRAIGHT PATH THAT FOLLOWS THIS
PATTERN: ▢■▢■ , HORIZONTAL OR VERTICAL
(NEVER DIAGONAL!), FROM THE TOP CHEVRON TO
THE CHEVRON AT THE BOTTOM OF THE GRID.

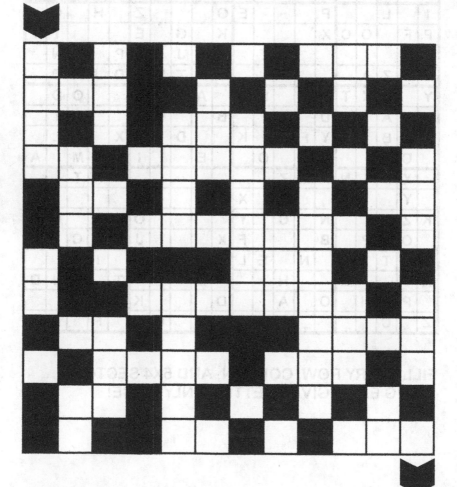

HOW MANY OF THESE FAMOUS TV LINES CAN YOU IDENTIFY?

"Yabba dabba do!"

SHOW:
....

YEAR:
....

SHOW:
....

YEAR:
....

"I'm a secret agent, trained to be cold, vicious, and savage. Not enough to be a businessman."

"Who loves you, baby?"

SHOW:
....

YEAR:
....

WORDFILL

WHICH 3-LETTER COMBINATIONS ON THE LEFT DO
YOU NEED TO COMPLETE THE 9-LETTER WORDS
ON THE RIGHT?

VAT	B	A	R				I	A	N
IPM	F	R	A				N	C	E
PBE	C	O	N				E	N	T
ACH	S	A	L				I	O	N
RON	P	R	O				L	E	R
SCI	M	E	T				O	M	E
PEL	E	Q	U				E	N	T
ITI	B	L	U				R	R	Y
GRA	R	A	S				R	R	Y
OMA	H	I	S				I	A	N
BAR	A	M	B				O	U	S
TOR	C	O	N				O	U	S
CHD	A	U	T				T	I	C
DIA	P	A	R				U	T	E
EBE	T	O	U				O	W	N
TIN	G	L	A				T	O	R

TRIVIA

1.

1926 ❱ Resigned as Detroit Tigers manager after 22 seasons.

2.

1939 ❱ Became the first journalist to report the upsurge of World War II.

3.

1947 ❱ Donated NYC East River site to the UN.

4.

1954 ❱ Became the first person to run a mile in under four minutes.

5.

1962 ❱ Won the Golden Lion award at the Venice Film Festival, for his first film, <u>Ivan's Childhood</u>.

6.

1975 ❱ Wrote the song which gave his band's second album its title: "Song for America."

7.

1983 ❱ Decided to leave his band, "The Police," while onstage during a concert at Shea Stadium.

8.

1986 ❱ Won the Best Artist and Best Black & White Comic Kirby Awards for <u>Love and Rockets</u> comic book.

DEFINITION SEARCH

```
L Z E M Q I U P P B U F F M E
N B J B U M S R R I S A S U D
Y A I E L S H O O O K I D N J
N L G E S T E C P T X E A K E
B I S P T N R R O E L N F N W
W R A S E E E A S C N D V O J
L O W E R P P S A H H P O W H
R A R A P L E T L N O R L N C
D O R O V L C I S O N E T A A
M Q R M P E O N H L G C A X N
E C L E P S A A R O K O G C T
U Z E S B I K T I G O P E R A
Y L Y U R Y T O L I N Y U I T
S O S U F U T R L E G O C S A
Q H D M C R L S L S P L O P S
```

- Axilla .
- Bleeps.
- Bioengineering.
- Vagrants.
- Arias.
- Brittle.
- Crop-yielding plant.
- Snip.
- —Adams.
- Expected.
- Fruits of the Durio tree.
- Xianggang (2 words).
- —puzzle.

- Grasslands.
- Cuts off.
- Lesser.
- Ribbed cotton fabric.
- Reflective thinkers.
- Floor plan w/ no walls (2 w.).
- Music-set drama.
- Stream.
- Dawdlers.
- Schemes.
- Copy again.
- Chauvinism.
- Ear-piercing.

- Insomniac.
- Wearing glasses.
- Soil under topsoil.
- Back-belted overcoat.
- Uncharted.
- Attendant.
- Electromotive force.
- Ripple.
- Toupee.

SPEECHES

CAN YOU COMPLETE THESE?

"Are we ruling over globalization or..."

WHAT:

. . . .
. . . .
. . . .

WHO:

. . . .
. . . .

WHAT:

. . . .
. . . .
. . . .

WHO:

. . . .
. . . .

"I cannot help asking those who have caused the situation..."

"The establishment protected itself but not the..."

WHAT:

. . . .
. . . .
. . . .

WHO:

. . . .
. . . .

MATCHMAKER

WHICH TWO ARE PERFECTLY ALIKE?

1.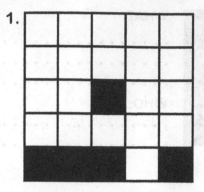

2.

3.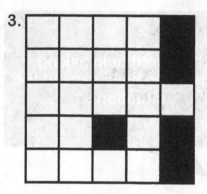

4.

5.

6.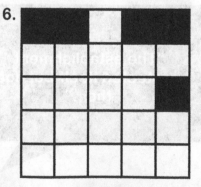

CRISSCROSS

ACROSS:
1. Artistic works.
4. Swimming and diving musical show.
7. Late risers.
9. Public meeting place.
10. Interconnected explosive charges (2 w.).
14. Caboose (2 w.).
15. Taking place in the morning.
16. —Island.
17. The lowest point.
18. Convulse.
19. Subatomic connection of matter (2 w.).
22. Dark stain.
24. Subduing.
25. Sea eagle.
26. Simultaneously.
27. Persistently harass.

DOWN:
1. Without advance preparation.
2. Wheel convergence.
3. Youngster.
5. Punditocracy.
6. Consular mail bags (2 words).
8. Hairstylist.
9. Befitting a father.
11. Loathe.
12. Shooting galleries (2 words).
13. Records officials.
20. Camelopards.
21. Offered as guarantee (archaic).
23. Submissive.

WORDSEARCH

```
R C K B W S B K O C T I F E Y K X
E X O Y U A Z P G G W F K P F T L
T T A M C R O C P O D V X X S H R
N Y D Y F H D E A B A L Y S Y C K
C F D V C R I O Q Y O G E Z D A F
I A E B X P E C C H E R V I L P A
N N R A Q V U Y O K C N A Y A E A
N G T A L C A G Y R D V N G L R C
A E O C W B E T O N Y O W E E S O
M L N H R A V C G X M A A D Z H N
O I G I A N Y L U I B E N N E T I
N C U C C E F Q R M C A T M I N T
D A E K C B B G C H I L L I L S E
C G A W L E A I S R S N O M D D E
Q A B E A R S F O O T V A V K J T
J K P E R R I C A M O M I L E N I
G Y G D Y Y L F O D Q Q F M W S Q
```

FIND 30 HERBS & SPICES STARTING WITH A, B, AND C.
CAN YOU THINK OF ANY OTHERS?

....
....
....
....
....
....
....
....
....
....

	I		S				Y	N	U				H		G	R	V	K			J		X	
J	U			M			S	P		V	T	F			B		L	X			N			
	T			A	X	Q		N	W	C	I	O			F			D		H	S	R		
Y	D	C			R		W	H		S				Q			O	N		M	E	P		
	O	N		U	T		K		D	B				C						Q				
F	K	Y		L				I		N				J			R							
S		X				T		A	D	P	L	N	O		G			F						
		E		I	Y	K	O			S		F					G			L				
B	M	P	Q			E	U		X		H		C		K	D								
V	A				S		F	D	Q		L			M		K				Y	N			
Q			F		V	G	M	R		X		U	O	T				B	W	A				
C	W			P		T		R			A		G		V					H	U			
K		N	A		Y			L		S		Q	R			C		P	I		V			
E	G			J		X		D			K		P	U		M				N	Q			
	V	L	H		U	O	T	W		Y		S	B	I		M			J					
L	X		A		T		O		G	W	R		J				M	H						
		X	E		A		N		B		K	H		Q	J	T	C							
G		T		Y		I			B	V	E	M	X											
	R		K	L	D	S	H	F	C		Q				Y		I							
	F		Q		M		U				B		D	R	K									
	P		M		E	I	W	D	B		L	S												
M	Q	B	J	N	L		D	U	R	V		T	G	E										
U	J	K	C	B	A	Y	P	M	F	H	T	E	X											
	V	H	F	P	G	W	O	C	Y		N	B	M											
N	H	Y	S	X	D	W	T	B	J		F	U												

FILL EVERY ROW, COLUMN, AND 5X5 SECTOR, USING EACH GIVEN LETTER ONLY ONCE!

MAZE

FIND A STRAIGHT PATH THAT FOLLOWS THIS
PATTERN: ⬛⬜⬛⬜⬛ , HORIZONTAL OR VERTICAL
(NEVER DIAGONAL!), FROM THE TOP CHEVRON TO
THE CHEVRON AT THE BOTTOM OF THE GRID.

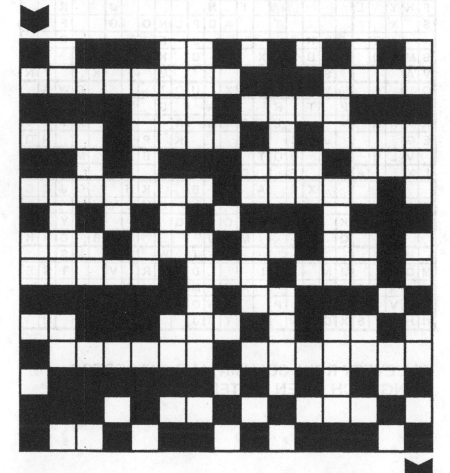

▶ NAME IT

HOW MANY MONOPOLY AVENUES CAN YOU NAME?

1.ATLANTIC AVE.

WORDFILL

WHICH 4-LETTER COMBINATIONS ON THE LEFT DO YOU NEED TO COMPLETE THE 12-LETTER WORDS ON THE RIGHT?

ERBA	A	L	L	I					T	I	O	N
LLIG	U	N	I	D					F	I	E	D
ESSI	I	N	T	E					T	E	N	T
KSGI	E	X	A	C					T	I	O	N
RMIT	I	N	D	E					E	N	C	E
TERA	I	N	T	E					E	N	C	E
NIZA	R	E	L	A					S	H	I	P
TION	T	H	A	N					V	I	N	G
ENTI	P	R	O	F					O	N	A	L
ADIC	O	R	G	A					T	I	O	N
ITIO	S	P	O	R					A	L	L	Y
PEND	I	N	T	I					T	I	N	G
ATOP	A	B	O	L					N	I	S	T
NCIA	O	N	O	M					O	E	I	A
ECIA	A	P	P	R					T	I	O	N
MIDA	A	N	N	U					T	I	O	N

▶ TRIVIA

FAMOUS PEOPLE FROM THE PAST.

1.

59AD ▶ Had Anicetus execute his mother, Agrippina.

2.

1182 ▶ Appointed as court physician and chief judge of Córdoba, Spain.

3.

1871 ▶ Founded America's most famous circus with partners Dan Castello and William C. Coup.

4.

1941 ▶ Five years after his exile, he returned to Addis Ababa and addressed the Ethiopian people.

5.

1952 ▶ Published his self-help best-seller, <u>The Power of Positive Thinking</u>.

6.

1972 ▶ His novella, <u>Johnathan Livingston Seagull</u>, sold more than one million copies that year.

7.

1977 ▶ Together with his four daughters, he was kidnapped and killed ("disappeared") by Argentina's military dictatorship.

8.

1978 ▶ Won his first Formula 1 World Drivers' Championship

DEFINITION SEARCH

```
A D I N T E R I M I X E D I N
F T H I C K S E T T L E C C M
P U T Z R W W I A C L O H H I
D E B R O S H Q I L L O E T N
P V F A U B C N E S I R E H E
L T U C C M A U U V E T S Y D
F G W C H S D I T T L I E O R
M Q O U I Y N R T U P D G L A
E V K R N E U A C S N I B O B
R P F S G G M C H A M I E G B
I D L E N E S S K E B N C I E
N K W X T O D O D I P O K S R
G O D I S M O U N T E D O T U
U V H I X H R Z V I S R N S N
E W U N P R E S E N T A B L E
```

- Anathematize.
- Temporary.
- Descended & settled.
- Lures.
- Entice.
- Brothers (abbr.).
- Rear freight-train car.
- Made from milk curds.
- Squatting down.
- Offspring of god & man.
- Dislodged.
- More pale.
- Fought in a duel.
- Presiding god.
- Ate greedily .
- High Energy Physics (abbr.).
- Strike.
- Metal fastener (3 words).
- Fish zoologists.
- Laziness.
- Intramuscular (abbr.).
- Yo-Yo—.
- Egg whites w/ sugar mix.
- Quarried.
- Embroiled (2 words).
- Unrefined metal.
- Petty.
- Dash.
- Sanicula europaea.
- Rabbit's tail.
- Short nap.
- Stocky.
- Gymslip.
- Ram.
- Disheveled.
- Veterans (abbr.).
- Brain tissue (2 w.).
- More disgusting.

NUTRITION FACTS

WHICH VITAMIN DOES THAT?

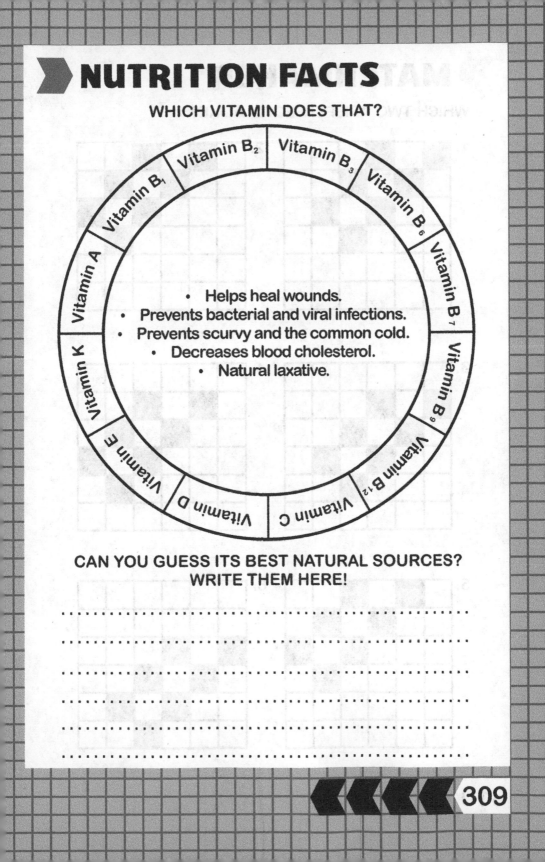

Vitamin B₂
Vitamin B₃
Vitamin B₁
Vitamin B₆
Vitamin A
Vitamin B₇
Vitamin K
Vitamin B₉
Vitamin E
Vitamin B₁₂
Vitamin D
Vitamin C

- Helps heal wounds.
- Prevents bacterial and viral infections.
- Prevents scurvy and the common cold.
- Decreases blood cholesterol.
- Natural laxative.

CAN YOU GUESS ITS BEST NATURAL SOURCES?
WRITE THEM HERE!

....

....

....

....

....

....

MATCHMAKER

WHICH TWO ARE PERFECTLY ALIKE?

1.
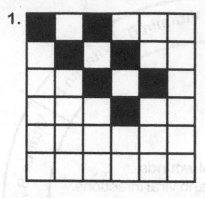

2.
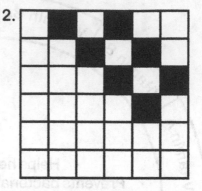

3.
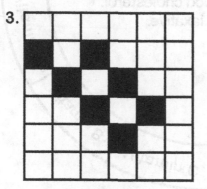

4.
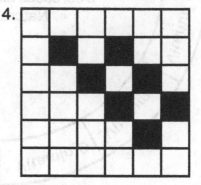

5.
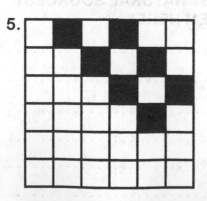

6.
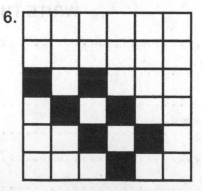

CRISSCROSS

ACROSS:

1. Atomic N° 30.
3. Rep.
6. Advanced Packaging Tool (abbr.).
8. Likelihood.
10. Self-assurance.
13. Directive.
15. Immigration and Customs Enforcement (abbr.).
16. So far.
18. Band.
20. Valve.
21. Indication.
22. Consortium.
24. Not any.
25. Omnibus.
26. Revolves.
27. —Club.
28. Competent.
31. Carry.
32. Appends.
33. Married.

DOWN:

1. Fasten.
2. Lid.
3. Acronym.
4. Expanded.
5. Completely.
6. Noah's—.
7. —Commandments.
9. Underneath.
11. Octopi.
12. Resoluteness.
14. Slant.
17. Motors.
19. Kayak.
21. Dawn.
23. Gullet.
25. Bible—.
26. Noise.
27. Paper money.
29. Small amount.
30. —Zeppelin.

```
N B W H C O F D J N R X H L S P G
G A L A N G A L W K C D M O P Q H
R Y E Y E B R I G H T Z I N P T O
O T M P V D X S D E X H A L W O R
U D O L I Q U O R I C E E E L D E
N R N U R V S O K C B N E T I G H
D A T Y A D B E O S N V O T H I O
S G H Q M E E N G E I W N U O N U
E O Y O L R I O F D R Y E C R G N
L N M L G F H E N B A N E E S E D
B S E U O Z C E L A V E N D E R I
W H N J U N I P E R P G E I R G T
S E S H E D G E H Y S S O P A G T
F A C R G A R L I C Q P F Y D A A
R D O G S C A B B A G E N T I A N
J L H H Y O S C Y A M U S I S L Y
F Y F G O O S E F O O T J V H G H
```

FIND 30 HERBS & SPICES STARTING WITH D, E, F, G, H, J, AND L. CAN YOU THINK OF ANY OTHERS?

. . . .
. . . .
. . . .
. . . .
. . . .
. . . .
. . . .
. . . .

▶ WORDOKU

**FILL EVERY ROW, COLUMN, AND 5X5 SECTOR,
USING EACH GIVEN LETTER ONLY ONCE!**

MAZE

FIND A STRAIGHT PATH THAT FOLLOWS THIS PATTERN: ■□□■, HORIZONTAL OR VERTICAL (NEVER DIAGONAL!), FROM THE TOP CHEVRON TO THE CHEVRON AT THE BOTTOM OF THE GRID.

▶ NAME IT

NAME 20 POP/ROCK BANDS STARTING WITH "THE"!

1. THE BAND

▶ WORDFILL

WHICH 4-LETTER COMBINATIONS ON THE LEFT DO YOU NEED TO COMPLETE THE 12-LETTER WORDS ON THE RIGHT?

LERA	A	R	C	H					T	U	R	E
TIPA	B	I	O	D					S	I	T	Y
LIZA	I	N	T	E					T	I	O	N
DEXT	A	C	C	E					T	I	O	N
RCEP	T	R	I	G					E	T	R	Y
IVER	C	O	M	M					A	T	O	R
PIRA	B	O	D	Y					D	I	N	G
RDIC	P	E	R	S					T	I	O	N
CIRA	R	E	S	U					T	I	O	N
ONOM	C	O	N	S					T	I	O	N
ITEC	V	E	L	O					P	T	O	R
OPOT	E	X	P	E					I	O	N	S
CTAT	A	M	B	I					R	O	U	S
BUIL	I	N	T	E					T	I	O	N
RREC	C	I	V	I					T	I	O	N
UNIC	H	I	P	P					A	M	U	S

▶ TRIVIA

FAMOUS PEOPLE FROM THE PAST.

1.
....
1346 ▶ Crowned as Emperor and Autocrat of Serbs and Romans.

2.
....
1475 ▶ Declared war on France, landing at Calais in support of Charles the Bold of Burgundy.

3.
....
1668 ▶ Sacked Puerto Príncipe (modern day Camagüey, Cuba).

4.
....
1703 ▶ Published his first medical paper, "Het Nut der Mechanistische Methode in de Geneeskunde."

5.
....
1746 ▶ Promoted to the post of chamber musician (Kammermusikus) by Frederick The Great.

6.
....
1865 ▶ Spent two years performing his pantomime routine in Rio de Janeiro, Brazil.

7.
....
1902 ▶ Found gold in what is now modern day Fairbanks, Alaska, starting a new Gold Rush.

8.
....
1910 ▶ Demonstrated his neon light invention at the Paris Motor Show.

```
X N H L R P U L W Z A K M R T B E
W V P H O T O C O P I E D S N U V
Y R R Y É V E N L I V E N E S S R
X C S A L L C U X K L E N Z S D T
H P I F T I O G T I R Z E E E S B
Y D G T Z L A Ï A I P A N P I P E
P M E Z A R B R S A C D P T L N M
E K T L E D D R G E N O E I M G B
S W L V T R E R G O T R O P I C T
U T O G I L D L F V C V M P N L Y
P R S H B N Y J I N F L I G H T L
P S T B L X E J Y E C L O S E S G
T R I O N Y X S P I N I F E R U S
Q N S P I D E R I S H D E A G H Y
H M S T R U E W A R B L E R S G E
L I P L L Q J W T X T S A D A M S
M O W S P E A R S E I V H H Q X N
```

- 2nd POTUS.
- Stronghold.
- Emerge from pupa.
- Active nervous system.
- Eng. Language Teaching (abbr.).
- Finished.
- Affection.
- Go away (2 words).
- Abbess of Paraclete.
- Gets overexcited.
- During a flight.
- Boiler.
- Edge.
- Reverberant quality.
- Learning Mgt. System (abbr.).
- Cuts down.
- Strike.
- Biters.
- Syrinx.
- Xeroxed.
- Medroxyprogesterone.
- 23rd Greek letter.
- Scorches.
- Mermaids.
- Slides violently.
- Lances.
- Resembling a spider.
- Shooting Star Press (abbr.).
- Unifier of beliefs.
- Electrical rail.
- It is (archaic).
- Surpassed.
- Spiny softshell turtle 2 words, Latin).
- Sylviidae birds (2 w.).
- Climber plants.

NUTRITION FACTS

WHICH VITAMIN DOES THAT?

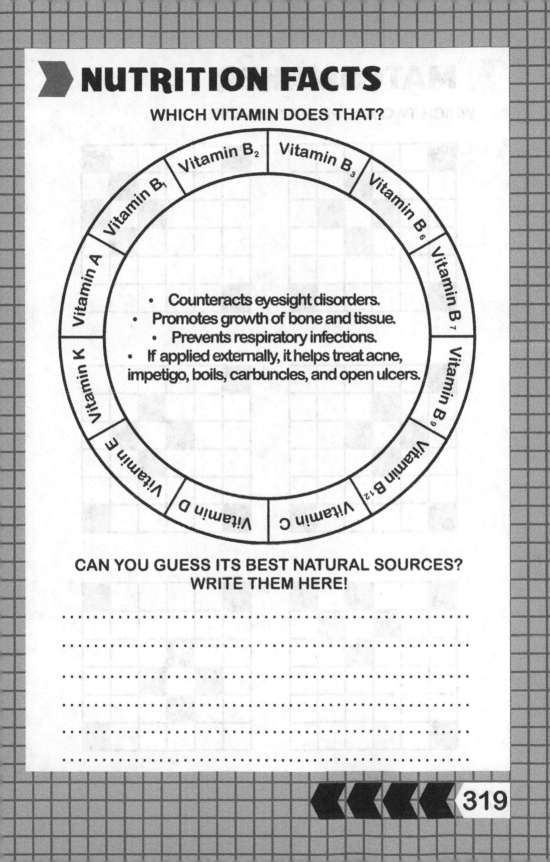

Vitamin B$_1$ · Vitamin B$_2$ · Vitamin B$_3$ · Vitamin B$_6$ · Vitamin B$_7$ · Vitamin B$_9$ · Vitamin B$_{12}$ · Vitamin C · Vitamin D · Vitamin E · Vitamin K · Vitamin A

- Counteracts eyesight disorders.
- Promotes growth of bone and tissue.
- Prevents respiratory infections.
- If applied externally, it helps treat acne, impetigo, boils, carbuncles, and open ulcers.

CAN YOU GUESS ITS BEST NATURAL SOURCES? WRITE THEM HERE!

. . . .

. . . .

. . . .

. . . .

. . . .

. . . .

MATCHMAKER

WHICH TWO ARE PERFECTLY ALIKE?

1.
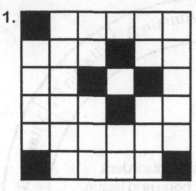

2.
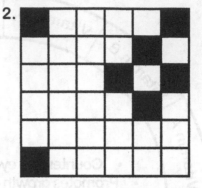

3.
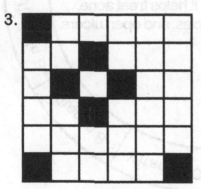

4.
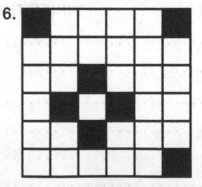

5.

6.

ACROSS:

2. State of knowing.
9. Row.
10. Japanese town.
11. Female knight.
13. Granny or Nanny.
14. Roman allies.
15. Small songbird.
16. CH_2:CHCO.
18. Fixed charge.
19. Not truly masculine.
22. Mat.
23. Writing down.
25. Salivary stones.
29. Turkish ship.
30. Tut— (Plural).
32. Unique Ref. Nº (abbr.).
34. Severe rebuke.
35. Petroleum.
36. Elm tree ooze.

DOWN:

1. Opposition (2 w.).
2. Promptly (Spanish).
3. Romp.
4. Electrodeposition.
5. Eva del— Bowles.
6. Natl. Eye Institute (abbr.).
7. Non-existent.
8. Current universe era.
12. Depth perception.
17. Fashionable.
20. Stream upwards.
21. Fully curved.
24. Contempt sound.
25. "Pirney" name variation (Scottish).
26. Day (Hebrew).
27. SE Indian language.
28. Eyot.
31. Formal "on".
33. Vietnam (slang).

WORDSEARCH

```
N H F U W W R C G J T M D L B O G
S Q W O O W M Y R R H A E W W R M
Y V Y L U P R D B N O R P I N E I
H O L R Y A W P R W R J E N U G N
N I I L M F O D P O O O N T T A E
W A T E R C R E S S U R N E M N T
M U S K R A M J U A G A Y R E O U
A O P Q T E W U C F H M R G G T R
R H T S C D O T C F W I O R E H M
I Z U C U A O A O R O N Y E B Y E
G M W D V T D R R O R T A E S M R
O B I S A V O R Y N T K L N A E I
L X W N N Z P A P R I K A S G E C
D A G N I W I G F M N T E L E O C
J H I I L Q G O P A R S L E Y L J
C W E Y L Q J N W C Z U L U E V U
D E D Q A U H E A E B L Q H N T A
```

FIND 30 HERBS & SPICES STARTING WITH M, N, P, R, S, T, V, AND W. CAN YOU THINK OF ANY OTHERS?

....
....
....
....
....
....
....
....
....
....

C	Q	Y	V	H	F	N						E			K		U					W		
			X		M		C				T		A	Q			G	B	F					
W					Z		E			I						O	X	B			S			
		I		H		T		K			X	Z		S		Y				V		E	M	
F			Y		B							I				A		Q	H	O	X			
E	W		A			Q	Y			V	N	U	Z		M	T				C				
	R		J		U	L		W			Z		K			V		C	F	E				O
		G		C		H			F			J		O				I	T	L				W
M		X		B	K	F				R			S	E			J			U		G		
	F	U			O	Z	S				X	B			Y		P		J	R		M		
	B	E				A	N			O	G			K	C		Q			M				
	T			S	I	Q			H			J		W	M	P	L			X	B			
U	Y			N		J					K				F				P				A	
		K	B		G					U	N	W		Y					S	O	V	C		
P	M		W		R								B	N	J		Z		H	E				
	N		C		E			R		P	I	F			B		H	Q			G			
	A	M			K			W	S		B			P	I		N			T	J			
Z	J				I			U			L				O		A	V	Y	H				
X	V			Y	P	R			O			K	S	U	E	L	Z	F	C					
		Y			H			L			E	G		R		V	K				I			
R	L	A	Z		P	S		G		C			N		X		E			W		V		
		Q	J	V	T		X			B	R		A						H	K			
	H		Q			L				R			V		Y		S	I						
S		F			O		B		Z		Y	W	N			J			A					
	K			F		O		Q	P	T	S		W	Z									

FILL EVERY ROW, COLUMN, AND 5X5 SECTOR, USING EACH GIVEN LETTER ONLY ONCE!

MAZE

FIND A STRAIGHT PATH THAT FOLLOWS THIS PATTERN: ■□■■□■ , HORIZONTAL OR VERTICAL (NEVER DIAGONAL!), FROM THE TOP CHEVRON TO THE CHEVRON AT THE BOTTOM OF THE GRID.

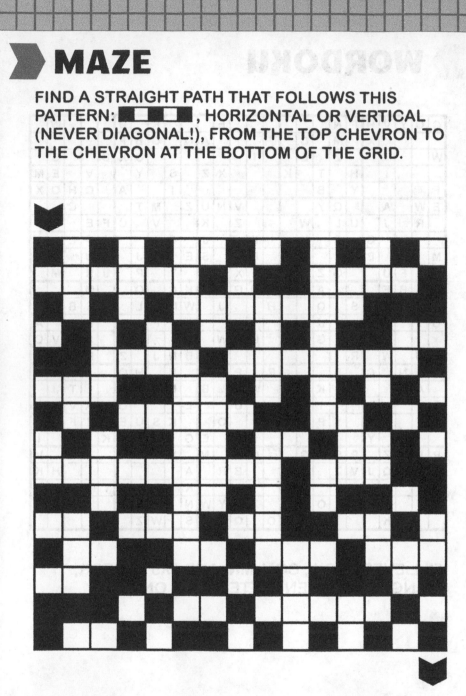

NAME 20 POP/ROCK BANDS NAMED AFTER REAL PLACES:

1. AMERICA

► WORDFILL

WHICH 4-LETTER COMBINATIONS ON THE LEFT DO YOU NEED TO COMPLETE THE 12-LETTER WORDS ON THE RIGHT?

PERA	G	R	A	N					E	N	T	S
HBOR	R	E	F	R					A	T	O	R
NIZA	E	X	A	S					T	I	O	N
DPAR	F	E	L	I					T	I	O	N
CIPA	C	A	N	T					R	O	U	S
ESTE	K	A	L	E					C	O	P	E
ENSA	E	X	H	I					T	I	N	G
IGER	A	B	B	R					T	I	O	N
CITA	C	O	L	O					T	I	O	N
ANKE	N	E	I	G					H	O	O	D
CRIP	A	N	T	I					T	I	O	N
CTIO	E	L	E	C					Y	I	N	G
LARA	A	F	F	E					N	A	T	E
TRIF	P	R	E	S					T	I	O	N
IDOS	C	O	N	D					T	I	O	N
EVIA	P	R	O	G					R	O	N	E

⯈ TRIVIA

FAMOUS PEOPLE FROM THE PAST.

1.

1345 ⯈ Arrived at the city of Quanzhou in Fujian Province, China.

2.

1418 ⯈ Discovered and claimed the Madeira Islands for Portugal.

3.

1623 ⯈ Adopted at age eleven by famous swordsman Miyamoto Musashi.

4.

1758 ⯈ Pushed the French out of Hanover and back across the River Rhine.

5.

1839 ⯈ Patented his invention, the steam shovel, which was the earliest type of excavator.

6.

1911 ⯈ His M1911 pistol served as the USAF standard issue sidearm from 1911 to 1986.

7.

1922 ⯈ Became Chairman of the Provisional Government of the Irish Free State until his assassination seven months later.

8.

1946 ⯈ Elected as the first United Nations Secretary-General.

```
W T V M I G E I W T P D Y E M A E
L B P T K C M L W I L O S P T T M
A J T V J Y H Q B B T I L U U G P
P Y O P H I W O M O U H D L S Q L
P U H R V Q L L I G W A O L U G O
A U D O U V V K S G Y S H U T T Y
R D S D V N L I T R B I S X T P E
E F J R L A D I S A S T A R V E D
N B R I B E U E V C N B W P C F D
T Q B O O S S P W E A P O N S W H
U I A Q X S F F M X D R E L J Y C
I V E G E T A T I O N I B B D E O
G I E R R O R R B B T L L D U A N
C S D H E A D Q U A R T E R S S Y
F H T J P S U S P E C T W E N T Y
R P I E S T O R E D E V O T I O N
F I D N W H B B E A S T S P P M H
```

- Complete.
- Obvious.
- Brutes.
- Brew.
- Exhaled.
- Pugilist.
- Occupied.
- Lower jaw apex.
- Specialized division.
- Fidelity.
- Masquerade.
- Gowns.
- Cardinal compass point at 90 degrees.
- Cubital joints.
- Hired.
- Mistake.
- Short prayer of thanks before a meal.
- HQ.
- Resided.
- Hazes.
- Good-natured tolerance.
- Tarts.
- Compassion.
- Contaminate.
- Spills.
- Draw.
- Close.
- Malnourish.
- Gumbo.
- Stockpiled.
- —of armor.
- Defendant.
- Stuffed toy bear.
- Salute.
- 20.
- Flora.
- Arms.
- Lacking.

WHICH VITAMIN DOES THAT?

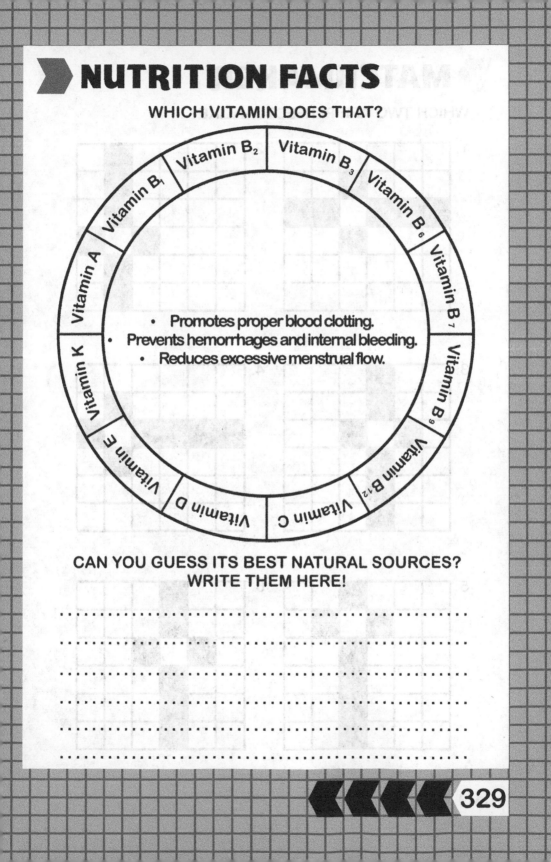

Vitamin B₂ · Vitamin B₃ · Vitamin B₆ · Vitamin B₇ · Vitamin B₉ · Vitamin B₁₂ · Vitamin C · Vitamin D · Vitamin E · Vitamin K · Vitamin A · Vitamin B₁

- Promotes proper blood clotting.
- Prevents hemorrhages and internal bleeding.
- Reduces excessive menstrual flow.

CAN YOU GUESS ITS BEST NATURAL SOURCES?
WRITE THEM HERE!

....

....

....

....

....

....

MATCHMAKER

WHICH TWO ARE PERFECTLY ALIKE?

1.

2.

3.

4.

5.

6.

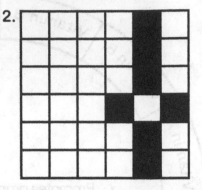
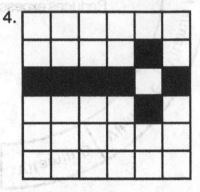
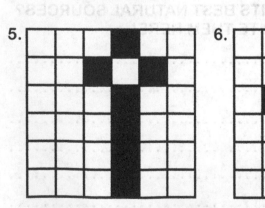
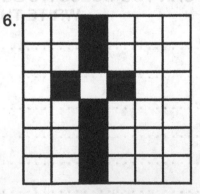

CRISSCROSS

ACROSS:

1. Make puffing sound.
4. Companions.
10. Taxation subject.
12. Accent (Spanish).
13. Dancing plant (2w.).
15. Trophies.
17. Sponsors.
18. Golf ball peg.
19. Inuit and Yupik.
20. Flaming torch.
22. Fart.
24. Takeoff (abbr.).
25. Equip.
26. Angry.
28. Trolls.
31. Family by marriage.
33. Incendiarism.
35. Ardent follower.
36. Rubbing.
39. Nipple.
41. Interface (abbr.).
42. Bribes (British).
43. Lambast.

DOWN:

2. Samovar.
3. Reynard the —.
4. Exploitation.
5. Straight people.
6. Waist pack w/ pouch.
7. Display device.
8. Previously.
9. Blurts.
10. Refusal to conform.
11. Newts.
14. Creative process.
16. Life of —.
17. Indian male title.
21. Diamond patterns.
23. Active Directory (abbr.).
27. Longest division of geological time.
29. Receding tide.
30. Arctic auk.
32. Ire.
34. Old Kinderhook (abbr.).
37. Also known as (abbr.).
38. G (pronunciation).
39. Time in Service (abbr.).
40. Spasm.

WORDSEARCH

```
R Y I J C H A R T R E U S E H A H
B U D W B O M T C S W X C A D N D
Y J B S L I N Z K D R A M B U I E
C C U Q A T K G B A G F H E B S W
R N R J C A N G O S T U R A O E C
E A G K K B O U R B O N H U N T H
M P U J R R R Z D R L H U J N T I
E E N E U A B C E G J U I O E E A
D R D V S M W H A M R S E L T B N
E I Y N S B V A U P T C L A R E T
C T S K I L Y B X Q P C A I H E I
A I W G A E F L I Q L L O S T R Y
S F B E N E D I C T I N E G I D G
S H I J P A B S I N T H E J N N B
I U H C H A M P A G N E X A A A O
S U J N T K U S Y W L P R U X C C
A J A Q U A V I T A E B F I O F K
```

FIND 30 BEVERAGES & COCKTAILS STARTING WITH A, B, AND C. CAN YOU THINK OF ANY OTHERS?

....
....
....
....
....
....
....
....
....
....

WORDOKU

S			P	E	J			D			T			G		N			Q	V				A
	Q	X		R		Z	A	U			B	J			W		G			C	L			
	Y	M	A	G		Q						K			U		L				B	S		
F			W	H	P	G			O		D	S						Z	J	R	T			
	U	V		L		T			W	C	E	Y			B				Z			D	M	N
			W	B				K			S	D	T				Q	Y	G	X				
		L		T		U			N	H		C			X			Z	R		A	M	O	P
	R	H			E				X				O	N	D			K	L					
K	F	Y	B				V			U			E	S						Q			H	
V		Z			A	L		W				B			F		M		P	G	S	U	N	
				O				T		C	V			J	P			S	W					M
E	O			Z		N		S			G	X							T	P	A			J
	H	J	M	U	D			X	Y	R	Z		O	Q	L	T			A	N	E	F	S	
C		A	K	F				S	E			R		X			U					L	Z	
X			R	M		F	B		N	P			L				Z							
	G	H	V	Q	R		J		P		L				O		C	U			X			D
	T		U				O	A		H				K					J	C	B	F		
			L	Z		P	E	M				C					H				K	Y		
	C	P	Z	Y		A	M		X		O		G	B			E		Q		V			
		D	O	H	B			U	Y	F		M			X	L								
D	B	E		X			R			V	H	M	O		S		C		U	T				
	F	Y	K	T				P	A		J			D	C	R	N						Q	
	U	V			S		L		F				J		H	D	E	Z						
	O	C			J		H		Q	Z		G	L	A		T		V	W					
H			P	V		M		D		R			E		N	X	K						Y	

FILL EVERY ROW, COLUMN, AND 5X5 SECTOR,
USING EACH GIVEN LETTER ONLY ONCE!

MAZE

FIND A STRAIGHT PATH THAT FOLLOWS THIS PATTERN: ▮▯▮▯▮ , HORIZONTAL OR VERTICAL (NEVER DIAGONAL!), FROM THE TOP CHEVRON TO THE CHEVRON AT THE BOTTOM OF THE GRID.

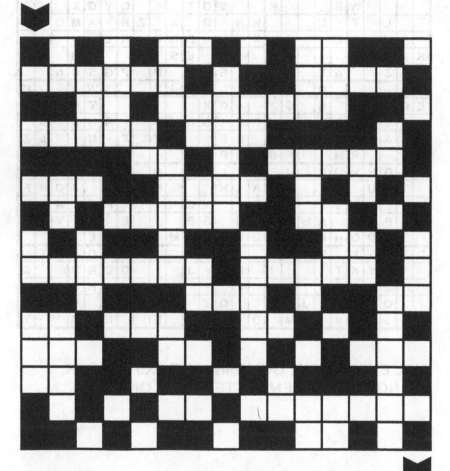

▶ NAME IT

DO YOU KNOW THE 20 MOST POPULAR LAST NAMES IN AMERICA TODAY? WRITE THEM DOWN.

1. SMITH

WORDFILL

WHICH 4-LETTER COMBINATIONS ON THE LEFT DO YOU NEED TO COMPLETE THE 12-LETTER WORDS ON THE RIGHT?

ILEC	V	E	T	E					R	I	A	N
LOCA	S	U	R	R					I	N	G	S
ERVA	A	N	N	O					M	E	N	T
MPAR	P	R	E	D					T	I	O	N
OACH	T	R	A	N					S	I	O	N
SMIS	E	C	H	O					T	I	O	N
WHEL	C	A	R	T					P	H	E	R
RNAT	E	N	C	Y					E	D	I	A
ITHE	C	O	N	S					T	I	V	E
UNCE	H	Y	P	O					A	M	U	S
ELGA	U	N	C	O					A	B	L	E
CLOP	O	V	E	R					M	I	N	G
THAL	A	P	P	R					A	B	L	E
OGRA	D	O	P	P					N	G	E	R
OUND	S	U	P	E					U	R	A	L
RINA	A	M	P	H					A	T	E	R

▶ TRIVIA

FAMOUS PEOPLE FROM THE PAST.

1. ....

1292 ❯ Conquered the kingdom of Hariphunchai, creating the Lanna Kingdom.

2. ....

1446 ❯ Commissioned by Cosimo de' Medici to illuminate choir books for the church of San Marco.

3. ....

1578 ❯ Held the first Thanksgiving celebration in North America, in Newfoundland.

4. ....

1779 ❯ Led a brigade in the victory at the Battle of Newtown.

5. ....

1928 ❯ Found the remains of a snail in her ginger beer, leading to a landmark lawsuit.

6. ....

1961 ❯ Rocketed into space aboard the Mercury-Redstone 2.

7. ....

1973 ❯ Assigned to the San Francisco Police Dept. team that investigated the "Zebra" murders.

8. ....

2006 ❯ Became editor of British weekly comic <u>The Beano</u>, after J. Euan Kerr stepped down.

```
D O X M U B I C R Y V P Q V R I Q
G U F R U A N A L O G S P E A K F
W G F V J L I G P E P T A L K Q C
T E W C T Z M V S W M S S A Y P N
B Y C O K A D L M T U E A T Z A C
T R A G I C A L I A L C N F O Y O
B L A C K F O R E S T G A T E A U
K S I Z P S Y C H I C S Y K I S N
L O V E S P O O R H O U S E N T
J U S T I C E O F T H E P E A C E
G G U A M A B S O A T E H U G E R
H O B S O U L G I R D E M E A N P
R H L W N R A L W E N Y A A A Z O
E Q I H I E C K E N C E T P L R I
Q G M G Z O K H E A P O S T L E S
D W E G E L E F L S R N E S A F E
Y X R S D E R X I K I S A W S Q S
```

- Eager to listen (2 w.).
- Parallels.
- Disciples.
- Stadiums.
- Bewildered.
- Circle of light.
- Honoré de—.
- Josef Keller's cake.
- More black.
- Gateau.
- Oh My Darling,—.
- Dutch oven.
- Counterbalances.
- Humiliate.
- Daughters.
- Germanic invaders.
- Mound.
- Listens.
- Concerning blood.
- Male ferrets.
- Larger.
- Yoke.
- Lay magistrate (UK).
- Trimmed w/ lace.
- Adores.
- Loch—.
- Encouraging speech (2 w.).
- Workhouse.
- Clairvoyants.
- Gouges.
- Strongbox.
- Most secure.
- Polished.
- Communicate.
- More elevated.
- Tragic.
- Sail (Spanish).
- Mexican cartel.

► NUTRITION FACTS

WHICH VITAMIN DOES THAT?

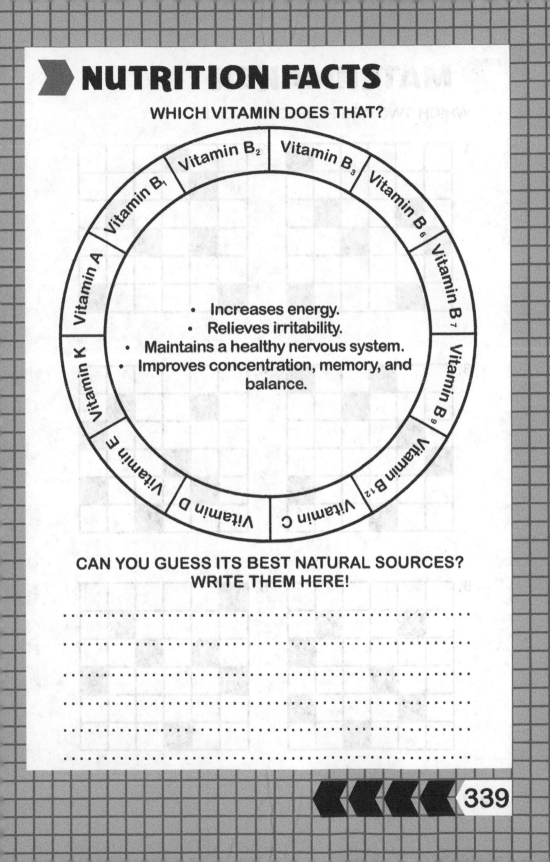

- Increases energy.
- Relieves irritability.
- Maintains a healthy nervous system.
- Improves concentration, memory, and balance.

Vitamin B_1, Vitamin B_2, Vitamin B_3, Vitamin B_6, Vitamin B_7, Vitamin B_9, Vitamin B_{12}, Vitamin A, Vitamin K, Vitamin E, Vitamin D, Vitamin C

CAN YOU GUESS ITS BEST NATURAL SOURCES?
WRITE THEM HERE!

....

....

....

....

....

....

MATCHMAKER

WHICH TWO ARE PERFECTLY ALIKE?

1.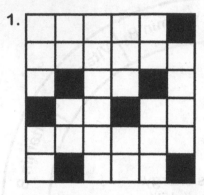

2.

3.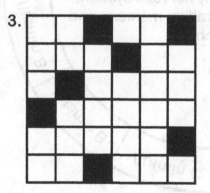

4.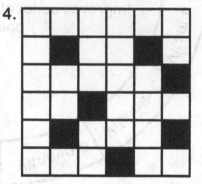

5.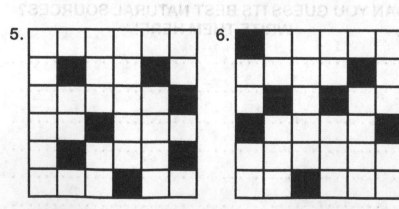

6.

CRISSCROSS

ACROSS:

2. Closely involved.
6. Withstand.
9. Dandy
10. Ardor.
11. Dildo.
13. Pitcher's measure (abbr.).
14. Cut slightly.
15. Tantrum.
16. Carpeting.
18. Hock.
19. Edible root (2 w.).
20. Court inspection (2 w.).
21. —Age.
23. Hypertension drugs.
27. Individual unit.
29. Wharf owners.
34. Writing point of a pen.
35. Genu varum.
36. Stanza.

DOWN:

1. Blame oneself.
3. The Soviet Union (abbr.).
4. Banderilla.
5. Marches (Scottish).
7. Noun acted upon (2w.).
8. Mr. Fantastic's first name.
9. Res Non Verba.
11. R Cygni (2 w.).
12. Beleaguer.
15. Dexterity.
17. Ivan S.—.
18. Providential.
22. Vet. Affairs Dept. (abbr.).
24. Doctrine.
25. Church bench.
26. To—is human.
28. Recede.
30. Crataegus shrub.
31. Cigarette (British).
32. Inflated pride.
33. So (Scots).

▶ **WORDSEARCH**

```
C E G J O H N C O L L I N S K B V
K K O U P T R J U L E P N C G N N
O V E E I P Z A A N H S E Y S O R
U A P Q A N U T I Y Y N K E I I Q
M S X F M L N D J L S G F T K E D
I S Z B H S A E E E O R C L T C I
S G H A P N I M S L N E F E I S K
S R K I E D M R L S N E N N H P I
G A F R G U O E I N P N V N Y D D
I V G F K H N X O S O V S E D R I
M E V U L R B C G B H E O E R A K
L S M U A I H A U C S S R K O M I
E G Z F I C R D L P N P Z V M B R
T R E E N C A T G L T E J N E U S
E L T E K A V A I N E R L H L I C
P G R A N D M A R N I E R I X E H
B F K A M I K A Z E I G R A P P A
```

FIND 30 BEVERAGES & COCKTAILS STARTING WITH D, F, G, H, I, J, AND K. CAN YOU THINK OF ANY OTHERS?

. . . .
. . . .
. . . .
. . . .
. . . .
. . . .
. . . .
. . . .
. . . .
. . . .

WORDOKU

		Z	F				I		O	X					A	P	S	T	B	E				R
	S				A			X		R	E		D		I			N	K	Z	G			
	H	N	A	D		F				V	W	L				Q				X		M		
	G			M	T		H	V							W				J	F	A			
	D		E	G		Y			I		T	J			X	R		W	C					
J	N			O	I	F		E	S			H		Z		A	P	X					C	
H						C	R			E	B	A		N	G		M							D
D				L	O	A				Q		Y	V	H	C			F	G	Z				
S	R	C		K	N		J			M	G	O		F			Y		A					
		X			G		T		J		Y		V	I		W					Q	H		
	G	D	Q	E			F	H		S				P			A			R				
	V	R	E	Z	C	H		D		G			K	O		M			P		F			
	W		I			R	N		E	A	P		G	X				L		V				
	A		J		S		Y	G		Q		C			F	B	O	D	T	X				
	X		J		D			F		W	N		V	Q	H	G								
N	I			H		Q	O		Z		E		B		G		M							
	V		B		M		T	G	J		E		P	F		N	Y	Q						
	X	F	L		C	I	N	T		Y		R	J	A				O						
Q			Y		P	L		N	R	W		F	K					V						
	P			Z	B	W		K		I		M	Y		N	S	X		D	T				
	O	R		E	P		V	J		M			N		W	D		Y						
	D	B	K		Z					H	J		Y	F		O								
	S		A		N		W	X	T			M		D	I	R	K							
	F	Y	Q	W		M		D		O	B		K		L			V						
M			P	I	H	V	R	J				X	T		O			N	B	L				

**FILL EVERY ROW, COLUMN, AND 5X5 SECTOR,
USING EACH GIVEN LETTER ONLY ONCE!**

MAZE

FIND A STRAIGHT PATH THAT FOLLOWS THIS PATTERN: ▮▯▮▯▮, HORIZONTAL OR VERTICAL (NEVER DIAGONAL!), FROM THE TOP CHEVRON TO THE CHEVRON AT THE BOTTOM OF THE GRID.

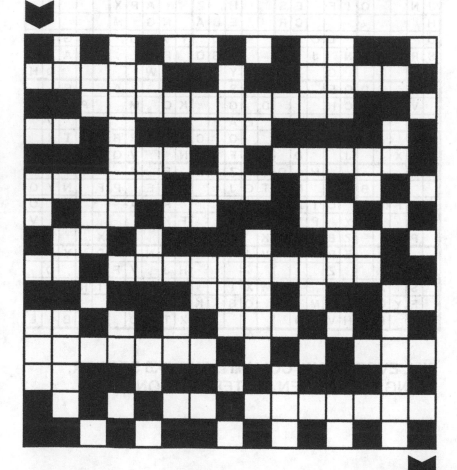

▶NAME IT

NAME 20 OF THE FUNNIEST COMEDIANS YOU KNOW.

1. LENNY BRUCE

▶ WORDFILL

WHICH 4-LETTER COMBINATIONS ON THE LEFT DO YOU NEED TO COMPLETE THE 12-LETTER WORDS ON THE RIGHT?

CEPT	C	O	N	D					N	I	N	G
TROL	A	S	P	H					T	I	O	N
HILA	A	N	N	I					T	I	O	N
LESS	I	D	E	A					T	I	O	N
TERA	U	N	A	T					A	B	L	E
SFAC	U	N	A	C					A	B	L	E
THER	E	L	E	C					Y	S	I	S
TBRE	A	D	U	L					T	I	O	N
DYNA	M	E	N	S					T	I	O	N
FICA	S	E	L	F					N	E	S	S
FICA	S	A	T	I					T	I	O	N
ITIO	T	O	G	E					N	E	S	S
YXIA	R	A	M	I					T	I	O	N
TRUA	A	E	R	O					M	I	C	S
TAIN	R	A	T	I					T	I	O	N
	H	E	A	R					A	K	E	R

▶ TRIVIA

FAMOUS PEOPLE FROM THE PAST.

1.
· ·

1221 ▶ Ascended to the Chrysanthemum Throne of Japan at age ten.

2.
· ·

1331 ▶ A missionary explorer to India, Sumatra, and China, he passed away in Udine, Italy.

3.
· ·

1441 ▶ Defeated the army of Stjepan Banic at Samobor, Croatia.

4.
· ·

1551 ▶ Began to write his <u>Suma y narración de los Incas</u>, a history of the Inca Empire in Peru.

5.
· ·

1661 ▶ Succeeded his father-in-law Diego Velázquez as court painter in Madrid.

6.
· ·

1771 ▶ Raised a militia to put down the long-running uprising against North Carolina's colonial government.

7.
· ·

1881 ▶ Published her supernatural fiction novel, <u>Asphodel</u>.

8.
· ·

1991 ▶ The first "Sonic The Hedgehog" video game he originally programmed was released in the US.

```
W G V H A J X U P D C D H E L A G
O J A L J N J Z N O O C A L Z U X
S K V V X I P C K R N L C C D M N
S Z Z I H R H M K I S C O O T E D
J A O J T H U S U V J Q N R B A O
M Q C C Y T A W K H Q M T R Y O N
H H G A A Q V L A C M K A J N Q G
B R L R P D I H T Y L L I I R W L
N J E U O A S A Q O S R N Y N Y E
W G B P N U C K Y D B U M B L E D
A A A Y L S T I F H R E E A B C T
J C U B U E A S T C A N N H W I S
K P L M H B T V L Y I H T T B Z G
K D D B U O Q E O S A X S O H M A
R H O R R O R S T R I C K E N U P
A Y O N C A R G U F Y I N G H W H
H Y N E T G M S W A G F W E L T C
```

- The Alphabet.
- Abominate.
- Mistflower (Latin).
- Lowest female voice.
- Altercating.
- Old (Scots).
- Contempt exclamation.
- Bended.
- Rosiness.
- Stammered.
- Capability.
- Restraints.
- Pain (Spanish).
- External device.
- Do not (contr.).
- Light conversation.
- Fungus puffball.
- Binds w/ plaster.
- Terrified.
- "Come again?"
- 1/12 of a foot.
- Slow down.
- Oman capital.
- Necrology.
- Unit of resistance.
- Larger rodent.
- Filled.
- Iranian monarch.
- —qua non.
- Quran chapter.
- Don.
- Offensive.
- Directions.
- Vitellus.
- Aku.

NUTRITION FACTS

WHICH VITAMIN DOES THAT?

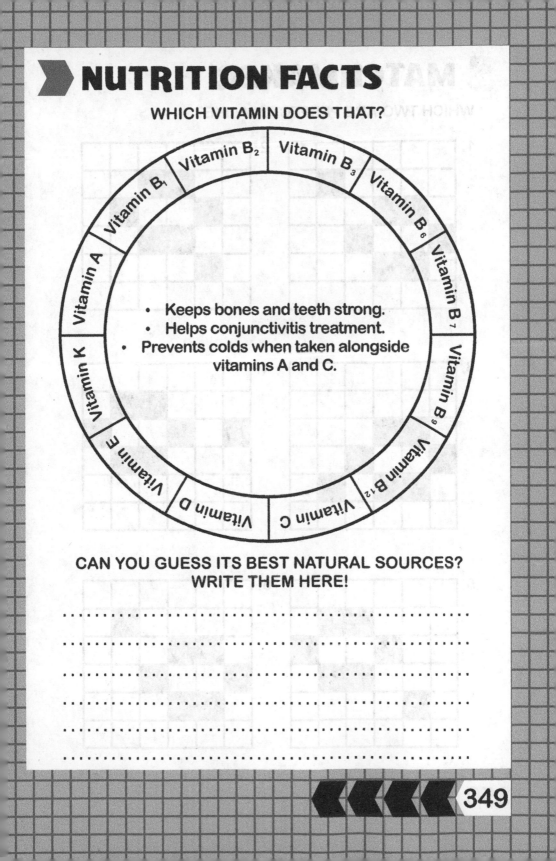

Vitamin B₂ · Vitamin B₃ · Vitamin B₆ · Vitamin B₇ · Vitamin B₉ · Vitamin B₁₂ · Vitamin C · Vitamin D · Vitamin E · Vitamin K · Vitamin A · Vitamin B₁

- Keeps bones and teeth strong.
- Helps conjunctivitis treatment.
- Prevents colds when taken alongside vitamins A and C.

CAN YOU GUESS ITS BEST NATURAL SOURCES?
WRITE THEM HERE!

....
....
....
....
....
....

MATCHMAKER

WHICH TWO ARE PERFECTLY ALIKE?

1.
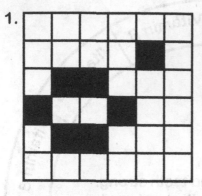

2.
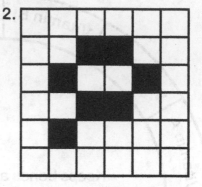

3.
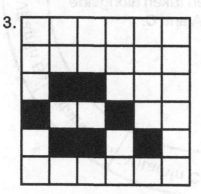

4.
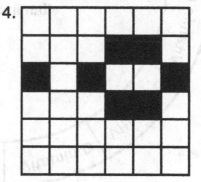

5.
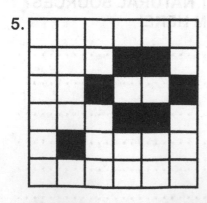

6.
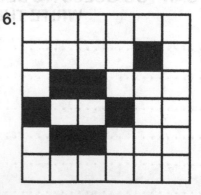

ACROSS:

1. —canto.
3. Holed up.
5. Eructs.
7. "I" problem.
9. Bawl.
10. Killing.
12. Beyond jurisdiction.
15. Knocked off.
17. Cephalopod.
18. Even if (abbr.).
20. Carpentry tool
21. Look sullen
22. National University of Singapore (abbr.).
23. Narrow-mindedly.
24. —Doubtfire.
25. Earlier than.
28. Hereafters.
30. Free from.
31. Lollipop man (UK).
35. Unheard-of.
36. Dash lengths.

DOWN:

1. Investors.
2. Ballad.
3. Exclamation of joy.
4. —DeLuise.
5. Baking soda.
6. Dominating.
7. Decorative case.
8. —Office.
11. Study of bones.
13. Payoffs.
14. Opposites.
16. —tzu.
19. Desert refuge.
21. Delayed.
26. —a high note (2 words).
27. Kitchen gadget.
29. Haitian currency.
32. Mythical monster.
33. Zod's henchman.
34. Physics units.

WORDSEARCH

```
M F O L D F A S H I O N E D K T P
A M O N K E Y G L A N D M Y Y W A
N P M V M Y F A I R L A D Y N H R
H I G H X M T D W M O S E L L E A
A S D P R A I R I E F I R E W P D
T C Y M I C H E L A D A Q C A O I
T O U E L U K M A R T I N I R R S
A M A R S A L A A P D P O R T C E
N G C W W L U E H L A F D S Q H Y
M A T A D O R U V Z A L U Q S C M
D J B F L X U R P Z P G O C D R A
P M O J I T O W R E E E A M E A D
E M U D S L I D E N K Y G N A W E
R P I N A C O L A D A O M U O L I
N E G R O N I S R E L C E L U E R
O O A W B C G Y M A I T A I Z R A
D O Z P N M U S C A T E L W O Q V
```

FIND 30 BEVERAGES & COCKTAILS STARTING WITH M, N, O, AND P. CAN YOU THINK OF ANY OTHERS?

....
....
....
....
....
....
....
....
....
....

WORDOKU

X		R	H	Z		J	O		C	P	T				L								I	
	K		O	W		G		U	Z	L	E	V		T		X								R
V		I			A		Q	J		U				F	P			X		K				
U	G		P	Y		H		R		X		D			M	O	Z			C	J			
S		N			L		V	F			I	Q		Y	D				Z	H				
	Q			R	X	U	V	F	D				G			Z								
		Y			R				F						S	G	O							
	X	F			Y	J		H	O	S	K	C	U	R	P	N			Z		T			I
D	J		G	P	A			I			Z	H			W	L					E			
M	E	U		I			N				J	T							F	R				X
		A	F		C		H	O	N	J		W			E	S		M			U			Q
	M	X	U		S		D	T	E								L	I	G		N			C
C		T		Q	P	I		M				E			Y	H	N			D				O
J	I		S	N	Z						A		S	I	P		O	M	Q		X		L	A	W
Q		G		O		M	N			A		S		I	P	Z		R		F	Y			
W		Z	C				Y	F							Q				V		O	J	M	
	Y			S	Q			R	E			J			D	X	T			G	W			
H		P		G	E	Z	A	V	X	O	Q	S	Y		I	T				K	U			
		Q	V	L			G						E			S				H				
			U		C				S	R	O	F	A	E				H						
	K	N		P	J	T	W			A	O		C				G		U					
	W	V	G	A	F		C		K	N		M	O	E		Q	T							
	H	M	O	C			P		R	D	T			Z		Y								
L		R	M	Y	Q	Z	V	X	W		C	N		S										
	Y		I			A	X	Z	U	L	P	W	M	F										

FILL EVERY ROW, COLUMN, AND 5X5 SECTOR, USING EACH GIVEN LETTER ONLY ONCE!

MAZE

FIND A STRAIGHT PATH THAT FOLLOWS THIS
PATTERN: ■■□■□■ , HORIZONTAL OR VERTICAL
(NEVER DIAGONAL!), FROM THE TOP CHEVRON TO
THE CHEVRON AT THE BOTTOM OF THE GRID.

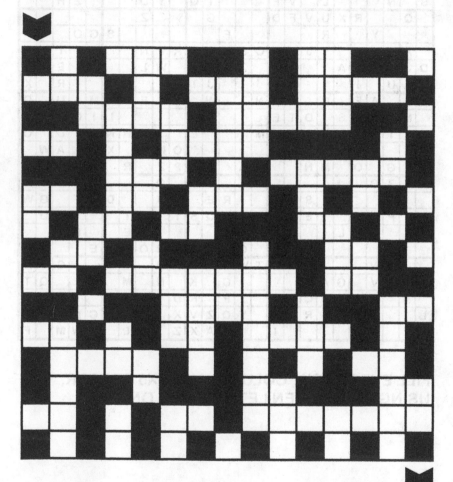

⏩ NAME IT

**DO YOU REMEMBER JIM HENSON'S <u>FRAGGLE ROCK</u>?
NAME 20 FRAGGLES!**

1. AUNT GRANNY

WORDFILL

WHICH 4-LETTER COMBINATIONS ON THE LEFT DO YOU NEED TO COMPLETE THE 12-LETTER WORDS ON THE RIGHT?

ERTA	Z	Y	M	O				N	I	C	S
VENA	S	H	A	P				F	T	E	R
STRA	I	N	T	E				T	I	O	N
TIZA	U	N	E	M				M	E	N	T
ICUL	D	I	S	S				T	I	O	N
RSEC	P	R	E	S				T	I	O	N
ANSI	I	N	T	E				T	I	O	N
ILLA	R	E	J	U				T	I	O	N
PLOY	A	S	T	R				I	C	A	L
NIZA	R	E	G	I				T	I	O	N
LLEC	A	M	O	R				T	I	O	N
TECH	R	E	C	O				T	I	O	N
ONOM	D	I	F	F				T	I	E	S
ESHI	I	M	M	U				T	I	O	N
RRUP	I	N	T	R				G	E	N	T
ERVA	D	I	S	T				T	I	O	N

► TRIVIA

FAMOUS PEOPLE FROM THE PAST.

1.

1865 ► Targeted by the plot that killed Lincoln, he was seriously wounded by conspirator Lewis Powell.

2.

1894 ► Founded Eragny Press with his wife and illustrated and printed books until it was closed in 1914.

3.

1905 ► The final episode of his comic <u>The Upside Downs of Little Lady Lovekins and Old Man Muffaroo</u> is published.

4.

1907 ► Blown up while driving a burning dynamite train away from a populated area in Sonora, Mexico.

5.

1911 ► Became the first MLB player in history to have more than twenty doubles, triples, home runs, and stolen bases in a season.

6.

1933 ► Attempted to assassinate president Franklin Delano Roosevelt, fatally wounding the Mayor of Chicago, Anton Cermak, instead.

7.

1946 ► She became the first mystery writer to be featured on the cover of <u>Time</u>.

8.

1971 ► Published his seminal <u>Design for the Real World: Human Ecology and Social Change</u>.

DEFINITION SEARCH

```
W L A W B I B L E U Y T J A L G R
O H M W R Y A Z P T U G E C H E B
R A I N P I E R M C U S X C S A V
D Y E P I N E B U O A Q E A L V E
M V E N R W I F Y P G F H C E Y Y
U N B S W O F N Q E I C O M E O N
S Y Q Y M Q W Q L N R N E D S L Q
I P T W C U Q O K U B V A F H A Y
C O O P T T T P P N O P A R O V B
I F O F D R S E O F N V L X R A Y
A A L X J A D O L H A U G U E L P
N L O A L I M I N O E S T E R I L
R W N C F L A U A R R Y J C S T O
A U G A L R G D F N S E K H R S T
I A N U X Y E T E P R L L L A A U
B O F O U R H O U R S I C S Y S B
B U R N N O S E N H O L D B E A M
```

- Cleans up (Spanish).
- Bag grapple.
- Unquestionable.
- Verified buyer.
- Nasal irritation.
- Au revoir.
- Subordinate story.
- Jackknife.
- Appoint.
- Color wood.
- Waldhorn.
- 240 minutes.
- Plenilune.

- Transverse pole.
- Catalytic substrates.
- Magma glow.
- Torah.
- Leeward (2 words).
- Non-equivalent stock.
- Ebalia tumefacta.
- Instead.
- Ox fence rail.
- Paddle opening.
- Rain-bird.
- Keep going.
- Ergot.

- Ultrasound beam.
- Gramineae.
- T-Section.
- Lengthy.
- Staple.
- Curved trim.
- Upside down.
- Advantage.
- Lyrics writer.
- EM waves.
- Antisubmarine gun.

NUTRITION FACTS

WHICH VITAMIN DOES THAT?

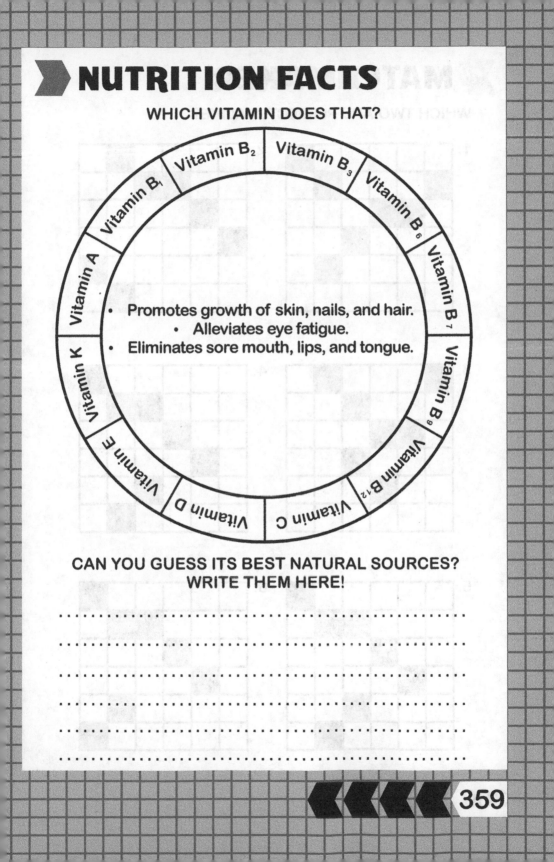

Vitamin B₂
Vitamin B₃
Vitamin B₁
Vitamin B₆
Vitamin A
Vitamin B₇
Vitamin K
Vitamin B₉
Vitamin E
Vitamin B₁₂
Vitamin D
Vitamin C

- Promotes growth of skin, nails, and hair.
  - Alleviates eye fatigue.
- Eliminates sore mouth, lips, and tongue.

CAN YOU GUESS ITS BEST NATURAL SOURCES?
WRITE THEM HERE!

....
....
....
....
....
....

MATCHMAKER

WHICH TWO ARE PERFECTLY ALIKE?

1.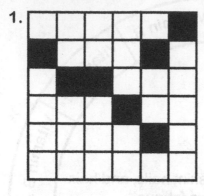

2.

3.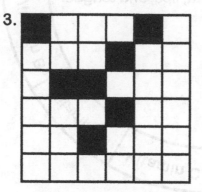

4.

5.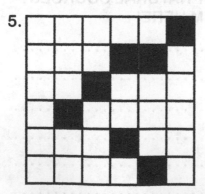

6.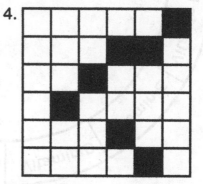

CRISSCROSS

ACROSS:
1. Decants.
3. Develops.
10. "O Sanctissima"
11. Mary had a little—.
12. Loosens up.
13. Vibraphone.
15. Bungle.
16. No more lonely—.
19. Signs.
20. Golly.
22. Final but important (4 words).
25. Seasonings plot (2 words).
26. Hungarian.
27. Woodlet.
28. Missions.
32. Hispaniola half (2 words).

DOWN:
1. PVC.
2. Conversion.
4. Spin (Spanish).
5. Eruptions.
6. Wusses.
7. Vagus nerve.
8. Remodels.
9. Orchid genus.
14. Liana.
17. Stomach surgery.
18. Luging.
21. Highway to—.
23. Harangue.
24. Sweated.
29. At no time (abbr.).
30. Short and erect tail.
31. —Arden.

▶ WORDSEARCH

```
U S N L U G S I D E C A R Q K R J S V
Y A R O Y A L A R R I V A L S G Y A Q
P U E J U C S U M A T R A K U L A N R
B T D R U L G C E R Z O U I F D G G A
S E R R B Q S H Q T K T P U F M C R R
E R U P U B E V I W O T B H E K E I Z
A N S T Y M X V A L S A K E R V W T C
B E S O R N O G I N T E Q U I L A A S
R R I D S V N P R Q U Y N R N Y H V A
E E A U I C T T C E D W D Q G T Q G Z
E D N L I S H R J E T W R E B I R H E
Z L S C E C E N N S E S T H A P R P R
E O N T T G B N A R A I I R S U A V A
C T P O N Y E C C P B L N N T N T S C
S U C I E K A S P E P P T V A C A H N
G S T K E Z C S K S C S G Y R H F E K
K S C S S R H A R M E W R V D A I R R
Y I O O S A N G A R E E A K B O A R L
R R X T B S Y V V T U X E D O I G Y Z
```

FIND 30 BEVERAGES & COCKTAILS STARTING WITH R, S,
AND T. CAN YOU THINK OF ANY OTHERS?

....
....
....
....
....
....
....
....
....
....

	A				B		F	Q		X	E	K	T	P			V			D	Y			
			M	V				Y			W					Z			B				Q	
K		C	H			D				X	U	N			S			A			P		F	
F	Q		Y				R						U	L			W	X	M			J		T
O			E				T	M				Q	R			K			L	N	Z	V	H	
B	H			W					S				T				O							V
X					Z	N		W	Y			R					B	J			O			
J		E						C	R	V		X			N		Y		K		Q			F
		S			P	E			O	H			K					U	X				Z	
P	Z	Y		O				H	E			J		F			W	G			S	R		D
V	J			A		L	E					R				N	M	Z			H		D	
	G	Q		T	H			B		N	O				D	S	F	K	V			L		
S	P						D	Q								G	E		U					
			R	K			J			P		Z	S	Y		B		X			C			
C	O				E	P			F	K	M		H			J			T	W	Q	Y		X
		N		C	B	Y		V						K		D		M	Q		A	L		
R	K		Z		Q		D				C		N	V			T	H	F					
		V	Y		M	O		E		U					G	L					B	W		
E					U	X	J	D				M			P	Q	F				H	C		
	H				L	R	N		F	X	Y		Z				A			K	U	T		
		K	B				C				H	O										A		
G				N	Q		L			K		V	D	H			S	T						
		X		F	G			W				Q		M								P	Y	
	A		D	X	E	K		P			F		W			S	L	N					R	
	V	F	L			A			T	M				X		U	P			Z	O	J	E	G

FILL EVERY ROW, COLUMN, AND 5X5 SECTOR, USING EACH GIVEN LETTER ONLY ONCE!

MAZE

FIND A STRAIGHT PATH THAT FOLLOWS THIS PATTERN: ■■□■□■■, HORIZONTAL OR VERTICAL (NEVER DIAGONAL!), FROM THE TOP CHEVRON TO THE CHEVRON AT THE BOTTOM OF THE GRID.

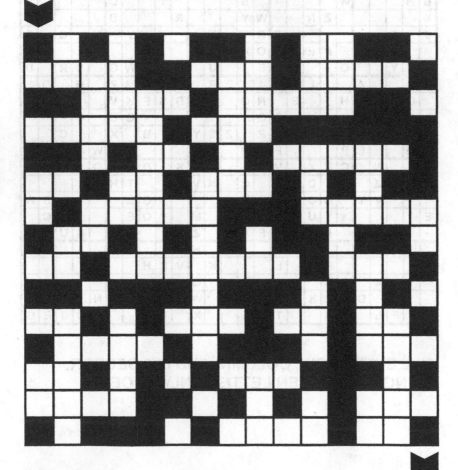

▶ NAME IT

NAME 20 OF YOUR FAVORITE <u>SESAME STREET</u> FRIENDS!

1. ABBY CADABBY

WORDFILL

WHICH 4-LETTER COMBINATIONS ON THE LEFT DO YOU NEED TO COMPLETE THE 12-LETTER WORDS ON THE RIGHT?

RVEN	H	A	N	D				H	I	E	F
ATRI	A	C	C	I				A	L	L	Y
STHE	C	O	N	S				T	I	O	N
STRA	C	A	L	I				N	I	C	S
IORA	S	U	P	E				T	I	O	N
ODUCT	E	X	T	I				S	H	E	R
DINA	P	E	D	I				C	I	A	N
FIGH	A	N	T	I				E	T	I	C
OGRA	P	H	O	T				P	H	E	R
KERC	A	M	E	L				T	I	O	N
CHED	W	R	E	T				N	E	S	S
TRUC	B	I	O	C				S	T	R	Y
HEMI	F	E	N	E				T	I	O	N
DENT	B	U	L	L				T	I	N	G
DIAB	I	N	T	R				T	I	O	N
NGUI	C	O	O	R				T	I	O	N

TRIVIA

FAMOUS PEOPLE FROM THE PAST.

1.

1789 ❯ Presented a unified view of new theories of chemistry, containing the law of conservation of mass, and defining the nature of elements.

2.

1824 ❯ Received the patent for Portland Cement on October 21st.

3.

1876 ❯ Begins marketing his "Budweiser" beer nationwide.

4.

1903 ❯ Assassinated in Belgrade by the "Black Hand" organization.

5.

1912 ❯ Made the first parachute jump from a flying airplane.

6.

1918 ❯ Appointed People's Commissar for Social Welfare, becoming the first female cabinet minister in Europe.

7.

1941 ❯ Published his classic novel <u>The Keys to the Kingdom</u>, which was made into a film three years later.

8.

1967 ❯ While created ten years earlier, his <u>Cheech Wizard</u> comic started to appear in print.

❯ DEFINITION SEARCH

```
P T N H I R F O A E V A S I V E V
C W S O P U F E U D O E R I L E X
K E U I D R V A N D A L G H S K R
F W H C T U I E U O T D W E N I Y
W C P K H O L J G D E I D U T T W
P A H C O A D E Q G N G H S D A L
A P O T A O R J J E S S A P E A L
I H N Z T T K L F R L U L L I L D
O L O Y Z F H Y O X L P D J T V X
J L R I L T U E F T C Q L I Y E W
V I S T S C O A C U T H M Y G K R
E X C U S E D G H T P E G M C H L
D S O Z Y H D S U S N G R O L T T
A J X N Z D T E C X P V S U I H Q
Z U X R E T I E W S B S U D S X E
E K X M K F N S B L U E S U Z S N
D M E J P S E J M T X G B Y T N E
```

- Contributes.
- Modify.
- Black music genre.
- George W.—.
- Arouse emotion.
- Ladyfingers and cream.
- —and Confused.
- God.
- Pigeon pea.
- Prepare (archaic).
- Unearths (2 words).
- Deceptive person.
- Cocoyam.

- Balls.
- Give off.
- Vague.
- Pardoned.
- Jerk.
- Distinctions.
- Attractive man.
- Aquifoliaceae tree.
- It will (contr.).
- Medieval combat.
- Jujitsu-based combat.
- Eccentric.
- Franz—.

- Tubercle.
- —bread.
- Prolonged ringing.
- Sound unit.
- Tie again.
- Agitate.
- Prong.
- Tuft.
- Vascular eye layer.
- Destructive person.
- Prohibition (Spanish).
- Vegetative.

NUTRITION FACTS

WHICH VITAMIN DOES THAT?

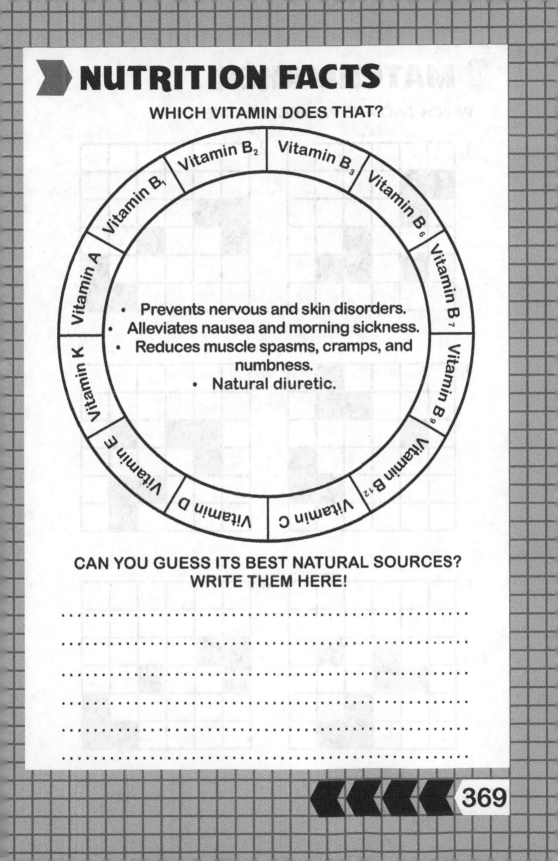

Vitamin B₂ · Vitamin B₃ · Vitamin B₆ · Vitamin B₇ · Vitamin B₉ · Vitamin B₁₂ · Vitamin C · Vitamin D · Vitamin E · Vitamin K · Vitamin A · Vitamin B₁

- Prevents nervous and skin disorders.
- Alleviates nausea and morning sickness.
- Reduces muscle spasms, cramps, and numbness.
- Natural diuretic.

CAN YOU GUESS ITS BEST NATURAL SOURCES?
WRITE THEM HERE!

....
....
....
....
....
....

MATCHMAKER

WHICH TWO ARE PERFECTLY ALIKE?

1.
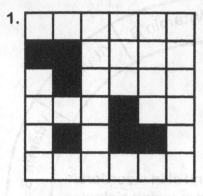

2.

3.

4.
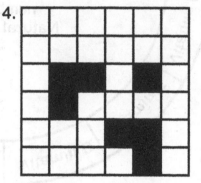

5.
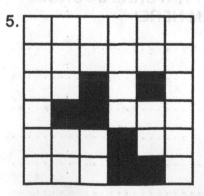

6.
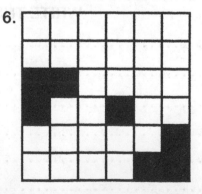

ACROSS:
1. Cares for nails.
5. Beg.
8. Predicate at the end.
11. Oglers.
13. Chippendale furniture.
15. The Matrix protagonist.
16. Ribonucleic.
18. Ginea-Bissau capital.
20. First-order—— (2 words).
25. Poetry verse w/ 8 metrical ft.
26. —Master.
27. Gauze.
28. Newhart setting.
29. "Call me—."
32. "A pox on you!"
33. Boer republic.

DOWN:
1. Blueprint.
2. —Jeane Mortenson.
3. Foreign market dump.
4. European Community (former).
5. Ballpoint.
6. Erave, Papua New Guinea (abbr.).
7. —Adkins.
9. Inconsistent.
10. Bowstring grooves.
11. —Franco.
12. Organisms.
14. Horsemen.
17. —Spiegelman.
18. —canto.
19. Blotchiest.
21. Selfishness.
22. Affix.
23. Disbelief exclamation (3 w.).
24. Kinswoman.
27. Summa—laude.
30. August (abbr.).
31. Anguish.

WORDSEARCH

CRISSC

```
V O D K A M C G O V E R N L K D D
O E Y V W H I T E R U S S I A N U
D O R E A B Z W A R D E I G H T P
K P Z D L M V G W L V T F T V P T
A V Y U E L P W W H S D Y U C M O
S P O G R S O I E T R C K A E N D
U K R D M R H W R D S S M K I Z A
N Z S F K E A O B O G Y W K Q W T
R F H H I A R C T I K U I O I H E
I Q U B K M G M A S R T E W P I W
S W M B Q D X I I P N D F H A T W
E O F J O C I H M O O D S I P E O
Z L C H D O W H V L Q T X S W L O
V F K C E V T Y M I E X E K L A W
V R M Z X G N H F X M T M E J D O
C A Z E N C O L L I N S G Y V Y O
K M B V E S P E R M A R T I N I C
```

FIND 21 BEVERAGES & COCKTAILS STARTING WITH U, V, W, Y, AND Z. CAN YOU THINK OF ANY OTHERS?

. . . .
. . . .
. . . .
. . . .
. . . .
. . . .
. . . .
. . . .

V	G		Y		E	K		N	S					M	Q		I		D				J	R	O
L	S	U				Y			R	D	K	B	X			N		J	Q	C	A	M			
		O	W			U	J			F	I				H	B	M	V	K			Q	S		
J	C							S				U	Y			F		R	L			N	F		
M		N				T			O	J	W					F		R	L						
B	W	F			X	J			U		M	Z				I		G					T		
	K			L		T		H	Y		D					N	U		G						
	V	I		G			B			Q			S	L			M		O		D				
O	E			Y		I	M			V			B			F									
D	Q		N	Z	O	K		F	A	I	H			S		W		X							
C	H		I		W	O		G		F	R					Z	Q								
	I	K			F	B		U	Y	D	C	O		E	G	R									
F	O	E	Q	K	C		L	D		G	T		X	S	B	N		Y	V						
	R	Z	J	Q	X	U	A	M		F	K				W		L								
T	V		N		Z	L		W	Y		M			C		I									
K	W	L		X	H	J	T		G	Q	I	O		S	C										
	M		T		N		Z	R		F			I	U											
I	Q	U		R	G	S		O			L	D	X												
	G	Y	W		I		U	J	K		X	Q													
H		M	C		D	Q	A		S	W		N	G	K											
	K	T	E	M	C	Y		L			D	N													
W	M	C		U	N		T				F	G													
U	N	B	D	X	Y	J		Z	E	M	O	H	V												
	E	X	V	F	I	Q	U	J	N	R	B	G		S	M	A									
Q	J	Z		S	G	O	X	V	I	E	C	U	W	L											

FILL EVERY ROW, COLUMN, AND 5X5 SECTOR, USING EACH GIVEN LETTER ONLY ONCE!

MAZE

FIND A STRAIGHT PATH THAT FOLLOWS THIS PATTERN: ▮▯▮▯▮ , HORIZONTAL OR VERTICAL (NEVER DIAGONAL!), FROM THE TOP CHEVRON TO THE CHEVRON AT THE BOTTOM OF THE GRID.

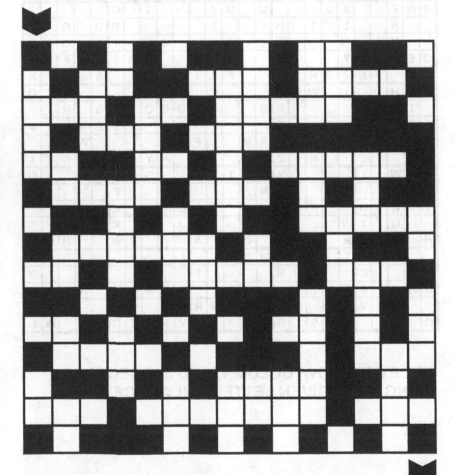

►► NAME IT

NAME 20 OF YOUR FAVORITE MUPPETS FROM <u>THE MUPPET SHOW</u> !

1. ANIMAL

WORDFILL

WHICH 4-LETTER COMBINATIONS ON THE LEFT DO YOU NEED TO COMPLETE THE 12-LETTER WORDS ON THE RIGHT?

LIGH	B	A	C	K					B	I	N	G
TOSA	D	E	S	A					T	I	O	N
NTAT	G	L	O	B					T	T	E	R
RTAI	B	R	O	N					U	R	U	S
MPLI	H	U	M	A					R	I	A	N
OSTE	E	X	H	I					T	I	O	N
LINA	M	O	O	N					T	I	N	G
ATIA	C	O	M	M					R	A	T	E
ETRO	O	S	T	E					I	O	U	S
LFUL	I	N	G	R					T	I	N	G
AMMA	A	C	C	O					S	H	E	D
STAB	S	T	O	N					L	I	N	G
EWAL	E	N	T	E					N	I	N	G
LARA	S	K	I	L					N	E	S	S
ENSU	I	N	F	L					T	I	O	N
NITA	P	R	E	P					R	O	U	S

▶ TRIVIA

FAMOUS PEOPLE FROM THE PAST.

1.

1792 ▶ Began experimenting with gas lighting as a replacement for oil and tallow-produced light.

2.

1804 ▶ Ordered the genocide of all French people in Haiti.

3.

1817 ▶ Successfully defended himself in a London court for the publication of his political satires.

4.

1838 ▶ Began his second term as Head of State in Costa Rica.

5.

1851 ▶ Conducted the premiere of his "Symphony No. 3" in Düsseldorf.

6.

1862 ▶ Observed white dwarf star "Sirius B" for the first time from a Northwestern University telescope.

7.

1876 ▶ Produced the first kosen-ga prints employing Western-style naturalistic light and shade.

8.

1924 ▶ His <u>Planck's Law and the Hypothesis of Light Quanta</u> is translated to German and published by Albert Einstein.

DEFINITION SEARCH

```
P R E C E S S L O V B E N T O L L
H R E F J Q U E M N K A X I H B E
X O N B L W N L S U N K B C P I N
S D T K O I R T R I R O U E B N T
D E R Q P R I V K R G O O A D G I
N O E S J L D N L O V K L V E K G
G S P A V D D E N A K L H Y C E O
M A R K E T L G R D Y A D R M N V
K Q E K E G E X W S P U E P E O S
A N N U L A R P D E G R I O N U F
U I E S S M J E U M U F E C C M O
A B U E U T T K W T T R S K O E N
S I R U R L E M P O S T E K I N D
S P I P A Y K A M E S J R D N O U
E M A M L X C L S W D A G D O N E
T S L E I W I J J E Q B J C O P T
E H S K C V R N Q O S N M N W J T
```

- In bed.
- Ring-shaped.
- Income-generating resource.
- Avow.
- Stooped.
- Heap.
- Captor.
- Currency.
- Native egyptian.
- Finished.
- Pair.
- Anguillidae.
- Enterprising.
- Melted cheese.
- Tattooed.
- Lotto game.
- Compassionate.
- Crazy person.
- Freckle.
- Made into malt.
- Mart.
- Inoperative (2 words).
- In itself.
- Command.
- Pustule.
- Mail.
- Precede.
- Do again.
- Iranian coin.
- Cattle roundups.
- Gone under.
- Curricula.
- Flirts.
- Price.
- Solve.
- NE European languages.
- Deplete (2 words).

NUTRITION FACTS

WHICH VITAMIN DOES THAT?

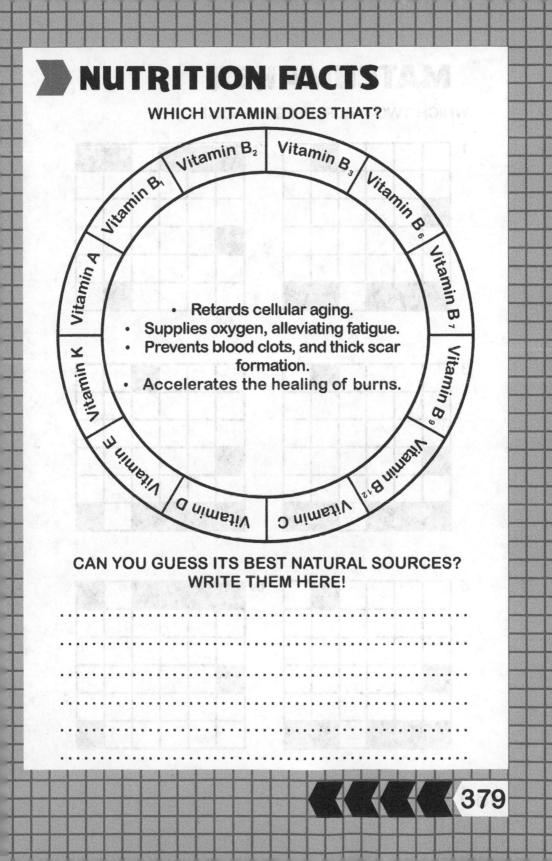

Vitamin B_2 · Vitamin B_3 · Vitamin B_6 · Vitamin B_7 · Vitamin B_9 · Vitamin B_{12} · Vitamin C · Vitamin D · Vitamin E · Vitamin K · Vitamin A · Vitamin B_1

- Retards cellular aging.
- Supplies oxygen, alleviating fatigue.
- Prevents blood clots, and thick scar formation.
- Accelerates the healing of burns.

CAN YOU GUESS ITS BEST NATURAL SOURCES? WRITE THEM HERE!

....

....

....

....

....

....

►MATCHMAKER

WHICH TWO ARE PERFECTLY ALIKE?

1.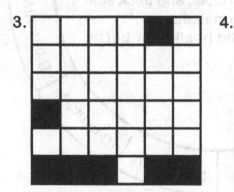

2.

3.

4.

5.

6.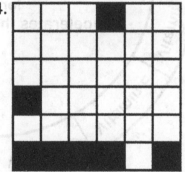

CRISSCROSS

ACROSS:
1. Cookware.
7. Bldg. extension.
9. Excitement (2 w.).
12. Large deer.
13. Fact-finding.
17. Ensign (abbr.).
18. Print heading (2 w.).
20. Eyebath.
22. Summer cooler (2 w.).
23. Sweetheart (2 w.).
29. Dynamite.
30. "Can you—it?"
32. Bug.
34. Aviation Administration (abbr.).
35. Ukelele.
36. Departure
37. Apply gently.
38. Absolutely.

DOWN:
1. Fragrant resin.
2. Listen in.
3. Cobra.
4. "Dig in!"
5. Watchtower Society (abbr.).
6. Breed.
8. 100 Albanian qintars.
10. Rules.
11. Starvation
14. Savings (2 words).
15. Ground cover.
16. Required.
19. Horned.
21. Uziel Gal's creation.
24. Unacceptable (2 w.).
25. Forays.
26. Automatic (abbr.).
27. Cost to cross.
28. Stupid man.
31. 34th POTUS (nickname).
33. Bar (UK).
34. Elfin.

```
L O R D V E R I S O P H T U X J O M T C P
J O N A S C H U Z Z L E W I T N B Z X L H
N A T H A N I E L W I N K L E P F G L A I
A N C A B X E H O B I L L S I K E S O R L
G U J O S I A H B O U N D E R B Y H U A I
N R P Y B D I C K S W I V E L L E R I P P
E I H B P M B R A S S S A M P S O N S E P
S A N J T A A T O M P I N C H I G I A G I
W H R I C H A R D C A R S T O N E S G G R
I H Q S A M U E L P I C K W I C K U R O R
C E D S T D A N I E L Q U I L P Q S A T I
K E M R J D L K F K Y B E S L R L A D T P
F P B E T S Y T R O T W O O D R N N G Y A
I G L C A L E B P L U M M E R V G N R N U
E B E N E Z E R S C R O O G E K C I I V L
L W I L L I A M D O R R I T L Y Y P N W D
D N E V I L L E L A N D L E S S J P D C O
D A V I D C O P P E R F I E L D I E C W M
J A C K D A W K I N S K R G B C G R P Z B
O L I V E R T W I S T T I N Y T I M O J E
A R T H U R C L E N H A M Y D O R R I T Y
```

FIND 30 CHARACTERS CREATED BY CHARLES DICKENS. CAN YOU THINK OF ANY OTHERS?

WORDOKU

	C	J	T			Z				S	Y		V		I	H		L	N					D
	L	G	D				O	T	I	B			E			U		F				H		
	K	B	W			G	P			Z		L	E	A			I					V		
	Q	O	U		I		E	H				T		P			S		J	G	A	X		B
				N		Q	L		A	G	X						K			Y		M		
A	I	V	M	L	C	T	J			D				H	Q	F			P				S	
				W	M		X		K		T				L		A	D	J			Q		
	Y				A			C					X		B	O	E	I						Z
		G	E		F	Y			Z		M			N		P			W			A	C	
	S				L		B		E	J	W	A					Z		T					
C	V			Y			N					D	P	F	I			Z					M	
M		U	I	O	Z	H				J	N	P	S				K	C	X	Q	A			
	A	Z	Y				M				H		X			Q				F	W	U		
	F	Q	S	X	P					V	I	L	G					Z	B	H	C	T		N
W			N			U	S	I	Q					H			T					B	K	
			N			X				Y	C	M	I		D		Q					P		
I	W			B			H		G			D		J		O	Y		Q	K				
H			Z	M	L	Q		K			P					B					G			
	Y		L	F	B		P			A		Q		U		V	T							
	G			Q				Y	D	S				T		A	F	H	C	M	I	X	L	
	F		C		M					J	G	B		K	E		S							
G		W	S	J	T		B			C		L				V	Y		N		O	U	D	
	Z			D			J	H	M		N					U	Q			V		S	T	
	B			Q		F			W			I	O	A	T					L	K	N		
O			V	U		Z	D			A		E	K					X			M	G	C	

FILL EVERY ROW, COLUMN, AND 5X5 SECTOR, USING EACH GIVEN LETTER ONLY ONCE!

MAZE

FIND A STRAIGHT PATH THAT FOLLOWS THIS PATTERN: ■□■□■ , HORIZONTAL OR VERTICAL (NEVER DIAGONAL!), FROM THE TOP CHEVRON TO THE CHEVRON AT THE BOTTOM OF THE GRID.

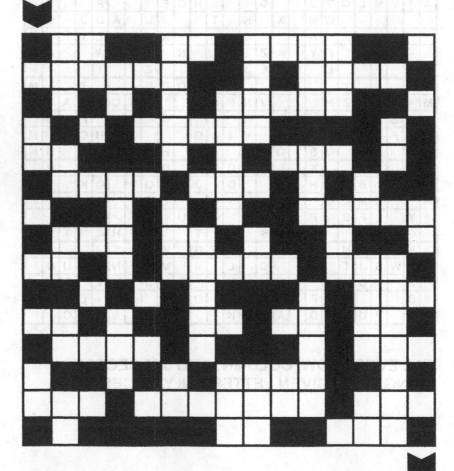

NAME IT

NAME 20 OF YOUR FAVORITE BOOKS BY PEARL BUCK.

1. THE GOOD EARTH

WHICH 4-LETTER COMBINATIONS ON THE LEFT DO YOU NEED TO COMPLETE THE 12-LETTER WORDS ON THE RIGHT?

ERGA	A	S	C	E					N	I	N	G
EHEN	T	H	U	N					T	O	R	M
TIFI	A	N	A	G					A	T	I	C
IFAC	K	I	N	D					R	T	E	N
INAC	O	V	E	R					E	V	E	R
DERS	A	C	A	D					A	L	L	Y
WOOD	P	E	T	R					T	I	O	N
NIST	F	E	M	I					T	I	O	N
RTAI	A	P	P	R					S	I	O	N
LERA	P	E	R	T					I	O	U	S
ACHI	A	C	C	E					T	I	N	G
ONSC	P	R	O	T					A	N	C	E
RAMM	I	D	E	N					A	B	L	E
UBER	B	A	C	K					S	M	A	N
NIZA	A	D	M	I					R	A	T	E
EMIC	S	U	B	C					I	O	U	S

FAMOUS PEOPLE FROM THE PAST.

1.

1889 ▶ Played first-class cricket for Lancashire as a fast bowler until 1901.

2.

1901 ▶ Released from prison after serving eighteen years for cannibalism.

3.

1925 ▶ Selected to teach a master class at the Städelschule Academy of Fine Art in Frankfurt.

4.

1951 ▶ Began to work with famous pin-up model Betty Page on a series of mail-order photographs.

5.

1956 ▶ Won the Pulitzer Prize for his 1955 interview of Nikita Khrushchev, premier of the USSR.

6.

1963 ▶ Reaches an altitude of 65.8 miles aboard an X-15 aircraft, making it a sub-orbital spaceflight by international standards.

7.

1978 ▶ Designed his own custom hardware and development tools in order to create the <u>Space Invaders</u> video game.

8.

1980 ▶ Redesigned Flash Gordon's rocket-cycle for that character's movie.

DEFINITION SEARCH

```
B N P X X K P E R S E P H O N E Q
L D I S X N E E N D O R S E D D A
S I X Z C Q H N W T E F M G E L Y
G C F W K S I M S L F B Q T F B D
U U G X A R E E D U H I N T R E Y
M D N W A É T U D E A E U S S L N
O I M P A I R E D N M N N I D R A
K S E D L X J E O E S E T R X A M
C H C C V A Z D S H S A M C N I
G E U D A U Y S D C A W L I X A T
W S X U O N G O T H P P P H Y F E
C I N M S D L I C U E F I H V H R
Z N E T I Y K B U L L I N L X P M
J X S T O N Y A P Z I A I I A A L
T U X J T A I E P L E T S G O R U
O V U I P M P O Y O R S T O W S X
A R E B L O B N N S K Z S U C F E
```

- Gnostic divine power.
- Mountaineers.
- Censured.
- Cuplike.
- Disturbed.
- Parabolic antennas.
- No good (UK).
- Revolutionary.
- Coil generator.
- Congers.
- Sponsored.
- Consequent.
- Bar by estoppel.
- Short solo composition.
- Edicts.
- 3ʳᵈ century Teutonic invader.
- Shootout.
- Lipo-Hepin.
- Diminished.
- Ceiba tree.
- Cookhouses.
- Suggestion to depart (2 w.).
- De—.
- Subordinate.
- Polyamide material.
- Equalities.
- Proserpina.
- Itches (Spanish).
- Hemingway's boat.
- Major Walter—, MD.
- Charles M.—.
- More bosomy.
- Obdurate.
- Packs.
- Establishment.
- From a lower to a higher position.
- Laundryman.

NUTRITION FACTS

WHICH VITAMIN DOES THAT?

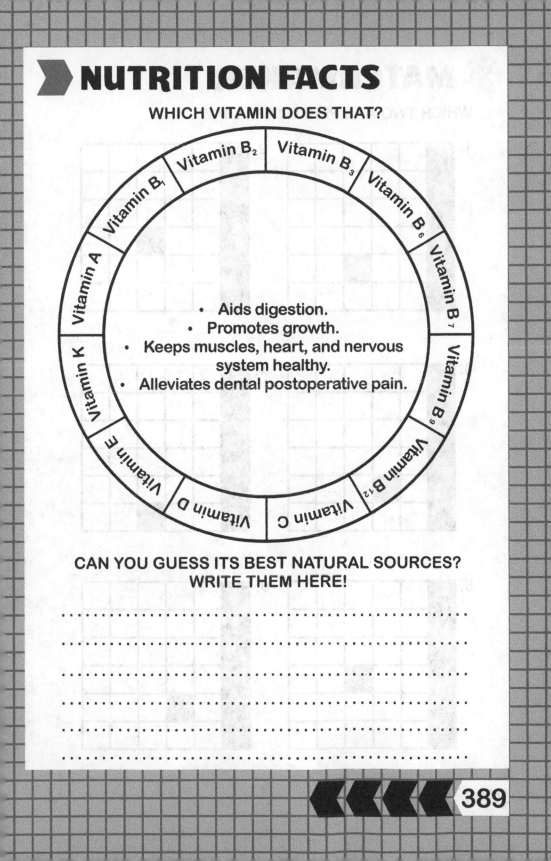

Vitamin B₂ · Vitamin B₃ · Vitamin B₆ · Vitamin B₇ · Vitamin B₉ · Vitamin B₁₂ · Vitamin C · Vitamin D · Vitamin E · Vitamin K · Vitamin A · Vitamin B₁

- Aids digestion.
- Promotes growth.
- Keeps muscles, heart, and nervous system healthy.
- Alleviates dental postoperative pain.

CAN YOU GUESS ITS BEST NATURAL SOURCES?
WRITE THEM HERE!

....

....

....

....

....

....

▶ MATCHMAKER

WHICH TWO ARE PERFECTLY ALIKE?

1.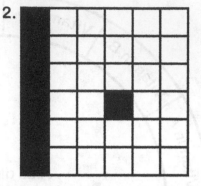

2.

3.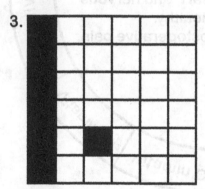

4.

5.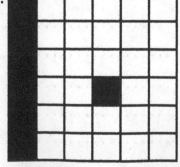

6.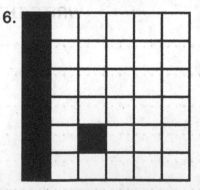

CRISSCROSS

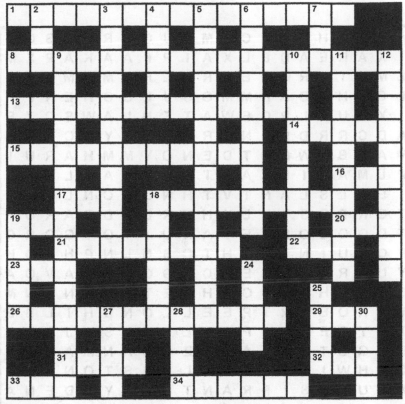

ACROSS:

1. Headaches relief.
8. Impossible to complete (nonexistent compound word).
13. Regrettable.
14. Half denier.
15. Collared lizard (Latin).
16. Low-grade wool.
17. Huang He river tributary.
18. Fovea-like.
19. —Guevara.
20. "I mean it" (abbr.).
21. 1-yr.-old bird (archaic).
22. Saint (Spanish).
23. "—por cual" (Spanish).
26. Alhambra style.
29. Key Largo, FL, airport (abbr.).
31. Steam boiler reinforcement.
32. Robust energy.
33. Quantity of money.
34. Downhill ski run.

DOWN:

2. Not a number (abbr.).
3. Cementing process.
4. Urticaceae plants.
5. Constrictiveness (archaic).
6. Albinism-related.
7. Auberge.
9. UK adherence (nonexistent compound word).
10. —of Córdoba
11. Ergot alkaloid.
12. Eglantine.
18. Healthier.
19. Etruscan goddess.
24. Drawn tight.
25. Like in (Slovak).
27. Gray plaid.
28. Nestling hawk .
30. Glowing solution (abbr.).

WORDSEARCH

```
W S D A H H E G C O M W J G H R Z J S Q F
I X A R E A D E L X A I P F A A K A P X M
L M V T R R W O E U R N L H R M N M E A P
L C I H B O A R M M G S J E O S H E N F N
I X D U E L R G E W A T F N L A W S C Z E
A D C R R D D E N R R O J R D Y Y C E S V
M A A B T W H C T D E N O Y M M H A R U I
P L M A A I E A A N T C H A A A E L P O L
I E E L S L A N T V T H N D C C N L E G L
T C R F Q S T N L X H U R D M D R A R O E
T D O O U O H I E T A R U I I O Y G C R C
P O N U I N T N E H T C S N L N P H E D H
Y U N R T A N G E E C H S G L A E A V O A
Q G D Y H R S U G R H I E T A L L N A N M
M L R O B E R T P E E L L O N D H I L B B
T A Y Q E L F W P S R L L N V S A J I R E
D S G U T G A L A A V Z J O H N M A J O R
Q H H W I L L I A M G L A D S T O N E W L
X O U V N S I F R A N T H O N Y E D E N A
B M P S T A N L E Y B A L D W I N E T J I
B E N J A M I N D I S R A E L I A R C T N
```

FIND 28 BRITISH PRIME MINISTERS. CAN YOU THINK OF ANY OTHERS?

. . . .
. . . .
. . . .
. . . .
. . . .
. . . .
. . . .
. . . .
. . . .
. . . .
. . . .

WORDOKU

			L				O		V	W	I			B					R	U	H	J	A	G
X			H		P	T		E	F		Q	L		A	W		S					V	C	N
	N			Q		H						P	F		X	D			A	K			L	S
V	K		D	G				Q	A	C		S				N	J			Z		T	W	B
			W	E	K		L	S		V					P			C	T				F	I
	B				S	A		H	L	F			V	E			N		U			P		
		O								D					A	Q		E		R		U		
	A	V				Z			N	X			P	Q	G	L		I	K		W		S	
C					X		D	I				O		Z			F	H	M		N	A	V	
U	S	E					G			B								J	V	Q	I	F		Z
B	H	C			U	M					A	T	I								K			L
	I	N	M	K			S	Z	W			U	L	F		E		T		A				P
		X		D		O					S		M					N		B		I		
S				J		R		X		K	Z	E			C	H	M			G	Q	W	N	
W			Z								B	H	X					Q	D			C	M	U
P		R	F	V	D	G								J			E					B	Q	M
	W	T	S		L	U	C			A		B				R	Z		H					V
	J		E		V	B		R	M	I	D			O	L			K				N	P	
		Z		A		K		J	P					L								O		
		U			Z		I			M	P			N	V	X		S	J				H	
N	M				O	S			C					H		F	B		I	P	V			
Q	O	H		Z			A	G				I		X	T	S				N	B		U	C
A	F			U	H			W	E		N	K						X		M			O	
I	E	D					X		Z	U		W	A		N	O		G	C		F			J
K	G	S	B	X	N					P			T	C	E		L				A			

FILL EVERY ROW, COLUMN, AND 5X5 SECTOR, USING EACH GIVEN LETTER ONLY ONCE!

MAZE

FIND A STRAIGHT PATH THAT FOLLOWS THIS PATTERN: ▮▯▮▯▮ , HORIZONTAL OR VERTICAL (NEVER DIAGONAL!), FROM THE TOP CHEVRON TO THE CHEVRON AT THE BOTTOM OF THE GRID.

▶NAME IT
NAME YOUR 20 FAVORITE JAMES BOND VILLAINS.

1. LE CHIFFRE

WHICH 4-LETTER COMBINATIONS ON THE LEFT DO YOU NEED TO COMPLETE THE 12-LETTER WORDS ON THE RIGHT?

ENTA	C	A	R	B					R	A	T	E
OPOL	O	R	T	H					T	I	C	S
AVAG	C	A	N	C					T	I	O	N
UIST	B	U	T	T					O	T	C	H
RTEN	F	E	R	M					T	I	O	N
ERSC	E	N	T	E					S	I	N	G
UMCI	C	O	S	M					I	T	A	N
UMST	W	I	T	H					D	I	N	G
STIA	E	X	T	R					A	N	Z	A
STAN	A	D	A	P					L	I	T	Y
ODON	C	O	N	Q					A	D	O	R
RVES	E	F	F	E					C	E	N	T
ELLA	C	H	R	I					N	I	T	Y
TABI	H	Y	P	E					S	I	O	N
RPRI	C	I	R	C					A	N	C	E
OHYD	C	I	R	C					S	I	O	N

▶ TRIVIA

FAMOUS PEOPLE FROM THE PAST.

1.

1875 ❯ Born in Arles, France, she went on to become the world's oldest person ever (122 years and 164 days).

2.

1887 ❯ Defended Pasteur's anti-rabies treatment in the in the Académie Nationale de Médecine.

3.

1893 ❯ His Symphony No. 9, "From the New World," premieres at Carnegie Hall in New York City.

4.

1902 ❯ Created The Failures of Kidoro Haikara for the magazine Jiji Manga.

5.

1906 ❯ Put on a train to Colton, California, by William Randolph Hearst to recover from tuberculosis.

6.

1913 ❯ His Fantomas five-episode movie serial was released in France to wide acclaim.

7.

1925 ❯ Sent one last telegram to his wife before disappearing in the Amazon jungle.

8.

1929 ❯ Piloted the world's first purpose-built rocket-powered aircraft in Frankfurt.

DEFINITION SEARCH

```
V D Z R I S M W G M H P L E A Q W
C U Y R M M T S N C R A E E T D B
R O I O O M L T N O D V C P E I L
F U M N Q I A E Z D P I L P P R G
H O R M S P E E D I N G P G H E C
E A O A U U X N L O G I Z A F C R
R P B W L N R S A S U E F U X U E
M P I A A I I R I Q T I K E V R S
E A N I N E Z T E D B R A C E R O
N L S T D E H E Y C E O O Z H E L
E A S T I R R E R S T A M M L N E
U C Q D P D R A P B E I R U F T D
T H O C L O T H C A P R O M S L U
I I S M O G G Y T C L P V N I Y E
C A L L W Y Q S P C M T F I A L T
S N Q M O M E N T A R Y R F C R O
V K R O I L P O U R E D L Y K E Y
```

- Vial.
- Mountain range.
- Wait for.
- Berry (Latin).
- Ocimum basilicum (plural).
- Mexican laborer.
- Long-distance—.
- Flat cap.
- Social work (2 w.).
- Methyl-phenol.
- Motherless calf.
- "Because of" (2 w.).
- Exegesis branch.
- Revolutionary.
- Acres.
- "For fear that."
- Vortex.
- —Manara.
- Fleeting.
- Postponed (2 words).
- Meager.
- Capsicum.
- Supplication.
- Turn over earth.
- Rained buckets.
- Promenades.
- Repeatedly.
- Flushed.
- Refurnished.
- Thrushes.
- Churn.
- Rusticate.
- Handgun.
- Polluted.
- Accelerating.
- Agitator (Australia).
- Adolescents.
- Cuban dance.

NUTRITION FACTS

WHICH VITAMIN DOES THAT?

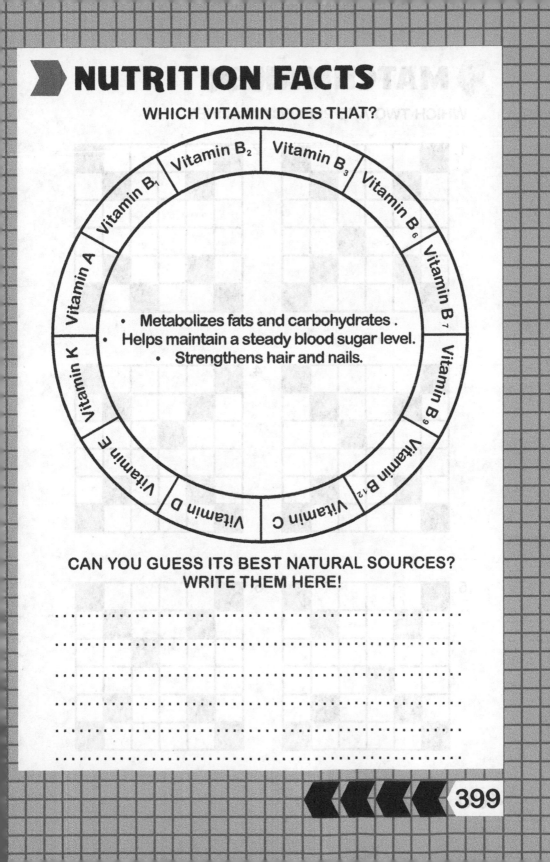

Vitamin B₁ Vitamin B₂ Vitamin B₃ Vitamin B₆ Vitamin B₇ Vitamin B₉ Vitamin B₁₂ Vitamin C Vitamin D Vitamin E Vitamin K Vitamin A

- Metabolizes fats and carbohydrates .
- Helps maintain a steady blood sugar level.
- Strengthens hair and nails.

CAN YOU GUESS ITS BEST NATURAL SOURCES?
WRITE THEM HERE!

....

....

....

....

....

....

► MATCHMAKER

WHICH TWO ARE PERFECTLY ALIKE?

1.

2.

3.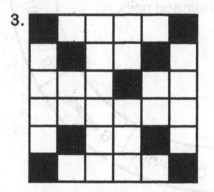

4.

5.

6.

LETTERCROSS

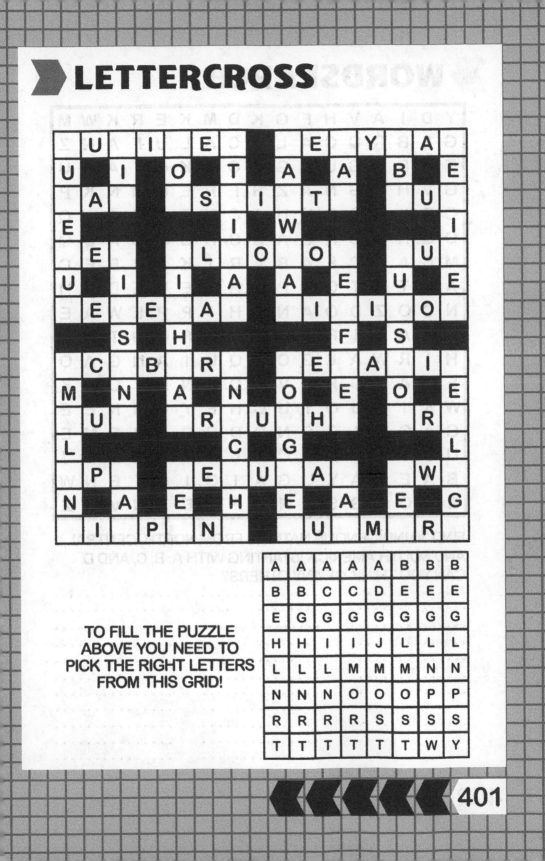

TO FILL THE PUZZLE
ABOVE YOU NEED TO
PICK THE RIGHT LETTERS
FROM THIS GRID!

A	A	A	A	A	B	B	B
B	B	C	C	D	E	E	E
E	G	G	G	G	G	G	G
H	H	I	I	J	L	L	L
L	L	L	M	M	M	N	N
N	N	N	O	O	O	P	P
R	R	R	R	S	S	S	S
T	T	T	T	T	W	Y	

```
Y D I A V H F G K D M K E R K W M
G F B R Q C A L A C A L U F A N Z
T N E A G U R G T C X K O Y A O U
G V H P G N A Z H F R E O H N K P
C R X A S P U U A C H O C T A W Q
O Q H H G R C A B C H B W C A D Q
M C A O C E A B A R I K A R E E C
A N T E T Q N P S H S E U E D L H
N C O Z D O A N C H I P P E W A E
C H A A I R B L A C K F O O T W R
H I R W A L G O N Q U I A N G A O
E C A M G P K V Z O V N H I O R K
W K I U U O I U C H E Y E N N E E
G A G U I Z S N D D C O F R E M E
U S Y M T N B C A L A M A R I B J
B A E C A Y U G A I G I C T E N W
Z W O F G S H R D P I E Z U V S Z
```

FIND 30 INDIGENOUS NATIONS FROM NORTH, CENTRAL, AND SOUTH AMERICA, STARTING WITH A, B, C, AND D. CAN YOU THINK OF ANY OTHERS?

....
....
....
....
....
....
....
....
....
....

SILHOUETTES

IDENTIFY THE CITY AND COUNTRY WHERE EACH LANDMARK IS LOCATED.

1. ....

2. ....

3. ....

4. ....

5. ....

6. ....

 # MAZE

FIND A STRAIGHT PATH THAT FOLLOWS THIS PATTERN: ■■□■□■ , HORIZONTAL OR VERTICAL (NEVER DIAGONAL!), FROM THE TOP CHEVRON TO THE CHEVRON AT THE BOTTOM OF THE GRID.

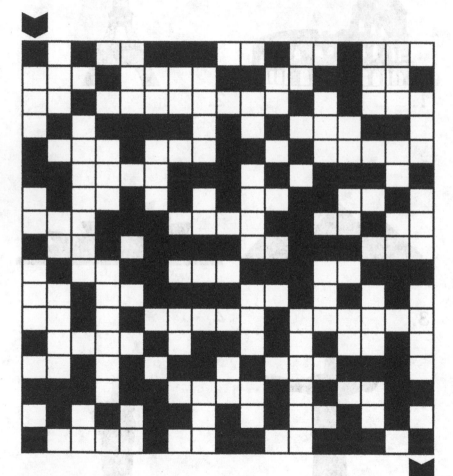

▶ NAME IT

NAME 20 OF YOUR FAVORITE DICK TRACY VILLAINS.

1. BIG BOY

WORDFILL

WHICH 5-LETTER COMBINATIONS ON THE LEFT DO YOU NEED TO COMPLETE THE 15-LETTER WORDS ON THE RIGHT?

TIFIC	P	R	O	C	R						A	T	I	O	N
CANIZ	P	E	R	S	O						A	T	I	O	N
BETIZ	C	H	A	R	A						S	T	I	C	S
POSSE	D	E	S	E	R						A	T	I	O	N
NIFIC	P	U	L	C	H						I	N	O	U	S
MATIZ	A	M	E	R	I						A	T	I	O	N
INOVE	A	B	D	O	M						S	I	C	A	L
LEDGE	C	O	N	G	R						T	I	O	N	S
CTERI	T	H	E	R	M						I	S	T	R	Y
PLISH	A	L	P	H	A						A	T	I	O	N
OCHEM	I	N	T	E	R						D	E	N	C	E
ENULT	A	C	C	O	M						M	E	N	T	S
DEPEN	U	N	P	R	E						S	S	I	N	G
ASTIN	A	C	K	N	O						M	E	N	T	S
ATULA	A	N	T	E	P						I	M	A	T	E
RITUD	A	C	C	L	I						A	T	I	O	N

▶ TRIVIA

FAMOUS PEOPLE FROM THE PAST.

1.
....

1407 ▶ Led a revolt against Bishop Georg von Liechtenstein in Trento, Italy.

2.
....

1576 ▶ Liberated Fray Luis de Leon, who was imprisoned for publishing a translation of the "Song of Solomon."

3.
....

1631 ▶ A Swiss painter, draftsman, and woodcut printmaker, he died penniless at age 73.

4.
....

1782 ▶ Published <u>Saggio sulla Storia Naturale del Chili</u> in Spain, the first account of the natural history of his native Chile.

5.
....

1874 ▶ The first man of African descent to receive a PhD, he was inaugurated as president of Georgetown University.

6.
....

1900 ▶ Took part in Baron Eduard Toll's Russian Polar Expedition aboard the ship Zarya.

7.
....

1910 ▶ Starred as the monster in the first horror film in history: <u>Frankenstein</u>.

8.
....

1932 ▶ Wrote <u>The Sign of the Cross</u> film screenplay for Cecil B. DeMille.

⏵ UNSCRAMBLE

ACROSS:
1. NESIAMAC
5. MOCAREYS
8. WOT
9. DANTMOR
10. NED
12. RON
13. POSHAMO
15. PAT
16. SEPHA
17. CHERT
19. XINDE
21. BAMAS
24. KIN

25. FULMIND
26. RAC
27. EGE
28. PEMTILY
30. WEY
31. FLATUSFA
32. ENTIMIES

DOWN:
2. ETRIGOP
3. SIM
4. RAFAREC
5. CAMPERS
6. TUC
7. MUTHBAD
8. ENETT
11. CHATN
13. ARSDOMT
14. TIMALPO
18. WGINS
19. KWELLNI
20. USPONEX

21. ICEFFUS
22. LYSTANA
23. WACAM
28. ATE
29. MAY

NUTRITION FACTS

WHICH MINERAL DOES THAT?

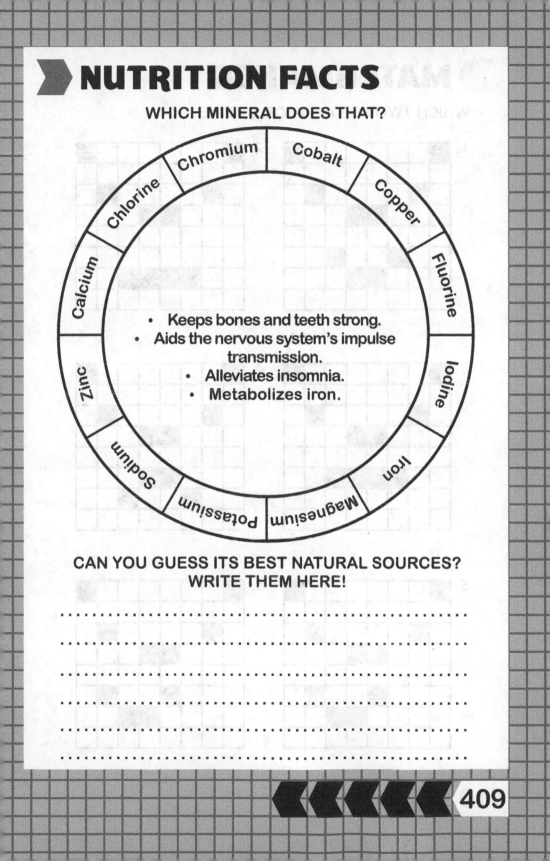

Chromium

Cobalt

Copper

Chlorine

Fluorine

Calcium

Iodine

Zinc

Iron

Sodium

Magnesium

Potassium

- Keeps bones and teeth strong.
- Aids the nervous system's impulse transmission.
- Alleviates insomnia.
- Metabolizes iron.

CAN YOU GUESS ITS BEST NATURAL SOURCES?
WRITE THEM HERE!

....
....
....
....
....
....

MATCHMAKER

WHICH TWO ARE PERFECTLY ALIKE?

1.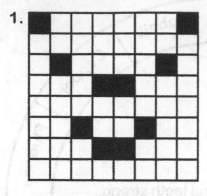

2.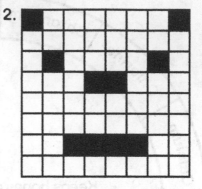

3.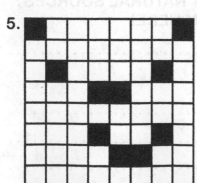

4.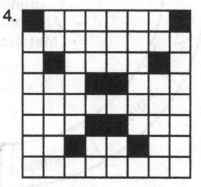

5.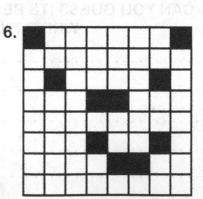

6.

LETTERCROSS

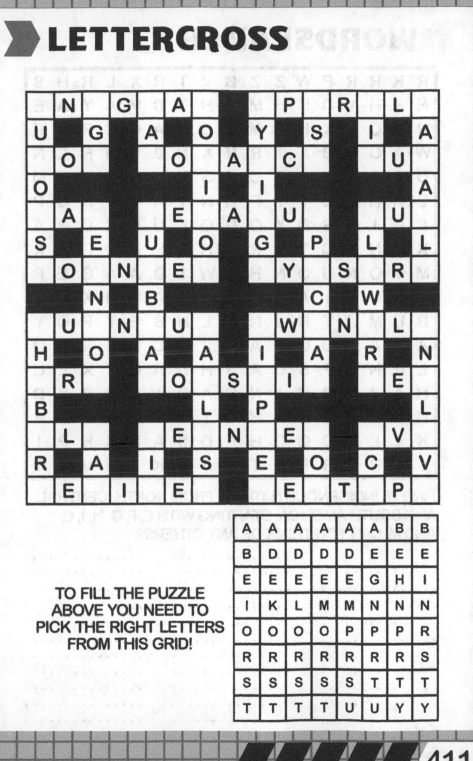

TO FILL THE PUZZLE
ABOVE YOU NEED TO
PICK THE RIGHT LETTERS
FROM THIS GRID!

WORDSEARCH

```
R K R R P W Z Z B V T R X L R H S
N X H Y D H H M C H T C M A Y A E
R R O I X K U M I C M A C C R I F
W A O K B X I R R X H J S H R L N
U F C P M I C C O S U K E E L E M
B H H E E T T F Q N I H L L H U P
F H I N S O X O U Q L U E K D R A
K X N G Q T F P O H L P N D G U X
M M O N U O N H I W I D A A G E P
H G U Y I A S U S M C A P N X H Z
B U M J T N J N F L H S E T P Q Y
A A A A O O C A T J E L N B R G O
L R N R P S U A J H D A O T X L U
H A J S P U I N G A R I K O D Y D
U N E F L E C H E I R O B L D O R
K I L N O G G H P D S A P C H P I
I V R I R F S T E A U K L O V F Q
```

FIND 28 INDIGENOUS NATIONS FROM NORTH, CENTRAL, AND SOUTH AMERICA, STARTING WITH E, F, G, H, I, L, AND M. CAN YOU THINK OF ANY OTHERS?

....
....
....
....
....
....
....
....

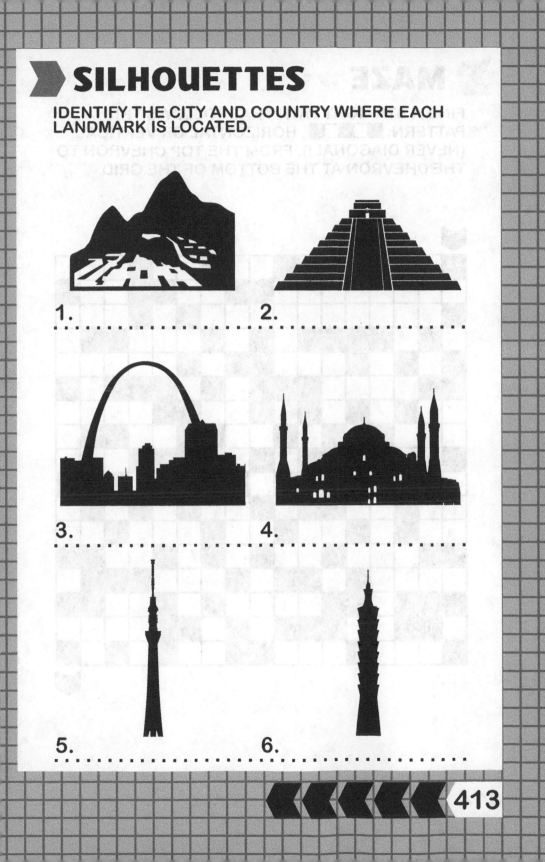

SILHOUETTES

IDENTIFY THE CITY AND COUNTRY WHERE EACH LANDMARK IS LOCATED.

1.

2.

3.

4.

5.

6.

▶ MAZE

FIND A STRAIGHT PATH THAT FOLLOWS THIS PATTERN: ■□■■□■ , HORIZONTAL OR VERTICAL (NEVER DIAGONAL!), FROM THE TOP CHEVRON TO THE CHEVRON AT THE BOTTOM OF THE GRID.

NAME IT
NAME 20 OF YOUR FAVORITE BATMAN VILLAINS.

1. ANARKY

▶ WORDFILL

WHICH 5-LETTER COMBINATIONS ON THE LEFT DO YOU NEED TO COMPLETE THE 15-LETTER WORDS ON THE RIGHT?

AMENT	T	R	U	S	T					I	N	E	S	S
ISSEU	M	I	S	A	P					N	S	I	O	N
NALIZ	N	A	T	I	O					A	T	I	O	N
OAGUL	I	N	S	U	B					A	T	I	O	N
TURIZ	K	I	N	D	H					D	N	E	S	S
SITIV	C	O	N	N	O					R	S	H	I	P
ALLIZ	E	X	C	O	M					A	T	I	O	N
NALIZ	M	I	N	I	A					A	T	I	O	N
WORTH	P	R	O	C	R					A	T	I	N	G
PREHE	M	E	D	I	C					A	T	I	O	N
ORDIN	C	O	N	F	I					A	L	I	T	Y
PRECI	A	C	Q	U	I					E	N	E	S	S
EARTE	I	N	T	E	R					A	T	I	O	N
ASTIN	M	I	S	A	P					A	T	I	O	N
DENTI	A	N	T	I	C					A	T	I	O	N
MUNIC	C	R	Y	S	T					A	T	I	O	N

TRIVIA

FAMOUS PEOPLE FROM THE PAST.

1.

1932 ▶ Failed to assassinate Emperor Hirohito of Japan with a hand grenade.

2.

1935 ▶ Under the direction of Wallace Carothers, he synthesized Nylon for the first time.

3.

1938 ▶ Gave the world's first public demonstration of a color television broadcast in London.

4.

1942 ▶ Escaped prison camp in Mauzac, and was later awarded the Military Cross.

5.

1947 ▶ Became the first pilot confirmed to have exceeded the speed of sound in level flight.

6.

1951 ▶ Began to illustrate the <u>Cisco Kid</u> newspaper comic strip for King Features.

7.

1956 ▶ Vanished during an MI6 reconnaissance diving mission around a Soviet cruiser.

8.

1960 ▶ As president of Cyprus, he survived four assassination attempts and a coup d'état.

► UNSCRAMBLE

ACROSS:

1. THUSANCA
5. RIDELOCH
8. OGH
9. ANSARCK
10. EAL
12. VAO
13. ESIAFRE
15. FOF
16. ESIMD
17. STOSC
19. BUICC
21. GERSD
24. BOS
25. TENAMAE
26. TIB
27. RAO
28. GYTULIR
30. VEE
31. THERICOL
32. BOOMARPD

DOWN:

2. GARDNIG
3. EHR
4. BENUSAM
5. SICSLAC
6. ELK
7. LONSLOR
8. HOYOE
11. FULAW
13. LEFRIBA
14. ASTEREU
18. MIOSG
19. RECABAT
20. CHETAPR
21. MAGRADI
22. ROBEZUS
23. THETI
28. EIL
29. PAY

NUTRITION FACTS

WHICH MINERAL DOES THAT?

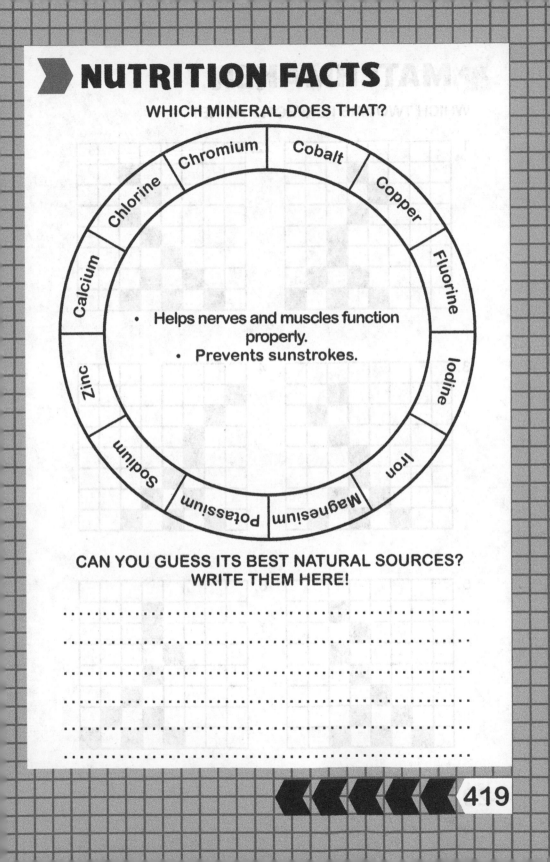

Chromium
Cobalt
Copper
Chlorine
Fluorine
Calcium
Iodine
Zinc
Iron
Sodium
Magnesium
Potassium

- Helps nerves and muscles function properly.
- Prevents sunstrokes.

CAN YOU GUESS ITS BEST NATURAL SOURCES? WRITE THEM HERE!

....

....

....

....

....

....

MATCHMAKER

WHICH TWO ARE PERFECTLY ALIKE?

1.

2.

3.

4.

5.

6.

LETTERCROSS

A	C	D		A	N		S	
A		I	N	A	T	O		A	Y
U			O	R	N			U	
V			R	P				C	
P			P	R	T		G		
S		R	A	N	N	C	M	P	
M		K	N		T	R	G		
	C	L			U	Z			
P		C	E		A	D	A		
E	S	N	E	Z	G	N	O		
	S		E	M	N		U		
L			R	R			F		
S			T	M	N		U		
N	E	E	T	N	I	H	S		
R	P	Z			I	L	S		

TO FILL THE PUZZLE
ABOVE YOU NEED TO
PICK THE RIGHT LETTERS
FROM THIS GRID!

A	A	A	A	A	A	A	A	A
A	A	A	C	C	C	D	E	
E	E	E	E	E	E	E	E	
E	G	G	G	I	I	I	I	
I	I	N	N	O	O	O		
P	P	R	R	R	R	S	S	
S	S	S	S	S	S	S	S	
S	S	S	T	T	T	T	T	

WORDSEARCH

```
X M Z X G Q F E J E O M N O S I Q
C K N Z N A E Q U S I O U X F R X
M U Y D Z N T Q M H S M E E U C O
H T L H W N L P Q A Q L V N W H N
G X W A I M I R I W O O Z O T T O
C H P T O L T E C N S N T O W G N
C S U L T P J W I E I W D T P B D
U T E I N T U M G E W N Z K A M A
D E L N X U E E M F A Y A A N W G
L H C G E S N Q B Y S A C C A Y A
S U H I X C C U W L H N O W R N A
C E E T S A A E X N O O L M E C Y
H L L L Z R P C A P S M K H Z A G
Y C B K T O S H H N H A A A Y W H
J H U R N R G U O K O M N H R D X
P E X Q P A T A G O N I A N A U H
A V I A Y F M G O N E I D A R H D
```

FIND 30 INDIGENOUS NATIONS FROM NORTH, CENTRAL, AND SOUTH AMERICA, STARTING WITH N, O, P, Q, S, T, W, AND Y. CAN YOU THINK OF ANY OTHERS?

....
....
....
....
....
....
....
....
....

SILHOUETTES

IDENTIFY THE CITY AND COUNTRY WHERE EACH LANDMARK IS LOCATED.

1.

2.

3.

4.

5.

6.

◢ MAZE

FIND A STRAIGHT PATH THAT FOLLOWS THIS PATTERN: ■□■■□■ , HORIZONTAL OR VERTICAL (NEVER DIAGONAL!), FROM THE TOP CHEVRON TO THE CHEVRON AT THE BOTTOM OF THE GRID.

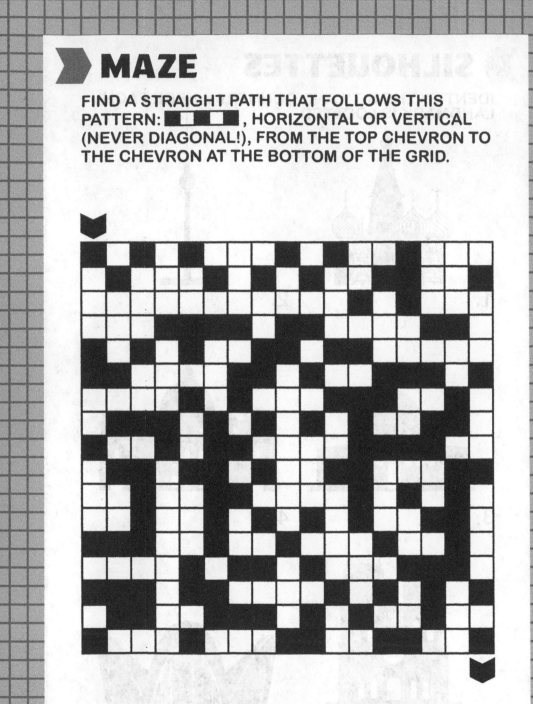

► NAME IT

NAME 20 OF YOUR FAVORITE TABLE GAMES.

1. BACKGAMMON

WORDFILL

WHICH 5-LETTER COMBINATIONS ON THE LEFT DO
YOU NEED TO COMPLETE THE 15-LETTER WORDS
ON THE RIGHT?

ITARI	E	X	P	E	R					A	T	I	O	N
NALIZ	A	C	C	O	M					I	N	G	L	Y
UMENT	E	L	E	C	T					A	T	I	O	N
OENTE	Z	I	N	J	A					P	U	S	E	S
UMINE	T	O	T	A	L					A	N	I	S	M
IMENT	I	N	A	C	C					I	L	I	T	Y
OEPHE	I	N	S	T	R					A	T	I	O	N
NTHRO	P	S	E	U	D					D	R	I	N	E
LARIZ	C	Y	C	L	O					P	R	I	N	E
DITIO	M	A	R	G	I					A	T	I	O	N
RIFIC	U	N	C	O	N					N	A	L	L	Y
MODAT	C	I	R	C	U					A	T	I	O	N
GANIZ	A	U	T	O	L					S	C	E	N	T
LECTU	G	A	S	T	R					R	I	T	I	S
BENZA	I	N	T	E	L					A	L	I	T	Y
ESSIB	D	I	S	O	R					A	T	I	O	N

▶TRIVIA

FAMOUS PEOPLE FROM THE PAST.

1.

1421 ▶ Received an imperial order to bring letters, silk products, and other gifts to various rulers around the Indian Ocean.

2.

1518 ▶ Published <u>A New Skill Book</u>, the first German bookkeeping manual.

3.

1615 ▶ Imposed a year's imprisonment for publishing Bibles without including the Apocrypha.

4.

1729 ▶ Painted portraits of Prince Charles Edward Stuart and his brother, Prince Henry.

5.

1830 ▶ His <u>Symphonie fantastique</u> had its world premiere in Paris.

6.

1946 ▶ Introduced a two-piece swimsuit design, which he named "Bikini."

7.

1966 ▶ Published the first explicitly erotic comics (<u>Goldrake</u>, <u>Messalina</u>, and <u>Isabella</u>).

8.

1978 ▶ Moved to Amsterdam to play bass guitar for a number of salsa and jazz bands until his return to Uruguay in 1984.

UNSCRAMBLE

ACROSS:

1. CITECLIP
5. BOLDENME
8. OWE
9. LEGARLY
10. BIF
12. OFE
13. GROINUP
15. YCI
16. FEFAG
17. RAGPH
19. SIFIN
21. REELD
24. ALE
25. TRUGHOY
26. XEV
27. PYA
28. TICASPE
30. DEO
31. RINECLAT
32. REERTAIN

DOWN:

2. BERGEIC
3. GUT
4. GOLONEC
5. LONGERE
6. UYB
7. FETISHL
8. WEFAR
11. YOUBA
13. IFANCYN
14. DIPLUTA
18. LIHLY
19. FERPLAP
20. MENTGES
21. TORQUAE
22. VIAROLI
23. XIEMO
28. WAN
29. TOC

NUTRITION FACTS

WHICH MINERAL DOES THAT?

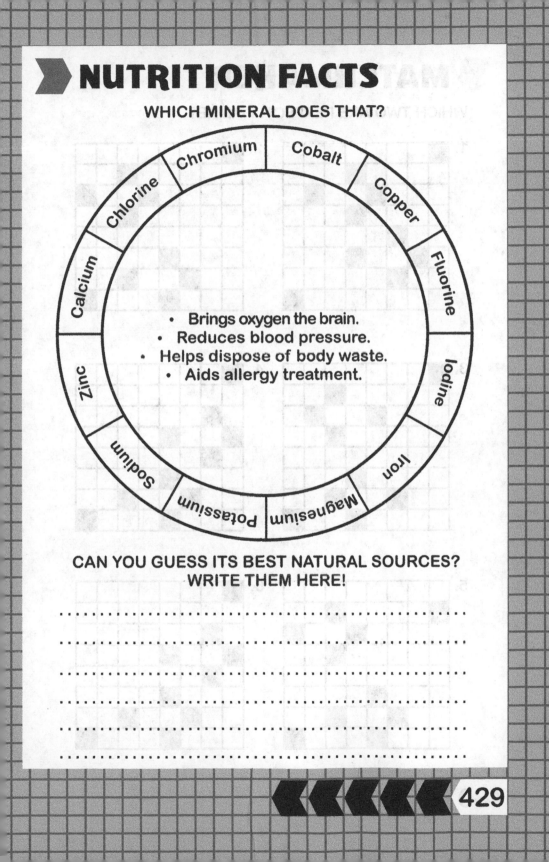

Chromium

Cobalt

Chlorine

Copper

Calcium

Fluorine

Zinc

Iodine

Sodium

Iron

Potassium

Magnesium

- Brings oxygen the brain.
- Reduces blood pressure.
- Helps dispose of body waste.
- Aids allergy treatment.

CAN YOU GUESS ITS BEST NATURAL SOURCES?
WRITE THEM HERE!

....

....

....

....

....

....

⟩ MATCHMAKER

WHICH TWO ARE PERFECTLY ALIKE?

1.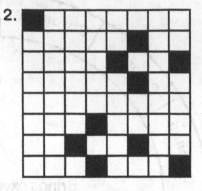

2.

3.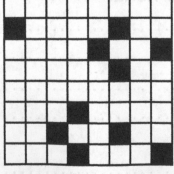

4.

5.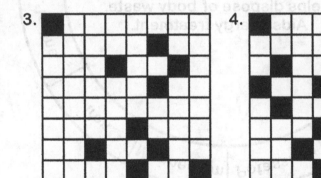

6.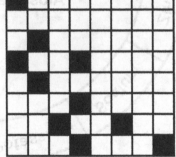

LETTERCROSS

TO FILL THE PUZZLE
ABOVE YOU NEED TO
PICK THE RIGHT LETTERS
FROM THIS GRID!

WORDSEARCH

```
Z G R M V B A N D A I D Y W A O U
J M U J Z I K L E E N E X R M S A
Z A B Z I J P U M S N D E A A C Z
V O B B L H L S V S T Z S N R R O
Z Y E Y H G P P I M T L P G V O N
V T R D Y I F D H L E K E L E O I
C K M Z L L A X E M A V P E L U C
P Y A L H V W S A D D I T R B T H
Y R I K K F A C O C A C O L A K R
C H D O E K H K C O L T B Q Y Y O
P T R B L U C K Y S T R I K E K M
L H N A L A I E L E G O S O R Q E
V E H R O S L P W Q E L M D M X Y
Z R V B G C R A Y O L A O J M E E
O M R I G C A T E R P I L L A R T
H O D E S B I A F V E H I S P O Z
O S C O T C H T A P E X T T H X O
```

FIND 29 FAMOUS BRANDS.
CAN YOU THINK OF ANY OTHERS?

. . . .
. . . .
. . . .
. . . .
. . . .
. . . .
. . . .
. . . .
. . . .

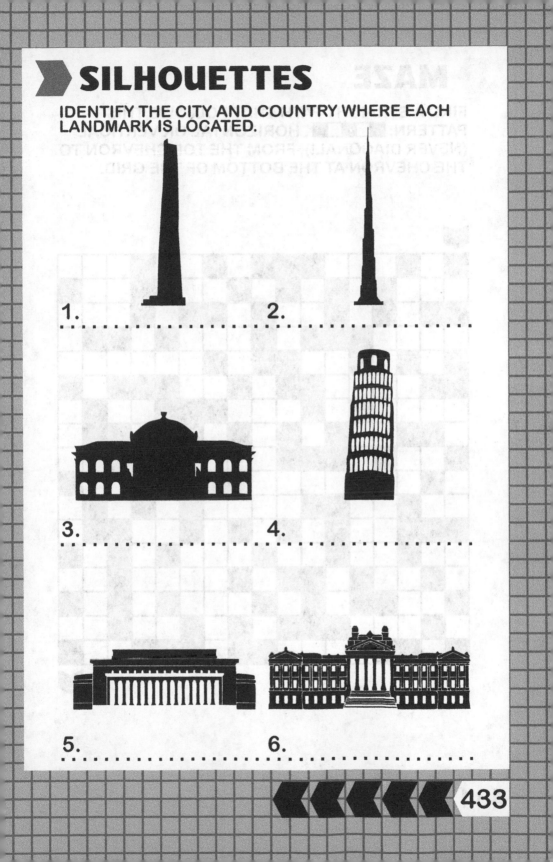

SILHOUETTES

IDENTIFY THE CITY AND COUNTRY WHERE EACH LANDMARK IS LOCATED.

1.

2.

3.

4.

5.

6.

FIND A STRAIGHT PATH THAT FOLLOWS THIS PATTERN: ■■□■□■■ , HORIZONTAL OR VERTICAL (NEVER DIAGONAL!), FROM THE TOP CHEVRON TO THE CHEVRON AT THE BOTTOM OF THE GRID.

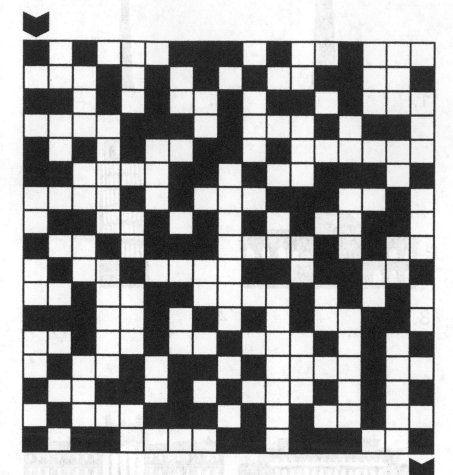

NAME IT

NAME 20 OF YOUR FAVORITE TV SHOWS FROM THE 60s.

1. BEWITCHED

WORDFILL

WHICH 5-LETTER COMBINATIONS ON THE LEFT DO
YOU NEED TO COMPLETE THE 15-LETTER WORDS
ON THE RIGHT?

IDUAL	P	I	C	T	U					E	N	E	S	S
GHTFO	I	M	P	O	N					I	L	I	T	Y
RESQU	I	N	T	E	R					E	A	B	L	E
UMENT	S	T	R	A	I					R	W	A	R	D
NTINU	M	A	T	E	R					A	T	I	O	N
RCEFU	R	E	S	P	O					E	N	E	S	S
NSIBL	S	T	A	N	D					H	N	E	S	S
CHANG	I	N	D	I	V					I	Z	I	N	G
SIFIC	I	N	S	T	R					A	L	I	S	T
NALIZ	D	I	V	E	R					A	T	I	O	N
ALLOG	C	O	M	F	O					E	N	E	S	S
MATIZ	C	R	I	M	I					A	T	I	O	N
RTABL	D	I	S	C	O					A	T	I	O	N
DERAB	S	Y	S	T	E					A	T	I	O	N
IALIZ	C	R	Y	S	T					R	A	P	H	Y
OFFIS	R	E	S	O	U					L	N	E	S	S

436

▶ TRIVIA

FAMOUS PEOPLE FROM THE PAST.

1.
....
1970 ▶ Became the first woman to be promoted to the rank of Brigadier General in the US Army.

2.
....
1971 ▶ Got kidnapped by Tupamaro guerrillas in Montevideo, Uruguay.

3.
....
1973 ▶ Published the first of his enduring <u>Hagar the Horrible</u> comic strips.

4.
....
1974 ▶ Awarded the Nobel Prize for his work in the field of polymers.

5.
....
1975 ▶ Played a solo improvisation at the Cologne Opera, which became the best-selling live piano recording in history.

6.
....
1976 ▶ Founded video game company Data East in Tokyo.

7.
....
1977 ▶ Joined the cast of NBC's <u>Saturday Night Live</u>, replacing Chevy Chase.

8.
....
1979 ▶ Found dead at age 21 of a heroin overdose in New York, the day after being released on bail from prison.

► UNSCRAMBLE

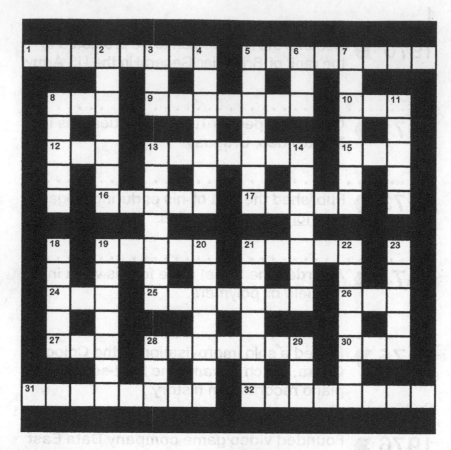

ACROSS:
1. RALAPELL
5. LUNEVOLY
8. SAG
9. BIBEMID
10. ORE
12. UMM
13. HUTWARY
15. BIN
16. NORDO
17. MAGOD
19. YEDEK
21. SAANU
24. UBN

25. DIEVNET
26. ROB
27. IMR
28. HERKING
30. TYR
31. IBN LONYO
32. CRODSSER

DOWN:
2. SUSAMED
3. LIE
4. BORALER
5. BUWODUN
6. ALD
7. DARANVE
8. MAGAM
11. BEDEM
13. TYPETIN
14. HURTGOY
18. CEBAR
19. NAMNIKS
20. VERIIND

21. SPEEKAR
22. BITERAR
23. ROSYP
28. BAG
29. DON

NUTRITION FACTS

WHICH MINERAL DOES THAT?

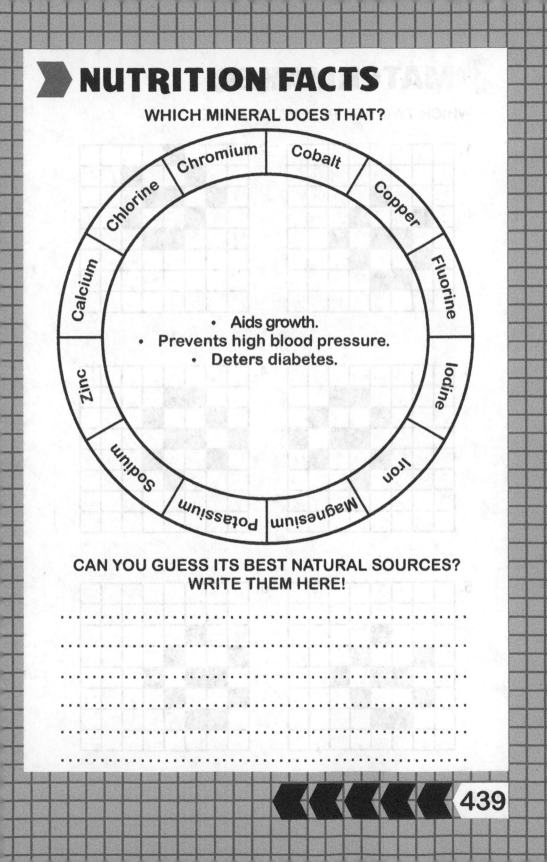

Chromium · Cobalt · Copper · Chlorine · Fluorine · Calcium · Iodine · Zinc · Iron · Sodium · Magnesium · Potassium

- Aids growth.
- Prevents high blood pressure.
- Deters diabetes.

CAN YOU GUESS ITS BEST NATURAL SOURCES? WRITE THEM HERE!

....

....

....

....

....

....

MATCHMAKER

WHICH TWO ARE PERFECTLY ALIKE?

1.
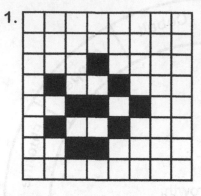

2.
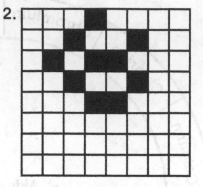

3.
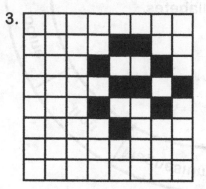

4.
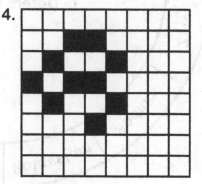

5.

6.

▶ LETTERCROSS

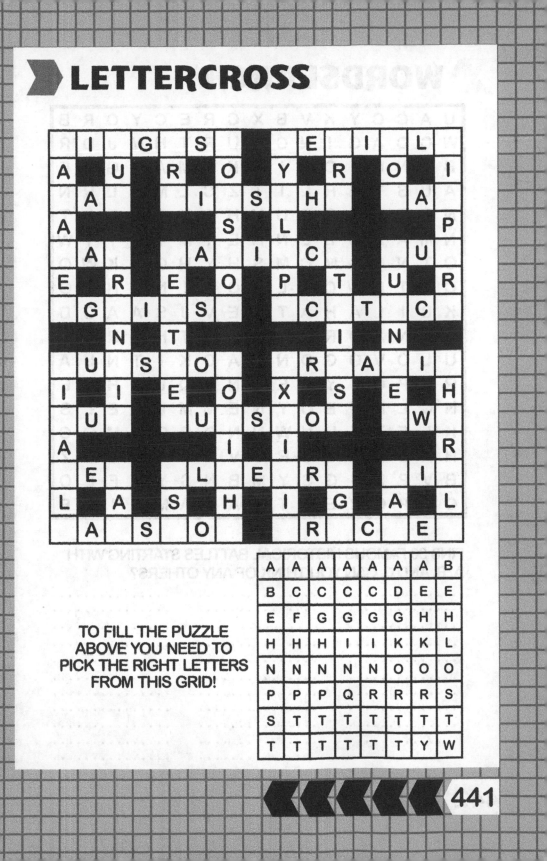

TO FILL THE PUZZLE
ABOVE YOU NEED TO
PICK THE RIGHT LETTERS
FROM THIS GRID!

A	A	A	A	A	A	A	B
B	C	C	C	C	D	E	E
E	F	G	G	G	H	H	
H	H	H	I	I	K	K	L
N	N	N	N	N	O	O	O
P	P	P	Q	R	R	R	S
S	T	T	T	T	T	T	T
T	T	T	T	T	T	Y	W

►WORDSEARCH

```
U A C C Y K V B X C R E C Y O R B
W Q O A G I N C O U R T H M J D R
B A N R I C H I C K A M A U G A E
A U S T E R L I T Z C L M N L R N
N L T H C O R U N H A Y P L Z L T
N M A A B L E N H E I M I Y T I W
O T N G S M C M S H Y H O K K W O
C X T E W C K L C O R I N T H X O
K B I L A H A T P E V J S A A O D
B A N X D R Q L K O A T H C R C U
U L O V O G D N O A C K I T N U A
R A P C Y Y U E Z N A Q L I H L E
N C L H F B O Y N E M M L U E L S
K L E T Z U U W N N D R O M M O C
H A C H A L G R O V E F I E L D Z
B V P S S G S Y M B N S Y R F E O
C A P O R E T T O A L A M E I N B
```

FIND 30 FAMOUS HISTORICAL BATTLES STARTING WITH
A, B, AND C. CAN YOU THINK OF ANY OTHERS?

. . . .
. . . .
. . . .
. . . .
. . . .
. . . .
. . . .
. . . .

SILHOUETTES

IDENTIFY THE CITY AND COUNTRY WHERE EACH
LANDMARK IS LOCATED.

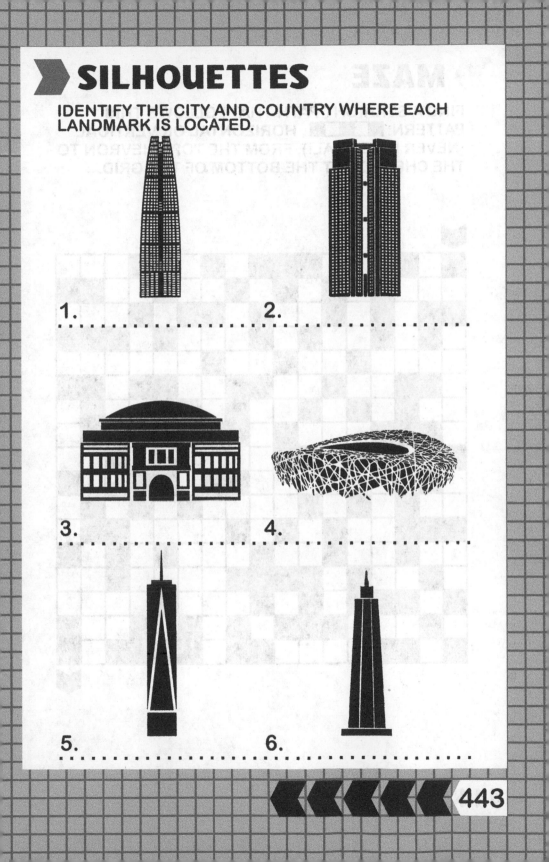

1.

2.

3.

4.

5.

6.

MAZE

FIND A STRAIGHT PATH THAT FOLLOWS THIS PATTERN: ■■□■□■■ , HORIZONTAL OR VERTICAL (NEVER DIAGONAL!), FROM THE TOP CHEVRON TO THE CHEVRON AT THE BOTTOM OF THE GRID.

▶ **NAME IT**

NAME 20 OF YOUR FAVORITE TV SHOWS FROM THE 70s.

1. ALL IN THE FAMILY

WORDFILL

WHICH 5-LETTER COMBINATIONS ON THE LEFT DO YOU NEED TO COMPLETE THE 15-LETTER WORDS ON THE RIGHT?

ORTIO	M	E	M	O	R					A	T	I	O	N
IALIZ	M	E	A	N	I					S	N	E	S	S
OPOMO	U	N	D	E	R					D	N	E	S	S
POTEN	W	E	A	T	H					R	D	I	N	G
HROMA	S	E	R	V	I					E	N	E	S	S
NGLES	R	E	A	P	P					N	M	E	N	T
ULTUR	P	L	E	N	I					T	I	A	R	Y
NETIZ	H	E	M	O	C					T	O	S	I	S
HANDE	A	G	R	I	C					A	L	I	S	T
IGHTE	H	O	S	P	I					A	T	I	O	N
RONIZ	D	I	S	A	D					G	E	O	U	S
ERBOA	T	H	E	R	A					C	A	L	L	Y
PEUTI	A	N	T	H	R					R	P	H	I	C
VANTA	S	Y	N	C	H					A	T	I	O	N
CEABL	D	E	M	A	G					A	T	I	O	N
TALIZ	N	E	A	R	S					D	N	E	S	S

▶ TRIVIA

FAMOUS PEOPLE FROM THE PAST.

1.
....

1941 ▶ Made the commander of the Leningrad Front, where he oversaw the city's defense.

2.
....

1958 ▶ Designated St. Clare of Assisi as the patron saint of television.

3.
....

1964 ▶ Became editor of Britain's best selling teen magazine, Jackie, which would last until 1993.

4.
....

1967 ▶ Together with Ed White and Roger Chaffee, he was killed when fire broke out in the Apollo I spacecraft.

5.
....

1972 ▶ Saved 35 games for the New York Yankees, becoming the first left-hander to save 100 career games in the League.

6.
....

1975 ▶ Invented the first portable digital camera at Eastman Kodak.

7.
....

1982 ▶ Attempted to assassinate Pope John Paul II with a bayonet in Fátima, Portugal.

8.
....

1987 ▶ Illustrated three issues of the Batman: Year Two mini-series.

►UNSCRAMBLE

ACROSS:
1. SOPIEDIC
5. LAMEHOND
8. QAF
9. TACCHOW
10. DUB
12. UDO
13. SHITPET
15. PAL
16. ORATA
17. IBITA
19. ORLOF
21. TERED
24. OBO
25. PASHALT
26. ABG
27. SEY
28. FIPUFER
30. VIY
31. PRESEMIS
32. HOLTALWN

DOWN:
2. AIQUOSE
3. COD
4. TICRAOA
5. THILITS
6. WOM
7. LIABELO
8. DERAF
11. THEPD
13. GOPERLA
14. THABITA
18. BYBAG
19. FLAMOTS
20. PORIFFS
21. ARIDIST
22. BISHBUR
23. GRYNA
28. SAP
29. WOR

NUTRITION FACTS

WHICH MINERAL DOES THAT?

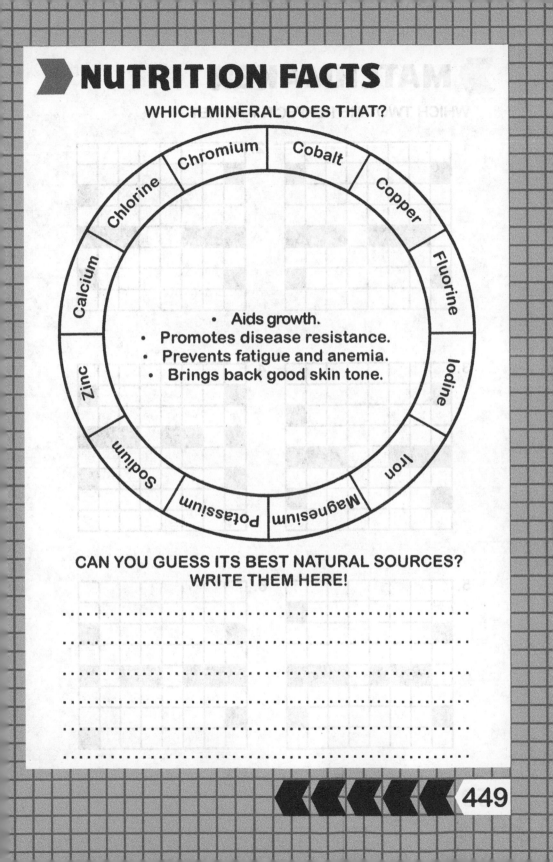

Chromium

Cobalt

Chlorine

Copper

Calcium

Fluorine

Zinc

Iodine

Sodium

Iron

Potassium

Magnesium

- Aids growth.
- Promotes disease resistance.
- Prevents fatigue and anemia.
- Brings back good skin tone.

CAN YOU GUESS ITS BEST NATURAL SOURCES? WRITE THEM HERE!

....

....

....

....

....

....

MATCHMAKER

WHICH TWO ARE PERFECTLY ALIKE?

1.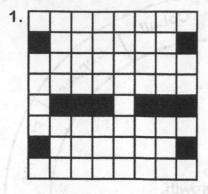

2.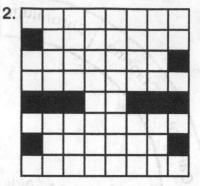

3.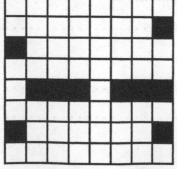

4.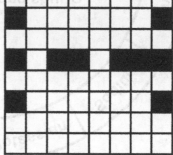

5.

6.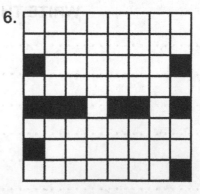

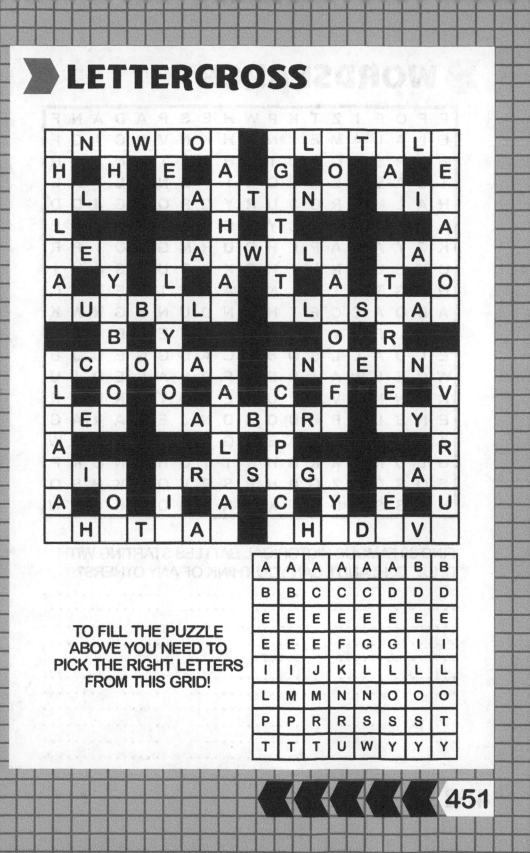

LETTERCROSS

TO FILL THE PUZZLE
ABOVE YOU NEED TO
PICK THE RIGHT LETTERS
FROM THIS GRID!

A	A	A	A	A	A	B	B
B	B	C	C	C	D	D	D
E	E	E	E	E	E	E	E
E	E	E	F	G	G	I	I
I	I	J	K	L	L	L	L
L	M	M	N	N	O	O	O
P	P	R	R	S	S	S	T
T	T	T	U	W	Y	Y	Y

WORDSEARCH

```
F F O P I Z T K P W H E S P A D A N F
E L A L A M E I N S H K N V D C I G F
W K R S F G A U T R H A T T I N X S R
I S A S Z E G F Q L I V S N E L Y K E
H A L M Y R O S U R Y Q R Q P G J D D
A P R J D M G C Y K O E D K P O G V E
K G Y A B A P L H D U R M G E O I P R
O U E U D N L I H G X J P U G S O H I
D A G T H I H I N D A N R I V E R I C
A D O A T C E T H A N D U N E G N W K
T A L F L Y L N N S H U Z E D R I O S
E L D A L L S O B R G A G G G E C J B
W C E L W A I B E I F D S A S E O I U
R A N K E V N P U R E U H T Z N B M R
E N S L S P B D O R D N J E I A V A G
A A P A G V O A E L G K P V I N B M W
U L U N Q K R B H R I I Q H N N G N P
F O R D L Z G P H P S R V Q U K H S Q
N L S S U D W T X O K K N D G K E D W
```

FIND 30 FAMOUS HISTORICAL BATTLES STARTING WITH D, E, F, G, H, AND I. CAN YOU THINK OF ANY OTHERS?

▶ SILHOUETTES

IDENTIFY THE CITY AND COUNTRY WHERE EACH LANDMARK IS LOCATED.

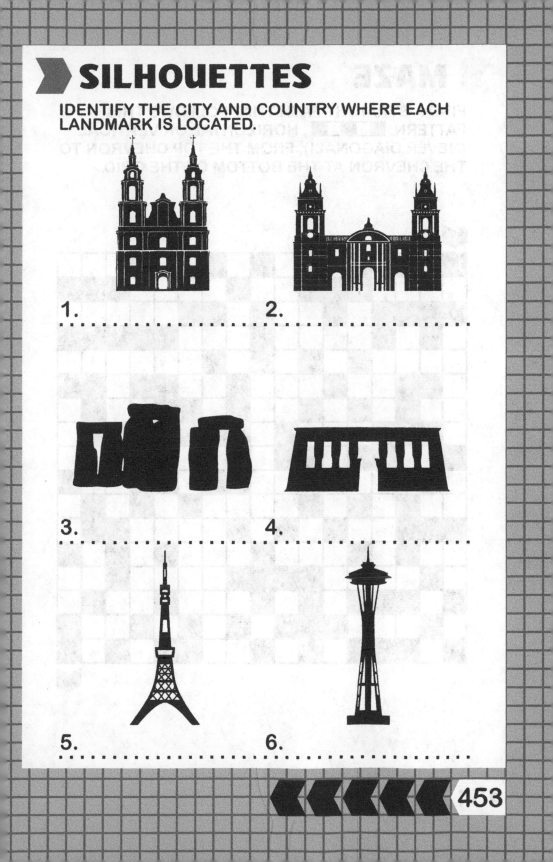

1. ....

2. ....

3. ....

4. ....

5. ....

6. ....

MAZE

FIND A STRAIGHT PATH THAT FOLLOWS THIS PATTERN: ▮▯▮▯▮ , HORIZONTAL OR VERTICAL (NEVER DIAGONAL!), FROM THE TOP CHEVRON TO THE CHEVRON AT THE BOTTOM OF THE GRID.

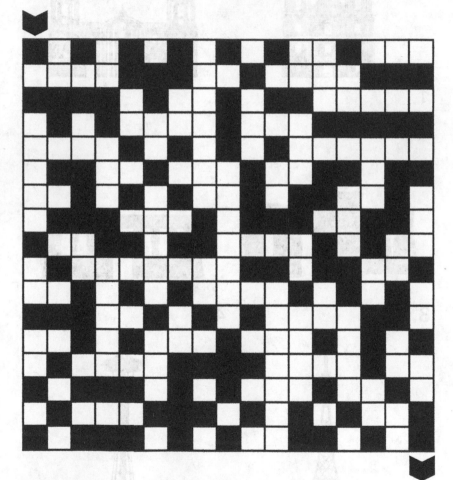

▶ NAME IT
NAME 20 OF YOUR FAVORITE TV SHOWS FROM THE 80s.

1. THE A-TEAM

WORDFILL

WHICH 5-LETTER COMBINATIONS ON THE LEFT DO YOU NEED TO COMPLETE THE 15-LETTER WORDS ON THE RIGHT?

Clue															
CUTIV	L	E	V	E	L				D	N	E	S	S
LIFIC	L	I	G	H	T				D	N	E	S	S
NHEAR	F	O	R	T	H				G	N	E	S	S
PREHE	C	O	N	S	E				E	N	E	S	S
HEADE	P	U	R	P	O				S	N	E	S	S
SITIZ	P	L	E	A	S				E	N	E	S	S
MATIZ	B	R	O	K	E				T	E	D	L	Y
COMIN	U	N	D	E	R				C	T	I	O	N
URABL	U	N	C	O	M				N	D	I	N	G
TERIZ	C	H	E	M	I				A	T	I	O	N
CALIZ	T	R	A	N	S				A	T	I	O	N
HEADE	D	E	S	T	A				A	T	I	O	N
PRODU	C	O	M	P	U				A	T	I	O	N
BILIZ	U	N	Q	U	A				A	T	I	O	N
FIGUR	A	C	H	R	O				A	T	I	O	N
SELES	D	E	S	E	N				A	T	I	O	N

456

▶ TRIVIA

FAMOUS PEOPLE FROM THE PAST.

1.
....

1900 ❯ His surprise attack on Sanna's Post on March 31st, was followed by the victory of Reddersburg on April 4th.

2.
....

1910 ❯ Elected to chair #26 of the Brazilian Academy of Letters.

3.
....

1920 ❯ Taken to a mental hospital in Berlin, where she claimed to be Anastasia of Russia.

4.
....

1930 ❯ Published the first study of the international distribution of lentils.

5.
....

1940 ❯ Defeated by Franklin Delano Roosevelt in the 1940 presidential election.

6.
....

1950 ❯ His film, <u>Escape at Dawn</u>, co-written with Akira Kurosawa, premiered in Japan.

7.
....

1960 ❯ Took a photograph of Ernesto "Che" Guevara, which would become an international icon.

8.
....

1970 ❯ Set a land speed record in a rocket-powered automobile called <u>Blue Flame</u>, fueled with natural gas.

► UNSCRAMBLE

ACROSS:

1. CINACVOL
5. COLICROB
8. PYG
9. SULETUP
10. YAL
12. NIA
13. DICLOME
15. OPX
16. KEDAN
17. ROTRE
19. WODNY
21. REVOP
24. KIS
25. DYARARM
26. SAG
27. DOD
28. DELEARN
30. REO
31. METILPAY
32. ALIROYST

DOWN:

2. NOPTICA
3. PIN
4. LETCADS
5. BERLUND
6. DOE
7. PSYCALO
8. PHARG
11. ISYAX
13. WAMAYKE
14. CROWMUT
18. SOSAB
19. RIDRYPD
20. GEADARY
21. NAPNERL
22. LOROGEG
23. TESTA
28. EIL
29. AYD

NUTRITION FACTS

WHICH MINERAL DOES THAT?

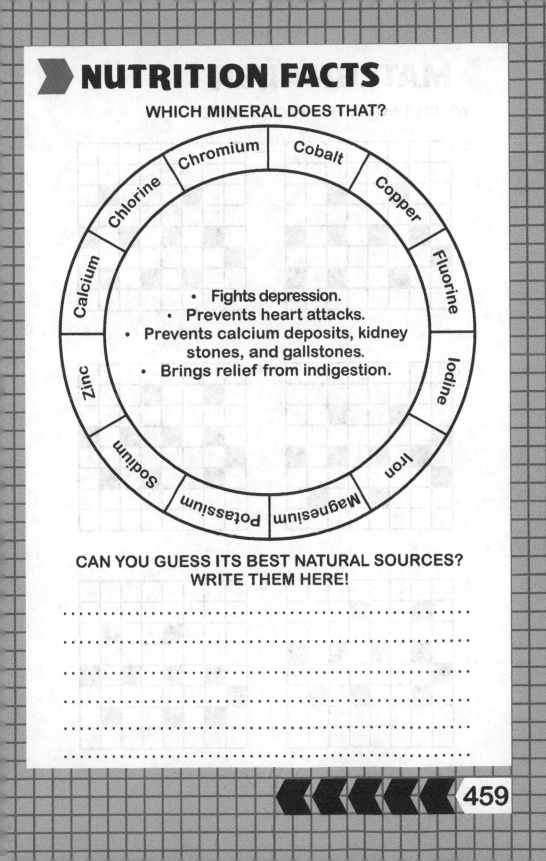

Chromium · Cobalt · Copper · Fluorine · Iodine · Iron · Magnesium · Potassium · Sodium · Zinc · Calcium · Chlorine

- Fights depression.
- Prevents heart attacks.
- Prevents calcium deposits, kidney stones, and gallstones.
- Brings relief from indigestion.

CAN YOU GUESS ITS BEST NATURAL SOURCES? WRITE THEM HERE!

....

....

....

....

....

....

MATCHMAKER

WHICH TWO ARE PERFECTLY ALIKE?

1.
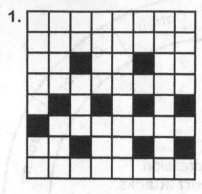

2.
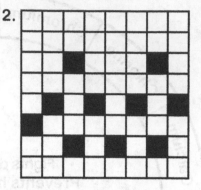

3.
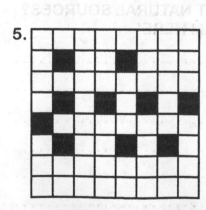

4.
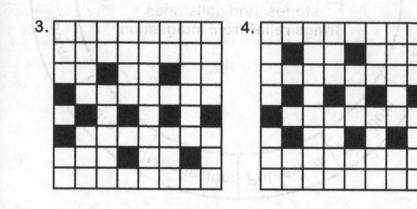

5.

6.
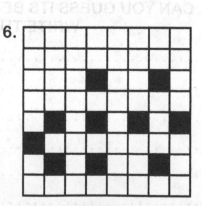

LETTERCROSS

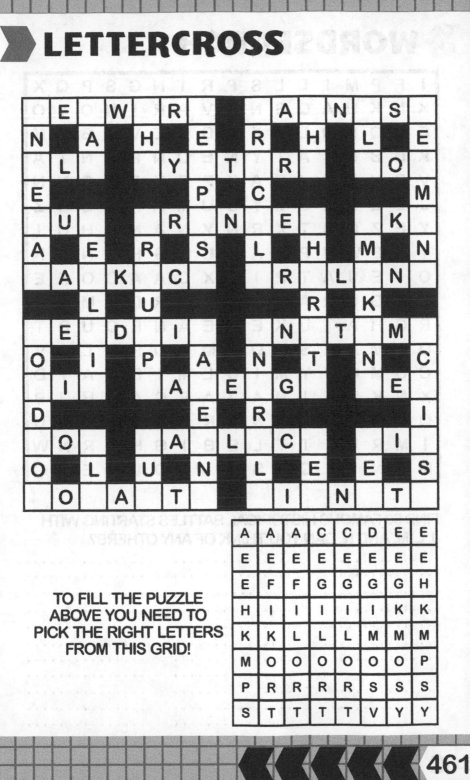

TO FILL THE PUZZLE
ABOVE YOU NEED TO
PICK THE RIGHT LETTERS
FROM THIS GRID!

A	A	A	C	C	D	E	E
E	E	E	E	E	E	E	E
E	F	F	G	G	G	G	H
H	I	I	I	I	K	K
K	K	L	L	L	M	M	M
M	O	O	O	O	O	O	P
P	R	R	R	R	S	S	S
S	T	T	T	T	V	Y	Y

WORDSEARCH

```
I F P M I L L S P R I N G S P Q X
K N K U A Q S N A V A R I N O Y O
E X Q K D L S X L D B L V A B G M
K D B D Y A T Y N E O N P E N T A
V G H E R J R A K P P Y S E Q N N
J L L N W U L Y O U M A R N E O Z
Y E Z G B T X R N Y N A N J H U I
Y X E W U P Y A Z E M S H T N O K
O I E J A T P I G X C A A O O F E
J N G B R A X O M A V R D E M O R
R G H A T U K E H E A N R Q U D T
Q T M A R S T O N M O O R D L Q V
C O M Q T Y M I U L M I D W A Y D
X N K D E I N A J A F G A R H J B
Q M I L V I A N B R I D G E O U U
I M R L I T T L E B I G H O R N W
M O N T E C A S S I N O L V E O G
```

FIND 30 FAMOUS HISTORICAL BATTLES STARTING WITH
J, L, M, AND N. CAN YOU THINK OF ANY OTHERS?

....
....
....
....
....
....
....
....

SILHOUETTES

IDENTIFY THE CITY AND COUNTRY WHERE EACH LANDMARK IS LOCATED.

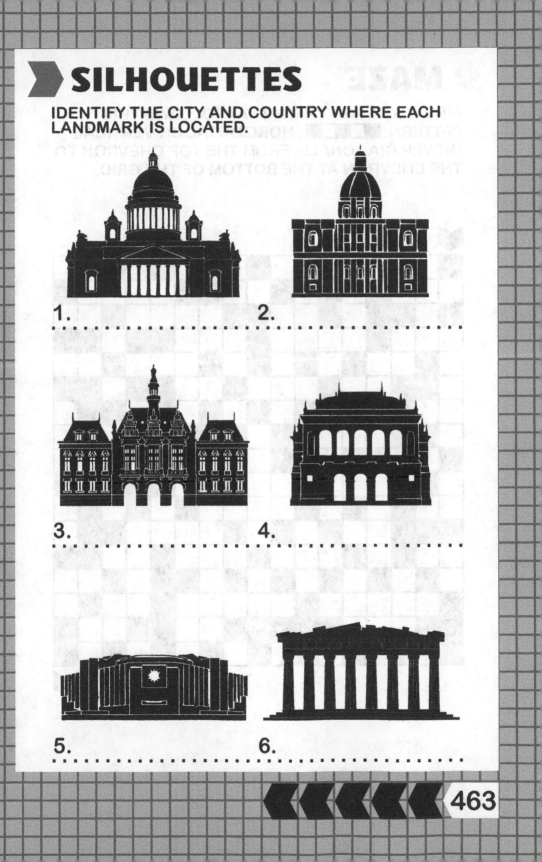

1.

2.

3.

4.

5.

6.

MAZE

FIND A STRAIGHT PATH THAT FOLLOWS THIS PATTERN: ▮□▮□▮ , HORIZONTAL OR VERTICAL (NEVER DIAGONAL!), FROM THE TOP CHEVRON TO THE CHEVRON AT THE BOTTOM OF THE GRID.

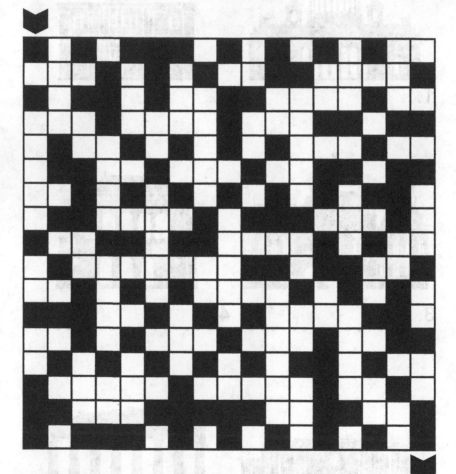

▶NAME IT

NAME 20 OF YOUR FAVORITE TV SHOWS FROM THE 90s.

1. ALLY MCBEAL

WORDFILL

WHICH 5-LETTER COMBINATIONS ON THE LEFT DO YOU NEED TO COMPLETE THE 15-LETTER WORDS ON THE RIGHT?

SCUOU	B	L	A	N	K				D	N	E	S	S	
MINDE	D	O	W	N	H				D	N	E	S	S	
TAMIN	M	E	A	S	U				S	N	E	S	S	
LOGIZ	G	E	N	T	L				I	N	E	S	S	
EARTE	T	H	O	U	G				S	N	E	S	S	
SIDER	P	R	O	M	I				S	N	E	S	S	
MMEND	A	N	T	H	R				N	T	R	I	C	
TATIZ	C	O	U	N	T				U	M	E	N	T	
HTLES	A	C	C	U	L				I	O	N	A	L	
OPOCE	M	Y	T	H	O				A	T	I	O	N	
RATIZ	D	I	S	C	O				A	T	I	O	N	
EMANL	D	E	C	O	N				A	T	I	O	N	
TICUL	D	E	M	O	C				A	T	I	O	N	
TURAT	I	N	C	O	N				A	T	I	O	N	
RELES	H	Y	P	O	S				A	T	I	O	N	
ERARG	D	I	S	A	R				A	T	I	O	N	

FAMOUS PEOPLE FROM THE PAST.

1.

1809 ▶ Deposed from the Swedish throne by the Riksdag of the Estates.

2.

1817 ▶ Discovered the old Roman emerald mines at Sikait, Egypt.

3.

1821 ▶ Began publishing the <u>Novelist's Library</u>, edited by Sir Walter Scott.

4.

1827 ▶ Painted a portrait of young Russian poet, playwright, and novelist, Alexander Pushkin.

5.

1836 ▶ Founded the Colony of South Australia, becoming its first Governor.

6.

1841 ▶ On a voyage to Anctartica, he discovered and named active volcanoes Mount Erebus and Mount Terror.

7.

1859 ▶ Performed "Dixie" for the first time in New York, alongside his Bryan's Minstrels troupe.

8.

1877 ▶ Born in Brussels, she would discover feminism by reading <u>Le Grand Catéchisme de la Femme</u> by Louis Frank.

UNSCRAMBLE

ACROSS:

1. FLETAFET
5. FLERMUFS
8. UBM
9. TIRYSTH
10. UGN
12. OBA
13. ENTLENI
15. PAC
16. CURIN
17. PHILD
19. UPPIN
21. THARE
24. PAL

25. LESNEDS
26. OCO
27. ELE
28. NITEGIL
30. YSL
31. ARLSTING
32. WAKECALK

DOWN:

2. NIPATIM
3. TAE
4. NERNITH
5. MEASLID
6. AFY
7. CALLOGI
8. BYBBO
11. PEGUN
13. SELICEN
14. THIRSTS
18. TEROA
19. PULAPOR
20. DAGOPEG

21. ELAGIEC
22. HAWCKAS
23. ODYWO
28. ILE
29. EKE

NUTRITION FACTS

WHICH MINERAL DOES THAT?

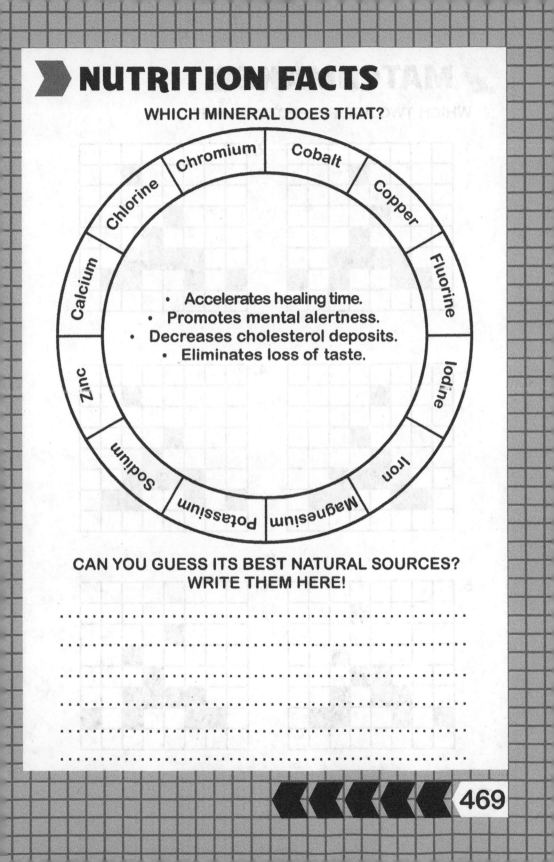

Chromium · Cobalt · Copper · Fluorine · Iodine · Iron · Magnesium · Potassium · Sodium · Zinc · Calcium · Chlorine

- Accelerates healing time.
- Promotes mental alertness.
- Decreases cholesterol deposits.
- Eliminates loss of taste.

CAN YOU GUESS ITS BEST NATURAL SOURCES?
WRITE THEM HERE!

....
....
....
....
....
....

⧁ MATCHMAKER

WHICH TWO ARE PERFECTLY ALIKE?

1.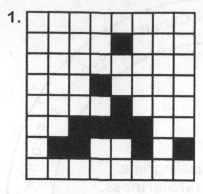

2.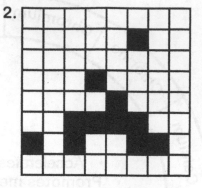

3.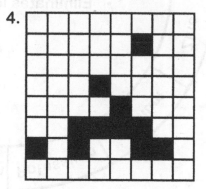

4.

5.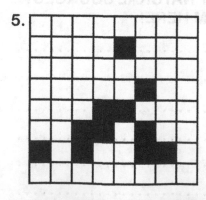

6.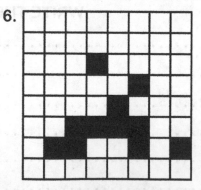

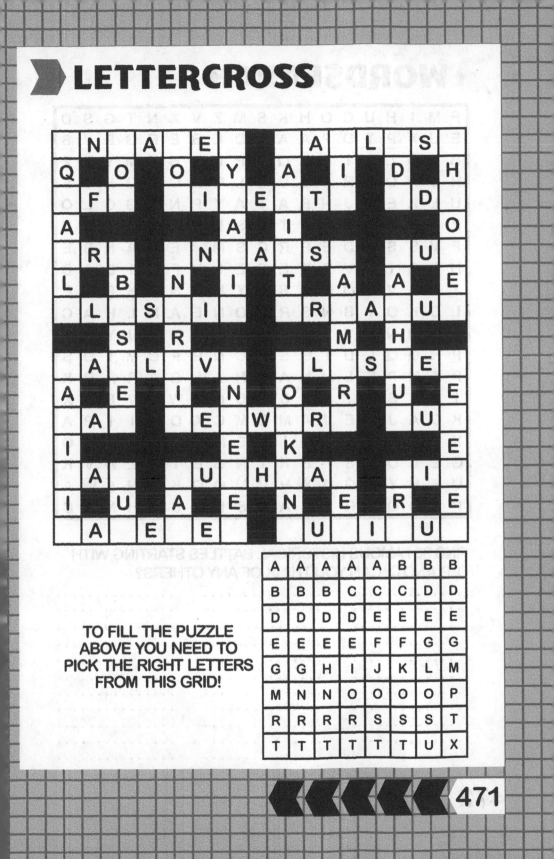

LETTERCROSS

TO FILL THE PUZZLE
ABOVE YOU NEED TO
PICK THE RIGHT LETTERS
FROM THIS GRID!

```
F M I H U C O H K S M Z V X N T G S D
E U X P T D P A A R D E B E R G E Y S
B L U L Z I R V Q T P U T B A M Y T Z
R D W O U R I Q U E L Q Z C O O H J E
U L K E T J N P A T A Y P N R G O L Q
Z Á H T G T C U T F S P M A I C E S U
P V S S L D E P R G S M J E N A N B E
H O Q I W V T R E O E L H F D I O A B
I U E V J O O E B Y Y N P N M H P E E
L D K O Y B N S R U O N E A N L H A C
I E N N M V T T A T R H A N O J Y A T
P N Q Q L D T O S E C N R P C M T O S
P A M P E L U N A S H A L B A R A R K
I R V S S I E R S Q O N H W N V E H X
K D A J L E J A M D M C A O A I I B A
K E C E U J P B I A E M R B T N D A O
G E L Q O S P E K I N G B I Z Z W V K
U E H Y K G D X H U U O O K I N A W A
P C O Q O R L E A N S P R S I H N H C
```

FIND 30 FAMOUS HISTORICAL BATTLES STARTING WITH O, P, AND Q. CAN YOU THINK OF ANY OTHERS?

. . . .
. . . .
. . . .
. . . .
. . . .
. . . .
. . . .
. . . .
. . . .
. . . .

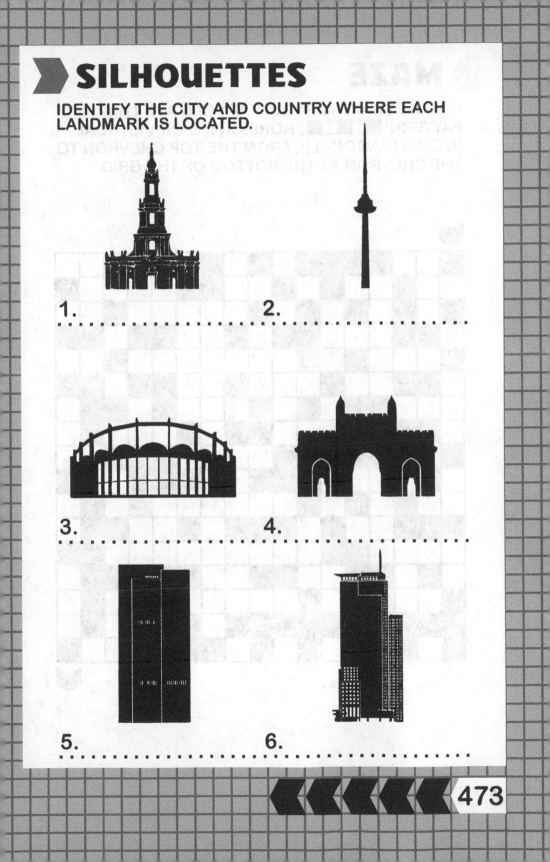

SILHOUETTES

IDENTIFY THE CITY AND COUNTRY WHERE EACH LANDMARK IS LOCATED.

1.

2.

3.

4.

5.

6.

 # MAZE

FIND A STRAIGHT PATH THAT FOLLOWS THIS PATTERN: ▗▖▗▖, HORIZONTAL OR VERTICAL (NEVER DIAGONAL!), FROM THE TOP CHEVRON TO THE CHEVRON AT THE BOTTOM OF THE GRID.

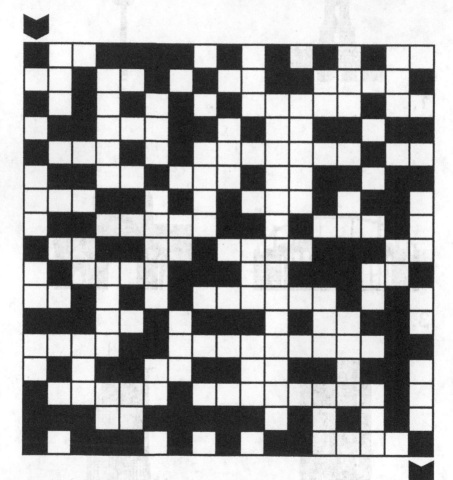

▶ NAME IT

NAME 20 OF YOUR FAVORITE FILMS DIRECTED BY STEVEN SPIELBERG!

1. A.I.

WHICH 5-LETTER COMBINATIONS ON THE LEFT DO YOU NEED TO COMPLETE THE 15-LETTER WORDS ON THE RIGHT?

OLOGI	S	O	F	T	H					D	N	E	S	S
TOMIZ	S	E	S	Q	U					E	N	A	R	Y
NMENT	M	A	C	R	O					C	A	L	L	Y
TISFA	P	H	Y	S	I					C	A	L	L	Y
SCOPI	U	N	A	C	C					A	T	I	N	G
PORIZ	O	P	H	T	H					O	G	I	S	T
MONIZ	U	N	D	E	M					A	T	I	V	E
ICENT	G	O	V	E	R					A	L	I	S	M
PROTE	P	H	O	T	O					A	L	I	S	M
ONSTR	E	L	E	C	T					I	T	I	V	E
EARTE	D	I	C	H	O					A	T	I	O	N
TIFIC	O	B	J	E	C					A	T	I	O	N
ROPOS	D	I	S	S	A					C	T	I	O	N
OMMOD	R	A	D	I	O					C	T	I	O	N
JOURN	R	E	H	A	R					A	T	I	O	N
ALMOL	E	X	T	E	M					A	T	I	O	N

476

⮞ TRIVIA

FAMOUS PEOPLE FROM THE PAST.

1.

1898 ⮞ Studied at the Royal Swedish Academy of Arts in Stockholm, and then at the Académie Colarossi in Paris.

2.

1906 ⮞ Published his novel, <u>The Paul Street Boys</u>, which would be translated into fourteen languages.

3.

1922 ⮞ Supported the September 11TH Revolution, which abolished the monarchy and declared the Second Hellenic Republic.

4.

1933 ⮞ Acquired the merchandising rights to Edgar Rice Burroughs' Tarzan character and produced a series of products.

5.

1954 ⮞ Wrote an important series of studies on the backgrounds of Supreme Court justices.

6.

1968 ⮞ Shot by the police in a protest for cheaper meals at a restaurant for low-income students.

7.

1976 ⮞ Became the artist on the Wonder Woman comics with issue #222 and drew the series until #286.

8.

1983 ⮞ Captured while on mission over Lebanon, he was held captive in Syria for over a month.

►UNSCRAMBLE

ACROSS:

1. WALNONCA
5. DOPETSOR
8. LEF
9. ETEVALE
10. REI
12. OTE
13. SENDLES
15. DAF
16. OTADY
17. NYNOS
19. ILEDO
21. RIMPP
24. YAP
25. LEBRUMT
26. FAT
27. PAZ
28. NURGLON
30. REA
31. CEBERUSE
32. HURTSGOY

DOWN:

2. FEBATOF
3. YEL
4. EKDEYWA
5. DREWARS
6. DOE
7. FITFLYS
8. TRYEN
11. DEERI
13. ULEPAET
14. DIALNUS
18. PAZTO
19. MYOLPIC
20. MINIDOE
21. TRAYOR
22. AUPLATE
23. TRAXE
28. ULE
29. ANG

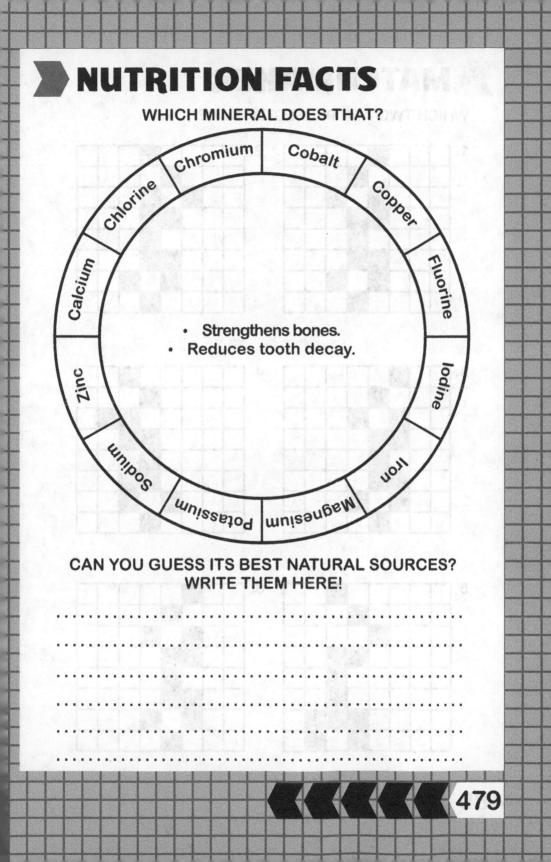

NUTRITION FACTS

WHICH MINERAL DOES THAT?

Chromium · Cobalt · Copper · Fluorine · Iodine · Iron · Magnesium · Potassium · Sodium · Zinc · Calcium · Chlorine · Chromium

- Strengthens bones.
- Reduces tooth decay.

CAN YOU GUESS ITS BEST NATURAL SOURCES?
WRITE THEM HERE!

....
....
....
....
....
....

▶ MATCHMAKER

WHICH TWO ARE PERFECTLY ALIKE?

1.

2.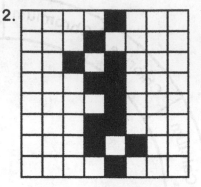

3.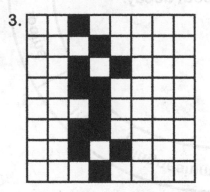

4.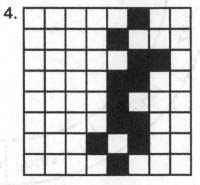

5.

6.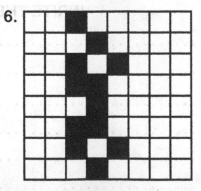

LETTERCROSS

TO FILL THE PUZZLE
ABOVE YOU NEED TO
PICK THE RIGHT LETTERS
FROM THIS GRID!

A	A	A	A	A	B	B	B
B	C	C	D	D	D	D	E
E	E	E	E	G	G	G	G
H	H	H	I	I	I	K	L
L	L	L	M	N	O	P	P
R	R	R	R	S	S	S	S
S	T	T	T	T	T	U	U
U	U	V	W	Y	Y	Y	Z

WORDSEARCH

```
L F I S N P T E N E R I F E S C C
X A O A F S B O A U T T O B R U K
W U K R F A C C R F Y N O D C Q Y
V P J A W S I H I C A E X U F O O
S N J T B E S R W C S Q J Y L T F
T A U O X V S U N E C E A B N O K
A H L G O E B E I G I B L A Y W N
L S Z A K N P L R H M N R B F T R
I A B R M P L U T I I A F S Y O O
N D U B I I B Z L R T P S U I N C
G O O T M N S U R A A B Y S R B H
R W E A E E S B N F R F R H S T E
A A R N O S A N D A H R A I N M S
D J N V L U E K M X I U C L M T T
G A D R A V T X B G L H U O G U E
T S E V A S T O P O L R S H A A R
V H O R A K V E R E R M E D L V R
```

FIND 30 FAMOUS HISTORICAL BATTLES STARTING WITH R, S, AND T. CAN YOU THINK OF ANY OTHERS?

....
....
....
....
....
....
....
....

SILHOUETTES

IDENTIFY THE CITY AND COUNTRY WHERE EACH LANDMARK IS LOCATED.

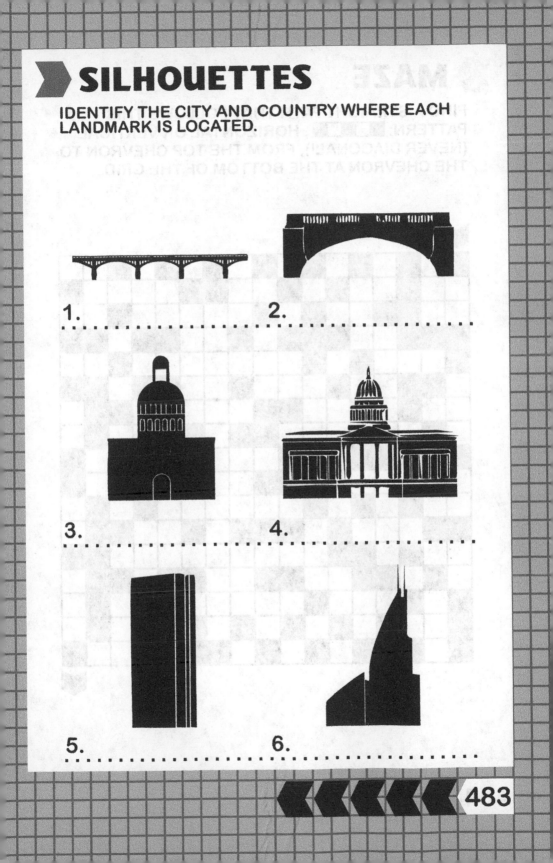

1.

2.

3.

4.

5.

6.

◤ MAZE

FIND A STRAIGHT PATH THAT FOLLOWS THIS PATTERN: ⬛⬜⬛⬜⬛ , HORIZONTAL OR VERTICAL (NEVER DIAGONAL!), FROM THE TOP CHEVRON TO THE CHEVRON AT THE BOTTOM OF THE GRID.

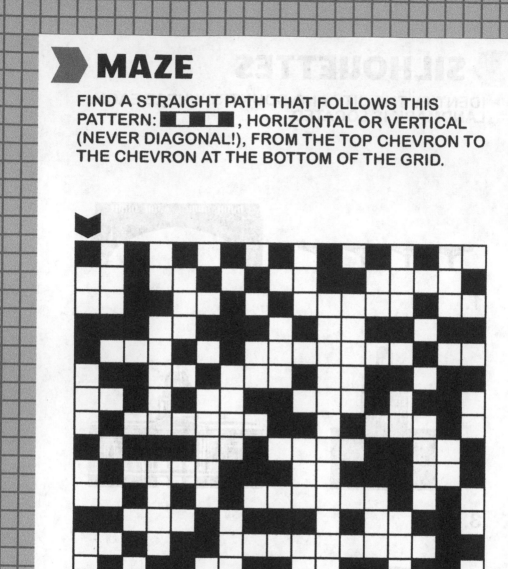

NAME IT

NAME 20 OF YOUR FAVORITE WWE SUPERSTARS FROM THE 1980s.

1. ANDRE THE GIANT

WORDFILL

WHICH 5-LETTER COMBINATIONS ON THE LEFT DO YOU NEED TO COMPLETE THE 15-LETTER WORDS ON THE RIGHT?

ETICA	P	H	A	R	M						E	R	A	P	Y
THSTA	R	E	M	O	R						S	N	E	S	S
CONDU	C	O	N	V	E						A	L	I	T	Y
ECTIV	E	N	E	R	G						L	N	E	S	S
SELES	P	R	E	C	I						S	N	E	S	S
CTION	I	N	E	P	H						E	N	E	S	S
CURRI	M	A	N	O	E						I	L	I	T	Y
HYPOP	E	N	V	I	R						T	A	L	L	Y
UVRAB	N	O	T	W	I						N	D	I	N	G
ONMEN	T	R	I	N	I						L	U	E	N	E
BIOLO	F	A	I	T	H						I	N	E	S	S
TROTO	N	E	U	R	O						G	I	C	A	L
WORTH	P	H	O	T	O						C	T	I	O	N
NTION	A	D	E	N	O						H	Y	S	I	S
PITOU	P	E	R	F	E						I	S	T	I	C
ACOTH	E	X	T	R	A						C	U	L	A	R

FAMOUS PEOPLE FROM THE PAST.

1.
....
1980 ⮞ Took his oath of office as Prime Minister of Zimbabwe.

2.
....
1981 ⮞ After losing touch for almost half a century, he reunited with his friend Hergé in Brussels.

3.
....
1982 ⮞ Piloted Japan Airlines Flight 350, which crashed into Tokyo Bay, killing 24 of the 174 passengers on board.

4.
....
1983 ⮞ Sentenced to imprisonment in a labor camp for dissident activity.

5.
....
1984 ⮞ Together with Ian Bell, he designed and developed revolutionary video game, ELITE.

6.
....
1985 ⮞ Wrote a story for <u>Heroes for Hope</u>, a benefit comic for African famine relief.

7.
....
1986 ⮞ Supervised a safety test gone awry at the Chernobyl Nuclear Power Plant, which resulted in a nuclear catastrophe.

8.
....
1987 ⮞ Starred on ABC TV series <u>AMERIKA</u> at age seventeen.

►UNSCRAMBLE

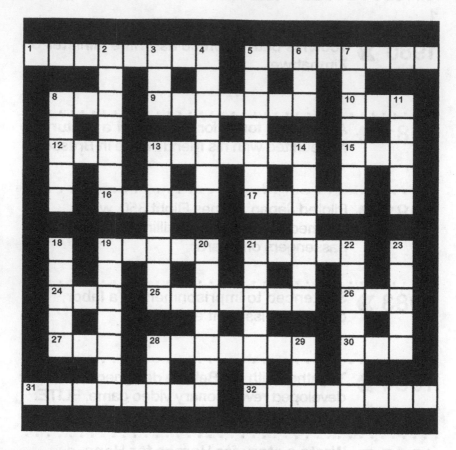

ACROSS:
1. MOTANAKYP
5. NEDIKYDOL
8. AST
9. CULAUST
10. TAN
12. EGO
13. LENICKS
15. SOI
16. GARTS
17. KINGE
19. TERAI
21. DERIP
24. MID
25. OGECROS
26. UGL
27. LIA
28. PEPEEYE
30. CAL
31. TEYESIGH
32. HORATCIC

DOWN:
2. THOUSON
3. UTA
4. SINGSEM
5. LEKNUCK
6. ELT
7. CINGNAD
8. GOLES
11. THOTO
13. PASSURS
14. ECFIDIE
18. DHIBO
19. MEATINS
20. ESTARNE
21. TROSECP
22. LIAUELA
23. LICOG
28. GEP
29. DEO

NUTRITION FACTS

WHICH MINERAL DOES THAT?

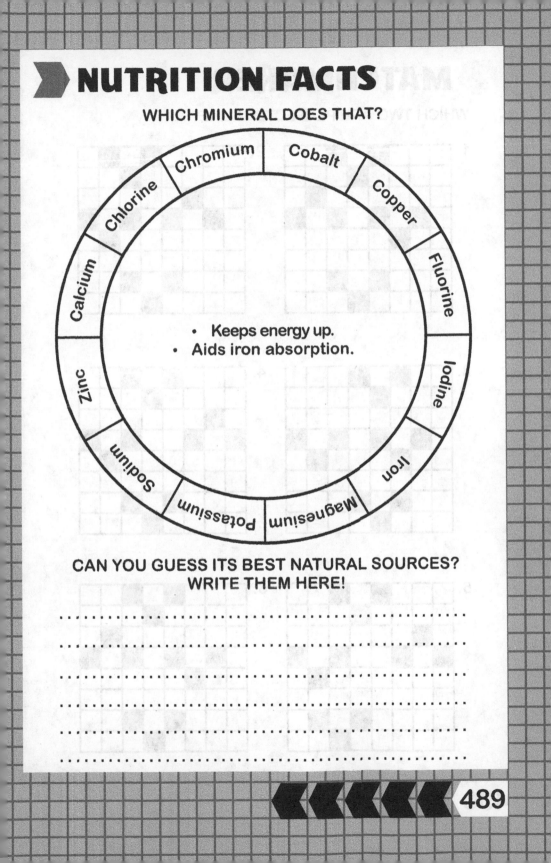

Chromium · Cobalt · Copper · Fluorine · Iodine · Iron · Magnesium · Potassium · Sodium · Zinc · Calcium · Chlorine

- Keeps energy up.
- Aids iron absorption.

CAN YOU GUESS ITS BEST NATURAL SOURCES?
WRITE THEM HERE!

....

....

....

....

....

MATCHMAKER

WHICH TWO ARE PERFECTLY ALIKE?

1.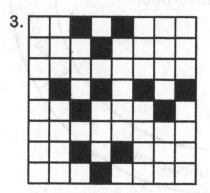

2.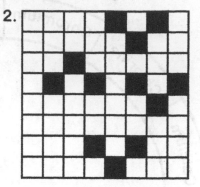

3.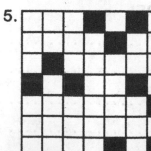

4.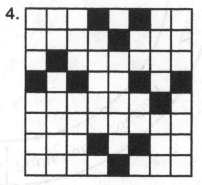

5.

6.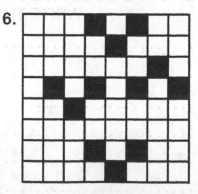

LETTERCROSS

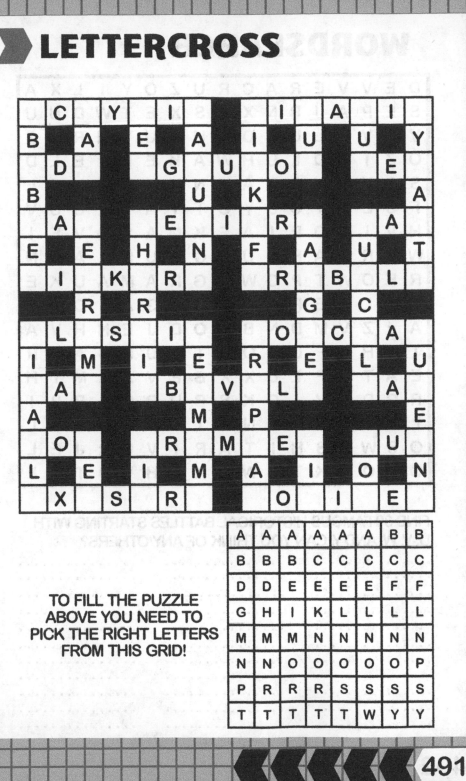

TO FILL THE PUZZLE
ABOVE YOU NEED TO
PICK THE RIGHT LETTERS
FROM THIS GRID!

A	A	A	A	A	A	B	B
B	B	B	C	C	C	C	C
D	D	E	E	E	E	F	F
G	H	I	K	L	L	L	L
M	M	M	N	N	N	N	N
N	N	O	O	O	O	O	P
P	R	R	R	S	S	S	S
T	T	T	T	T	W	Y	Y

WORDSEARCH

```
D E V V E R A C R U Z O Y I L X A
S E P A J B N X U S X E T W D U U
V T V U L U N D I H R U Y H R C Z
O Z I Z D L U H W A K E F I E L D
S S M R H E E A V N V L H T K E L
F U E W T O S Y O T I A I E U S V
H V I T O R I A F K M A S P V F I
W H R Y A R M U K O Y U S L A J N
R K O W T P C W A G R A M A U K E
W I L D E R N E S S I G A I C I G
A J Z V M D N B S O D J E N H V A
T T H U F D B Q U T G U N S A N R
E A T K F L U X X B E V A L M Y H
R C D O V I C K S B U R G J P P I
L D D V A L E N C I E N N E S R L
O S W A S H I T A R I V E R J E L
O Y O R K T O W N K O H V D T S L
```

FIND 30 FAMOUS HISTORICAL BATTLES STARTING WITH
U, V, W, AND Y. CAN YOU THINK OF ANY OTHERS?

. . . .
. . . .
. . . .
. . . .
. . . .
. . . .
. . . .
. . . .

SILHOUETTES

IDENTIFY THE CITY AND COUNTRY WHERE EACH LANDMARK IS LOCATED.

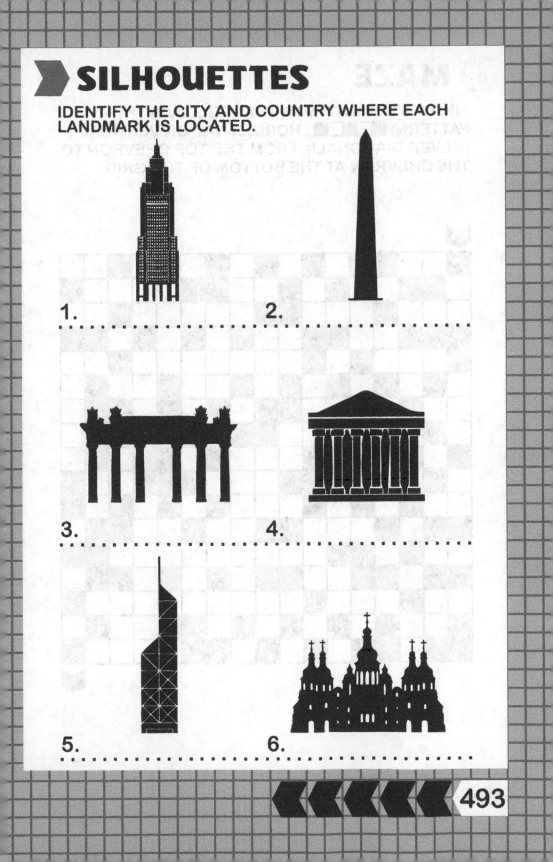

1.

2.

3.

4.

5.

6.

MAZE

FIND A STRAIGHT PATH THAT FOLLOWS THIS PATTERN: ■□□■□■ , HORIZONTAL OR VERTICAL (NEVER DIAGONAL!), FROM THE TOP CHEVRON TO THE CHEVRON AT THE BOTTOM OF THE GRID.

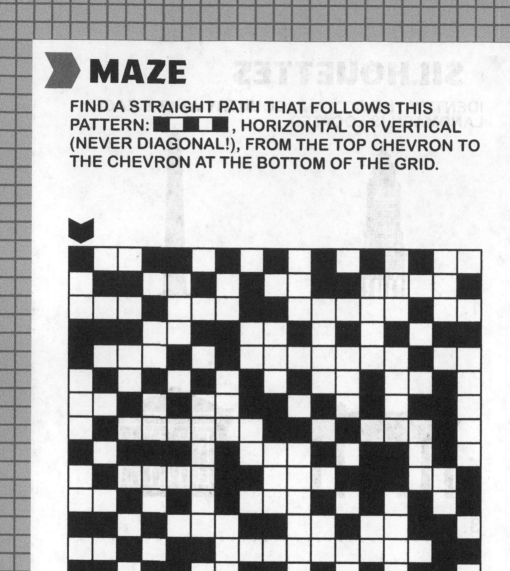

▶ NAME IT

NAME 20 OF YOUR FAVORITE G.L.O.W. PERFORMERS
FROM THE 1980s.

1. AMERICANA

WORDFILL

WHICH 5-LETTER COMBINATIONS ON THE LEFT DO YOU NEED TO COMPLETE THE 15-LETTER WORDS ON THE RIGHT?

TICIZ	D	E	S	T	R						E	N	E	S	S
UCTIV	C	O	M	M	U						A	T	I	O	N
CORRE	D	E	C	A	L						A	T	I	O	N
EMENT	R	O	M	A	N						A	T	I	O	N
ONSTR	E	L	E	C	T						A	T	I	O	N
OTELI	P	A	L	A	E						O	G	I	S	T
NALIZ	T	R	A	N	S						A	T	I	O	N
TERVE	H	Y	P	E	R						C	T	I	O	N
ANSFE	U	N	C	O	M						A	T	I	V	E
ONTOL	I	N	D	E	M						A	T	I	O	N
THYRO	S	U	P	P	L						A	T	I	O	N
NIFIC	V	A	S	O	C						I	C	T	O	R
MUNIC	A	R	I	S	T						A	N	I	S	M
PLANT	N	O	N	I	N						N	T	I	O	N
CIFIC	H	Y	P	E	R						I	D	I	S	M
ROLIZ	N	O	N	T	R						R	A	B	L	E

▶ TRIVIA

FAMOUS PEOPLE FROM THE PAST.

1.

1988 ▶ Implicated in World War II deportations by a Nazi document.

2.

1989 ▶ Agreed to sell his stake in Carolco Pictures to co-founder Mario Kassar for $106 million.

3.

1990 ▶ Became the first elected woman president in the Americas.

4.

1991 ▶ Passed away at 78, his <u>Fred Basset</u> comic strip being continued by his daughter Arran Keith.

5.

1992 ▶ Released ViolaWWW, the first popular web browser, in the United States.

6.

1993 ▶ Sworn in to become the first female Attorney General of the United States.

7.

1994 ▶ Began his 437.7 day orbit, setting the world record for days spent in orbit.

8.

1995 ▶ Announced the resumption of nuclear tests in French Polynesia.

▶ UNSCRAMBLE

ACROSS:
1. BITORRUA
5. SOMENEGO
8. UFT
9. HAAMLEB
10. LAF
12. UNN
13. PSYCOLA
15. GUL
16. CRAIV
17. ENTES
19. ORAXI
21. CAYAC
24. LEK
25. TELADAU
26. CAZ
27. HUP
28. DENACTO
30. ERO
31. HALISECH
32. STANBIKA

DOWN:
2. VENATOR
3. IBM
4. CHOLAIC
5. POTLIGA
6. INB
7. LESMACS
8. NYNAF
11. GEOFY
13. LAVOCLA
14. CLEPERO
18. HEAPA
19. KINBUSH
20. CUSARUN
21. RAEYOCK
22. OKSZODA
23. CESYE
28. LIT
29. LEB

498

NUTRITION FACTS

WHICH MINERAL DOES THAT?

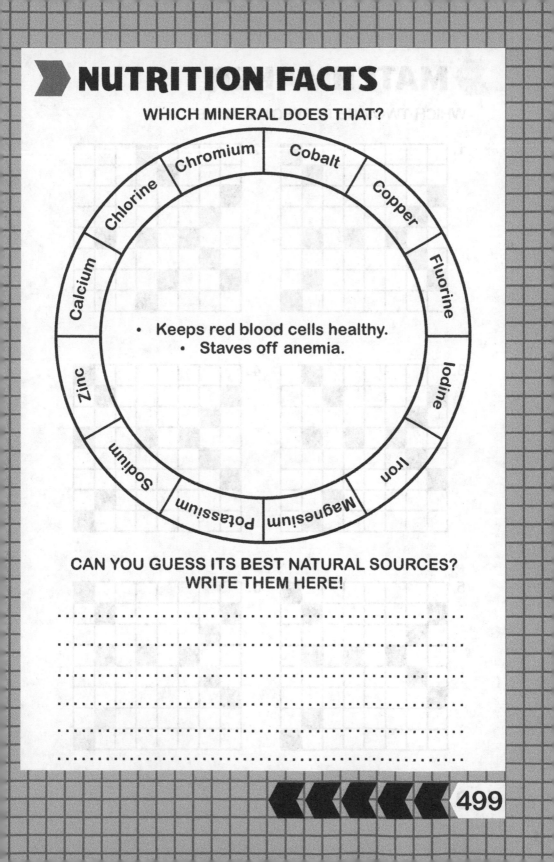

Chromium · Cobalt · Copper · Fluorine · Iodine · Iron · Magnesium · Potassium · Sodium · Zinc · Calcium · Chlorine

- Keeps red blood cells healthy.
- Staves off anemia.

CAN YOU GUESS ITS BEST NATURAL SOURCES? WRITE THEM HERE!

....
....
....
....
....
....

MATCHMAKER

WHICH TWO ARE PERFECTLY ALIKE?

1.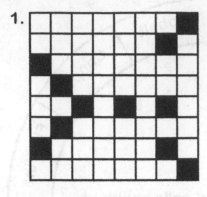

2.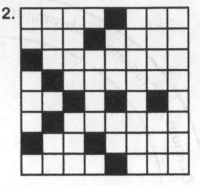

3.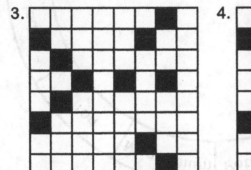

4.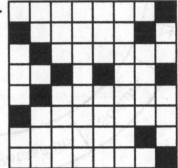

5.

6.

LETTERCROSS

BONUS PUZZLE!

TO FILL THE PUZZLE ABOVE YOU NEED TO PICK THE RIGHT LETTERS FROM THIS GRID!

A	A	A	A	A	A	B	C
C	C	C	C	D	D	D	E
E	E	E	E	E	F	F	F
F	H	H	I	K	K	L	L
L	L	L	M	M	M	M	N
N	N	N	O	O	O	O	R
R	R	R	R	S	S	S	T
T	T	T	U	U	X	Y	Y

501

WORDSEARCH

```
Q R O J S H I D E M E R A T U S L
S S B V V J O I R M T O C H R T S
I Y R Z V O Z A N A M N W L K N T
A M W W Z O Q I R I I M L T R I C
X P A K Y V U J J C Q O P A L A L
B H K C S C R A C J R H G A Q D J
N O L F L E K A I R O L D I W U W
I S X A B A N M A Q L Q P J Y D D
S I A E O O R C O Y K H U D N E E
H U W A B G M E I S H I D A N N M
I S N I L F I B T K Y G O N E E E
O T F N Q H Y S P I L S B U R Y Z
M A L E S K A G A R D N E R E U I
R R V A Z E M R U L H A V H S A R
I N M K F K O L I P N S H P R J I
X K S W I F T H F R A N K L I N A
I A K A A O O A Q T I D L U H Z C
```

FIND 24 FAMOUS AND OBSCURE PUZZLE CREATORS.
CAN YOU THINK OF ANY OTHERS?

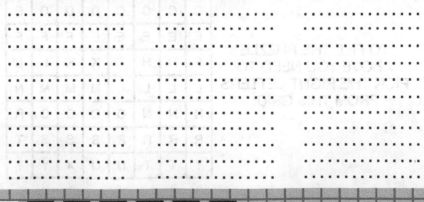

PIX-CROSS

CAN YOU CRACK THE NONOGRAM?

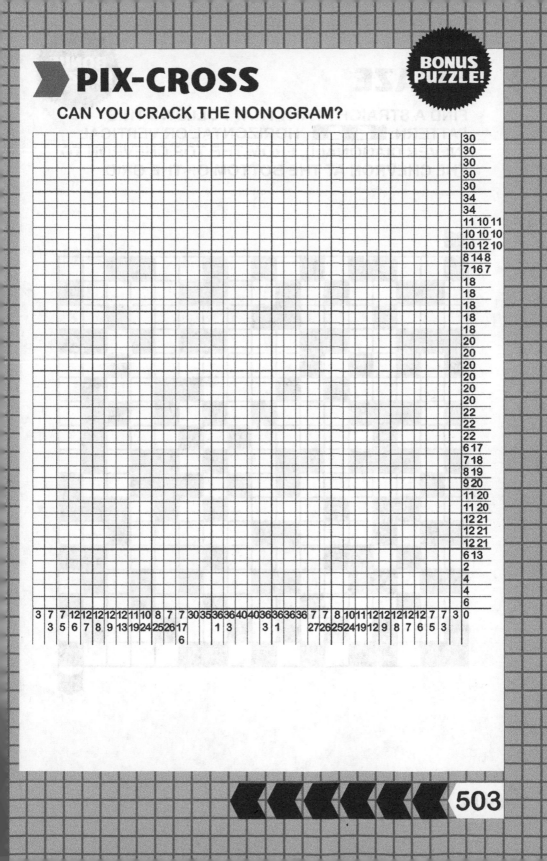

MAZE

FIND A STRAIGHT PATH THAT FOLLOWS THIS PATTERN: ▮▯▯▮ , HORIZONTAL OR VERTICAL (NEVER DIAGONAL!), FROM THE TOP CHEVRON TO THE CHEVRON AT THE BOTTOM OF THE GRID.

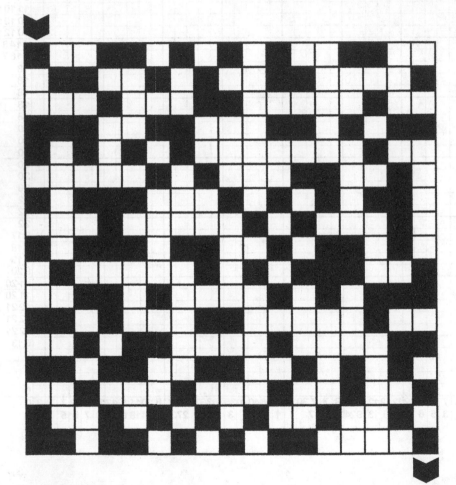

▶NAME IT

**NAME 20 OF YOUR FAVORITE HEROES
AND VILLAINS CREATED BY STAN LEE.**

1. BLACK PANTHER

DOT-TO-DOT

▶ TRIVIA

FAMOUS PEOPLE FROM THE PAST.

1. ....

1970 ▶ Kidnaped by Quebec separatists on October 5th.

2. ....

1972 ▶ Died in Paris after being hit by a car.

3. ....

1978 ▶ Recorded his fifth solo album, <u>Pacific</u>.

4. ....

1983 ▶ Published his <u>Dal Tokyo</u> graphic novel.

5. ....

1985 ▶ Portrayed a demented grandma in the iconic Argentinian comedy <u>Waiting for the Hearse</u>.

6. ....

1986 ▶ Elected as the first civilian president of Portugal.

7. ....

1988 ▶ A cartoon show based on his "Anpanman" character debuted in Japan.

8. ....

1990 ▶ Dropped out of school to pursue a career in music.

➤ 25 DIFFERENCES

FIND ALL THE SUBTLE AND NOT-SO-SUBTLE DETAILS THAT DON'T MATCH.

WHAT WAS THIS FORMER HOLLYWOOD POWER-COUPLE NICKNAMED?

► MATCHMAKER

WHICH TWO ARE PERFECTLY ALIKE?

1.
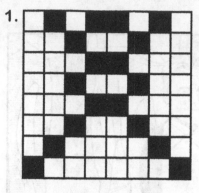

2.
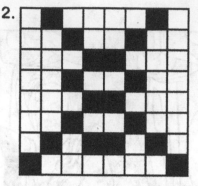

3.
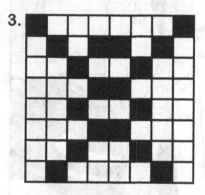

4.
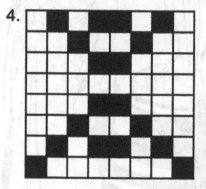

5.
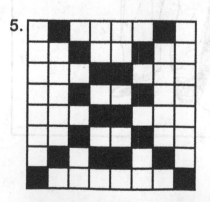

6.
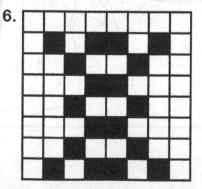

►SOLUTIONS

001

A	D	D			E	M	S
R	O	A	D	M	A	P	
A		S	I	B			R
B	E	T	A	R	A	Y	
I		A	N	A			E
C	A	R	A	C	A	S	
A	N	D			E	S	T

002

003

A	M	U	I	E	J	K	O	L
E	J	O	K	A	L	U	I	M
K	L	I	U	O	M	A	J	E
J	I	A	O	U	E	M	L	K
M	E	K	L	J	I	O	A	U
O	U	L	M	K	A	J	E	I
I	A	J	E	M	U	L	K	O
U	O	E	J	L	K	I	M	A
L	K	M	A	I	O	E	U	J

004

THE WIZARD OF OZ
1939 | Judy Garland
CASABLANCA
1942 | Humphrey Bogart
THE GRADUATE
1967 | Dustin Hoffman

005

1. USA
2. RUSSIA
3. CHINA
4. BRAZIL
5. FRANCE
6. BRITAIN

006

B	O	X	E	R		H	I	K	E	R
U			I		B					O
N		B	E	D	R	O	O	M		W
C		E		G		M		I		E
H	E	D	G	E		B	A	N	A	L
		O					D			
B	R	U	S	H		R	E	F	I	T
R		I		U		E		U		O
I		N	U	M	E	R	A	L		N
E				P		U				N
F	I	F	T	H		N	I	C	H	E

007

1. Christopher Columbus
2. Benjamin Franklin
3. George Washington
4. Mark Twain
5. Thomas Edison
6. Theodore Roosevelt
7. Philo Farnsworth
8. Hedy Lamarr

▶ SOLUTIONS

008

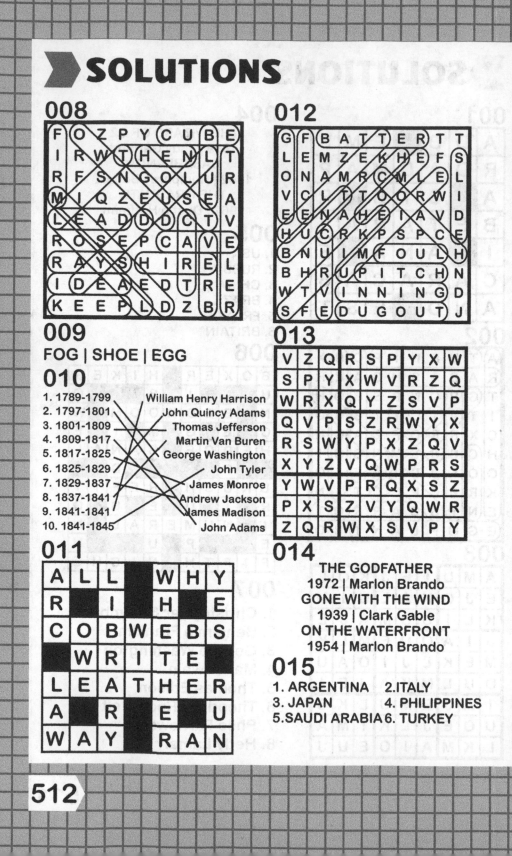

009

FOG | SHOE | EGG

010

1. 1789-1799
2. 1797-1801
3. 1801-1809
4. 1809-1817
5. 1817-1825
6. 1825-1829
7. 1829-1837
8. 1837-1841
9. 1841-1841
10. 1841-1845

William Henry Harrison
John Quincy Adams
Thomas Jefferson
Martin Van Buren
George Washington
John Tyler
James Monroe
Andrew Jackson
James Madison
John Adams

011

A	L	L		W	H	Y
R		I		H		E
C	O	B	W	E	B	S
	W	R	I	T	E	
L	E	A	T	H	E	R
A		R		E		U
W	A	Y		R	A	N

012

013

V	Z	Q	R	S	P	Y	X	W
S	P	Y	X	W	V	R	Z	Q
W	R	X	Q	Y	Z	S	V	P
Q	V	P	S	Z	R	W	Y	X
R	S	W	Y	P	X	Z	Q	V
X	Y	Z	V	Q	W	P	R	S
Y	W	V	P	R	Q	X	S	Z
P	X	S	Z	V	Y	Q	W	R
Z	Q	R	W	X	S	V	P	Y

014

THE GODFATHER
1972 | Marlon Brando
GONE WITH THE WIND
1939 | Clark Gable
ON THE WATERFRONT
1954 | Marlon Brando

015

1. ARGENTINA   2.ITALY
3. JAPAN   4. PHILIPPINES
5.SAUDI ARABIA 6. TURKEY

▶SOLUTIONS

016

C	R	E	P	T		C	O	L	I	C
E			E			L		O		O
L		S	E	R	V	A	N	T		S
E		P		M		N		R		T
B	E	A	N	S		G	R	A	S	S
		S						I		
S	A	T	I	N		T	O	N	G	S
L		I		E		R		E		A
E		C	R	E	M	A	T	E		B
E			D			P				L
T	E	E	N	S		S	P	I	T	E

017

1. Julius Caesar
2. Marco Polo
3. Kublai Khan
4. Süleyman I
5. John Knox
6. Florence Nightingale
7. Walt Whitman
8. Abraham Lincoln

018

019

GRAPES | IMAGINATION | LOVE

020

11. 1845-1849
12. 1849-1850
13. 1850-1853
14. 1853-1857
15. 1857-1861
16. 1861-1865
17. 1865-1869
18. 1869-1877
19. 1877-1881
20. 1881-1881

James A. Garfield
Zachary Taylor
Ulyses S. Grant
James Buchanan
Rutherford B. Hayes
Millard Fillmore
Abraham Lincoln
Andrew Johnson
James K. Polk
Franklin Pierce

021

N	O	R		V		N	O	B
O	P	E	R	A	T	I	V	E
	T	S	A	R	I	N	A	
C		U	N	I	T	E		S
B	U	R		A		P	A	P
S		F	A	B	L	E		A
	S	A	I	L	I	N	G	
S	A	C	R	E	D	C	O	W
O	D	E		S		E	Y	E

022

►SOLUTIONS

023

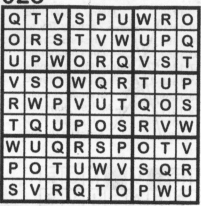

Q	T	V	S	P	U	W	R	O
O	R	S	T	V	W	U	P	Q
U	P	W	O	R	Q	V	S	T
V	S	O	W	Q	R	T	U	P
R	W	P	V	U	T	Q	O	S
T	Q	U	P	O	S	R	V	W
W	U	Q	R	S	P	O	T	V
P	O	T	U	W	V	S	Q	R
S	V	R	Q	T	O	P	W	U

024

STAR WARS
1977 | Harrison Ford
FORREST GUMP
1994 | Tom Hanks
PLANET OF THE APES
1968 | Charlton Heston

025

1. CANADA 2. MEXICO
3. ISRAEL   4. PORTUGAL
5. FINLAND 6. DENMARK

026

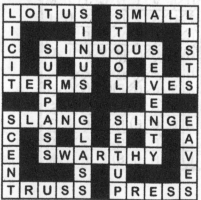

027

1. Alexander The Great
2. Marcus Aurelius
3. Avicenna (Ibn Sina)
4. Elizabeth I
5. Rider Haggard
6. Helen Keller
7. Walt Disney
8. Ernest Hemingway

028

029

MAP | LANTERN | MAN

030

21. 1881-1885 ——— Chester A. Arthur
22. 1885-1889 — William H. Taft
23. 1889-1893 — Stephen G. Cleveland
24. 1893-1897 — Warren G. Harding
25. 1897-1901 — Woodrow Wilson
26. 1901-1909 — William McKinley
27. 1909-1913 — Benjamin Harrison
28. 1913-1921 — Calvin Coolidge
29. 1921-1923 — Theodore Roosevelt
30. 1923-1929 — Stephen G. Cleveland

SOLUTIONS

031

I	S	M		S	E	A	S
L	E	A		L	A	T	T	E
L	A	N	C	E	T		A	M
		T	O	W		S	K	I
T	A	I	L		W	H	E	T
O	L	D		S	A	T		
P	I		H	E	R	E	S	Y
S	K	I	E	R		T	H	E
	E	T	N	A		L	E	T

032

C	S	E	A	E	L	E	P	H	A	N	T	R
A	H	L	S	E	A	L	I	O	N	Q	A	Y
P	B	L	U	E	W	H	A	L	E	E	T	S
Y	W	Q	U	Q	Y	K	U	S	B	A	I	W
B	O	W	I	E	K	E	G	R	C	Q	T	L
A	Z	Y	Q	Y	E	E	A	R	V	X	P	Y
R	Q	R	K	T	F	L	O	C	P	N	M	K
A	L	S	A	F	O	E	R	Q	L	O	A	C
G	B	N	A	P	S	W	H	Y	K	Z	M	T
R	A	R	K	O	D	I	A	K	B	E	A	R
M	I	U	O	F	P	B	I	S	O	N	R	A
G	K	M	R	H	I	N	O	C	E	R	O	S
H	I	P	P	O	P	O	T	A	M	U	S	F

033

D	I	X	Y	J	E	P	Z	A
Z	J	P	A	D	I	X	E	Y
E	Y	A	P	Z	X	I	J	D
Y	X	I	Z	E	J	A	D	P
A	D	E	I	Y	P	J	X	Z
J	P	Z	D	X	A	Y	I	E
I	E	Y	J	A	Z	D	P	X
P	Z	D	X	I	Y	E	A	J
X	A	J	E	P	D	Z	Y	I

034

WHITE HEAT
1949 | James Cagney
JAWS
1975 | Roy Scheider
FIELD OF DREAMS
1989 | Kevin Costner (hears it)

035

1. S. KOREA 2. N. KOREA
3. NORWAY 4. SWEDEN
5. PERU 6. BOLIVIA

036

G	A	M	E	R		Y	O	U	R	S
R			O			U				E
U		O	P	T	I	C	A	L		V
E		P		O		C		A		E
L	I	T	E	R		A	D	D	O	N
		I						Y		
C	O	M	F	Y		R	E	B	U	S
H		U		A		O		U		L
I		M	A	H	J	O	N	G		O
R		O		M		M				T
P	R	O	M	O		Y	O	U	T	H

037

1. Wolfgang A. Mozart
2. Immanuel Kant
3. John Adams
4. Queen Victoria
5. Alfred Hitchcock
6. Katharine Hepburn
7. Winston Churchill
8. Charles Schulz

▶ SOLUTIONS

038

039

- Be thankful for what YOU have.
- Take advantage of the moment.
- Things are not always what they seem.

040

31. 1929-1933 — Richard M. Nixon
32. 1933-1945 — Lyndon B. Johnson
33. 1945-1953 — Harry S. Truman
34. 1953-1961 — Franklin D. Roosevelt
35. 1961-1963 — John F. Kennedy
36. 1963-1969 — Gerald R. Ford
37. 1969-1974 — Herbert C. Hoover
38. 1974-1977 — James E. Carter
39. 1977-1981 — Dwight D. Eisenhower
40. 1981-1989 — Ronald W. Reagan

041

R U E | | P U B
T | P A R S L E Y
A S | G E I S H A
U N F E D | T A P
| A I R | R E V
P I N | H A R E M
A L I N E D | S O
P E T U N I A | O
| D E N | O N E

042

T R O B I N S O N C R U S O E
J H U N C L E T O M C A B I N
W A R O F T H E W O R L D S E
B T R E A S U R E I S L A N D
S Q J R E W H I T E F A N G J
S P M Q R M F E O S P I D B U
W N E L D K U W I T K V P G N
D R K P N N P S F L M A B N G
X S B N E Q K I K P L N U L E
N A O D Y S S E Y E B H L I E
F Z L S E O A J X A T O R R B
J A M O B Y D I C K M E X Z O
W G R E A T G A T S B Y E P O
M T H E G O O D E A R T H R K
G R A P E S O F W R A T H Q S

043

P	S	O	K	I	U	J	H	A
H	I	K	P	J	A	S	U	O
J	A	U	S	O	H	K	P	I
O	J	H	U	A	P	I	K	S
K	U	S	I	H	J	O	A	P
A	P	I	O	S	K	U	J	H
U	O	J	A	P	S	H	I	K
S	H	A	J	K	I	P	O	U
I	K	P	H	U	O	A	S	J

►SOLUTIONS

044

ALL ABOUT EVE
1950 | Bette Davis
COOL HAND LUKE
1967 | Strother Martin
MOMMIE DEAREST
1981 | Faye Dunaway

045

1. SPAIN   2. URUGUAY
3. CUBA   4. CHILE
5. VIETNAM   6. THAILAND

046

047

1. Robert Fulton
2. Alfred Nobel
3. Ulysses Grant
4. Laura Ingalls
5. John Ford
6. Hank Ketcham
7. Frank Sinatra
8. Rosa Parks

048

049

- Can't have too many people doing the same thing at the same time.
- Having opposite desires leads to nothing.
- Be a polite guest wherever you visit.

050

2 and 3

051

▶ SOLUTIONS

052

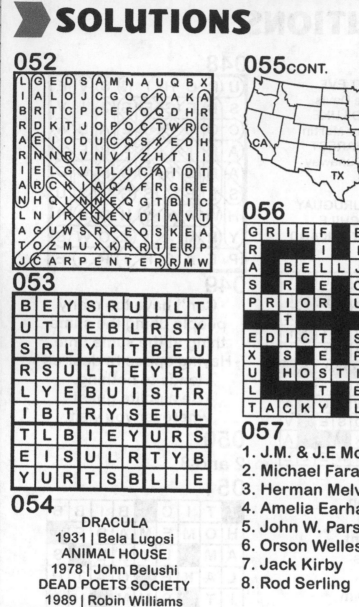

```
L G E D S A M N A U Q B X
I A L O J C G O C K A K A
B R D K T C P O C E F O Q D H R
R E E N N R V N V I Z H T I D E
A R I O D U U C Q S X E D R A C
R I E L G L A Q A F R G I R C H
I N R C K I A A F R T I B V I T
A L H Q L N N E O G T D I E T C
N L N I R E T E Y D I S K E R T
A G U W S R P E O S T E R A P
T O Z M U X K R R R T E P
J C A R P E N T E R R M W
```

053

B	E	Y	S	R	U	I	L	T
U	T	I	E	B	L	R	S	Y
S	R	L	Y	I	T	B	E	U
R	S	U	L	T	E	Y	B	I
L	Y	E	B	U	I	S	T	R
I	B	T	R	Y	S	E	U	L
T	L	B	I	E	Y	U	R	S
E	I	S	U	L	R	T	Y	B
Y	U	R	T	S	B	L	I	E

054

DRACULA
1931 | Bela Lugosi
ANIMAL HOUSE
1978 | John Belushi
DEAD POETS SOCIETY
1989 | Robin Williams

055

1. CALIFORNIA   2. FLORIDA
3. NEW YORK   4. TEXAS

055 CONT.

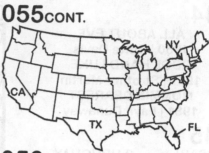

056

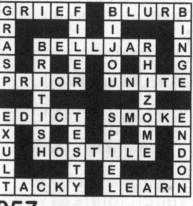

```
G R I E F   B L U R B
R       I   I       I
A   B E L L J A R   N
S   R   E   O   H   G
P R I O R   U N I T E
    T       Z
E D I C T   S M O K E
X   S   E   P   M   N
U   H O S T I L E   D
L   T   E   E       O
T A C K Y   L E A R N
```

057

1. J.M. & J.E Montgolfier
2. Michael Faraday
3. Herman Melville
4. Amelia Earhart
5. John W. Parsons
6. Orson Welles
7. Jack Kirby
8. Rod Serling

058

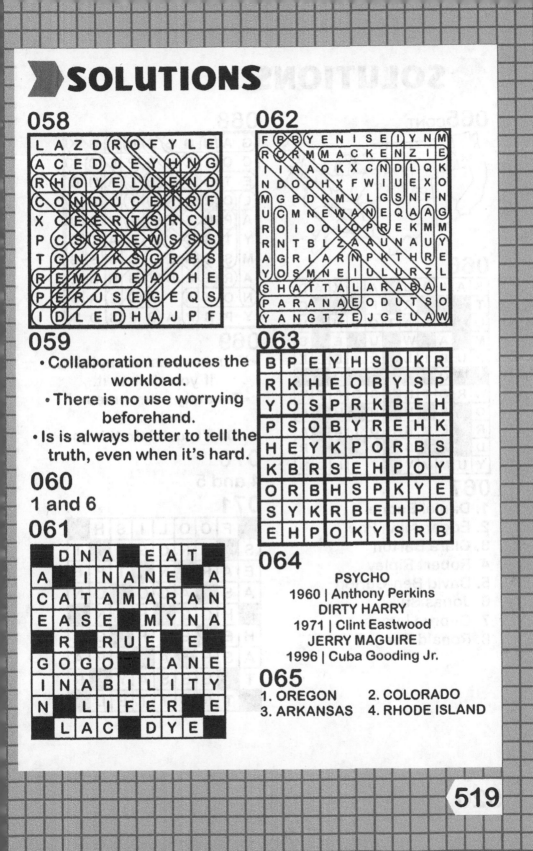

```
L A Z D R O F Y L E
A C E D O E Y H N G
R H O V E L L E N D
C O N D U C E T R F
X C E E R T S R C U
P C S S T E W S S S
T G N I R S G R B S
R E M A D E A O H E
P E R U S E G E Q S
I D L E D H A J P F
```

059

- Collaboration reduces the workload.
- There is no use worrying beforehand.
- Is is always better to tell the truth, even when it's hard.

060

1 and 6

061

```
  D N A   E A T
A   I N A N E   A
C A T A M A R A N
E A S E   M Y N A
  R   R U E   E
G O G O   L A N E
I N A B I L I T Y
N   L I F E R   E
  L A C   D Y E
```

062

```
F B B Y E N I S E I Y N M
R O R M M A C K E N Z I E
I A A O K X C N D L Q K
N D O O H X F W I U E X O
M G B D K M V L G S N F N
U R C M N E W A N E Q A G
R I O O L O P R E K M M
R N T B L Z A A U N A Y E
A G R L A R N P K T H R L
Y O S M N E I U L U R Z L
  S H A T T A L A R A B A O
  P A R A N A E O D U T S O
  Y A N G T Z E J G E U A W
```

063

```
B P E Y H S O K R
R K H E O B Y S P
Y O S P R K B E H
P S O B Y R E H K
H E Y K P O R B S
K B R S E H P O Y
O R B H S P K Y E
S Y K R B E H P O
E H P O K Y S R B
```

064

PSYCHO
1960 | Anthony Perkins
DIRTY HARRY
1971 | Clint Eastwood
JERRY MAGUIRE
1996 | Cuba Gooding Jr.

065

1. OREGON 2. COLORADO
3. ARKANSAS 4. RHODE ISLAND

► SOLUTIONS

065 CONT.

066

067

1. Daniel Boone
2. Edgar Allan Poe
3. Clara Barton
4. Robert Ripley
5. David Ben-Gurion
6. Jonas Salk
7. George Lucas
8. Ronald Reagan

068

069

- You can master anything if you stick to it.
- Tenacity overcomes all obstacles.
- Don't rush into things.

070

4 and 5

071

▶SOLUTIONS

072

```
R E Y K J A V I K M X
H E L S I N K I C E
L S E O U L Z N O X
M O S C O W I R P I
P T G I L L G O E C
R O L B B N Y M N O
A K P U I F P E H C
G Y D J Q S A C A I
U O I C A I R O G T
E E M A D R I D E Y
B E R L I N S K N M
```

073

```
K R A I S N T W M
N T W K M R S A I
M S I A T W R N K
A W R T K S I M N
T M S N A I K R W
I N K R W M A S T
W K N S I A M T R
R A T M N K W I S
S I M W R T N K A
```

074

MIDNIGHT COWBOY
1969 | Dustin Hoffman
AIRPLANE!
1980 | Leslie Nielsen
THE MASK
1994 | Jim Carrey

075

1. NEVADA   2. NEW MEXICO
3. NEBRASKA   4. PENNSYLVANIA

075 CONT.

076

```
A U D I O ■ T E N T H
N ■ ■ R ■ O ■ ■ E
T ■ C L A P P E D ■ N
I ■ H ■ T ■ A ■ E ■ N
C H U T E ■ Z E B R A
■ C ■ ■ ■ ■ A ■ ■
T A K E R ■ W A C K Y
H ■ L ■ A ■ H ■ L ■ O
R ■ E V I L E Y E ■ D
O ■ ■ T ■ L ■ ■ E
E D E M A ■ P U P I L
```

077

1. Napoleon Bonaparte
2. John Quincy Adams
3. Solomon Northup
4. Rockwell Kent
5. Edward L. Stratemeyer
6. Marjorie H. Buell
7. Mikhail Gorbachev
8. Toni Morrison

521

SOLUTIONS

078

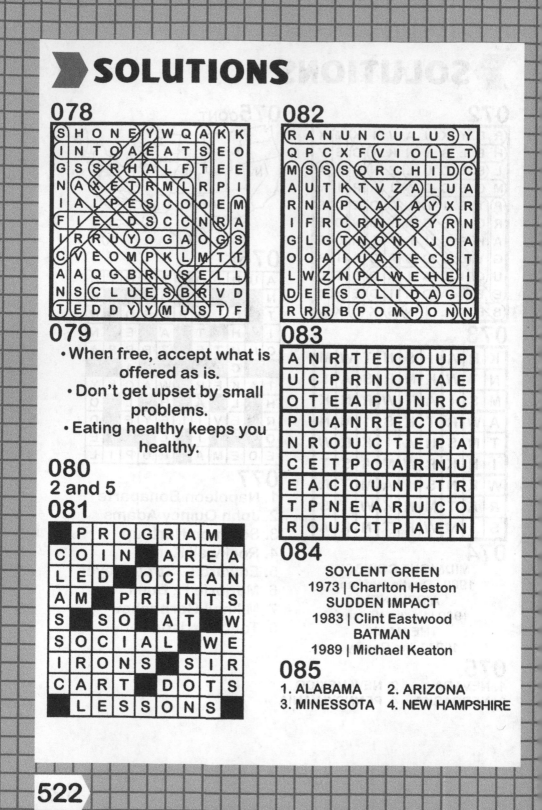

079

- When free, accept what is offered as is.
- Don't get upset by small problems.
- Eating healthy keeps you healthy.

080

2 and 5

081

	P	R	O	G	R	A	M
C	O	I	N		A	R	E	A
L	E	D		O	C	E	A	N
A	M		P	R	I	N	T	S
S		S	O		A	T		W
S	O	C	I	A	L		W	E
I	R	O	N	S		S	I	R
C	A	R	T		D	O	T	S
	L	E	S	S	O	N	S	

082

083

A	N	R	T	E	C	O	U	P
U	C	P	R	N	O	T	A	E
O	T	E	A	P	U	N	R	C
P	U	A	N	R	E	C	O	T
N	R	O	U	C	T	E	P	A
C	E	T	P	O	A	R	N	U
E	A	C	O	U	N	P	T	R
T	P	N	E	A	R	U	C	O
R	O	U	C	T	P	A	E	N

084

SOYLENT GREEN
1973 | Charlton Heston
SUDDEN IMPACT
1983 | Clint Eastwood
BATMAN
1989 | Michael Keaton

085

1. ALABAMA   2. ARIZONA
3. MINESSOTA   4. NEW HAMPSHIRE

522

▶ SOLUTIONS

085 CONT.

086

087

1. Horatio Nelson
2. Horatio Alger Jr.
3. Vincent Van Gogh
4. J. Edgar Hoover
5. Franklin D. Roosevelt
6. Gregory Peck
7. Margaret Thatcher
8. Steven Spielberg

088

089

- Being early gives you the advantage.
- At least show up.
- The secret's been revealed.

090

3 and 4

091

▶ SOLUTIONS

092

093

R	J	P	A	N	O	E	U	D
D	N	U	J	E	P	A	O	R
A	E	O	U	D	R	P	N	J
P	U	A	O	R	J	D	E	N
N	O	E	P	U	D	R	J	A
J	D	R	E	A	N	O	P	U
O	A	D	N	J	E	U	R	P
E	R	J	D	P	U	N	A	O
U	P	N	R	O	A	J	D	E

094

TO HAVE AND HAVE NOT
1941 | Lauren Bacall
GHOSTBUSTERS
1984 | Ernie Hudson
TITANIC
1997 | Leonardo DiCaprio

095

1. WASHINGTON 2. VERMONT
3. UTAH   4. VIRGINIA

095 CONT.

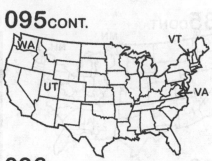

096

V	A	T	I	C		P	A	I	N	S
I						R				P
R		D	R	A	W	E	R	S		R
U		O		M		S		A		A
S	U	N	U	P			S	A	D	L	Y
W		G						N		
S	A	L	E	S			S	H	E	E	T
W		E		I		C		S		A
E		S	I	N	U	O	U	S		W
E				U		W				N
P	I	O	U	S			L	E	F	T	Y

097

1. Thomas Jefferson
2. Thomas Cochrane
3. Nikola Tesla
4. Norman Rockwell
5. Grace Kelly
6. Martin Luther King Jr.
7. Truman Capote
8. Nelson Mandela

⏵ SOLUTIONS

098

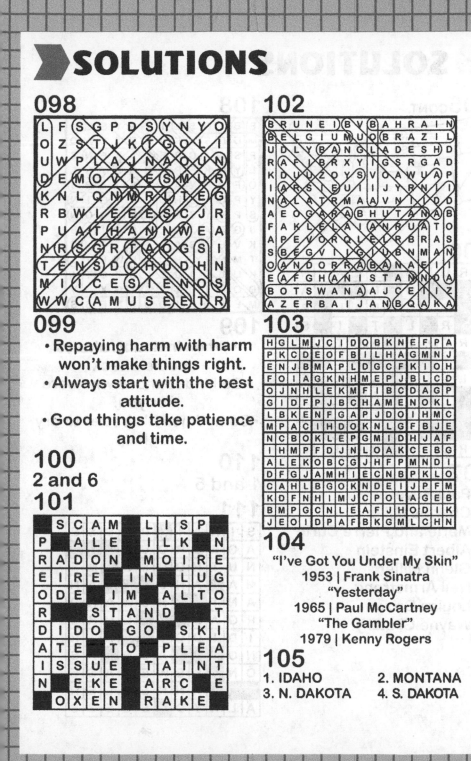

099

- Repaying harm with harm won't make things right.
- Always start with the best attitude.
- Good things take patience and time.

100

2 and 6

101

	S	C	A	M		L	I	S	P	
P		A	L	E		I	L	K		N
R	A	D	O	N		M	O	I	R	E
E	I	R	E		I	N		L	U	G
O	D	E		I	M		A	L	T	O
R			S	T	A	N	D			T
D	I	D	O		G	O		S	K	I
A	T	E		T	O		P	L	E	A
I	S	S	U	E		T	A	I	N	T
N		E	K	E		A	R	C		E
	O	X	E	N		R	A	K	E	

102

103

104

"I've Got You Under My Skin"
1953 | Frank Sinatra
"Yesterday"
1965 | Paul McCartney
"The Gambler"
1979 | Kenny Rogers

105

1. IDAHO   2. MONTANA
3. N. DAKOTA   4. S. DAKOTA

◥ SOLUTIONS

105 CONT.

106

107

1. Paul Revere
2. Charles Miller
3. Marie and Pierre Curie
4. Albert Einstein
5. Glenn Miller
6. Neil Armstrong
7. Louise Brown
8. Wayne Gretzky

108

109

- When in doubt, always double-check.
- Be kind to those who care for you.
- Sometimes it's better to cry for help.

110

1 and 5

111

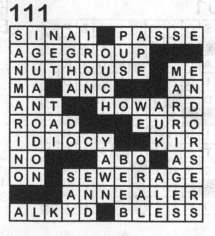

▶SOLUTIONS

112

113

114

"La Bamba"
1958 | Ritchie Valens
"Imagine"
1971 | John Lennon
"Bohemian Rapsody"
1975 | Freddie Mercury

115

1. MARYLAND 2. MASSACHUSETTS
3. LOUISIANA 4. KENTUCKY

115 CONT.

116

117

1. Matthew C. Perry
2. G. Westinghouse
3. William F. Cody
4. Pedro Flores
5. Edward VIII
6. Elvis Presley
7. Bill Gates
8. Jim Henson

▶ SOLUTIONS

118

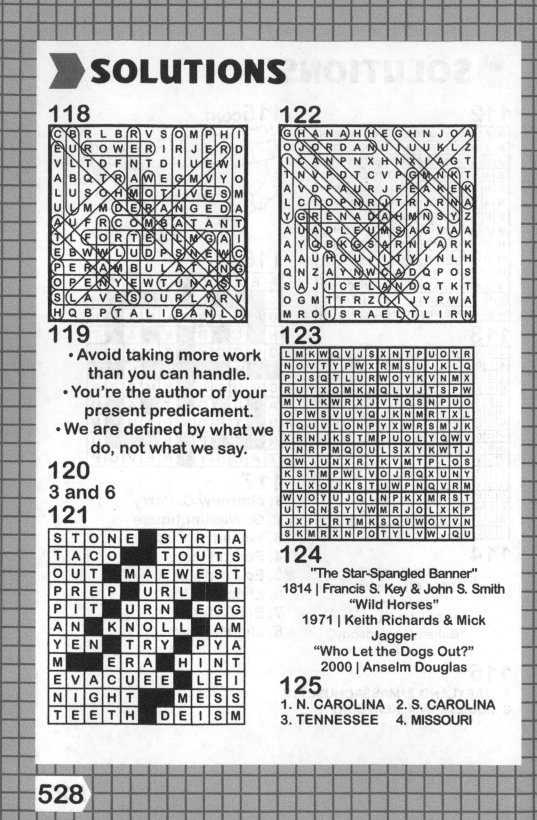

119

- Avoid taking more work than you can handle.
- You're the author of your present predicament.
- We are defined by what we do, not what we say.

120

3 and 6

121

122

123

124

"The Star-Spangled Banner"
1814 | Francis S. Key & John S. Smith
"Wild Horses"
1971 | Keith Richards & Mick Jagger
"Who Let the Dogs Out?"
2000 | Anselm Douglas

125

1. N. CAROLINA   2. S. CAROLINA
3. TENNESSEE   4. MISSOURI

► SOLUTIONS

125 CONT.

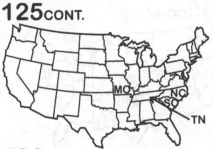

126

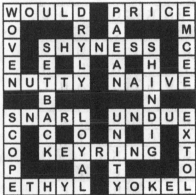

127

1. Wilhelm Röntgen
2. Ernest Rutherford
3. Woodrow Wilson
4. Dwight D. Eisenhower
5. Erich von Däniken
6. Uri Geller
7. Stephen King
8. Ridley Scott

128

129

- When it comes to couples, both are responsible.
- Don't make plans based on expectations.
- Complaining won't solve anything.

130

2 and 5

131

▶ SOLUTIONS

132

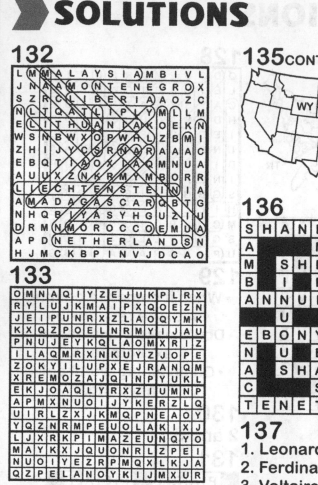

133

134

"Pennies from Heaven"
1936 | Bing Crosby
"Bridge over Troubled Water"
1970 | Simon & Garfunkel
"Born in the USA"
1982 | Bruce Springsteen

135

1. OKLAHOMA
2. OHIO
3. WYOMING
4. KANSAS

135 CONT.

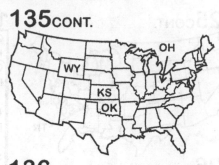

136

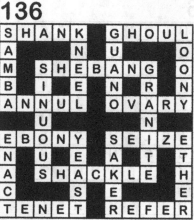

S	H	A	N	K		G	H	O	U	L
A			N			U			O	
M		S	H	E	B	A	N	G	O	N
B		I		E		N		R		Y
A	N	N	U	L		O	V	A	R	Y
		U					N			
E	B	O	N	Y		S	E	I	Z	E
N		U		E		A		T		T
A		S	H	A	C	K	L	E		H
C				S		E				E
T	E	N	E	T		R	E	F	E	R

137

1. Leonardo DaVinci
2. Ferdinand Magellan
3. Voltaire
4. Rudolf Diesel
5. Jack Dempsey
6. Charles Lindbergh
7. Buddy Holly
8. Ray Croc

▶ SOLUTIONS

138

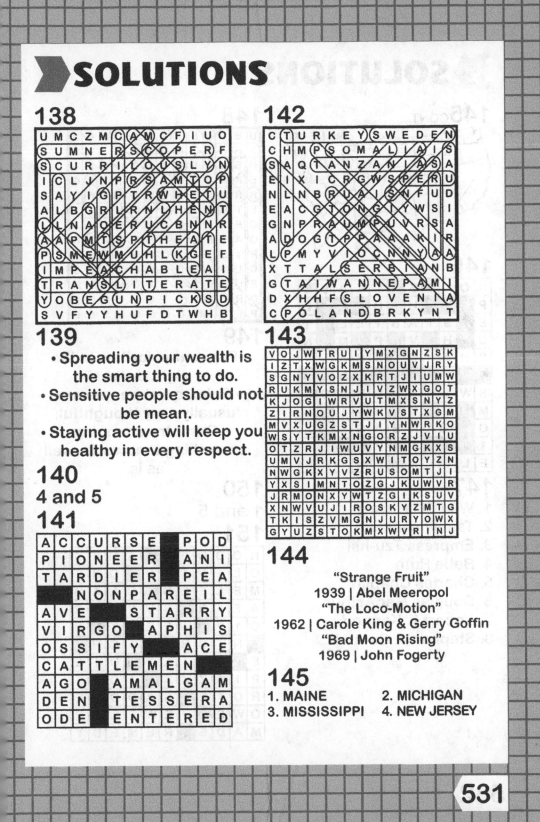

142

139

- Spreading your wealth is the smart thing to do.
- Sensitive people should not be mean.
- Staying active will keep you healthy in every respect.

140

4 and 5

141

143

144

"Strange Fruit"
1939 | Abel Meeropol
"The Loco-Motion"
1962 | Carole King & Gerry Goffin
"Bad Moon Rising"
1969 | John Fogerty

145

1. MAINE
2. MICHIGAN
3. MISSISSIPPI
4. NEW JERSEY

► SOLUTIONS

145 CONT.

146

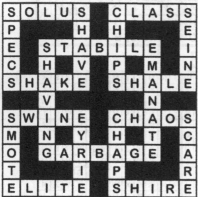

147

1. Wild Bill Hickok
2. Tsar Nicholas II
3. Empress Tzu-hsi
4. Babe Ruth
5. Charles Chaplin
6. Douglas MacArthur
7. Robert F. Kennedy
8. Stephen J. Cannell

148

149

• Put your priorities in the right order.
• Calm, quiet people are usually very thoughtful.
• Don't try changing something that works well as is.

150

1 and 5

151

▶ SOLUTIONS

152

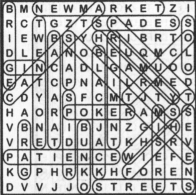

153

154

"The Twist"
1959 | Hank Ballard
"Fox on the Run"
1974 | A.Scott & M. Tucker
"Panama"
1984 | Van Halen

155

1. W. VIRGINIA   2. CONNECTICUT
3. IOWA   4. WISCONSIN

155CONT.

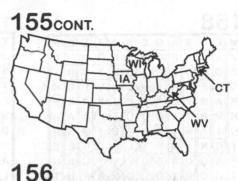

156

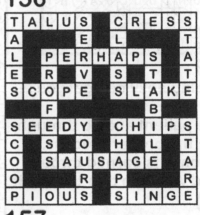

157

1. James Brooke
2. Robert L. Stevenson
3. Giacomo Puccini
4. Thomas J. Watson
5. Christian Dior
6. Arnold Drake
7. Marvin Gaye
8. Ozzy Osbourne

►SOLUTIONS

158

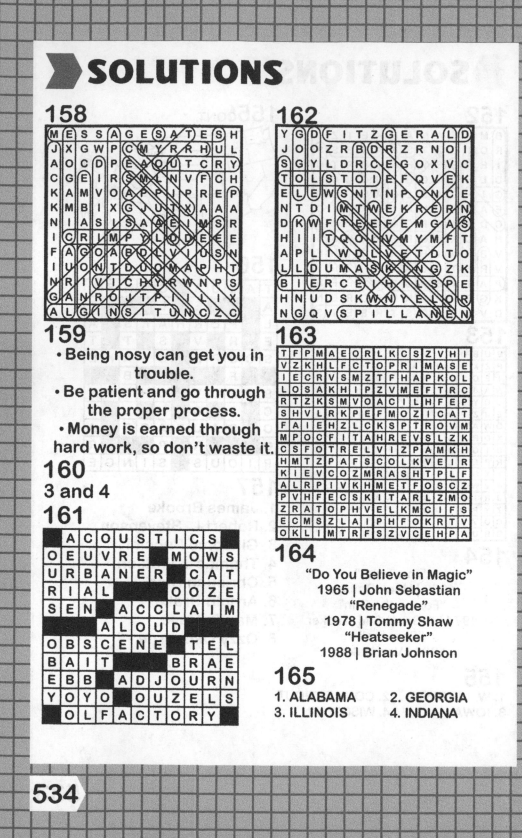

159

- Being nosy can get you in trouble.
- Be patient and go through the proper process.
- Money is earned through hard work, so don't waste it.

160

3 and 4

161

162

163

164

"Do You Believe in Magic"
1965 | John Sebastian
"Renegade"
1978 | Tommy Shaw
"Heatseeker"
1988 | Brian Johnson

165

1. ALABAMA   2. GEORGIA
3. ILLINOIS   4. INDIANA

►SOLUTIONS

165 CONT.

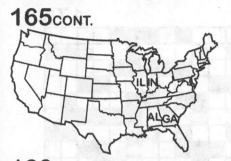

166

S	T	A	V	E		C	L	A	S	S
K			E			R				H
E		C	A	R	C	A	S	S		A
I		A		I		S	H			V
N	E	R	V	E		S	H	A	L	E
		D				T				
C	H	I	P	S		S	E	T	U	P
R		A		E		C				R
O		C	E	N	T	A	U	R		I
S		S		S		N				D
S	K	A	T	E		T	H	A	N	E

167

1. Don Bosco
2. Pyotr Ilyich Tchaikovsky
3. J. P. Morgan
4. Manfred von Richthofen
5. Harry Truman
6. Gary Cooper
7. Yuri Gagarin
8. John Glenn

168

169

- Can't do what I would like to do.
  - A little sign of a larger problem lying below.
- Knowing nothing may be difficult, but better than receiving bad news.

170

2 and 6

171

D	I	P	S	O	M	A	N	I	A	C
	T	R	I	V	A	L	E	N	T	
M		E	R	A		S	O	S		R
I	M	P		L	A	O		E	R	E
L	O	S	S		D		S	C	A	G
D	O	C		D	I	E		T	I	N
E	C	H	O		E		P	I	T	A
W	H	O		J	U	S		C	A	N
S		O	B	I		T	A	I		T
	G	L	I	S	S	A	N	D	I	
P	O	S	T	M	O	R	T	E	M	S

►SOLUTIONS

172

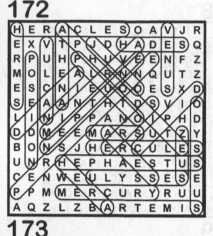

175

173

176

A	I	T	C	H			I	N	L	A	Y
V			O			O		D			U
O		C	O	N	F	I	R	M			M
I		H		O		O		I			M
D	R	E	A	R		M	I	N	T		Y
		V						A			
S	T	R	U	T		L	A	R	V	A	
T		O		A		E		E		W	
E		N	A	S	C	E	N	T		A	
I				T		R				S	
N	A	S	T	Y			Y	O	U	T	H

174

"Spider-Man"
1967 | Webster & Harris
"Wonder Woman"
1970 | Fox & Gimbel
"Believe It or Not"
1981 | Joey Scarbury

177

1. Salvador Allende
2. Phyllis Diller
3. Howard Stern
4. Eduardo Barreto
5. Prince Charles
6. Kareem Abdul-Jabbar
7. Hulk Hogan
8. Maya Angelou

▶ SOLUTIONS

178

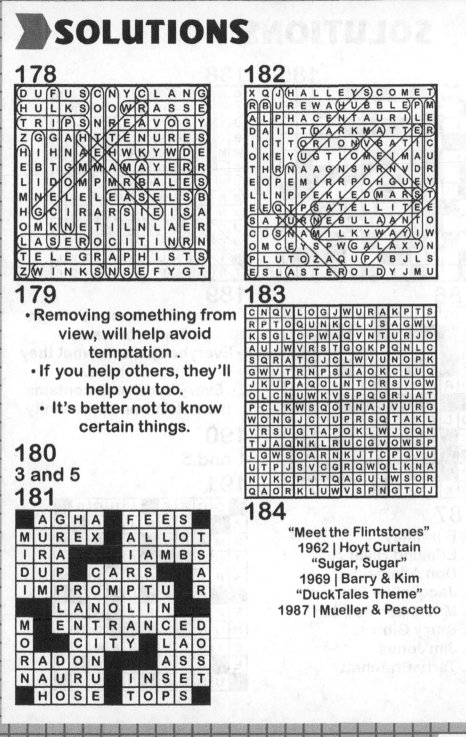

179

- Removing something from view, will help avoid temptation.
- If you help others, they'll help you too.
- It's better not to know certain things.

180

3 and 5

181

182

183

184

"Meet the Flintstones"
1962 | Hoyt Curtain
"Sugar, Sugar"
1969 | Barry & Kim
"DuckTales Theme"
1987 | Mueller & Pescetto

185

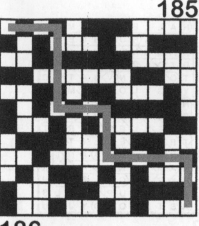

188

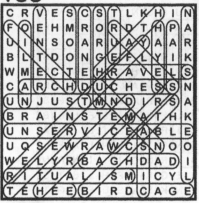

186

189

- Only what comes through hard work lasts.
- Everybody wants what they can't have.
- Every bad break contains the seed of an opportunity.

190

1 and 5

191

187

1. Bill Haley
2. Edmund Hillary
3. Don Adams
4. Jacqueline Susann
5. Muammar Gaddafi
6. Barry Gibb
7. Jim Jones
8. Terry Pratchett

►SOLUTIONS

192

```
P F L I N T S T O N E S O D S X
P M X J S W H H A P P Y D A Y S
T S T A R T R E K D L G Z U L G
W I I K G B R E A K I N G B A D
Q F G E T S M A R T A Y K D W W
Q R F K A P S R H N E H B I A G
H I G H W A Y T O H E A V E N E
M V F A T A L B E R T W M C D I
S F A N T A S Y I S L A N D O U
K O J A K N I G H T R I D E R S
D B A T M A N S D F R I E N D S
A Q S I M P S O N S X F R Z E D
L O V E B O A T M G A I A O R W
L I F E O N M A R S S V R C K W
A G I N C R E D I B L E H U L K
S A N F O R D A N D S O N E Q D
```

195

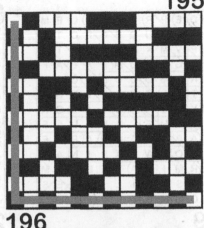

193

```
O M P E U I K A H S G C T L W N
W S T C H P L M N K I E O U A G
N H K G C E O T W A L U I M S P
U A L I G N W S O T M P K C E H
L C A N P T E H G O W S M K I U
H O W S L U A I M E K N C G P T
E I U T O G M K L C P A W H N S
M K G P N S C W I U T H E O L A
A E C U S M N G T I O L P W H K
G L I O A H U E K P S W N T M C
T P N M K W I O A H C G L S U E
S W H K T C P L U N E M A I G O
I U O L E K G N S W A T H P C M
C N E W M O T U P G H I S A K L
K G M H I A S P C L N O U E T W
P T S A W L H C E M U K G N O I
```

196

194

"Spirit in the Sky"
1969 | Norman Greenbaum
"Girls Just Want to Have Fun"
1983 | Cyndi Lauper
"Holyanna"
1984 | Porcaro & Paich

197

1. Juan Ponce de Leon
2. John Winthrop
3. John Hancock
4. Gail Borden
5. Margaret Mitchell
6. Leon Uris
7. Carl Sagan
8. Pierre Culliford ("Peyo")

198

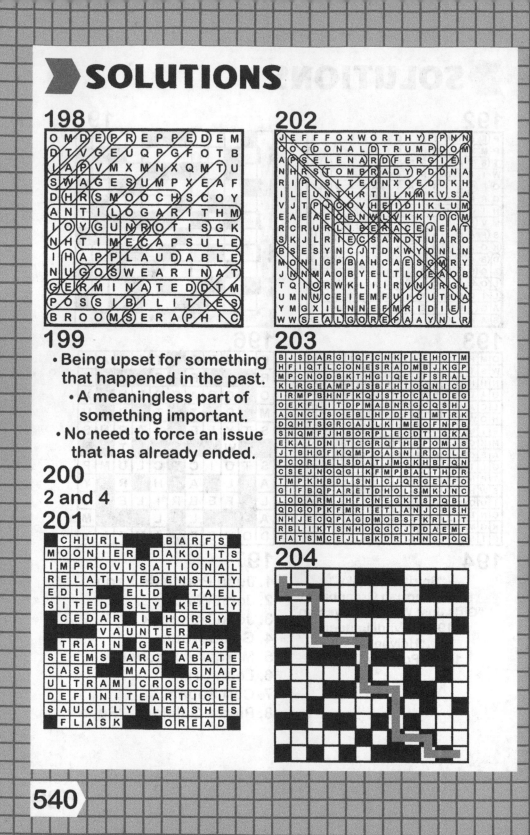

199

- Being upset for something that happened in the past.
- A meaningless part of something important.
- No need to force an issue that has already ended.

200

2 and 4

201

202

203

204

▶ SOLUTIONS

205
"Star Trek" | 1966
"Buffy The Vampire Slayer" | 1997
"How I Met Your Mother" | 2005

206
IDENTICAL	IMPORTANT
CHOCOLATE	CONSONANT
CHRISTMAS	CHRISTIAN
BEAUTIFUL	DANGEROUS
HAPPINESS	MASCULINE
WEDNESDAY	CELEBRATE
CHALLENGE	AUSTRALIA
ADVENTURE	IRREGULAR

207
1. Franz Kafka
2. Charles "Lucky" Luciano
3. Jimmy Stewart
4. George Reeves
5. Rubin "Hurricane" Carter
6. Erno Rubik
7. Gary Kasparov
8. Gordon Gould

208

209
"We are not interested in the possibilities of defeat; they do not exist."
Queen Victoria

"We shall defend our island, whatever the cost may be, we shall fight on the beaches, we shall fight on the landing grounds, we shall fight in the fields and in the streets, we shall fight in the hills; we shall never surrender."
Sir Winston Churchill

"Mr. Gorbachev, open this gate! Mr. Gorbachev, tear down this wall!"
Ronald Reagan

210
2 and 6

211

▶ SOLUTIONS

212

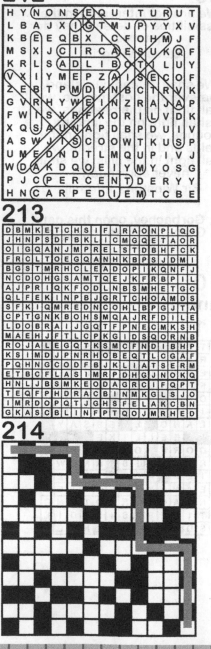

213

214

215

"Emergency!" | 1972
"Frasier" | 1993
"The Office" | 2005

216

SOMETHING	UNDEFINED
KNOWLEDGE	HALLOWEEN
POLLUTION	AMBULANCE
PRESIDENT	ALLIGATOR
WRESTLING	SEVENTEEN
PINEAPPLE	AFFECTION
ADJECTIVE	CONGRUENT
SECRETARY	COMMUNITY

217

1. Burt Reynolds
2. Donald B. Hamilton
3. Grace Bumbry
4. Bob Dylan
5. Andy Warhol
6. Gary Larson
7. Michael Landon
8. Neil Gaiman

218

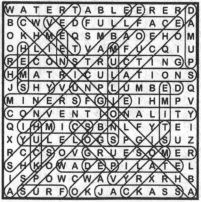

219

"Those who refuse to learn from history are condemned to repeat it."
George Santayana

"So, first of all, let me assert my firm belief that the only thing we have to fear is fear itself-nameless, unreasoning, unjustified terror which paralyzes needed efforts to convert retreat into advance."
Franklin Delano Roosevelt

"Revolution is not a dinner party, not an essay, nor a painting, nor a piece of embroidery; it cannot be advanced softly, gradually, carefully, considerately, respectfully, politely, plainly, and modestly."
Mao Tse-tung

220

4 and 5

221

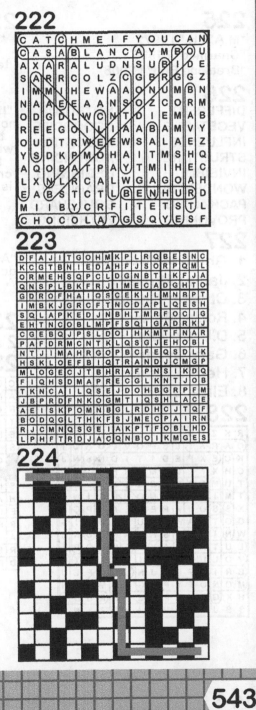

222

223

224

▶ SOLUTIONS

225
"M.A.S.H." | 1972
"Charmed" | 1998
"Breaking Bad" | 2008

226
DIFFERENT	NUTRITION
VEGETABLE	CROCODILE
INFLUENCE	EDUCATION
STRUCTURE	ABOUNDING
INVISIBLE	BEGINNING
WONDERFUL	BRAINLESS
PACKAGING	BOULEVARD
PROVOKING	WITHERING

227
1. Geoffrey Chaucer
2. James Murray
3. Chester Gould
4. Rocky Marciano
5. D.B. Cooper
6. Gary Gygax
7. Herbie Hancock
8. Elizabeth II

228

229
"You must not fight too often with one enemy, or you will teach him all your art of war."
Napoleon Bonaparte

"It is not the critic who counts; not the man who points out how the strong man stumbles, or where the doer of deeds could have done them better. The credit belongs to the man who is actually in the arena, whose face is marred by dust and sweat and blood..."
Theodore Roosevelt

"Ask not what your country can do for you; ask what you can do for your country."
John Fitzgerald Kennedy

230
2 and 3

231

▶ SOLUTIONS

232

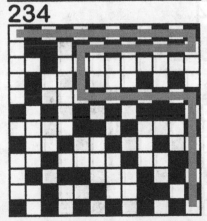

233

234

235

"Lost in Space" | 1965
"The Incredible Hulk" | 1977
"Fantasy Island" | 1977

236

BREATHING	CHARACTER
SOPHOMORE	BLESSINGS
SEPTEMBER	ADVERSITY
IMPERFECT	CONFUSION
BREAKFAST	ABDUCTING
XYLOPHONE	AFTERLIFE
HAMBURGER	SUFFERING
INTEGRITY	EVERYBODY

237

1. Ambrose Bierce
2. Louise Brooks
3. Joe Louis
4. Veronica Lake
5. Charles Addams
6. Brooke Shields
7. Victor Arriagada ("Vicar")
8. Richard Pryor

238

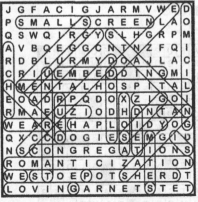

239

"You and I, gentlemen, have shared the labour and shared the danger, and the rewards are for us all. The conquered territory belongs to you; from your ranks the governors of it are chosen…"

Alexander The Great

"Hear me, my Chiefs! I am tired; my heart is sick and sad. From where the sun now stands I will fight no more forever."

Chief Joseph

"But has the last word been said? Must hope disappear? Is defeat final? No!

Believe me, I who am speaking to you with full knowledge of the facts, and who tell you that nothing is lost for France. The same means that overcame us can bring us victory one day. For France is not alone! She is not alone! She is not alone!"

Charles de Gaulle

240

1 and 5

241

	L	A	P	U	P			F	U	M	E	R
C	U	R	L	S	U	P		B	O	N	E	L	E	T
I	S	R	A	E	L	I		U	R	I	N	A	T	E
S	T	A	N	D	E	E		G	E	T	I	T	O	N
C	E	N	T			T	H	E	W		S	I	R	S
O	R	G	A	N		Y	O	Y	O		C	O	T	E
	S	E	R	U	M		R	E	M	A	I	N	S	
			L	A	U	N	D	E	R			
	H	E	M	L	I	N	E		N	I	C	H	E
L	A	S	E		N	E	T	T		A	L	O	N	G
O	R	C	A		M	A	S	H		O	T	T	O
F	L	A	T	C	A	R		E	M	I	T	T	E	R
T	O	P	M	O	S	T		T	I	N	T	I	N	G
S	T	E	A	L	T	H		A	L	D	E	N	T	E
	S	E	N	D	S			L	O	D	G	E	

242

243

244

►SOLUTIONS

245

"Leave It to Beaver" | 1957
"Sanford and Son " | 1972
"The A-Team" | 1983

246

CURIOSITY
CELEBRITY
DELICIOUS
TURQUOISE
ATTENTION
COMPANION
ELOCUTION
WHIMSICAL

DIFFICULT
AGITATION
NECESSARY
LIGHTNING
CHEMISTRY
RECYCLING
TREATMENT
SPAGHETTI

247

1. Henry Morton Stanley
2. Annie Oakley
3. Orville and Wilbur Wright
4. D.W. Griffith
5. Edward V. Rickenbacker
6. Roscoe "Fatty" Arbuckle
7. Esther Williams
8. Louis Armstrong

248

249

"Having now finished the work assigned me, I retire from the great theater of Action; and bidding an Affectionate farewell to this August body under whose orders I have so long acted, I here offer my Commission, and take my leave of all the employments of public life."
George Washington

"In the democracy which I have envisaged, a democracy established by non-violence, there will be equal freedom for all. Everybody will be his own master. It is to join a struggle for such democracy that I invite you today."
Mahatma Gandhi

"In the councils of government, we must guard against the acquisition of unwarranted influence, whether sought or unsought, by the military-industrial complex. The potential for the disastrous rise of misplaced power exists and will persist. We must never let the weight of this combination endanger our liberties or democratic processes."
Dwight D. Eisenhower

250
3 and 6

▶ SOLUTIONS

251

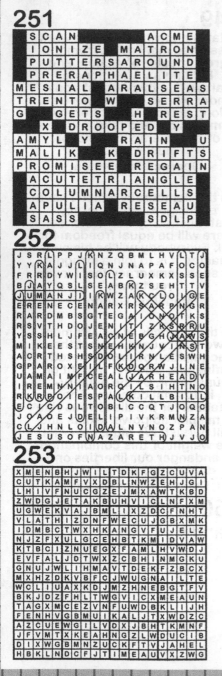

```
  S C A N         A C M E
  I O N I Z E   M A T R O N
  P U T T E R S A R O U N D
  P R E R A P H A E L I T E
M E S I A L   A R A L S E A S
T R E N T O   W     S E R R A
G     G E T S     H   R E S T
    X   D R O O P E D   Y
A M Y L   Y   R A I N     U
M A L I K   K   D R I F T S
P R O M I S E E   R E G A I N
  A C U T E T R I A N G L E
  C O L U M N A R C E L L S
  A P U L I A   R E S E A U
  S A S S       S D L P
```

252

253

254

255

"Columbo" | 1968
"Scooby-Doo" | 1969
"Seinfeld" | 1989

256

BILLBOARD
AGREEMENT
TERRITORY
AMENDMENT
ARCHITECT
FLEDGLING
ECOSYSTEM
MAGNESIUM

TWENTIETH
DECEPTION
CARIBBEAN
GENERATOR
PERIMETER
AMPHIBIAN
RADIATION
ORANGUTAN

257

1. William Randolph Hearst
2. Rudolph Valentino
3. E.C. Segar
4. Wernher Von Braun
5. Godtfred Kirk Christiansen
6. Julia Child
7. Louise Fletcher
8. Chuck Wagner

►SOLUTIONS

258

259

"It is this fate, I solemnly assure you, that I dread for you, when the time comes that you make your reckoning, and realize that there is no longer anything that can be done. May you never find yourselves, men of Athens, in such a position!"

Demostenes

"Of course, in one sense, the first essential for a man's being a good citizen is his possession of the home virtues of which we think when we call a man by the emphatic adjective of manly."

Theodore Roosevelt

"Fans, for the past two weeks you have been reading about a bad break I got. Yet today I consider myself the luckiest man on the face of the earth."

Lou Gehrig

260

2 and 4

261

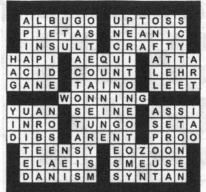

262

U	J	L	M	O	M	H	B	J	M	Q	R	O	M	L	C	G
Z	X	N	I	R	T	Y	M	P	L	N	A	U	I	N	Z	Y
N	I	Z	S	D	I	N	M	Y	F	A	I	R	L	A	D	Y
D	A	X	S	I	O	N	H	Q	C	T	E	M	L	P	S	X
Y	E	P	C	N	C	O	I	I	M	I	M	A	I	O	O	T
P	J	E	O	A	E	R	M	A	A	O	D	N	O	L	F	M
H	O	U	N	R	A	M	E	J	G	N	K	I	N	E	F	Y
J	U	T	G	Y	N	A	N	M	N	A	G	N	O	O	I	L
U	T	O	S	E	P	S	R	I	J	O	L	R	H	O	N	C	E
B	O	S	N	E	E	A	N	D	L	T	M	A	L	D	E	F
H	F	Q	I	O	L	E	B	T	I	R	I	V	L	Y	S	T
D	A	Y	R	A	P	E	U	L	M	A	E	C	A	A	N	P
F	F	R	L	L	V	S	A	M	I	A	H	A	B	M	C	O
L	R	E	I	T	E	N	C	A	J	S	A	A	U	E	N	J
H	I	H	T	N	S	K	A	A	U	E	N	A	I	T	E
S	C	K	Y	R	T	U	N	Y	P	R	L	R	B	T	V	D
M	A	G	N	U	M	F	O	R	C	E	L	R	Y	E	W	Q

263

N	P	Z	R	C	O	L	K	T	J	Y	X	M	D	V	B	I	Q	A	S
S	O	D	K	T	X	A	R	C	I	Q	B	P	N	J	Z	M	L	V	Y
Y	Q	V	B	J	D	M	N	P	S	I	Z	L	A	C	K	X	O	R	T
X	L	A	M	I	Q	Y	Z	V	B	O	T	R	K	S	P	C	D	N	J
C	K	T	J	S	V	O	D	L	M	X	A	Z	B	Y	R	P	N	Q	I
B	R	I	X	N	J	Z	A	Y	T	P	L	K	M	Q	V	O	C	S	D
M	D	Y	A	P	N	R	Q	B	C	T	S	O	V	I	L	K	J	Z	X
Q	Z	L	O	V	I	K	P	S	X	D	R	C	J	N	A	Y	B	T	M
P	X	K	D	Z	B	Q	I	N	L	C	O	V	S	T	Y	J	R	M	A
O	A	B	N	R	C	J	M	D	Z	K	P	Y	I	X	S	Q	T	L	V
L	I	M	S	Q	K	V	T	A	Y	B	J	N	R	Z	X	D	P	O	C
V	J	C	T	Y	R	P	S	X	O	A	D	Q	L	M	N	B	Z	I	K
R	V	X	Q	A	T	N	L	I	K	S	Y	B	C	P	J	Z	M	D	O
I	B	O	P	M	Z	D	J	R	Q	V	K	A	T	L	C	S	Y	X	N
J	C	N	L	K	S	X	Y	O	V	R	M	I	Z	D	Q	T	A	P	B
T	Y	S	Z	D	P	C	B	M	A	J	N	X	Q	O	I	L	K	J	Z	X
A	N	P	Y	O	M	B	C	Z	D	L	V	S	X	K	T	R	I	J	Q
Z	S	J	V	B	L	T	X	Q	N	M	I	D	Y	R	O	A	K	C	P
K	M	R	C	X	Y	I	V	J	P	Z	Q	T	O	A	D	N	S	B	L
D	T	Q	I	L	A	S	O	K	R	N	C	J	P	B	M	V	X	Y	Z

►SOLUTIONS

264

268

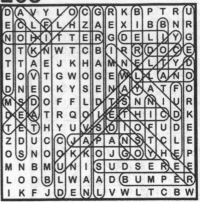

265

"The Honeymooners" | 1955
"Hawaii Five-O" | 1968
"The Six Million Dollar Man" | 1974

266

INNOCENCE	SUNFLOWER
DANDELION	AUTHORITY
NIGHTMARE	MOUSTACHE
COMMODITY	INCEPTION
ABUNDANCE	FIREWORKS
DIRECTION	AWARENESS
DIVERGENT	HURRICANE
REFERENCE	LISTENING

267

1. Joseph Pulitzer
2. Frédéric A. Bartholdi
3. Lon Chaney
4. Cole Porter
5. Crockett Johnson
6. Hugh Hefner
7. Jack Finney
8. Christine Evert

269

"... and if I say again that daily to discourse about virtue, and of those other things about which you hear me examining myself and others, is the greatest good of man, and that the unexamined life is not worth living, you are still less likely to believe me."
Socrates

"I believe that man will not merely endure: he will prevail. He is immortal, not because he alone among creatures has an inexhaustible voice, but because he has a soul..."
William Faulkner

"And like the old soldier of that ballad, I now close my military career and just fade away, an old soldier who tried to do his duty as God gave him the light to see that duty."
Douglas MacArthur

270

4 and 6

▶ SOLUTIONS

271

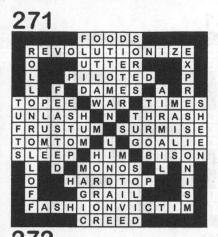

```
          F O O D S
  R E V O L U T I O N I Z E
  O       U T T E R       X
  L     P I L O T E D     P
  L   F   D A M E S   A   R
T O P E E   W A R   T I M E S
U N L A S H   N   T H R A S H
F R U S T U M   S U R M I S E
T O M T O M   L   G O A L I E
S L E E P   H I M   B I S O N
  L   D   M O N O S   L
  O     H A R D T O P     I
  F       G R A I L       S
F A S H I O N V I C T I M
        C R E E D
```

272

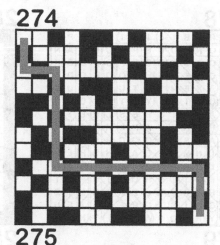

273

274

275

"Hogan's Heroes" | 1965
"The Andy Griffith Show" | 1968
"Fat Albert" | 1972

276

CRITICISM	ACCORDION
TRADITION	BRILLIANT
SCORCHING	FANTASTIC
PROFESSOR	AWAKENING
CHAMELEON	TANGERINE
GATHERING	LEGENDARY
SCIENTIST	WATERFALL
ASTRONAUT	DEDICATED

277

1. Robert E. Howard
2. Dino De Laurentiis
3. Ron Cobb
4. Gerry Lopez
5. Oliver Stone
6. John Milius
7. Arnold Schwarzenegger
8. Sven-Ole Thorsen

278

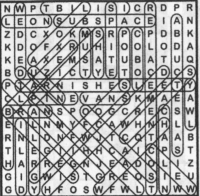

279

"So died these men as became Athenians. You, their survivors, must determine to have as unfaltering a resolution in the field, though you may pray that it may have a happier issue."

Pericles

"Is life so dear, or peace so sweet, as to be purchased at the price of chains and slavery? Forbid it, Almighty God! I know not what course others may take; but as for me, give me liberty, or give me death!"

Patrick Henry

"With malice toward none, with charity for all, with firmness in the right as God gives us to see the right, let us strive on to finish the work we are in, to bind up the nation's wounds..."

Abraham Lincoln

280

1 and 5

281

J	A	P	I	N	G			I	D	I	O	M	S
E	D	I	T	O	R		C	A	S	K	E	T	
T				G	O	R	E	D				I	
P		K	N	O	T		C	O	L	A		C	
R		N		T		A		I	N			K	
O	P	O	R	T	O		P	A	P	Y	R	I	
P	A	W						W	A	N			
U	N	H	U	R	T		B	U	S	I	N	G	
L		O	F		I		A		A	S		P	
I		W	O	R	N		R	I	C	E		O	
			A	D	L	I	B					I	
O	H	M	A	G	E		T	E	U	T	O	N	
N	E	A	T	E	R		E	X	P	O	R	T	

282

(word search grid — SCHINDLER'S LIST, TOP GUN, TARANTULA, TRUE GRIT, SCENT OF A WOMAN, STAND BY ME, FOX, etc.)

283

(word search grid)

▶ SOLUTIONS

284

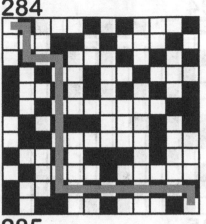

285

"Dragnet" | 1967
"All in the family" | 1971
"Nip/Tuck" | 2003

286

ADMIRABLE   SIGNATURE
JELLYFISH   SHRIEKING
BALLISTIC   FAIRYTALE
BUTTERFLY   MECHANISM
FORGOTTEN   SENSATION
SLEEPOVER   PENINSULA
TREASURER   SAXOPHONE
SANCTUARY   ADVERTISE

287

1. John André
2. Benedict Arnold
3. J.M.W. Turner
4. Rudyard Kipling
5. Willis Carrier
6. Juliette Gordon Low
7. Ray Chapman
8. Walter Chrysler

288

```
E E N O B B E X R R S B P T H
H G V E A P A P P R O V A L S
L M E G A F L O P E U O S H P
B B H R E D L T O G R V S H Z
A W C F N Z T V O E Z E E A O
C S T E E P E R P N G R R I L
K R C G A B L E B E L B E R A
O Y A R S S E A T R O U T R C
R E N A P R I E R A A R R I I
D B A D C B O M S T T D O N N
E R L A X A G E O I S E C E I
R E S T R I C T I V E N E S S
T A M E S T U N N E L E D S M
R D Z C L E A R H E A D E D A
D O U B L E J E O P A R D Y I
```

289

"Blessed are the poor in spirit: for theirs is the kingdom of heaven.
Blessed are they that mourn: for they shall be comforted.
Blessed are the meek: for they shall inherit the earth."
Jesus of Nazareth

"I am not included within the pale of this glorious anniversary! Your high independence only reveals the immeasurable distance between us. The blessings in which you this day rejoice are not enjoyed in common."
Frederick Douglass

"This is our hope. This is the faith that I go back to the South with. With this faith we will be able to hew out of the mountain of despair a stone of hope."
Martin Luther King Jr.

290

3 and 6

SOLUTIONS

291

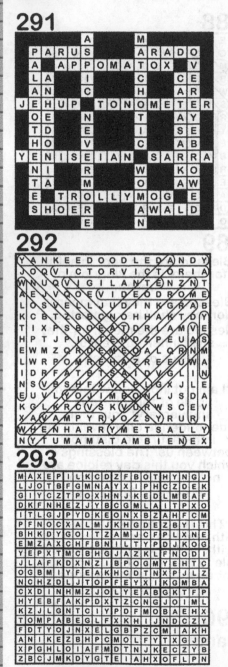

A M
PARUS ARADO
A APPOMATOX V
LAN I C CE
AN C AR
JEHUP TONOMETER
OE N T AY
TD E I SE
HO V C AB
YENISEIAN SARRA
NI R W KO
TA M O AW
E TROLLYMOG E
SHOER AWALD
E N

294

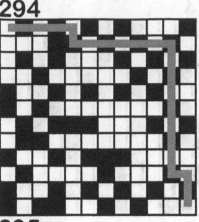

292

YANKEEDOODLEDANDY
VICTORVICTORIA
VIGILANTE
VIDEODROME
WHENHARRYMETSALLY
NYTUMAMATAMBIENEX

293

(letter grid)

295

"The Flintstones" | 1960
"Get Smart" | 1965
"Kojak" | 1973

296

BARBARIAN	RASPBERRY
FRAGRANCE	HISTORIAN
CONTINENT	AMBITIOUS
SALVATION	CONSCIOUS
PROPELLER	AUTOMATIC
METRONOME	PARACHUTE
EQUIPMENT	TOUCHDOWN
BLUEBERRY	GLADIATOR

297

1. Ty Cobb
2. Clare Hollingworth
3. John D. Rockefeller Jr.
4. Roger Bannister
5. Andrei Tarkovsky
6. Kerry Livgren
7. Gordon Sumner ("Sting")
8. Xaime Hernandez

▶ SOLUTIONS

298

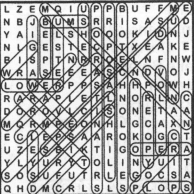

299

"Are we ruling over globalization or is globalization ruling over us? Is it possible to speak of solidarity and of 'being all together' in an economy based on ruthless competition? How far does our fraternity go?"
José Mujica

"I cannot help asking those who have caused the situation, do you realize now what you've done?"
Vladimir Putin

"The establishment protected itself but not the citizens of our country. Their victories have not been your victories. Their triumphs have not been your triumphs. While they have celebrated there has been little to celebrate for struggling families all across our land."
Donald J. Trump.

300

2 and 3

301

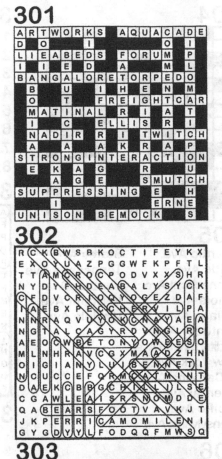

302

303

►SOLUTIONS

304

305

Atlantic Ave.	States Ave.
Baltic Ave.	Tennessee Ave.
Connecticut Ave.	Ventnor Ave.
Illinois Ave.	Vermont Ave.
Indiana Ave.	Virginia Ave.
Kentucky Ave.	
Mediterranean Ave.	
New York Ave.	
N. Carolina Ave.	
Oriental Ave.	
Pacific Ave.	
Pennsylvania Ave.	

306

ALLITERATION	PROFESSIONAL
UNIDENTIFIED	ORGANIZATION
INTERMITTENT	SPORADICALLY
EXACERBATION	INTIMIDATING
INDEPENDENCE	ABOLITIONIST
INTELLIGENCE	ONOMATOPOEIA
RELATIONSHIP	APPRECIATION
THANKSGIVING	ANNUNCIATION

307

1. Nero
2. Ibn Rushd (Averroes)
3. P. T. Barnum
4. Haile Selassie
5. Norman V. Peale
6. Richard Bach
7. Hector G. Oesterheld
8. Mario Andretti

308

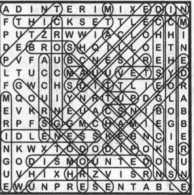

309

Vitamin C
Sources: Citrus fruits, berries, green and leafy vegetables, tomatoes, cauliflower, and sauerkraut.

310

2 and 5

►SOLUTIONS

311

	Z	I	N	C					A	G	E	N	T	
	I		A					B		N		O		
A	P	T		P	R	O	B	A	B	I	L	I	T	Y
R		E					E		R		A		A	
C	O	N	F	I	D	E	N	C	E		R	U	L	E
T		C			E			V		G		L		
I		T		T	A		I	C	E			Y	E	T
L	O	R	C	H	E	S	T	R	A		D		N	
T	A	P		A	R	H		T		S	I	G	N	
	N		M			I		I			U			
A	S	S	O	C	I	A	T	I	O	N		N	O	N	E
	E		E		N	H		N		R		E		
B	U	S		A		R		S	P	I	N	S		
E			C	O	T	T	O	N		O		S		
	L		A		I		A		U	S	E	F	U	L
T	R	A	N	S	P	O	R	T		N		E	E	
		H		N		A	D	D	S		W	E	D	

314

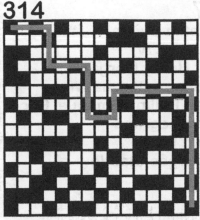

315

The Band
The Beach Boys
The Beatles
The Bee Gees
The Byrds
The Cars
The Clash
The Commodores
The Doors
The Grateful Dead
The Guess Who
The Kinks
The Platters
The Police
The Ramones
The Rolling Stones
The Supremes
The Temptations
The Who
The Yardbirds

312

(word search grid)

313

(word search grid)

316

ARCHITECTURE	RESURRECTION
BIODIVERSITY	CONSTIPATION
INTERDICTION	VELOCIRAPTOR
ACCELERATION	EXPECTATIONS
TRIGONOMETRY	AMBIDEXTROUS
COMMUNICATOR	INTERCEPTION
BODYBUILDING	CIVILIZATION
PERSPIRATION	HIPPOPOTAMUS

▶ SOLUTIONS

317

1. Stefan Dušan
2. Edward IV
3. Sir Henry Morgan
4. Herman Boerhaave
5. Carl Philipp Emanuel Bach
6. Paul Legrand
7. Felix Pedro
8. Georges Claude

318

319

Vitamin A

Sources: Liver, cod liver oil, green and yellow fruits and vegetables, carrots, milk and dairy products.

320

1 and 4

321

322

323

►SOLUTIONS

324

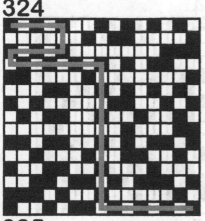

325

America	Japan
Asia	Kansas
Atlanta	L.A. Guns
Alabama	London
Beirut	Nazareth
Berlin	New York Dolls
Boston	Orleans
Brownsville Station	Phoenix
Chicago	
Detroit Spinners	
Dresden Dolls	
Europe	

326

GRANDPARENTS	COLONIZATION
REFRIGERATOR	NEIGHBORHOOD
EXASPERATION	ANTICIPATION
FELICITATION	ELECTRIFYING
CANTANKEROUS	AFFECTIONATE
KALEIDOSCOPE	PRESCRIPTION
EXHILARATING	CONDENSATION
ABBREVIATION	PROGESTERONE

327

1. Ibn Battuta
2. João Gonçalves Zarco
3. Miyamoto Iori
4. Ferdinand of Brunswick
5. William Otis
6. John Browning
7. Michael Collins
8. Trygve Lie

328

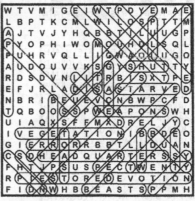

329

Vitamin K
Sources: Yogurt, egg yolk, alfalfa, kelp, leafy green vegetables, safflower oil, and soybean oil.

330

3 and 6

331

```
C H U F F   C O H A B I T A N T S
  R     O   O   E   U   E   E   P
N O N E X E M P T   T I L D E   L
O   F     M   E   T   E       U
N     T E L E G R A P H P L A N T
C U P S   R   O   A   R   R   T
O   I   B A C K S   C   O   T E E
N   A   I   E S K I M O       R
F L A M B E A U X     P   G A S
O   R   U   L   U     T O   D
R I G S   I R A T E   E
M   Y   Z   L   O G R E S     P
I N L A W   A R S O N     B   U
S   E   R   T     K   B U F F
M A S S A G I N G   T I T     F
  K     T   O   E   I   F     I
B A C K H A N D E R S   C   P A N
```

332

```
R Y I J C H A R T R E U S E H A H
B U D W B O M T C S W X C A D N D
Y J B S L I N Z K D R A M B U I E
C C U Q A T G B A G F H E B S B S
R N R J C A N G O S T U R A O E C
E A G K K B O U R B O N H U N T H
M P E U A A R R Z D R L H U J N T
E E N U C E G J U I O E E A I A I
D R D V S M W H A M R S E L T B N
E I Y N S B V A U P T C L A R E T
C T S K I L Y B X Q P C A I H E I
A I W G A E L I Q L L O S T R Y
S F B E N E D I C T I N E G I N B
S H I J P A B S I N T H E N N R
I U H C H A M P A G N E X A A B O
S U J N T K U S Y W L A R U X C C
A J A Q U A V I T A E B F I O F K
```

333

```
S Z C P E J K B D M L T X F G R N Y O Q V W H U A
T N Q X D R V Z A U H B J M P W S G F E Y C L K O
O Y M A G X Q H N C W V Z K R T U D L J F B S E P
F K B W H P G E Y L O U D S N C A V M Z J R T Q X
J U V R L S T F O W C E Y Q A P B X H K Z G D M N
P A N E W B M R H K V J S D T U F O Q Y G X Z C L
G D L S T F U Y Q J N H K C W X V Z R B A M O P E
U R H Q J E C P Z S X G M A O N D T K L B F Y V W
K F Y B M G X O V N Z L U P E S C J A W D Q R H T
V X Z O C A L T W D Q R B Y F E M H P G S U N J K
Y G D N Q Z O L E R T A C V K J P F U S W H B X M
E O W L Z C N U S Q F M G X H B Y K V D T P A R J
B H J M U D P K X Y R Z W O Q L T C G A N E F S V
C P A K F W J Z T V Y S E B D H R N X M U O Q L Z
X V S T R M H A F B J N P U L Q W E Z O K Y G D C
M W G H V Q R S J F P K L T Z Y O B C U E A X N D
L T R U S N Y D G O A Q H E X Z K P W V M J C B F
Q J X F B L Z V P E M D N W C A G R T H O S K Y U
N C P Z Y U A M K X S O R G B D J L E F Q T V W H
A E K D O H B W C T U Y F J V M Q S N X L Z P G R
D B E J X Y F N R A K W V H M O Z Q S P G L U T G
Z S F Y K T E X U G B P A L J V H W D C R N M O Q
W Q U V A O S C L P G F T N Y K X M J R H D E Z B
R M O C N K D J B H E X Q Z U G L A Y T P V W F S
H L T G P V W Q M Z D C O R S F E U B N X K J A Y
```

334

335

336

VETERINARIAN	CONSERVATIVE
SURROUNDINGS	HYPOTHALAMUS
ANNOUNCEMENT	UNCOMPARABLE
PREDILECTION	OVERWHELMING
TRANSMISSION	APPROACHABLE
ECHOLOCATION	DOPPELGANGER
CARTOGRAPHER	SUPERNATURAL
ENCYCLOPEDIA	AMPHITHEATER

▶ SOLUTIONS

337

1. **Mangrai the Great**
2. **Zanobi Strozzi**
3. **Martin Frobisher**
4. **Enoch Poor**
5. **May Donoghue**
6. **Ham The Astrochimp**
7. **Dave Toschi**
8. **Alan Digby**

338

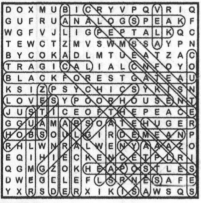

339

Vitamin B$_{12}$
Sources: Liver, kidney,
beef, pork, eggs,
milk and cheese.

340

4 and 5

341

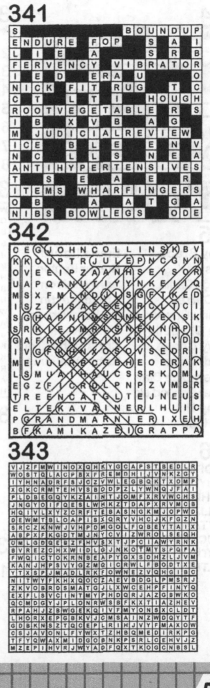

342

343

◢ SOLUTIONS

344

345

Lenny Bruce
Louis C. K.
George Carlin
Jim Carrey
Johnny Carson
Dave Chapelle
Chevy Chase
David Cross
Andrew Dice Clay
Rodney Dangerfield
Benny Hill
Bob Hope

Eddie Izzard
Buster Keaton
Sam Kinison
Steve Martin
Richard Pryor
Chris Rock
Christopher Titus
Robin Williams

346

CONDITIONING
ASPHYXIATION
ANNIHILATION
IDEALIZATION
UNATTAINABLE
UNACCEPTABLE
ELECTROLYSIS
ADULTERATION

MENSTRUATION
SELFLESSNESS
SATISFACTION
TOGETHERNESS
RAMIFICATION
AERODYNAMICS
RATIFICATION
HEARTBREAKER

347

1. Emperor Go-Horikawa
2. Odoric of Pordenone
3. Ulrich of Celje
4. Juan de Betanzos
5. Juan Bautista Martínez
6. William Tryon
7. Mary Elizabeth Braddon
8. Yuji Naka

348

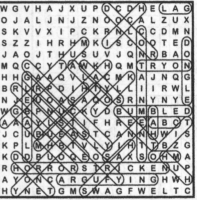

349

Vitamin D
Lichen, eggs, liver,
sardines, and shiitake
mushrooms.

350

1 and 6

►SOLUTIONS

351

354

352

355

Aunt Granny	Lambo
Beige	Lou ("Louise")
Bigmouth	Mokey
Bonehead	Noodlenose
Boober	Red
Brio	Side Bottom
Cantus	Uncle Matt
Chuchu	Wembley
Convincing John	
The Dimpleys	
Fishface	
Gobbo	

353

356

ZYMOTECHNICS	ASTRONOMICAL
SHAPESHIFTER	REGISTRATION
INTERSECTION	AMORTIZATION
UNEMPLOYMENT	RECOLLECTION
DISSERTATION	DIFFICULTIES
PRESERVATION	IMMUNIZATION
INTERRUPTION	INTRANSIGENT
REJUVENATION	DISTILLATION

▶ SOLUTIONS

357
1. William H. Seward
2. Lucien Pissarro
3. Gustave Verbeek
4. Jesús García Corona
5. Frank Schulte
6. Giuseppe Zangara
7. Craig Rice
8. Victor Papanek

358

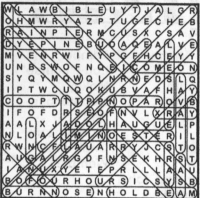

359

Vitamin B$_2$
Sources: Eggs, fish, liver, kidney, leafy green vegetables, yeast, milk and cheese.

360
4 and 5

361

362

363

▶ SOLUTIONS

364

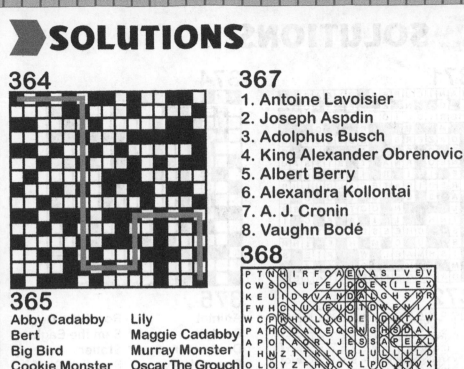

365

Abby Cadabby	Lily
Bert	Maggie Cadabby
Big Bird	Murray Monster
Cookie Monster	Oscar The Grouch
Count Von Count	Prairie Dawn
Elmo	Rosita
Ernie	Sherlock Hemlock
Granny Bird	Zoe
Grover	
Guy Smiley	
Herry Monster	
Julia	

366

HANDKERCHIEF	PHOTOGRAPHER
ACCIDENTALLY	AMELIORATION
CONSTRUCTION	WRETCHEDNESS
CALISTHENICS	BIOCHEMISTRY
SUPERVENTION	FENESTRATION
EXTINGUISHER	BULLFIGHTING
PEDIATRICIAN	COORDINATION
ANTIDIABETIC	INTRODUCTION

367

1. Antoine Lavoisier
2. Joseph Aspdin
3. Adolphus Busch
4. King Alexander Obrenovic
5. Albert Berry
6. Alexandra Kollontai
7. A. J. Cronin
8. Vaughn Bodé

368

369

Vitamin B$_6$
Sources: Wheat germ and bran, milk, eggs, beef, liver, kidney, heart, cantaloupe, and cabbage.

370

2 and 6

▶ SOLUTIONS

371

372

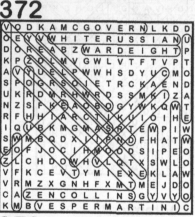

374

375

Animal
Beaker
Dr. Bunsen
Crazy Harry
Floyd Pepper
Fozzie Bear
Gonzo
Janice
Kermit the Frog
Lew Zealand
Miss Piggy
Rizzo the Rat

Rowlf the Dog
Sam the Eagle
Statler
Swedish Chef
Sweetums
Dr. Teeth
Waldorf
Zoot

373

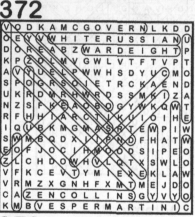

376

BACKSTABBING	OSTENTATIOUS
DESALINATION	INGRATIATING
GLOBETROTTER	ACCOMPLISHED
BRONTOSAURUS	STONEWALLING
HUMANITARIAN	ENTERTAINING
EXHILARATION	SKILLFULNESS
MOONLIGHTING	INFLAMMATION
COMMENSURATE	PREPOSTEROUS

▶SOLUTIONS

377

1. William Murdoch
2. Jean-Jacques Dessalines
3. William Hone
4. Braulio Carrillo
5. Robert Schumann
6. Alvan Graham Clark
7. Kobayashi Kiyochika
8. Satyendra Nath Bose

378

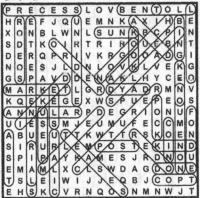

379

Vitamin E
Sources: Whole grain cereals, soybeans, vegetable oils, broccoli, Brussels sprouts, and eggs.

380

3 and 5

381

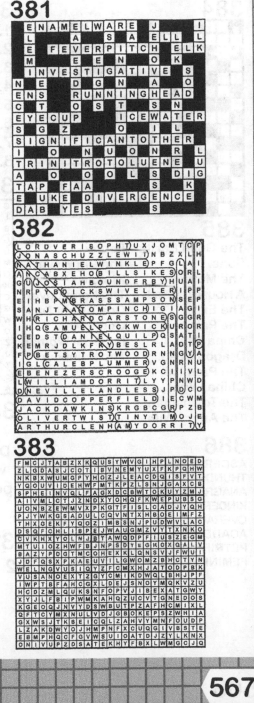

382

383

▶ SOLUTIONS

384

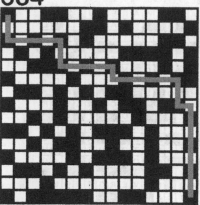

385

The Good Earth.
Sons.
The Mother.
A House Divided.
The Exile.
The Patriot.
China Sky.
Dragon Seed.
The Promise.
China Flight.
The Townsman.
The Angry Wife.

Peony.
The Big Wave.
Kinfolk.
The Long Love.
One Bright Day.
God's Men.
Imperial Woman.
The Rainbow.

386

ASCERTAINING
THUNDERSTORM
ANAGRAMMATIC
KINDERGARTEN
OVERACHIEVER
ACADEMICALLY
PETRIFACTION
FEMINIZATION

APPREHENSION
PERTINACIOUS
ACCELERATING
PROTUBERANCE
IDENTIFIABLE
BACKWOODSMAN
ADMINISTRATE
SUBCONSCIOUS

387

1. Arthur Mold
2. Alferd Packer
3. Max Beckmann
4. Irving Klaw
5. Frank Conniff
6. Joe Walker
7. Tomohiro Nishikado
8. Chris Foss

388

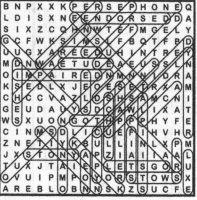

389

Vitamin B_1
Dried yeast, rice husks,
whole wheat, oatmeal,
peanuts, pork, milk, and
most vegetables.

390

2 and 5

▶SOLUTIONS

391

A	N	T	I	C	E	P	H	A	L	A	L	G	I	C	
	A			E		I		S		L		N			
I	N	C	O	M	P	L	E	T	A	B	L	E	N	E	S	S
	O			E		R		I		U		R		W	
L	A	M	E	N	T	A	T	I	O	N	A	L		G	E
	M		T			C		I		O	B	O	L	E	
C	R	O	T	A	P	H	Y	T	U	S		G		T	
	N		T			I		T		I		A	B	B	
	W	E	I		F	O	V	E	I	F	O	R	M		R
C	H	E		O		E		C		U		I	M	I	E
A		A	N	N	O	T	I	N	E		S	A	N		E
T	A	L		T		E		T		A			E		
H		T		E		S		A		A					
A	L	H	A	M	B	R	E	S	Q	U	E		K	Y	L
	A			A		Y		T		O			U		
	S	P	U	T		A						V	I	M	
S	U	M		D		S	C	H	U	S	S		E		

394

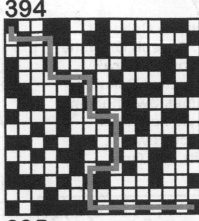

395

Le Chiffre
Mr. Big
Sir Hugo Drax
Jack Spang
Seraffimo Spang
Rosa Kleb
Grubozaboyschikov
Dr. Julius No
Auric Goldfinger
Von Hammerstein
Hector Gonzales
Milton Krest

Emilio Largo
Ernst Stavro Blofeld
Mr. Sanguinetti
Paco Scaramanga
"Horror" Horowitz
"Sluggsy" Morant
Dexter Smythe
Trigger

392

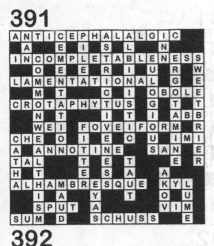

393

T	C	P	L	S	M	D	O	N	V	W	I	X	E	B	Z	K	Q	F	R	U	H	J	A	G
X	U	M	H	I	P	T	Z	E	F	J	Q	L	K	A	W	G	S	B	O	D	R	V	C	N
J	N	B	O	Q	W	H	U	C	G	Z	R	P	F	T	X	D	I	V	A	K	E	M	L	S
V	K	F	D	G	I	X	R	Q	A	C	M	S	O	U	H	N	J	L	E	Z	P	T	W	B
Z	R	A	W	E	K	J	L	S	B	V	H	G	N	D	P	M	U	C	T	X	O	Q	F	I
D	B	I	X	T	S	A	Q	H	L	F	W	M	V	E	R	C	N	Z	U	O	J	P	G	K
L	Z	O	G	W	J	F	V	P	K	D	C	N	H	I	A	Q	X	E	S	R	M	U	B	T
F	A	V	R	M	E	Z	B	U	N	X	T	J	P	Q	G	L	O	I	K	C	W	D	S	H
O	Q	K	J	P	X	W	D	J	I	R	S	U	O	G	Z	B	T	F	H	M	L	N	A	V	E
U	S	E	N	H	T	C	G	M	O	B	L	A	K	K	D	P	W	J	V	Q	I	F	X	Z
B	H	C	Q	O	U	M	F	D	J	N	A	T	I	P	S	W	G	R	X	V	K	E	Z	L
R	I	N	M	K	C	Q	S	Z	W	G	J	U	L	F	O	E	V	T	B	A	X	H	D	P
E	P	X	U	D	G	O	K	V	H	Q	S	C	M	W	J	Z	A	N	L	B	T	I	R	F
S	T	L	A	J	B	R	P	X	I	K	Z	E	D	V	C	H	M	U	F	G	Q	W	N	O
W	V	G	Z	F	A	N	E	L	T	O	B	H	X	R	K	I	P	Q	D	J	S	C	M	U
P	X	R	F	V	D	G	H	A	S	T	K	Z	C	J	I	U	E	O	N	W	L	B	Q	M
M	W	T	S	N	L	U	C	O	X	A	E	B	Q	G	F	R	Z	P	H	I	D	K	J	V
H	J	Q	E	C	V	B	W	R	M	I	D	F	U	O	L	A	T	K	G	S	Z	N	V	Z
G	D	Z	I	A	F	K	N	J	P	H	X	V	S	L	M	B	C	W	Q	E	U	O	T	R
O	L	U	K	B	Z	E	I	T	H	D	C	W	M	P	R	W	N	V	X	D	S	J	F	C	G	H	A
N	M	W	T	L	O	S	J	K	C	R	G	D	Z	H	U	F	B	A	I	P	V	X	E	Q
Q	O	H	V	Z	R	P	A	G	D	E	F	I	J	X	T	S	K	M	W	N	B	L	U	C
A	F	J	C	U	H	I	T	W	E	L	N	K	B	S	Q	V	R	X	P	M	G	Z	O	D
I	E	D	P	R	Q	L	X	B	Z	U	V	W	A	M	N	O	H	G	C	T	F	S	K	J
K	G	S	B	X	N	V	M	F	U	P	O	Q	T	C	E	J	L	D	Z	H	A	R	I	W

396

CARBOHYDRATE
ORTHODONTICS
CANCELLATION
BUTTERSCOTCH
FERMENTATION
ENTERPRISING
COSMOPOLITAN
WITHSTANDING

EXTRAVAGANZA
ADAPTABILITY
CONQUISTADOR
EFFERVESCENT
CHRISTIANITY
HYPERTENSION
CIRCUMSTANCE
CIRCUMCISION

►SOLUTIONS

397
1. Jeanne Calment
2. Dr. Joseph Grancher
3. Antonin Dvorak
4. Kitazawa Rakuten
5. James Swinnerton
6. Louis Feuillade
7. Percy Fawcett
8. Fritz von Opel

398

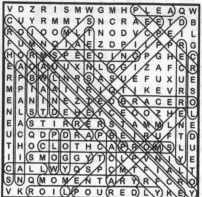

399

Vitamin B$_7$
Sources: Raw egg yolk, liver, peanuts, and leafy green vegetables.

400
3 and 6

401

402

403
1. ROME, ITALY.
2. PARIS, FRANCE.
3. CAIRO, EGYPT.
4. SYDNEY, AUSTRALIA.
5. RIO, BRAZIL.
6. NEW YORK CITY, USA.

◢ SOLUTIONS

404

405

Big Boy
Black Pearl
The Brow
The Brush
Coffyhead
Dude Tonsils
Flattop
Flyface
Gargles
Hypo
Influence
Jojo Nidle

Krome
Mambo
Measles
The Mole
Mumbles
Rhodent
Scorpio
Shoulders

406

PROCRASTINATION
PERSONIFICATION
CHARACTERISTICS
DECERTIFICATION
PULCHRITUDINOUS
AMERICANIZATION
ABDOMINOVESICAL
CONGRATULATIONS

THERMOCHEMISTRY
ALPHABETIZATION
INTERDEPENDENCE
ACCOMPLISHMENTS
UNPREPOSSESSING
ACKNOWLEDGMENTS
ANTEPENULTIMATE
ACCLIMATIZATION

407

1. Rudolfo Belenzani
2. Gaspar de Quiroga y Vela
3. Gregorius Sickinger
4. Juan Ignacio Molina
5. Patrick Francis Healy
6. Nikifor Begichev
7. Charles Ogle
8. Waldemar Young

408

409

CALCIUM
Sources: Milk and dairy products, salmon, sardines, sunflower seeds, dried beans, peanuts and walnuts.

410

5 and 6

►SOLUTIONS

411

A	N	A	G	R	A	M		S	P	A	R	K	L	E
U		G		A		O		Y		S		I		A
T	O	E		M	O	N	A	R	C	H		T	U	T
O				I		I								A
P	A	R		T	E	T	A	N	U	S		B	U	B
S		E		U		O		G		P		L		L
Y	O	U	N	G	E	R		E	Y	E	S	O	R	E
		N		B				C		W				
R	U	I	N	O	U	S		D	W	I	N	D	L	E
H		O		A		A		I		A		R		N
U	R	N		T	O	P	S	O	I	L		Y	E	S
B				L		P								L
A	L	P		R	E	E	N	T	E	R		O	V	A
R		A		I		S		O		C		V		
B	E	S	I	D	E	S		R	E	D	T	A	P	E

414

412

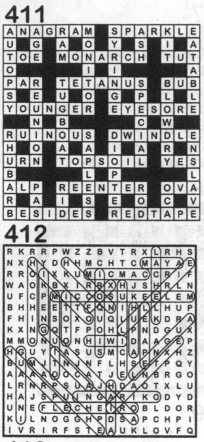

413

1. CUZCO, PERU.
2. PISTE, MEXICO.
3. ST. LOUIS, USA.
4. ISTANBUL, TURKEY.
5. TOKYO, JAPAN.
6. TAIPEI, TAIWAN.

415

Anarky
Black Mask
Bane
Catwoman
Clayface
Deadshot
Harley Quinn
Hugo Strange
Joker
Killer Croc
Mad Hatter
Man-Bat

Mr. Freeze
Penguin
Ra's al Ghul
Riddler
Scarecrow
Two-Face
Ventriloquist
Zsasz

416

TRUSTWORTHINESS
MISAPPREHENSION
NATIONALIZATION
INSUBORDINATION
KINDHEARTEDNESS
CONNOISSEURSHIP
EXCOMMUNICATION
MINIATURIZATION

PROCRASTINATING
MEDICAMENTATION
CONFIDENTIALITY
ACQUISITIVENESS
INTERNALIZATION
MISAPPRECIATION
ANTICOAGULATION
CRYSTALLIZATION

▶SOLUTIONS

417

1. Lee Bong-chang
2. Gérard Berchet
3. John Logie Baird
4. Georges Bégué
5. Chuck Yeager
6. José Luis Salinas
7. Lionel Crabb
8. Makarios III

418

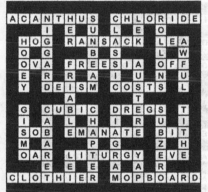

419

SODIUM
Sources: Salt, shellfish, carrots, beets, artichokes, dried beef, and bacon.

420

2 and 5

421

422

423

1. MOSCOW, RUSSIA.
2. BERLIN, GERMANY.
3. JERUSALEM, ISRAEL.
4. VATICAN CITY, VATICAN.
5. PARIS, FRANCE.
6. VALENCIA, SPAIN.

►SOLUTIONS

424

425

Backgammon
Bergen
Bezique
Bridge
Chess
Craps
Dominoes
D&D
Go
Hex
Mah Jong
Mikado

Piquet
Pinocle
Persian
Poker
Rummy
Roulette
Star
Wari

426

EXPERIMENTATION
ACCOMMODATINGLY
ELECTRIFICATION
ZINJANTHROPUSES
TOTALITARIANISM
INACCESSIBILITY
INSTRUMENTATION
PSEUDOEPHEDRINE

CYCLOBENZAPRINE
MARGINALIZATION
UNCONDITIONALLY
CIRCULARIZATION
AUTOLUMINISCENT
GASTROENTERITIS
INTELLECTUALITY
DISORGANIZATION

427

1. Zheng He
2. Henricus Grammateus
3. George Abbot
4. Antonio David
5. Hector Berlioz
6. Louis Réard
7. Renzo Barbieri
8. Jaime Roos

428

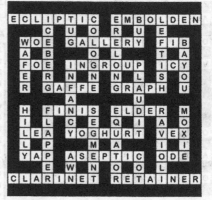

429

POTASSIUM
Sources: Citrus fruits,
bananas, potatoes,
watercress, mint leaves,
and leafy green
vegetables.

430

4 and 6

►SOLUTIONS

431

S	T	O	P	G	A	P			E	N	D	U	S	E	R
P		F		O		H		P		A		E			O
O	U	T		O	U	R	L	A	D	Y		T	A	M	
N				A		U									A
S	I	R		I	N	S	U	L	A	R		O	W	N	
O		E		N		A		E		E		B			O
R	E	M	O	V	A	L		T	E	L	A	V	I	V	
		A		E				I		I					I
P	E	R	S	I	S	T		R	A	V	I	O	L	I	
A		R			G		E		E	E		U		M	
S	K	Y		H	A	N	G	U	P	S		S	A	P	
T				A				N						I	
E	A	R		S	U	N	D	I	A	L		P	I	N	
U		U		O		C		O		E		R			
P	A	G	E	B	O	Y		N	O	I	S	O	M	E	

432

433

1. SHANGHAI, CHINA.
2. DUBAI, UAE
3. PALERMO, ITALY
4. PISA, ITALY
5. MANILA, PHILIPPINES
6. MONTEVIDEO, URUGUAY

434

435

Bewitched
Bonanza
Combat!
The Flintstones
The Fugitive
Gilligan's Island
Green Acres
Gunsmoke
Hawaii Five-O
Hogan's Heroes
The Jetsons
McHale's Navy

Mister Ed
The Mod Squad
The Munsters
Perry Mason
The Saint
Star Trek
Twilight Zone
Wild Wild West

436

PICTURESQUENESS
IMPONDERABILITY
INTERCHANGEABLE
STRAIGHTFORWARD
MATERIALIZATION
RESPONSIBLENESS
STANDOFFISHNESS
INDIVIDUALIZING

INSTRUMENTALIST
DIVERSIFICATION
COMFORTABLENESS
CRIMINALIZATION
DISCONTINUATION
SYSTEMATIZATION
CRYSTALLOGRAPHY
RESOURCEFULNESS

◗ **SOLUTIONS**

437

1. Anna Mae Hays
2. Geoffrey Jackson
3. Dik Browne
4. Paul J. Flory
5. Keith Jarrett
6. Tetsuo Fukuda
7. Bill Murray
8. Sid Vicious

438

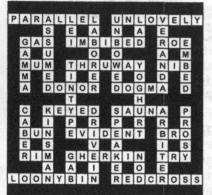

439

CHROMIUM
Sources: Meat, shellfish, clam, chicken, corn oil, and brewer's yeast.

440

1 and 5

441

P	I	G	G	I	S	H		C	E	D	I	L	L	A
A		U		R	O	Y		Y		R	O			I
N	A	N		K	I	T	S	C	H	Y		W	A	R
A					S		L							P
C	A	T		T	A	P	I	O	C	A		Q	U	A
E		R		E		O	P		T		U			R
A	G	A	I	N	S	T		S	C	H	T	I	C	K
		N		T						I		N		
F	U	S	S	P	O	T		E	R	R	A	T	I	C
I			E		X		S		E			E		H
N	U	T		G	U	N	S	H	O	T		T	W	O
A			I				I							R
G	E	T		A	L	G	E	B	R	A		B	I	T
L		A		S		H		I		G	A	L		
E	A	R	S	H	O	T		T	R	O	C	H	E	E

442

(word search grid)

443

1. SANTIAGO, CHILE.
2. BUENOS AIRES, ARGENTINA.
3. LONDON, ENGLAND.
4. BEIJING, CHINA.
5. NEW YORK, USA.
6. HAVANA, CUBA.

►SOLUTIONS

444

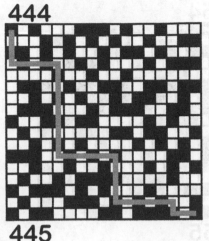

445

All In The Family	Laverne & Shirley
Bionic Woman	Love Boat
Charlie's Angels	M*A*S*H
ChiPs	Maude
Dallas	Mork & Mindy
Diff'rent Strokes	Sanford and Son
Dukes of Hazzard	Starsky & Hutch
Facts of Life	Wonder Woman
Good Times	
Happy Days	
Incredible Hulk	
The Jeffersons	

446

MEMORIALIZATION	AGRICULTURALIST
MEANINGLESSNESS	HOSPITALIZATION
UNDERHANDEDNESS	DISADVANTAGEOUS
WEATHERBOARDING	THERAPEUTICALLY
SERVICEABLENESS	ANTHROPOMORPHIC
REAPPORTIONMENT	SYNCHRONIZATION
PLENIPOTENTIARY	DEMAGNETIZATION
HEMOCHROMATOSIS	NEARSIGHTEDNESS

447

1. Georgy Zhukov
2. Pius XII
3. Gordon Small
4. Gus Grissom
5. Sparky Lyle
6. Steve Sasson
7. Juan M. Fernández y Krohn
8. Todd McFarlane

448

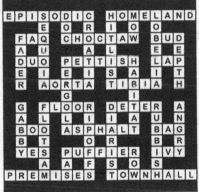

449

IRON
Sources: Red meat, heart, liver, kidney, egg yolk, raw clams and oysters, nuts, beans, and oatmeal .

450

2 and 3

▶ SOLUTIONS

451

S	N	O	W	J	O	B		A	L	L	T	O	L	D
H		H		E		A		G		O		A		E
E	L	M		T	A	T	T	I	N	G		T	I	C
L				H		T				L		A		
L	E	E		P	A	Y	W	A	L	L		S	A	G
A		Y		L		A		T		A		T		O
C	U	E	B	A	L	L		E	L	Y	S	I	A	N
	B		Y					R			O			R
A	C	R	O	B	A	T		I	N	F	E	R	N	O
L		O		O		A		C		F		E		V
M	E	W		Y	A	B	B	E	R	S		D	Y	E
A						L		P						R
N	I	B		P	R	E	S	A	G	E		L	A	D
A		O		I		A		C		Y		E		U
C	H	A	T	E	A	U		K	H	E	D	I	V	E

452

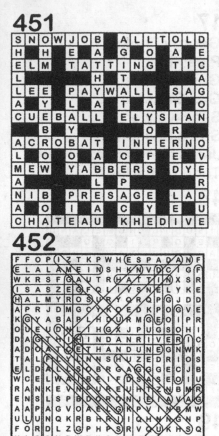

453

1. MINSK, BELARUS
2. LIMA, PERU
3. WHILTSHIRE, UK
4. LUXOR, EGYPT
5. TOKYO, JAPAN
6. SEATTLE, USA

454

455

A-Team
ALF
Cagney & Lacey
Cheers
Equalizer
Family Ties
Full House
Golden Girls
Golden Years
Knight Rider
Magnum P.I.
Max Headroom

Miami Vice
Moonlighting
Murder She Wrote
Murphy Brown
Newheart
Remington Steele
Stingray
Wonder Years

456

LEVELHEADEDNESS
LIGHTHEADEDNESS
FORTHCOMINGNESS
CONSECUTIVENESS
PURPOSELESSNESS
PLEASURABLENESS
BROKENHEARTEDLY
UNDERPRODUCTION

UNCOMPREHENDING
CHEMICALIZATION
TRANSFIGURATION
DESTABILIZATION
COMPUTERIZATION
UNQUALIFICATION
ACHROMATIZATION
DESENSITIZATION

578

▶SOLUTIONS

457
1. Christiaan de Wet
2. João do Rio
3. Anna Anderson
4. Elena Ivanovna Barulina
5. Wendell Willkie
6. Senkichi Taniguchi
7. Alberto Korda
8. Gary Gabelich

458

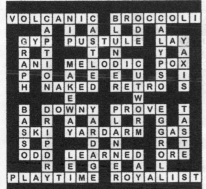

459

MAGNESIUM

Sources: Figs, lemons, grapefruit, apples, dark-green vegetables, seeds, and nuts.

460
4 and 5

461

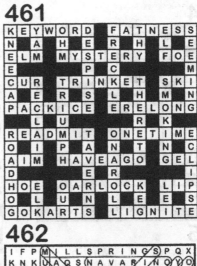

462

463
1. ST. PETERSBURG, RUSSIA
2. LISBON, PORTUGAL
3. LA PAZ, BOLIVIA
4. BUDAPEST, HUNGARY
5. SOFIA, BULGARIA
6. ATHENS, GREECE

▶ SOLUTIONS

464

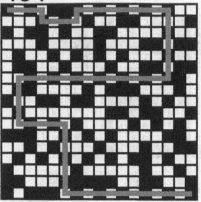

465

Ally McBeal
Buffy
Dr. Quinn
ER
Frasier
Freaks and Geeks
Highlander
Friends
King of Queens
Law & Order
Lois & Clark
Mad About You

Martin
My So-Called Life
NewsRadio
NYPD Blue
Power Rangers
Seinfeld
That 70's Show
X-Files

466

BLANKMINDEDNESS
DOWNHEARTEDNESS
MEASURELESSNESS
GENTLEMANLINESS
THOUGHTLESSNESS
PROMISCUOUSNESS
ANTHROPOCENTRIC
COUNTERARGUMENT

ACCULTURATIONAL
MYTHOLOGIZATION
DISCOMMENDATION
DECONTAMINATION
DEMOCRATIZATION
INCONSIDERATION
HYPOSTATIZATION
DISARTICULATION

467

1. Gustav IV Adolf
2. Frédéric Cailliaud
3. James Ballantyne
4. Orest Kiprensky
5. John Hindmarsh
6. James Clark Ross
7. Jerry O'Neill
8. Louise Van den Plas

468

F	L	A	T	F	E	E	T		M	U	F	F	L	E	R	S
		I		A		H		I		A				O		
B	U	M		T	H	I	R	S	T	Y		G	N	U		
O		P				N		L				I		N		
B	O	A		L	E	N	I	E	N	T		C	A	P		
B		N		I		E		A		S		A		E		
Y		I	N	C	U	R		D	P	H	I	L				
		E								I						
O		P	I	N	U	P		E	A	R	T	H		W		
R		O		S		E		L		T		A		O		
A	L	P		E	N	D	L	E	S	S		C	O	O		
T		U				A		G			K		D			
E	E	L		L	I	G	N	I	T	E		S	L	Y		
A		A		E		O		A		E			A			
S	T	A	R	L	I	N	G		C	A	K	E	W	A	L	K

469

ZINC

Sources: Steak, lamb chops, pork loin, wheat germ, eggs, pumpkin seeds, and ground mustard.

470

2 and 4

471

E	N	G	A	G	E	D		B	A	L	L	A	S	T
Q		O		O		Y		A		I		D		H
U	F	O		D	I	N	E	T	T	E		O	D	E
A				A		I				T				O
B	R	A		E	N	M	A	S	S	E		B	U	R
L		B		N		I		T		A		A		E
E	L	A	S	T	I	C		E	R	R	A	T	U	M
		S		R				M		H				
P	A	H	L	A	V	I		B	L	A	S	T	E	D
A		E		I		N		O		R		U		E
C	A	D		N	E	T	W	O	R	K		B	U	S
I				E		E		K				E		E
F	A	G		J	U	G	H	E	A	D		F	I	X
I		U		A		N		R		E		R		E
C	A	T	E	R	E	R		D	U	B	I	O	U	S

474

472

473

1. DRESDEN, GERMANY
2. VILNIUS, LITHUANIA
3. BUCHAREST, ROMANIA
4. MUMBAI, INDIA
5. PHOENIX, USA
6. MONTREAL, CANADA

475

A.I.	Minority Report
Always	Munich
Amistad	Savage
1941	Schindler's List
The Color Purple	Something Evil
Duel	Sugarland
Empire of the Sun	Express
E.T.	The Terminal
Hook	
Jaws	
Jurassic Park	
Lincoln	

476

SOFTHEARTEDNESS	PHOTOJOURNALISM
SESQUICENTENARY	ELECTROPOSITIVE
MACROSCOPICALLY	DICHOTOMIZATION
PHYSIOLOGICALLY	OBJECTIFICATION
UNACCOMMODATING	DISSATISFACTION
OPHTHALMOLOGIST	RADIOPROTECTION
UNDEMONSTRATIVE	REHARMONIZATION
GOVERNMENTALISM	EXTEMPORIZATION

► SOLUTIONS

477
1. Anna Cervin
2. Ferenc Molnar
3. Theodoros Pangalos
4. Stephen Slesinger
5. John R. Schmidhauser
6. Edson Luís de Lima
7. José Delbo
8. Bobby Goodman

478

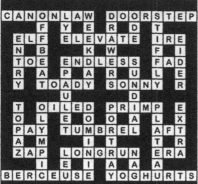

479

FLUORINE
Sources: Fluoridated drinking water, seafoods, and gelatin.

480
3 and 6

481

482

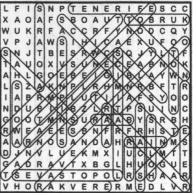

483
1. AUSTIN, USA
2. KALISZ, POLAND
3. VENICE, ITALY
4. SINGAPORE
5. BOSTON, USA
6. SOFIA, BULGARIA

►SOLUTIONS

484

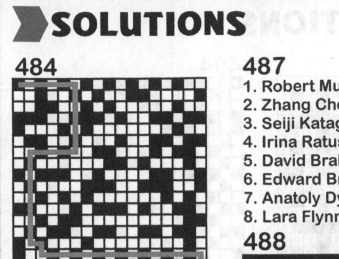

485

Andre the Giant	Pedro Morales
Big John Studd	Rick Flair
Don Muraco	Rick Rude
Harley Race	Ricky Steamboat
Honky Tonk Man	Roddy Piper
Hulk Hogan	Ted DiBiase
Iron Sheik	Tito Santana
Jake Roberts	Ultimate Warrior
Jim Duggan	
Jimmy Snuka	
King Kong Bundy	
Macho Man	

486

PHARMACOTHERAPY	NOTWITHSTANDING
REMORSELESSNESS	TRINITROTOLUENE
CONVENTIONALITY	FAITHWORTHINESS
ENERGETICALNESS	NEUROBIOLOGICAL
PRECIPITOUSNESS	PHOTOCONDUCTION
INEFFECTIVENESS	ADENOHYPOPHYSIS
MANOEUVRABILITY	PERFECTIONISTIC
ENVIRONMENTALLY	EXTRACURRICULAR

487

1. Robert Mugabe
2. Zhang Chongren
3. Seiji Katagiri
4. Irina Ratushinskaya
5. David Braben
6. Edward Bryant
7. Anatoly Dyatlov
8. Lara Flynn Boyle

488

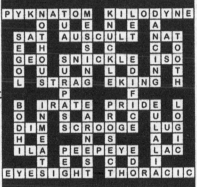

489

COPPER
Sources: Beef liver, prunes, peas, beans, and most seafood.

490

1 and 6

▶ SOLUTIONS

491

A	C	R	Y	L	I	C		K	I	W	A	N	I	S
B		A		E		A		I		U		U		Y
A	D	Y		A	G	L	U	C	O	N		B	E	N
B				U		K				N				A
D	A	R		S	E	M	I	O	R	B		S	A	P
E		E		H		N		F		A		U		T
H	I	C	K	O	R	Y		F	R	I	B	B	L	E
		R						R		G		C		
B	L	A	S	T	I	D		C	O	N	C	E	A	L
I		M		I		E		R		E		L		U
T	A	P		A	B	S	V	O	L	T		L	A	C
A				M		P				A				E
B	O	N		G	R	O	M	M	E	T		F	U	R
L		E		I		M		A		I		O		N
E	X	O	S	T	R	A		N	O	M	I	N	E	E

492

494

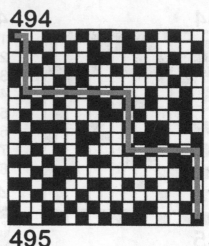

493

1. SAO PAULO, BRAZIL
2. BUENOS AIRES, ARGENTINA
3. ST. PETERSBURG, RUSSIA
4. LISBON, PORTUGAL
5. HONG KONG, CHINA
6. KIEV, UKRAINE.

495

Americana	Dallas
Angel	Debbie
Ashley Cartier	Debutante
Attache	Dementia
Beastie	Ebony
Big Bad Mama	Matilda The Hun
Broadway Rose	Palestina
Brunilda	Zelda The Brain
California Doll	
Cheyenne Cher	
Col. Ninotchka	
Daisy	

496

DESTRUCTIVENESS	UNCOMMUNICATIVE
COMMUNALIZATION	INDEMNIFICATION
DECALCIFICATION	SUPPLEMENTATION
ROMANTICIZATION	VASOCONSTRICTOR
ELECTROLYZATION	ARISTOTELIANISM
PALAEONTOLOGIST	NONINTERVENTION
TRANSPLANTATION	HYPERTHYROIDISM
HYPERCORRECTION	NONTRANSFERABLE

▶SOLUTIONS

497

1. Kurt Waldheim
2. Andrew G. Vajna
3. Violeta Chamorro
4. Alex Graham
5. Pei-Yuan Wei
6. Janet Reno
7. Valeri Polyakov
8. Jacques Chirac

498

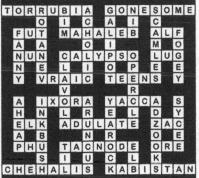

499

COBALT
Sources: Meat, liver, kidney, milk, oysters, and clams.

500

5 and 6

501

502

503

►SOLUTIONS

504

505

Black Panther	Quicksilver
Cyclops	Scarlet Witch
Daredevil	Silver Surfer
Dr.Doom	Spiderman
Green Goblin	Dr.Strange
The Hulk	The Thing
Iceman	Thor
Iron Man	Professor X
The Kingpin	
Loki	
Magneto	
The Mandarin	

506

507

1. James Cross
2. Stanley Loomis
3. Haruomi Hosono
4. Gary Panter
5. Antonio Gasalla
6. Mário Soares
7. Takashi Yanase
8. Billie Joe Armstrong

508-509

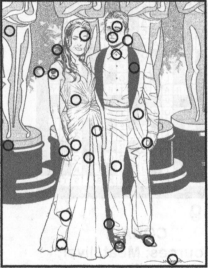

BRANGELINA

510

2 and 5

◗ ACKNOWLEDGMENTS

I am indebted to my editor, Jesse McHugh, for his continued enthusiasm and support.

A huge GRACIAS to assistant editor Jessica Burch, whose mad editing skills make me look good.

Tip of the hat to authors William Sunners, Stan Kurzban, Mel Rosen, Gary David Bouton, and Roger E. Sanders for teaching me so much through their books —they certainly keep my mind sharp!

◗ ABOUT THE AUTHOR

Diego Jourdan Pereira is a leading puzzle designer and nonfiction writer with a background in illustration, comic-books, and graphic design.

In addition to his own books for children and adults, he has worked on licensed properties such as Teenage Mutant Ninja Turtles, Transformers, Donald Duck, Grumpy Cat, LEGO, Mars Attacks!, Regular Show, Sesame Street, Star Wars, Toy Story, and WWE, for an international clientele including DC Comics, DC Thomson Media, Dover Publications, IDW Publishing, Skyhorse Publishing, and The Topps Company.